D0330811

THE DISASTER EXPERTS

The Disaster Experts

MASTERING RISK
IN MODERN AMERICA

SCOTT GABRIEL KNOWLES

PENN

UNIVERSITY OF PENNSYLVANIA PRESS

PHILADELPHIA

HV
551.3
.K65
2011

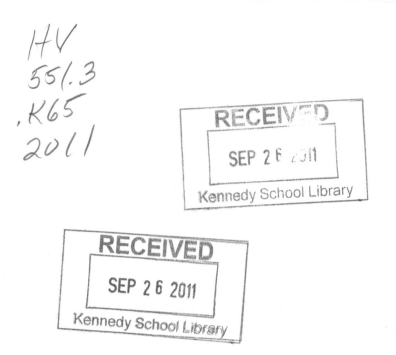

Philadelphia Copyright © 2011 University of Pennsylvania Press

All rights reserved. Except for brief quotations used
for purposes of review or scholarly citation, none of this
book may be reproduced in any form by any means without
written permission from the publisher.

Published by
University of Pennsylvania Press
Philadelphia, Pennsylvania 19104-4112
www.upenn.edu/pennpress

Printed in the United States of America
on acid-free paper

10 9 8 7 6 5 4 3 2 1

Library of Congress Cataloging-in-Publication Data
ISBN 978-0-8122-4350-5

To Julia, patience expert . . .

CONTENTS

ABBREVIATIONS

ASCE   American Society of Civil Engineers
BPAT   Building Performance Assessment Team
CD   Civil Defense
DCPA   Defense Civil Preparedness Administration
DRC   Disaster Research Center (Ohio State University/University of
          Delaware)
EMI   Emergency Management Institute
FCDA   Federal Civil Defense Administration
FEMA   Federal Emergency Management Agency
HSC   House Science Committee
NBFU   National Board of Fire Underwriters
NBS   National Bureau of Standards
NEHRP   National Earthquake Hazards Reduction Program
NFIP   National Flood Insurance Program
NFPA   National Fire Protection Association
NGA   National Governors Association
NIST   National Institute of Standards and Technology
NSF   National Science Foundation
NORC   National Opinion Research Center (University of Chicago)
ODM   Office of Defense Mobilization
UL   Underwriters Laboratories, Inc.

INTRODUCTION

"Here is an example of a steel structure subjected to the impacts of a fully loaded, fueled 747 airplane." With the lights dimmed in the hearing chamber, engineering professor Abolhassan Astaneh-Asl narrated a computer simulation for the House Science Committee. "Here is the plane approaching that building at 450 miles per hour. Close up here, you can see the damage to the structures." In the front row sat Sally Regenhard, among the dozens of family members in the audience, clutching a portrait of her son Christian. A "proby," a probationary firefighter still new to the job, he was covering for someone in Engine Company 279 on the morning of September 11. Christian Regenhard was one of the more than 1,100 victims of the World Trade Center attacks whose remains were never identified.[1] "We can analyze . . . the spread of temperature and weakening of steel and the final collapse," the engineer explained. "This is what we would like to do for the World Trade Center." Unfortunately, Astaneh continued, he had encountered "impediments" to his work, impediments like "not having access to Ground Zero and surrounding damaged buildings, not having enough time to inspect the World Trade Center steel . . . not having the drawings, videotapes, photographs, and other data on the building to conduct our analysis of the collapse." As such, he concluded that as of March 2002, "we are unable to proceed with our study."[2]

Officials from the Federal Emergency Management Agency (FEMA), the American Society of Civil Engineers (ASCE), and the National Institute of Standards and Technology (NIST) each offered in their testimony a rather different take on the investigation, stressing that they had been necessarily delayed early on by the imperatives of looking for victims. Lacking subpoena power had hampered evidence collection they conceded, but overall they were confident that their work would translate the tragedy into actionable steps for safer buildings, particularly through the work of the multi-disciplinary Building Performance Assessment Team (BPAT). The

BPAT was a voluntary collaboration between FEMA and the ASCE, scheduled to publish its report in May and then hand over the remaining research tasks to NIST, the pre-eminent national laboratory for fire research. As FEMA's Robert Shea put it, "What we learn from this tragedy is probably beyond the current generation of buildings. But we can influence the next generation of buildings."[3]

In his turn before the Committee fire science professor Glenn Corbett blasted this cautious optimism, zeroing in on the fact that the World Trade Center steel had been sent away—to recycling yards in New Jersey, and as far away as Shanghai—before experts could begin to examine it. "The Building Performance Assessment Team is composed of an elite group of engineers and scientists," Corbett conceded. Nevertheless, they had "allowed valuable evidence in the form of the towers' structural steel to be destroyed." Committee chairman and New York Representative Sherwood Boehlert picked up on Corbett's line of argument. "We need to understand a lot more about the behavior of skyscrapers and about fire if we are going to prevent future tragedies," he warned. In his view the investigation thus far had "faced numerous obstacles," including a lack of coordination and a slowness to react, matched by a lack of initiative in gathering evidence and asserting investigative authority. "No organized team was at the site for weeks. Potentially valuable evidence has been irretrievably lost," he worried. "What this experience clearly points up," Boehlert concluded, "is that the Federal Government needs to put in place standard investigative protocols and procedures right now so we don't have to reinvent the wheel each time we face a building failure."[4]

Angry and frustrated in his attempts to understand exactly who among the experts was in control, New York Representative Anthony Weiner asked a seemingly simple question. "Will the person who is in charge of the investigation raise their hand?" Two hands went up, and then a third. "I want to know who is in charge," Weiner demanded. "Where does the buck stop . . . on this investigation?"[5] When NIST director Ander L. Bement, Jr., answered that it was, in fact, now NIST's investigation to run, Weiner wanted to know more about why the steel analysis was so crucial. "You said that we have the capability to determine the impact of heat on structural failure in buildings. . . . Do you believe that if we had that information before September 11, some of the people that are sitting behind you would not have lost loved ones?" This was the question that really mattered—did the disaster experts have the knowledge to prevent the worst from happening, and if so could they have used it to save lives *before* September 11? "Perhaps. Yes."[6] Bement replied.

Here before the House Science Committee were the disaster experts—specialists in predicting the unpredictable and managing the unmanageable—working at the cutting-edge of fire protection, engineering, and emergency management. Disagreements over the technical details of a complex investigation could be expected, even heralded as evidence of a self-critical and scientific process. But, the brief and honest exchange between Arden Bement and Anthony Weiner revealed a more deeply unsettling and mostly obscured feature of life in the modern technological age. When it comes to mastering risk, knowledge is usually not the problem. In the case of the World Trade Center disaster, what began as a technical investigation had turned into a bureaucratic soul-search, and a lament for the failure of the experts to transform their knowledge into action.

When it did appear in May, the BPAT's *World Trade Center Performance Study* took pains to point out the seemingly remarkable fact that each building had withstood the impact of a collision with a commercial jet. In fact it is fair to speculate based on reading the *Performance Study* that the buildings might have stood, albeit in shambles, had the fire and emergency systems performed effectively. But, they had not, and what followed was a grim tale of failure.[7] The fireproofing material surrounding the structural columns and beams was of little use, swept away by airplane fuselage tearing through the buildings. Jet fuel ignited infernos on multiple floors, burning hot enough to weaken the steel, particularly the light "bar truss" members supporting each floor. Emergency exits, elevators, and communications systems were overtaxed almost immediately, and failing to perform as designed they placed first responders in added danger and thwarted the evacuation effort.

A troubling question emerged: might other skyscrapers worldwide not suffer the same fate as the Twin Towers, whether or not they absorb the impact of jet airliners, whether or not they are the targets of terrorism? In fact the 47-story World Trade Center Building 7 answered this question. Though not hit by a plane, Building 7 collapsed late on the afternoon of September 11 after sustaining heavy damage by falling debris, and burning throughout the day.[8] Not confident in implicating the specific design features of the Twin Towers or the building and fire codes under which they were regulated, the authors of the *Performance Study* emphasized a generic need for more fire protection research, and more robust interaction among building designers and engineers, fire protection experts, emergency personnel, and building users as possible safeguards against similar future disasters.[9]

Sally Regenhard and the other victims' family members—now organized into the Skyscraper Safety Campaign, with Glenn Corbett as an expert advisor—knew that a technical study could obviously not bring back their loved ones, but they wondered, could it cause real change? It was Regenhard, speaking with the moral authority of the mother of a fallen firefighter who had provoked the media and eventually elected officials to pay attention to the failures of the disaster experts in the first place.[10] Corbett dismissed the *Performance Study* as a technocratic "book report," a failure to seize the moment and carry out the type of investigation that would prompt immediate change to the nation's fire and building codes. He exhorted NIST to conduct the next stage of the research with urgency and with an eye towards making specific "fast track" recommendations for building code changes.[11]

The House Science Committee accepted NIST's argument for continuing the investigation, and pushed forward a 16 million dollar appropriation to support a long-term 9/11 building safety study. At the same time Representatives Boehlert and Weiner, strongly influenced by the Skyscraper Safety Campaign's call for meaningful reform, also introduced a new piece of legislation, granting subpoena power in disaster investigations to NIST under the authority of the National Construction Safety Team Act. On the floor of the House, Boehlert would describe it as "in many ways, a memorial to those who lost their lives on September 11 and a tribute to their families who have joined together to advocate for this measure in the Campaign for Skyscraper Safety."[12] The bill passed overwhelmingly in both houses of congress. In its haste to do something productive and answer to the American people for the collapse of the World Trade Center, congress had bestowed new authority and greater responsibility on the nation's fire disaster experts. But it was an ambiguous charge: were the experts meant to challenge the status quo of American high-rise construction, emerging as aggressive investigators and enforcers of public safety? Or were they supposed to tend mainly to their technical research in the hopes that new knowledge about fire disasters would filter its way into public policy and eventually lead to safer cities? Both? The message from Washington was mixed, and there was no more time for debate.

By the time the National Construction Safety Team Act passed the House, the Lower Manhattan Development Corporation, an appointed body charged with the redevelopment of the 16-acre site, announced its first six design possibilities for the next World Trade Center. The last of the rubble had been cleared in May, and though opinions swirled about how to rebuild without forgetting, it was a foregone conclusion that the 16-acre site would not sit empty for long. Whether or not a high rise could be built in that location that could withstand another terrorist attack, or even just a bad fire, was entirely unknown. Only a few voices were heard raising this concern and they were drowned out by the cries to rebuild in the name of patriotic and defiant reconstruction.[13]

Why rush to build at the very moment when the disaster experts had been empowered to transform the World Trade Center disaster into new knowledge that could lead to safer future buildings? The answer is straight-forward: disasters are not external in some magical way to the realities of the human-shaped environment or political culture in which they occur. In fact, it is probably best understood the other way around. In the patterns of property destruction, in the communities damaged and those protected, in the technologies and policies available to limit or avoid them, a disaster mirrors the prevailing values of the society in which it occurs. And the same holds true for disaster experts as well. This is not to say that expert knowledge created to predict, mitigate, and recover from disasters has proven itself of no value; it is instead to suggest that the creation and application of such knowledge reflects struggles and priority-setting through which we can learn a great deal about, among other things, the efficacy of the modern state in confronting complex emerging problems, and the evolution of the modern urban environment. How disaster experts have understood risks, how these understandings shaped their research and the ways they applied their research, and how they found funding to continue and promote their findings in law and the built environment are worth a closer look. History shows that disasters are not random or "natural" acts. If and when people take time to study them, disasters reveal patterns of risk and vulnerability built in the environment and the technological systems that undergird modern society. This demand for time to study and ask hard questions about the risks of modern society, however, frequently runs out of phase with the logic of investment and development, and the shortness of public attention spans, and political life spans.

With the Taliban government in Afghanistan gone and debate over the war in Iraq heating up, the first anniversary of September 11 arrived. It was a windy day, the names of the dead echoed across the open pit where the

Twin Towers had stood. The national conversation revolved around the anguish of memory, the enthusiasm for rebuilding, and the thirst for revenge. The World Trade Center disaster was by now largely understood as an act of war, evidence of an external threat to Americans, a horror standing somehow outside the reality of two risky buildings where 50,000 people had gone to work every day, taller but not dissimilar from buildings where Americans went to work every day across the nation. The nation was getting back to business as usual, risk-taking as usual, and the disaster experts and their ongoing World Trade Center collapse investigation were largely forgotten.

Investigating the Disaster Experts

The World Trade Center disaster was not a bolt from the blue. The buildings were evaluated for airplane crash resiliency during their design stage in the 1960s, in part because of the memory of an infamous B-25 crash into the Empire State Building in 1945. Tenants and New York City firefighters expressed misgivings about successfully fighting a fire that high in the sky.[14] Radio communications, insufficient water pressure, and the sheer exhaustion of fighting such fires and evacuating victims from high floors were well-known challenges, illustrated dramatically during the 1993 World Trade Center bombing, a disaster that killed six and injured over 1000 people. But after the 1993 bombing the New York City Fire Department did not solve the radio communications problems they had encountered, evacuation remained mostly unaddressed, and the Port Authority of New York and New Jersey (owner of the land and exempt from New York City building and fire codes) made only small upgrades in building safety overall —no comprehensive disaster mitigation strategy was created for the Twin Towers, and no building-wide evacuation drills were ever held.[15] Fire experts' knowledge of the risks at the World Trade Center were not sufficient to force either comprehensive public or private efforts towards mitigating those risks.

Not too long after the 1993 attack the Twin Towers were back to normal —that is to say they were a bundle of risks dangerous enough to watch and safe enough to use. This type of normal is not an objectively provable condition of safety in any sense, not a guarantee against disaster, but instead reflects a "disaster consensus," a frequently contentious and impermanent agreement among experts over what to protect against disaster, and how to protect it. Cost is a factor, so is knowledge, and of course politics play a role in defining any sort of consensus. The historical record preserves many, many artifacts of consensus moments around risks and disasters, ranging from fire safety codes and flood insurance programs to bomb shelters and color-coded threat charts. It is a varied and at times confusing collection of artifacts, but each reflects the constant interaction of disaster experts and governmental actors, always with input from society and shaped by the physical environment.

The historical literature has tended to treat American disasters episodically, emphasizing the twin dramas of destruction and blame.[16] However, what may seem like disconnected repetitions of natural or technological wrath often, when studied over a longer period of time, offer insight into a more coherent and interconnected story of American risk-taking. It is a story in which disasters repeat themselves because of fundamental American commitments to unrestrained land development, technological innovation, and federalism. Those same commitments have also spurred the development of new knowledge and new methods of risk control designed to keep the builder, the corporation, the citizen, and the elected official one step ahead of catastrophe. Seen in this light, the cinematic "man v. nature" narratives to which we are accustomed leave unexplained the many creative efforts to control disasters, and the reasons for success and failure among those efforts. This more complete history of American disasters also illustrates a recurring conflict between the creation of knowledge—in this case the knowledge of risks and how to prevent or best react to disasters—and the many and varied barriers towards its application.

The Disaster Experts constructs an extensive disaster chronology, shifting the historical focus to a diverse and powerful group of experts who have made the knowledge and control of disasters their special concern. For example, in the complex interplay among disaster experts, elected officials, the media, and victim's families that emerged after the World Trade Center collapse—and that in some instances continues ten years later—we are witnessing a historically-significant period of intense argument over the meanings of, and appropriate responses to, a disaster. While the press and the public have followed along and sometimes made their voices heard, the most influential figures are speaking a highly specialized language. Theirs is the discourse of risk and disaster, and the socio-technical causalities that give these terms form and meaning. Blame for a manifest failure to protect is always a possibility, as is credit for orchestrating an acceptable level of loss. Between these two poles the disaster experts do their main work: creative adjustment to new risks and management of old ones. And when a disaster does occur they are immediately working to make sense of what happened, and to make their way forward in the form of new standards, new technologies, new practices of protection and response. Making sense of the attacks in New York City, disaster experts went to work reconstructing its salient moments, allocating responsibility, finding lessons in the rubble, and offering the possibility of a safer future. Despite limitations on their authority in the months after September 11—limitations highlighted by the Science Committee hearings—the disaster experts charged ahead with their investigations, and the work of reshaping best practices in design, and in building and fire codes. Policies and practices of risk mitigation and disaster response that affect us all have and will continue to be crafted from their recommendations. The intensity of the moment, the immediacy of needing to understand demanded by the public and elected officials, shows us a core problem for disaster experts. Their methods tend to be slow, scientific, and consensus-driven, useful for establishing broad-based, multidisciplinary knowledge and best practices, but far less than ideal for making on-the-spot policy recommendations to politicians or "never again" guarantees to grieving families.

The disaster experts of September 11 did not materialize instantaneously, any more than did the Twin Towers or New York City itself. Their areas of specific knowledge and their claims to authority stretch back decades. It is an exceptionally diverse collection of experts, drawn from various public, private, non-profit, and academic settings. The fire protection experts and the institutions they represent like the National Fire Protection Association, Underwriters Laboratories, and NIST (formerly the National Bureau of Standards) have been active and powerful for more than a century. Federal disaster experts have been on the scene since the Cold War, epitomized by FEMA, with emergency managers also coming in at the state and local levels in the past few decades. Physical scientists and engineers, geographers and social scientists have all contributed to ongoing disaster research programs, aiming to understand disasters and use their understanding to influence the built environment and public disaster policy. Important as these myriad experts are to modern American life, though, there have been correspondingly few attempts to examine them critically, and even fewer efforts to follow them across a long stretch of historical time. *The Disaster Experts* provides this examination, following these experts as they gain and exert authority, and analyzing their work as it consistently defined and redefined urban risks and disasters from the mid nineteenth century into the present century.

The history of disaster experts challenges the conventional wisdom about the relationship between modern knowledge creation and the solving of complex problems.[17] As disaster knowledge began to increase in the late nineteenth century and proliferated in the twentieth century it never led in a linear way to the eradication of, or in many cases even a substantial reduction of risks; in some cases the risks actually increased and disasters remained costly to lives and property. Another surprise: as the number of expert-led institutions charged with protecting the public from disasters has increased, the scale of risk-taking has expanded by leaps and bounds. In other words, in their work towards ending disasters, the experts have supplied much of the confidence necessary to take bigger risks, particularly in the expansion of cities—sometimes in ways that citizens find sustainable, and sometimes in ways that mask tremendous disasters waiting to happen, like the collapse of the Twin Towers or the drowning of New Orleans after Hurricane Katrina in 2005. One feature of this is the fact that risk-taking tends to expand in quanta, not increments. To take one example, once skyscrapers started to be built, and could be protected from collapse or fire, adventurous architects did not pause to make them incrementally taller. Fire protection experts met the challenge by testing steel and a thousand other components along the way, and insurance companies supplied the confidence that enabled construction of the 285-foot Flatiron Building (1902), the 792-foot Woolworth Building (1913), the 1250-foot Empire State Building (1931), and finally the 1368-foot North Tower of the World Trade Center (1970). The same sorts of quantum leaps in risk-taking can be shown in the Cold War era's rapid and terrifying nuclear arms stockpiling, and likewise in the rapid postwar extensions of urban and suburban development into earthquake, wildfire, and flood zones. Each triumph of technology over risk helps to build confidence that is at times built on faulty assumptions. In the first 9/11 House Science Committee hearing of March 2002, Professor Astaneh-Asl put it this way:

What we have done is we have gone up and up over the last century or so without looking into the fact that you cannot expand everything without limit. There is a size effect in everything, in all our engineering work, that when you get to a certain size, you have to change the concept that you are using. We have, unfortunately, added up these floors without looking at the fact that you cannot reach the upper floors for fire fighting and you cannot really protect them against airplanes and other objects. . . . But I think what we . . . missed—and did not pay attention [to] is that, in our effort to build tall buildings, we have not paid attention to protecting them.[18]

It is not surprising that the modern response to the threat of disasters has been to create expert, specialized knowledge. The rise of the modern corporation, the emergence of the industrial metropolis, the use of science and technology both for war and for extending human life, are all phenomena dependent on the creation of more and more specialized knowledge. From research universities and industrial R&D labs to policy think tanks and management consultancies we find the modern American landscape crowded with institutions and experts who define problems, research solutions, and transform abstract knowledge into products and laws. This is a central part of the modernization narrative in western society and remains a standard prescription for "developing" nations.[19] What the narrative leaves unexplained, however, is the difficulty posed when the best of the experts have difficulty solving the trickiest problems, the degradation of the environment, or nuclear arms stockpiling, for example. Is it the experts themselves, the ways they organize their work? Or is it the society, not ready to mobilize their solutions? The struggle of experts to master risk and disaster in modern America provides a perfect case through which to explore such questions, a way to build a contextualized understanding of why American history does not reveal a linear pathway from danger to safety, and why disasters still occur with high loss of life and property every year.

Disasters are by their nature interdisciplinary problems, and cut across jurisdictional boundaries. As such, disaster experts have often struggled to overcome disciplinary boundaries, public/private boundaries, and geographical challenges posed by the rapid environmental changes in modern cities and metropolitan regions. The impediments have been many and varied, including at one time or another federalism and the challenge of working simultaneously through multiple levels of government, public mistrust of big business, public mistrust of government, public mistrust of experts, and the consistently powerful interests of land development and construction. Additionally, though disaster consensus has proven possible in specific times and places, and though saving lives and reducing loss often provides a broadly shared set of values for disaster experts, the fact is that technical experts, social scientists, and government bureaucrats are motivated by different reward structures, speak different professional languages, and compete for authority and access to power in ways that frequently pit them against one another.

At a broader level one might also consider the difference between European society, where a "precautionary principle" holds sway, and an American society that frequently celebrates risk-taking. Tied to economic and even personal development, risk-taking is often heralded as a core feature of the American way of life. In the realm of disasters this has evolved over time into a sort of fatalism, an acceptance that Americans will build in harm's way and take what comes to them. Another factor to consider is that while the memory of disaster runs deep in many American communities, there is a difficulty inherent in transforming memory into mitigation and proactive restrictions on development, especially since disasters occur in multiple locations and at irregular time intervals, and since legal requirements to "remember" through local zoning laws or hazard maps are often nonexistent or erratically enforced. If all of this sounds familiar to debates about public health measures or global warming, it should. The disaster experts are one among many types of experts who are focused on safety and the protection of property who have frequently found their authority challenged or their policy prescriptions ineffective. What they can accomplish in the lab has not always been possible on the floor of the Congress, or in the court of public opinion.

At the same time there have been victories for the disaster experts, moments when their knowledge and skills aligned with opportunities to influence the built environment and disaster policy. These include: voluntary code and standard-setting practices, the creation of non-profit disaster research institutions, public/private partnerships in risk mitigation, innovations in assembling multidisciplinary research teams, the creation of new government agencies at all levels to control risk and disasters, intergovernmental coordination in policy implementation, policy opportunism after disasters, risk education at the grass roots level and the empowerment of "citizen experts." I am not focused on providing objective metrics of success, but rather demonstrating contexts in which disaster experts have set and achieved (or not achieved) their own goals of risk and disaster control. In other words, this is not a history of America becoming more or less safe.

There are plenty of measures out there to make the case in both directions: we have no cities burning down now, but losses over a billion dollars from a single disaster today are common, a rarity a century ago. This is instead a set of stories of how different experts define safety in different eras and work to achieve it.

This book charts the multiple historical trajectories of disaster experts in the making of modern America, with one central question structuring the analysis: what is the relationship between the creation of disaster knowledge and the application of that knowledge toward risk reduction and disaster mitigation? To answer this we find ourselves watching as new risks emerge, and as the demand for expert knowledge grows and the knowledge is produced. We also watch as this knowledge is applied effectively, or not, through channels of public policy, private entrepreneurship, and nonprofit persuasion.

Three key arguments emerge—these define the analytical project of the book. First, effective disaster knowledge usually crosses and often redraws disciplinary boundaries. This reality confounds the faith that any single profession or body of knowledge will be adequate to once-and-for-all manage disasters. Understanding fire, for example, requires facility with chemistry and physics. Understanding fire protection in a city involves the basic science but also local geography, city planning, public policy, and much, much more. In their full complexity disasters present themselves among the most difficult interdisciplinary puzzles in the modern world, encompassing realms technical and social, private and public. Disaster sociologist Russell R. Dynes explains the challenge, and the enticement from a researcher's point of view, posed by disasters: "disaster tends to affect all aspects of a community in a cross-sectional fashion—governmental, legal, religious, industrial, and commercial, health, communications, welfare, educational, and other organizational aspects."[20] There is not a single discipline or collection of disciplines that effectively claims to understand disasters in their totality. This reality has inspired some very innovative multi-disciplinary and interdisciplinary solutions, sometimes sponsored by the private sector— fire insurance for example—sometimes in engineering and the physical and social sciences, and at times by the hand of government.

Second, moving disaster expertise into action has generally required the creation of innovative organizational forms, crossing and sometimes defying public/private and jurisdictional boundaries. Sometimes private sector firms, unable to affect public policy to their advantage, have built their own de facto disaster policy structures through private and non-profit institutional arrangements. This is all strongly conditioned by the federal system of government in the United States, a system in which local needs and state and federal power are constantly at odds, where the constant push and pull of stakeholders ranging from citizens and interest groups to private interests with varying degrees of wealth and influence constantly wrangle to shape the law.

Disasters also provide a thorny issue when it comes to meting out blame—this may in part at least explain why the "act of God" concept was used for so long as an explanation. A deity—or his proxy, nature—cannot be sued, voted out of office, or easily blamed for anything. In a modern capitalist state like the United States, however, finding and fixing blame is a key aspect in adjusting behaviors, policies, and markets to deal with shifting realities, and so it is a subject we must consider. Additionally, private firms have worked hard to influence government's role in managing risk and allocating disaster-related resources. When unable to rely on government, private firms often take matters into their own hands, creating "shadow governments" for risk and disaster control, such as the voluntary fire safety standard system in the United States. Government has in some cases completely taken over a disaster issue—like nuclear attack—for example, where in other areas like local land use policy or building codes the federal government's influence has been halting at best. I consider these concerns, and show how they have been met over time, resulting in the historically shaped disaster system we have today. It is an expert-led system, very talented in gathering and producing knowledge about risks and disasters, but constrained in forcing policy changes, especially changes in land use policy and industrial/technological development.

Last, the American city provides an unprecedented crucible for disasters—modern urbanization itself emerging as a process marked by fires, floods, and the imminent risks inherent in new and untested meetings of people, material, and environment. As such the city serves as the dominant geographical setting for the disaster experts and their work. Urban government in the modern United States has been strongly shaped by disasters, showing creativity amidst the terrors, and establishing hand in hand with private firms realms of expertise that have proven successful over time in defining and managing risk. The disaster experts and their greatest successes have been decidedly urban-focused; fire protection, land use policy, city planning, structural engineering, emergency management, and sustainable development are all areas of expertise that have emerged in one way or another from the concern over the creation and maintenance of urban spaces that are safe. When and where the experts in disaster have failed we generally see established disaster expertise straining against the demands of new urban forms—a dialectic of trial and error tremendously productive of new disaster knowledge. This urban geographical history of disaster expertise has major implications, however, for the prospects of applying disaster expertise in suburban or rural geographies. A tension also exists between the ideal of creating abstract disaster knowledge applicable across space and time, and the reality that disasters often reflect ecologically and socially specific characteristics as unique as the places and eras in which they strike. The appropriate disaster mitigation regime for Chicago will be different from that of Miami, or Los Angeles—despite the dreams of profit and efficiency entailed by "one-size" risk reduction tactics. In this conflict we see the problem of the modern city as one where individual cities may suffer from a poverty of protection as a result of the very forces driving modernization itself: standardization, speed, and laissez-faire federalism.

Looking across historical eras we can see why turning disaster knowledge into practice and disaster policy is not a straightforward task—this book recounts three major historical cases showing how and under what circumstances the process has unfolded. In the end, the nation's faith in autonomous disaster professionals or enlightened policymakers has never been repaid with much success in controlling risk or disaster in America. Intrepid firemen alone could save the nineteenth century city no more than civil defense experts could force Americans into bomb shelters or Jimmy Carter could end flood and earthquake losses by the stroke of the pen that created FEMA. Of more lasting impact have been networks of experts coming together around disaster concerns—working across disciplinary boundaries and often creating ad hoc institutions—and interacting with lawmakers intermittently to push their research and practices out into comprehensive, mandated use. Again, the results have never been a perfect realm of safety, but a disaster consensus holding at a particular place and time around a particular risk.

To develop a century-plus long examination of disaster experts I chronicle three critical eras in the history of American disaster history: the "Conflagration Era" (1860s–1940s), the "Civil Defense Era" (1940s–1980s), and the "All-Hazards Era" (1960s–present). Each era witnessed the American city and its inhabitants confronting its own existential threats—each shaped and was shaped by the development of tools to anticipate, mitigate, or in the worst case explain and recover from a disaster.

The Conflagration Era was the time of most rapid growth in the history of the American city, but conflagrations leveled whole or large sections of cities in this period. Disasters arrived in the form of flood, hurricane, riot, and disease in this era as well. I focus on fire as it was the most consistent, costly, and widely-experienced risk to both life and property in the period. Certainly each of the other types of disasters have inspired close and useful study, and are worthy of continued research. When and where possible I have made connections among the other types of disasters to the fire case.

The rapid growth of the nineteenth-century American industrial metropolis threw cities off balance in their abilities to guard property and citizens against the existential threat of fire. Between the 1860s and 1940s an urban fire crisis precipitated the creation of a new type of expert knowledge, fostered by fire insurance companies, and tailored to understanding the urban fire disaster environment and meeting it with new multi-disciplinary tools of technical analysis. The experts in fire safety worked quickly to revoke the "devil's privilege" of burning the cities, but they met significant barriers to change: construction industry power, political inertia and underdeveloped laws to protect citizens and property, and traditionally low cultural expectations of safety in cities.

Manifold impediments faced fire experts as they worked to harden their research and techniques into laws that would regulate construction and establish norms of safety for the risky technologies—from electric irons to entire factory complexes—that were becoming ubiquitous in the urban environment. That they faced any difficulty at all throws into question the scholarly paradigm of the Progressive Era as a time when the "rule of experts" saved the American city. New analytical tools and a call for objectivity over localism and cronyism certainly marked the period, evidenced by the Iroquois Theater Fire (1903) in Chicago and the resulting investigations into its causes. But fire expertise was caught in a paradox of the Progressive Era, considering that so much of its growth was fostered by one of the nation's largest industries. Public fear of fire disasters coming from one direction collided with public outrage against the amalgamation of monopoly power coming from the other, a situation that resulted in new opportunities for nonprofit sector fire protection institutions to assert authority.

Fire safety experts' work as they transformed their knowledge into building codes and safety standards strongly curtailed the urban conflagration hazard in the United States by the eve of World War II. Led by Underwriters Laboratories and the National Fire Protection Association the fire experts developed claims to neutrality and expertise in research and policy prescription that helped to form a consensus around the meaning of fire safety in the United States; this consensus grew into a flexible standard-setting system that was largely voluntary in nature, thriving somewhere between private sector autonomy and comprehensive public regulation. This work combined with that of urban planners, building code councils, and a growing state and federal regulatory sector successfully extinguished the conflagration threat in American cities from center city business districts.

A new era of urban risk was dramatically initiated by the development of the atomic bomb. While fire experts were reaching the high point of their skills in American cities by World War II, physicists in Los Alamos would in three short years undermine their efforts. In this Civil Defense Era the threat of nuclear attack on American cities led to the rise of federally-directed civil defense experts who oversaw the preparation of cities for nuclear attack while all other urban disaster risks were demoted to lesser significance. A strong consensus formed at all levels of government around the need to prioritize nuclear war preparedness through fall-out shelter construction, post-attack planning, and citizen mobilization around civil defense goals. A top-down military command and control mindset marked this type of disaster expertise, while at the same time other disaster experts were developing more contextual tools of social science, fire protection, and ecological analysis that from the perspective of cities were more useful and appropriate to their safety needs.

The idea that disasters are primarily caused by external threats (like the Soviet Union's nuclear arsenal)—a central idea of the Civil Defense Era—came under intense scrutiny from the 1960s forward. In the 1970s the "civil defense consensus" gave way to an "all hazards consensus" as cities and states rejected the federal command and control structure of disaster preparedness. In this All-Hazards Era social science disaster researchers, geography-based hazards researchers, as well as weather and climate experts and geophysical scientists all developed significant new paradigms for understanding disasters and their causes and impacts. This redrew the lines of inquiry within which risks and disasters were analyzed, and policy makers responded with new programs and federal funding to incentivize risk mitigation across the full spectrum of disasters that might strike the nation. A rising tide of research and legislation emerged in these years around the idea of mitigating disasters to avoid or minimize their impact, focusing on understanding and addressing the underlying hazards facing a given environment.

A remarkable quantity and diversity of disaster research was performed by social scientists in the 1950s–1970s, funded by federal civil defense agencies, as civil defenders struggled to model the potential results of a nuclear attack on American cities. By examining earthquakes, floods, industrial accidents and other disasters, the social scientists developed a key set of findings about communities under stress, findings that in many cases demonstrated nuclear civil defense efforts to be misguided at best and useless at worst. Though their research was ground breaking, the social science disaster knowledge created by the end of the 1960s had done very little to reshape risk and disaster policy at the federal, state, or local level.

Following the rise of all-hazards analysis informed by geography and physical sciences research, and a shift towards mitigation as a method of disaster avoidance, a broad-based rejection of nuclear-focused civil defense as a workable national disaster strategy began to unfold in the 1960s. In this context the profession of emergency management began to take shape, marked by the Carter Administration's creation of the Federal Emergency Management Agency in 1979. Emergency management grew rapidly as an area of disaster expertise, taking within its purview all functions in disaster mitigation, preparedness, response, and recovery. The research core of emergency management contains social science, public health, geography, and ecology while at the same time its practical application rests in public administration first response training. As cities faced the hurricanes, earthquakes, fires, and other disasters of the 1970s-1990s emergency managers grew in number and authority.

By the end of the 1990s FEMA had been elevated to Cabinet-level status and the idea that "there is no such thing as a natural disaster" was broadly held by disaster experts who looked at vulnerabilities in communities and geographies as co-creations of human and environmental interaction. The strong leadership and mitigation mindset of James Lee Witt as FEMA administrator, and the subsequent move of FEMA to a Cabinet-level organization were emblematic of the rising profile of emergency management in the 1990s. With its success, emergency management at the turn of the century nevertheless displayed a profound split between those who would focus on mitigating disasters in the first place and others who emphasized the profession's strengths in disaster response. Squabbles with critics of the civil defense mindset, and the ever-present difficulties presented in disasters by federalism remained as artifacts of the Cold War era, impossible for emergency managers to completely cast aside. September 11, 2001 and the year that followed threw into plain view the competition that persisted, even with the Cold War over, between and among risk and disaster experts focusing on all hazards approaches and mitigation, and experts who wished to revive the command and control mindset of the Civil Defense Era.

A note on terminology is required at the outset. Within the contemporary disaster research community there exists a lively debate—spawning many articles and books—on the definitional range of the term "disaster."[21] As this is a work of history, I strive to supply historical context in order to understand how different actors chose to define the term over the past century and a half. Attempts to define disaster by body or dollar counts might be considered "objective," but would hardly be historically nuanced in a way that might explain why some disaster concerns have inspired concerted research and policy actions and others not.

Where historical actors make use of specific terminology I work to cite the usage, and to explain its significance and evolution. This becomes important particularly in the latter section of the book as the disaster research community begins to grow rapidly, especially in the fields of sociology and geography, and their debates over terminology begin to shape their research methodologies and conclusions. Additionally, where the federal government began to create what we might broadly term "federal disaster policy" in the 1960s it is necessary to pay attention to definitions as they are reflected in policy language, and as they ultimately shaped disaster mitigation and response patterns on the ground.

Historical actors themselves are inexact in their usage of "disaster language" most of the time. That inexactitude is itself a subject of inquiry that this book addresses. Terms often used interchangeably in the historical record include: disaster, catastrophe, calamity, emergency, and crisis. Also used interchangeably are: risk, threat, vulnerability, hazard, and menace. Where historical actors describe their concerns over specific types of disasters, a "conflagration," or "deluge," or less prosaically a fire or flood, I use their terms—especially when the word implies a degree of intensity for a fire or flood that rises to significance from the actor's perspective. It is historically accurate in many cases to use terms like disaster and risk broadly and loosely constructed, especially when looking at actors who do not feel compelled to speak in an objective or scientific manner, but instead wish to make more general points about the universal nature and validity of their concerns. When specific terms are not used in the historical record, or when I am speaking in a more synthetic manner, I use the words "disaster" and "risk." I derive these words and their definitions from a sort of "average" usage evident in the period and places under examination in this book. I take "disaster" to mean "an event focused in time and place causing significant disruptions to normal activities and incurring unacceptably high losses of property and/or life." I take risk to mean "a likelihood, which may be described either quantitatively or qualitatively, that a disaster will occur." My approach to the use of the word "expert" follows this logic as well. Where appropriate I defer to the historical actors themselves as they define their roles as experts, specialists, scientists, engineers, or managers. In general, though, I take an expert to be "a person with a defensible claim to authority based on possession of specialized knowledge and/or practice." Developing context to see where and under what circumstances claims to expertise are successful, and where not, is a major task of the book.

There is contingency lurking in these definitions, factors of time, place, and causality waiting to be revealed. For example, "unacceptably high losses" immediately prompts the need for context. Unacceptable to whom? High by what measure? Can an event with no loss of life still be a disaster? The same holds with the "possession of specialized knowledge." Is everyone in possession of specialized knowledge equally powerful, and if not, why not? What limits the utilization of expert knowledge? Under what conditions does it shape public policy? The answer to each of these questions is, unavoidably: it depends. But to say that it depends is not a rhetorical shoulder shrug; it is an invitation to historical analysis.

Engineers, scientists, civil defense officials and emergency managers, and social scientists all appear in these pages. Though the work of disaster experts has often been interdisciplinary, professional identities did and still do shape expert perceptions of their achievements in theory and practice. I have chosen case studies that intentionally look across these disciplinary, as well as governmental, divides—a strategy that I hope leads to some spirited conversations about the real barriers that traditional modes of professionalization often pose towards the solving of major societal problems. An additional point to make before going further: the absence of key disaster researchers and practitioners from this history should not be seen as diminishing their roles in American history—the fire service is not, for example, treated in detail, nor are geophysical scientists, civil and earthquake engineers, public health experts and many, many others. Excellent studies already exist for these groups in many cases, and it is hoped that many of the trends outlined in these pages will prove applicable to further historical analysis of an even more diverse cast of disaster experts in future studies. Finally, contemporary disaster researchers and practitioners might find it odd to consider themselves as part of a larger American historical narrative in which technical, social, and policy innovations in response to disaster threats are all considered together. My hope is that connectivity and historical parallels emerge that might stimulate fresh thinking about how disaster experts have historically defied, and could continue to defy professional and disciplinary boundaries, as well as obstacles to intergovernmental cooperation, in the cause of disaster mitigation.

It is a standard lament heard after an American disaster: "We have to learn from this tragedy so that it never happens again." The fact is that the historical record is full and available; disasters do not recur in the United States because of a poverty of knowledge. Forgetfulness about risks and disasters is no accident. This book addresses one aspect of our national disaster amnesia, a disjunction between knowledge and action that is frustrating, but that history shows is capable of being overcome.

1

The Devil's Privilege

Industrialism, the main creative force of the nineteenth century, produced the most degraded urban environment the world had yet seen. . . . Extraordinary changes of scale took place in the masses of buildings and the areas they covered; vast structures were erected almost overnight. Men built in haste, and had hardly time to repent of their mistakes before they tore down their original structures and built again, just as heedlessly. . . . It was a period of vast urban improvisation: makeshift hastily piled upon makeshift. . . . Every man was for himself; and the Devil, if he did not take the hindmost, at least reserved for himself the privilege of building the cities.

—Lewis Mumford

Disasters threatened and destroyed industrializing American cities in the nineteenth and early twentieth centuries with a ferocity that challenged the notion of modernity itself as a sustainable urban condition. Chicago's infamous 1871 fire leveled whole neighborhoods as well as the entire business district in a three-day blaze. Boston (1872) and Seattle (1889) fared only slightly better. Financial losses from fires in the United States were just under $75 million dollars in 1880 and had more than quadrupled to $330 million in 1920 —with over $250 million lost in the 1904 Baltimore conflagration year alone, and $359 million lost in the 1906 San Francisco Earthquake and Fire year.[1] The Iroquois Theater Fire (1903), breaking out in a Chicago building advertised as "fireproof," took 602 lives in less than fifteen minutes; the Triangle Shirtwaist Factory Fire (1911) killed 146 immigrant textile workers, many of whom leaped out of windows to their deaths. Among the 20 deadliest fires in American history, 18 occurred between 1865 and 1945.[2] Though hurricanes and floods, earthquakes, and epidemic disease struck frequently, fire consumed lives and property with a regularity that truly marked this time in American history as a "Conflagration Era."

Fire in industrializing America presented a threat encompassing every aspect of urban life, including the grave possibility of exterminating entire cities. Fire presented two complex and intertwined problems. First, fire risk was not equally allocated across the urban landscape; it was contingent on factors that changed from building to building, block to block, neighborhood to neighborhood. In the rapidly changing urban environment it was difficult to predict where the next fire might break out—to even begin to do so would require a massive effort toward understanding the science of fire and materials, construction history and vulnerabilities across the urban landscape, and comparative success of fire mitigation techniques from city to city. Second, a nuanced understanding of fire risk was not consistently fostered among city government officials, who might have exercised strong police powers in zoning and building code enforcement. Sporadic attempts to do so followed in the wake of major disasters like the 1871 Chicago Fire; but, such attempts were overcome time and again in every city by the daunting task of collecting the information necessary to standardize fire safety, and by the powerful interests of development. Elected officials found this situation risky to their political lives when disaster struck, but in most cases the risks of fire were tolerated in the nineteenth century by citizens with relatively low expectations of strong government action toward public safety, and high hopes for rapid construction and economic growth.

Before the Civil War private and volunteer firefighting companies proliferated in American cities, manned in many cases by firemen inspired to join by the neighborhood-level cultural appeals of ethnicity and race. By the latter part of the nineteenth century firefighting became too important to leave disorganized and chaotic, so cities took over this function and the fire service and its techniques became standardized and trusted. At this time fire departments and small building inspection departments comprised the sum total of publicly available knowledge about, and authority over, fire risk. Municipal water and fire alarm telegraph systems incrementally made the fire service more effective, but the overall situation was still a reactive and mostly passive government response to fire at a time of steadily heightening risk. In this risky environment heroic firemen were apparently expected to save the industrial city from itself. And when the firemen failed, as they inevitably would against unsafe high rise office buildings and theaters, factories and tenements, the public would just have to accept destruction by fire as a constant of the urban experience.[3]

The specter of fire in the Conflagration Era exposed a conflict at the heart of industrialization, a condition of "reflexive modernity" explained by sociologist Ulrich Beck in which the exact processes making the industrial metropolis possible also manufactured a startlingly high level of risk. The technological and financial achievements of the industrial age brought with them a corresponding emphasis on standard setting, performance, and invention. Delivering high performance and reliability from technological systems sat at the center of new claims to authority from technically minded elites in American cities.[4] And yet it was this very same cadre of industrial entrepreneurs and managers, engineers, scientists, and financiers bringing about the changes that were making cities increasingly likely to burn. One group of experts among them was acutely aware of this paradox. Threatened consistently with massive losses and bankruptcies the fire insurance industry took on the twin challenges of fire: understanding it, and bringing about the reforms necessary to prevent it.

From the 1860s forward, an emerging vanguard of fire experts, many of them connected with the fire insurance industry, worked to influence the built city through creation and dissemination of knowledge about fire risks and disasters. Some objective basis on which to define safety was badly needed for the fire insurance industry to set profitable rates for coverage—not an easy task in hodgepodge cities full of wood and machinery jammed next to steel and glass, and with no standard approaches to municipal government control over fire risk. Generalization and abstraction, with so many technical and regulatory variations, were not easy to accomplish. However, valuable knowledge about fire risks was being created on the job by the fire insurance experts, and as knowledge expanded, fires and conditions causing them began to fall into what observers believed were discernible patterns. This led to new efforts to influence the built environment through both market pressure in the form of higher rates and public policy pressure in the form of more stringent building and fire codes. With both strategies progressing in fits and starts throughout the late nineteenth century, the insurance industry also created novel nonprofit organizations geared toward understanding fire risk systematically and scientifically, and disseminating the knowledge widely. When their work veered toward the theoretical they found willing collaborators in university science and engineering departments. When their work pitched toward the applied, they found partners in the fire service, the architecture and city planning professions, and among muckraking journalists and consumer advocates.

A fire disaster expert network expanded its knowledge and authority in the United States in the late nineteenth century, rooted in the activities of two different segments of the fire insurance industry. One was the National Board of Fire Underwriters (NBFU), a collection of companies that had grown frantic after the Civil War at the prospect of keeping up with increasing urban fire risks. A second industry organization, the Associated Factory Mutual Fire Insurance Companies (Factory Mutuals), had for decades before the Civil War been championing fire safety in the design and maintenance of factories in New England. The Factory Mutuals and NBFU over time came to collaborate in the name of fire protection and the profitability it made possible. Despite their accomplishments in information-gathering and risk analysis, at the height of the period of industrialization—a moment marked by the deification of electricity in Chicago at the 1893 World's Columbian Exposition—the risks continued to aggregate. The disaster experts saw themselves behind the pace of urban change no matter how fast they worked. In the midst of this uncertainty, the introduction of laboratory testing methods in order to quantify and rate electrical and structural materials marked a new approach to the broad goal of achieving urban fire safety, one that found immediate legitimacy through its reliance on scientific and engineering practice that elevated it above mounting criticism of big business in the late nineteenth century. In the pioneering work of William H. Merrill, founder of Underwriters Laboratories (UL) in Chicago, we see the invention of fire safety moving to the laboratory. This held implications not only for the growth of knowledge about fire safety but also the ability of the fire insurance industry to work toward preventing or at least mitigating fires in a climate of reactionary and sporadic government attention to fire risk. By the end of the nineteenth century it was possible for the fire experts to collect what had been learned over the previous decades, codify it, and teach it, signified by the innovative "fire protection engineering" program taught at Chicago's Armour Institute of Technology. In each of these ways the explosion of risk in the Conflagration Era prompted an emerging cadre of disaster experts to ask new questions and develop new techniques with which they hoped to revoke the "Devil's privilege" in the American city.

The National Board of Fire Underwriters

There is no better way to map the landscapes of risk in industrializing America than to chart the history of the fire insurance industry.[5] Fire insurance in the United States is traceable back to the colonial period, but in general municipal governments and lenders did not require property owners to purchase it. Many fire insurance customers were, as might be expected, merchants who stood to lose their businesses if docks and warehouses went up in flames. In Philadelphia, Benjamin Franklin helped found an insurance company that provided protection for homeowners, tied to an integrated firefighting-insurance connection followed also by some European cities. Experimentation and variability in municipal firefighting capabilities and insurance requirements marked American urbanization until the twentieth century.[6]

The fire insurance industry was (and is) divided into two general types: stock companies and mutuals. Stock companies make up the larger share of the industry, and are marked by a profit-based model, dependent on writing policies and collecting premiums that surpass losses paid out to policyholders. The stock companies are often publicly traded (hence the term "stock"). Stock companies derive much of their profitability from returns on investments made with the premiums collected. Mutuals are often cooperatively or privately owned and reflect the interests of a particular class of risks, usually large-scale industrial risks. Mutual policyholders have traditionally been more willing to adopt fireproofing technologies in exchange for lower premiums and have been interested in insurance policies less as investment instruments than as more specific methods of risk mitigation.

In 1866, after staggering fire losses at the end of the Civil War, stock fire insurance companies banded together into a nationwide organization, the National Board of Fire Underwriters (NBFU).[7] Previously, individual companies and local associations operated largely without sharing information about rate-setting techniques and standards for coverage. The NBFU emerged as an instrument through which to try to bring standards and order to a geographically dispersed industry. The founding goals of the

NBFU included provisions for establishment of uniform rates and premiums and payment of agents, arson reduction, and promotion of the value of insurance for both businesses and individual consumers.[8] Small and isolated fires could even be good for business by encouraging customers to take out policies and governments to require coverage. But in order to profit by risk, the NBFU had to begin to measure, calculate, and attempt to control the largest fire disasters.

To "establish and maintain . . . a system of uniform rates of premiums . . . and maintain a uniform rate of compensation to agents and brokers" were the NBFU's first two founding principles.[9] Both indicate a desire for price standardization across the industry—a need that required a hitherto unrealized level of statistical knowledge about insured and potentially insurable structures. A clear goal was comprehensive, timely, accurate information.[10] If fires were perceived as inevitable (and necessary to business), the most profitable way to run insurance companies involved knowing what sorts of buildings are most likely to burn, and charging premiums that reflected the accurate level of danger by region or city and by class of structure. By sharing information from around the country, individual underwriters would now be able to see a more comprehensive map of dangers than was ever before possible.

In good times fire insurance companies might stray from organizational cohesion and information sharing, but the NBFU's work took on new urgency after the Chicago Fire of 1871.[11] The Chicago Fire—still the most storied in American history—killed as many as 300 people, rendered 90,000 homeless, and left a "Burnt District" four miles long and roughly three-quarters of a mile wide; damages totaled 200 million dollars, and almost every fire insurer doing business in the city failed, leaving the industry demoralized and policyholders stranded.[12] Coming as it did in the midst of an election season, the conflagration turned fireproofing and building standards into a political issue, with a "Fire Proof Party" taking most of the seats on the Board of Aldermen with its pledge to rebuild Chicago as a fireproof city.

As historian Christine Meisner Rosen explains, difficulties emerged immediately after the election around the exact nature of the legislation needed to end the conflagration risk. Fire Proof Party officials and many middle- and upper-income Chicagoans, along with the downtown business community, advocated a total ban on wooden frame construction in the city. Working-class, mostly immigrant Chicagoans pushed back against the ban, fearing the high costs of building brick homes. Protests and debate animated a season in which compromise finally emerged in the form of a "comprehensive ordinance" establishing a sizable inner urban zone where wooden frame construction was banned and risky industries like explosives manufacturing and planing mills were prohibited. Wooden construction was permitted in the outer zones. Such an approach was far-sighted, as it addressed individual property-owners' responsibilities as well as introducing a zoning concept of planning at a larger scale to define and spatially organize acceptable and unacceptable land uses. While building and fire codes stretched back to the founding of American cities, zoning for risk mitigation was not yet standard practice.[13]

The new fire ordinance in Chicago reflected the possibility for open democratic dialogue and policy action around consensus risk and disaster standards in the industrializing city. However, as it turned out, the restrictions on wooden construction did not include flammable roofing materials, wooden sidewalks, or other wooden architectural elements. The ordinance also "contained no provisions for effective enforcement of its prohibitions. Thus it did little to stop people from building wooden houses even in the inner zone." Rosen concludes that industrializing cities like Chicago—even in the aftermath of extraordinary disasters—"were not able to use their police powers to condemn or compel the renovation of structures that violated building laws in any sweeping way until the twentieth century."[14] Elected officials did not have the expertise in fire protection to frame a truly effective fireproofing law in the first place, and if they had they still lacked the authority or manpower to punish scofflaws. Meanwhile, in the midst of the election and legislative wrangling, the city was being rapidly rebuilt, largely out of wood. In the end, the Chicago that rose from the ashes was very much like the one it replaced.

An early test of the NBFU's abilities to control insurance premiums and standards of coverage at the local city level came in 1874, as Chicago was still dealing with the aftermath of the 1871 conflagration. After receiving reports that the city was just as ready to burn again as it had been in 1871, the NBFU Executive Committee sent two investigators to the city in the summer of 1874, who found "alarming defects." The fire department was in disarray; fire stations exhibited "no pride" in their appearance. Wooden frame structures still dominated buildings in the city. The NBFU investigators judged that fire inspectors were politically motivated and neglected their duties, leading them to conclude that "It would appear that buildings

can be erected in any way or style that suits the convenience of the interested parties, irrespective of the law . . . no effort being made to enforce the
law." The citizens might be "indifferent" to such dangers, but the NBFU
resolved to act.[15]

The NBFU called for a complete fire insurance boycott in the city until
Chicago adopted permanent fire limits or zones, a stringent building law,
reorganization and eradication of political influence in the fire department,
increase in water facilities, establishment of a Fire-Marshal's Bureau, and a
law to compel the gradual removal of hazards.[16] To a surprising degree, the
action worked, at least in terms of organizing NBFU member companies
around a common set of goals and demands from city government. Companies affiliated with the NBFU refused to insure Chicago's buildings for
almost six weeks in the autumn of 1874, and only slowly resumed previous
rates of coverage.[17] The NBFU drew from the boycott a rising confidence
—and a belief that through unified action it might gain the power to influence the built environment of a city.

Such unified action, however, required data about urban fire risks and
standards for the analysis of such risks. Gathering and analyzing these data,
establishing building codes, and embarking on a crusade of civic persuasion
stand as the NBFU's primary innovations throughout this period. The existence of "wildcat" insurance companies—willing to write policies on any
structure in any city—seems to have been the undoing of the NBFU's
efforts in this case and would continue to disrupt its abilities to force public
sector fire safety initiatives. The era was marked by a constant back and
forth between stock insurers who saw profitability as necessitating control
of the built environment and others who saw writing more policies and
charging the highest possible rates as the best strategy. The excesses of the
latter strategy would become the basis for a sustained populist reaction
against the fire insurance industry in the 1880s, resulting in a wave of regulatory actions over the industry in the 1890s–1900s.

The NBFU's risk mitigation strategy in these early years also involved
the introduction of a set of information gathering and risk categorization
techniques. Beginning in 1866, and for many years after, the NBFU annual
proceedings teemed with statistics. Comparative rates of fire losses in specific parts of the country and around the world, analysis of specific types of
fires as to their causes, and fluctuations in profits as a function of building
materials used are just a few examples of the new information gathered by
the underwriters. Also in 1874 the NBFU undertook an ongoing series of

studies on specific fire departments and water delivery systems throughout the United States. The first report of the Committee on Fire Departments, Salvage Corps, and Water Supply discussed the reliability of such services in 660 locations around the country.[18] The Committee paid particular attention to the larger cities in the survey and felt compelled to make recommendations that were then used to help in the establishment of rates. The standards could be very specific. For example, it judged that "No city . . . of 30,000 inhabitants should have less than two trucks of eight ladders each, including an extension ladder, carrying six short hooks, two of medium size of nine feet and two long hooks of fifteen feet, besides axes and fire extinguishers, and no town should be without at least one truck; these should be manned by not less than five men. It is one of the most valuable means of fire protection, and is of the utmost consequence when skillfully handled in preventing the spread of a conflagration."[19]

The NBFU also considered the composition and construction of buildings. Tentatively at first, this soon became the NBFU's most significant innovation. NBFU "suggested" building codes appeared in their yearly proceedings and in circulars sent around to civic officials and fire departments. The codes themselves dealt with a range of topics, including building height in relation to the width of local streets, use of materials such as wood and concrete, stairways and windows, heating, and wall and roof dimensions.[20]

The NBFU Committee on Construction of Buildings published a report in 1875 that set out a city classification system based on the existence and enforcement of building codes. While the NBFU preferred cities to adopt its suggested codes, fire codes established at the local level were often recognized as well. Cities were divided into four classes, from first, where "laws are regarded as approximating a standard of excellence, and also including cities where the law is regarded as adequate to the size of the place," to fourth, "having no laws either as to construction of Buildings or Fire Limits." Anything below a first class rating for large cities like Chicago was considered an egregious failing. First class cities included Boston and New York; Chicago was second-class along with Philadelphia; Atlanta, Detroit, Providence, and St. Paul were in the third class; and Baltimore and San Francisco were rated fourth class—both would burn catastrophically, in 1904 and 1906 respectively.[21]

Ruinous price competition among member companies eroded the NBFU's cohesiveness and powers of collective action over safety standards in the 1880s, leaving urbanites more exposed than ever to risk taking in construction. Alongside the national network, though, local boards and associations of underwriters evolved.[22] These boards were often highly effective, like that founded in Philadelphia by mapmaker and "fire engineer" Charles Hexamer, in influencing local construction and fire safety codes. Local insurance board members might be active in local business and political circles, giving them influence that a national insurance expert might not enjoy. A tight fit between fire insurance experts and policymakers could be accomplished in this way, especially in cities like Philadelphia, Boston, and New York, where government was more established and where development was happening at a less frenetic pace than that witnessed in the western industrial cities like Chicago, Seattle, and St. Louis. In the stock insurance local boards we find many of the fire safety experts who began to see a way forward in sustained fire safety through private pressure on both customers and government.[23]

Building codes at this time, though they could be quite specific as to allowable heights, materials, and occupancies, were sporadically enforced, with very small inspection departments even in cities like New York and Chicago. The NBFU and the local insurance boards assumed the role of classifying and codifying acceptable building methods more systematically than any municipal government of the late nineteenth century. Against the backdrop of social and technological upheavals that marked the late nineteenth-century American city, the NBFU had realized that simply reacting to fire dangers was not good enough. Their efforts to influence building codes signified a hope that local government might assist in limiting their losses (and build their profits) through adoption of the new standards that they suggested. In these years, underwriters began to also increasingly see scientific analysis and invention as tools with which to build their dream: the insured, yet fireproof city.

In an 1889 speech, NBFU president D. A. Heald recounted the organization's innovations; however, he was quick to point out that such innovations were not enough to meet the changing tide of new technologies in the cities. He explained that "Many of these . . . changes, and injurious tendencies it has been the purpose of this Board to control . . . where it could not entirely prevent their introduction or ward off their injurious effects. Turning to our classification lists we can scarcely point to a single class of insurable property that has not been affected by hazards of which little or nothing was known twenty-five or thirty years ago. So radically has the nature of our business changed, that to keep pace with its demands and meet its ever-increasing hazards, require the utmost activity at our command."[24] The "utmost activity" still found the NBFU often racing from behind to keep up in a business where the emergence of a new technology could force a reconsideration of all that was known about the risks of the city before. Electricity was just such a technology.

From about 1880 electric power and light began its ascent as a visible economic and cultural force in the United States. First used in hotels and public lighting demonstrations, direct current systems and arc lights connoted status and wealth, as well as changing the way America did business. The famous "battle of the systems" erupted in the 1880s between Thomas Edison's direct current system and George Westinghouse's alternating current, as central generator systems began to creep across the nation and form a patchwork of electrified towns and cities. This was a time of great uncertainty in the commercial utilities industry, and a time when forward-looking businessmen, such as Elihu Thomson and Samuel Insull, stood to reap enormous profits.

What the standard narrative of electrification often leaves out is that electricity posed a serious threat to insurance companies and consumers who bore the economic and physical burden in the event that this highly prized new invention should fail. While electricity did replace a dangerous set of technologies— open fires, oil lamps, and gas heaters—it should be noted that the blessing of electricity was decidedly mixed. First of all, in Chicago for example, electricity did not advance along a steady front in the city. Wealthier residents and businesses in the central business district enjoyed electric lighting, while workers on the city's South Side relied on more traditional fuels for light and heat. Also, the advent of electricity allowed for a range of consumer goods unimaginable in a time when power delivery resided mainly in coal and petroleum products. Electric stoves, lamps, and irons simply replaced their wood- or gas-powered ancestors. However, new inventions such as elevators, telephones, and burglar alarms illustrated a new range of applications available for electricity. While electricity may have replaced or modified a number of risky technologies, it likewise added to the overall number of unproven and potentially dangerous technologies in the city.[25] Chairman of the NBFU Committee on Statistics F. O. Affeld voiced concern over this situation in 1892, pointing out the dangers of "the unscrupulous business man who . . . employs cheap laborers to look after boilers and electric light apparatus, and who hires bell hangers and the cheapest kind of labor to put in electric light equipments."[26] For this reason it remained crucial to the NBFU to work in areas where it might exert the most influence in keeping the number of electrical fires down.

When the NBFU met in 1892, on the eve of Chicago's Columbian Exposition, electricity in the expanding American city was at the very top of the list of concerns. In the words of one underwriter, "There is so little that we do understand about electricity, and our ignorance is so dense that we may well stand appalled in the presence of dangers which we know are great but the magnitude of which we are too ignorant to appreciate."[27]

The Associated Factory Mutual Fire Insurance Companies

An organization of New England insurance companies—the Associated Factory Mutual Fire Insurance Companies—emerged in the mid-nineteenth century, working primarily to reduce fire losses by compelling their clients to adopt fireproof construction. The Boston Manufacturers Mutual Fire Insurance Company, founded by Zachariah Allen in 1835, led the way. Allen ran a cotton mill and found that despite the fact that his mill contained "every appliance for putting out a fire that he could find," he received no reduction in premiums from stock insurance companies.[28] Allen's idea was to organize factory owners as members of a cooperative (mutual), who would, in effect, own their own insurance company and set strict building design and maintenance guidelines for membership. Cotton mill owners oversaw factories full of highly flammable raw materials, with plenty of dust and moving machine parts ready to ignite the mill. For this reason, they believed they really had no choice about whether to insure. Mutuals could keep premiums low if buildings were constructed and maintained using fireproofing technologies.

Mutual insurance companies represent a niche of institutional innovation in the business history of the United States. Mutuals emerged as an alternative at a time of profound market centralization in the insurance industry, a sort of middle way between strong government regulation on one side and the stock corporation model on the other. Of the mutuals in business in the early twentieth century, an overwhelming number were founded in the years of greatest urban growth, as well as greatest Gilded Age market centralization, the 1890s and 1900s.[29] Mutual companies were focused primarily on specific cities or regions and specific classes of risks, factories, for example, allowing them to gain a depth of knowledge not possible if they had been more geographically dispersed or less specialized. Unlike stock companies that invested policyholders' premiums, mutuals tended to be cooperatively owned and managed by their policyholders, a fact that reduced operating costs and limited the interest in functions beyond policy writing and inspection.

The mutuals philosophy resulted in the first efforts to innovate in fire-proof construction on a scale that had previously been practiced only in very specific types of buildings, primarily courthouses and seats of government, hospitals, prisons, and banks. Over the next forty years the Factory Mutuals prospered and the business model spread; by the 1870s the Factory Mutuals network included 17 member companies throughout New England, with members meeting regularly to discuss standards and to exchange information on risks.[30]

Analysis by sociologist Marc Schneiberg reveals that mutuals came in two forms in the late nineteenth century. One variety focused on large-scale industrial risks in the Northeast; the others were "small, locally operating class mutuals associated with farmers, merchants and small manufacturers in the Midwest and the rural communities of a few eastern states." Both types "formed a well-defined and recognized alternative to the for-profit, joint stock corporation."[31] Purely economic explanations would predict that mutuals were necessary only in places where customers could not get insurance from a stock company, or where stock companies had low reputations for paying out on claims. Like stock insurers, mutuals offered consumers a measure of control over the built environment through private means, in the absence of meaningful state or municipal oversight of fire risks. Mutuals, though, often emerged in places where a strong antimonopoly politics was ascendant, and where consumers wanted more responsive, "homegrown" institutions to address their insurance needs. Additionally, mutuals (like the New England Factory Mutuals) paid extra attention to fire mitigation and specialized in insuring the most dangerous industrial customers (textile and paper mills, for example). In such settings mutuals could grow to be large and geographically dispersed, and often succeeded over decades in direct competition with stock insurers.[32]

By the 1870s the mutual insurance organizational method had proven its stability. Meanwhile, the pace of industrialization was picking up markedly, and fire risks now encompassed larger rural factories, as well as the dynamic and dangerous urban industrial environment. The most significant figure involved in meeting these challenges, guiding and expanding the Factory Mutuals influence during this period was a man named Edward Atkinson. Atkinson was born in Brookline, Massachusetts, in 1827.[33] In 1878, he gave up his activities in cotton manufacturing and shifted to the world of fire insurance, assuming a post as president-treasurer of the Boston Manufacturers Mutual Fire Insurance Company, which had been active since 1850. Atkinson had served on the board of directors of the company since 1865. The Factory Mutuals strategy that Atkinson inherited involved "confining their risks to one general type . . . expanding their territory only as they were able to supervise the extended area." The Mutuals recognized "the principle that the primary function of the fire insurance company was to prevent losses and not merely to distribute them after fires had occurred." It was a cautious approach, too cautious for a shrewd businessman like Atkinson, who was out to market his reformer's zeal for combating what he saw as the unaccountably wasteful yearly fire losses of the country.[34] Up to 1878, Atkinson believed that Factory Mutuals inspections "had been made in a desultory manner by the presidents or secretaries of the several companies about once a year, usually a few weeks before the expiration of the policy. Modern safeguards had not been thoroughly investigated. Automatic sprinklers were known, but had secured little or no attention. There were no experience tables, no classification of risks, and no real comprehension of the relative hazards on different classes."[35]

Atkinson attacked each of these shortcomings, remaking the Factory Mutuals into an extremely active and innovative fire safety institution whose work soon extended beyond the narrow confines of factory insurance. He proposed a comprehensive method for fireproof construction in factories that came to be called "slow-burning" mill construction. The "slow-burning" theory emphasized both structural design features and fire-mitigation technologies in the mill. This involved incremental changes in construction methods, capped off by the introduction of the automatic sprinkler. About the time Atkinson joined the Factory Mutuals, they were beginning to suggest sprinklers to customers, and between 1880 and 1910 most members adopted the technology.[36] Atkinson also worked to involve factory employees themselves in the fire protection of their workplace. In 1878, the Boston Mutual organized an inspection department that would eventually pursue a regular regime of quarterly inspections for all risks. The inspections were used to standardize factory conditions and to connect the company with its customers on a regular basis. Atkinson also called for the drafting of complete plans of the premises of each risk, so that the Factory Mutuals might study them and make suggestions for the elimination of hazards. Lastly, Atkinson reviewed policies and acted to have dangerous risks removed from the companies' books over the next two years. It was an ambitious program, and one that opened up opportunities to both guide the construction of new factories, and to learn more from the risks "in the field."

At first, according to Atkinson, he and his staff learned: "by experience . . . without much reference to science or statistics. The inspectors were all mill men; men of very great capacity and of wonderful memory; but they were few in number. They visited the risks but once a year; and there was no general distribution of special information. In the lapse of time the size of mills increased; the new hazards of petroleum, of high speed, of spontaneous combustion of chemicals, and of electricity had to be met."[37] Atkinson saw this type of enhanced inspection work as critical to a new role for the Factory Mutuals as promoters for the "slow-burning" method, and mitigation of fire risks more generally as a principle that might extend beyond the confines of the factory. Motivated necessarily by growing the Factory Mutuals business, Atkinson displayed a type of risk and disaster entrepreneurship, a technical expertise that was symbiotic with that of the system builders and inventors we are so accustomed to studying from this time period. They built the risks, and Atkinson worked to control them.

The array of new risks presented by urbanization and industrialization, associated as they were with what seemed like an inevitable expansion in the scale and scope of factory production, worried the Factory Mutuals. Electricity, for example, proved viable for factory lighting after 1879, and was soon adopted by many New England mills. One inspector reported that by 1883, 82 mills under Mutuals protection had at least partial electric lighting, including 2,518 (extremely fire prone) arc lights and 10,481 incandescent lamps. In the 82 mills, 23 fires had been reported, none of them with serious damage—not yet.[38] Atkinson had already launched his idea to respond to these new factory conditions, standardize the best practices in mill construction and protection, and publish them in a textbook that the Factory Mutuals would make widely available. However, there was one problem, Edward Atkinson was a skilled organizer, publicist, public speaker, and writer, but he had no formal scientific or engineering training.

If the Factory Mutuals were going to reorganize factories along fireproof lines, then the risks of the modern factory needed to be analyzed, tabulated, and codified—skills he did not possess.

With this in mind, Atkinson began grooming a team of factory inspectors, drawing many of them from technical colleges, to go out in the field, inspect factories, and bring back valuable risk information. He intended to apply this information to the Factory Mutuals specific business and, as it turned out, also to the more general national problem of fire waste. "Having no truly scientific mastery of any of the applied sciences," Atkinson later recalled, "it has been my function to select men who might each in his own branch of science work out the problems as they have been presented."[39]

One of the Factory Mutuals inspectors immediately commanded Atkinson's attention. Charles J. H. Woodbury, a former civil engineering student at the Massachusetts Institute of Technology, was traveling around Pennsylvania and New Jersey for the Mutuals in 1879 testing fire sprinklers and pumps in insured factories. In the field Woodbury came across some difficult situations, once testing a sprinkler system that gave forth a deluge of water, flooding part of the mill. Woodbury's reports on sprinklers and electricity managed to translate the varieties of inspection experience into the kinds of statistical and technical analyses Atkinson was looking for.[40]

Atkinson turned over his textbook project to Woodbury, who published *The Fire Protection of Mills* in 1882.[41] This was the first of many widely circulated publications the Factory Mutuals would turn out over the next two decades. In it, readers found the principles of slow-burning mill construction explained. Most cotton mill floors were of joist construction, and were assembled of two wooden layers an inch thick. Because of the partitions formed by the joists, it was difficult to reach all parts of the ceiling with hoses or sprinklers. Attics and other obstructed spaces were hard to clean and harder to extinguish, and allowed spaces for mice and rats to hoard trash and oily rags. Slow-burning mill construction consisted of specific measures to make an entire factory space both fire resistant and accessible to fire fighting equipment: heavy and solid masses of wood with exposures easily reached by hoses in case of fire and no "hidden" spaces; brick walls; beams resting on cast iron caps; floors separated by incombustible materials and the floors themselves composed of planks 3–4 inches thick; stairways and shaftways separated from the main floors with brick or other incombustible materials;

fireproof ceiling materials; and thick, nearly flat plank roofs with fire-resistant coverings like gravel or tin. All these elements added up to a style of construction that forced fire, if it broke out, to proceed slowly through the structure, allowing time to extinguish the blaze: hence the denotation "slow burning." Water buckets, fire hoses, automatic sprinklers, and fire drills to prepare mill hands for emergencies were also part of this Factory Mutuals fireproofing system.[42]

Next, Atkinson set out to analyze the causes of fires in the mills and found three main culprits: broken lanterns, spontaneous combustion, and friction. He gave addresses on these subjects and pushed for safer lanterns, after investigating factories and finding that "Not a single safe lantern could be found in use." On the friction issue, he "persuaded the several mutual companies and some of the stock companies to contribute jointly for the purpose of making a scientific investigation of lubricating oils" and hired MIT chemistry professor John Ordway to undertake the experimental laboratory work. This marked the first of many collaborations between the Factory Mutuals and MIT—a significant collaboration considering that the Factory Mutuals did not have laboratories or many inspectors with science training.[43] The MIT connection allowed them to deepen their fire risk knowledge without hiring their own scientists or building labs. Ordway set out to determine the rate of evaporation, viscosity, flash points, and other qualities that would determine the usefulness of the lubricants. The research indicated that the flash points of various oils used for lubrication ranged widely, but only one was deemed safe. Atkinson "served notice" to the makers of oils that unless their product was improved, warnings would be sent "to members of the insurance companies not to buy or use these inferior oils under any circumstances." When some oil manufacturers threatened a lawsuit, Atkinson kept on with his campaign. A year later, wanting to test some of the volatile oil, Atkinson claimed that none could be found on the market.[44] Though his statement was probably an exaggeration, Atkinson was at pains to demonstrate the viability of the new fire safety system he was building. Fire experts would isolate risks, convert them to technical problems, solve the problems and translate the solutions into new practices, and then promote the new practices. Forcing customers and the broader construction world to accept the Factory Mutuals methods and standards required persuasion, threats, and constant demonstrations of success—all skills at which Atkinson was working throughout the 1870s and 1880s.

An Insurance Engineer at Work

Traditional methods of assessing knowledge creation in the modern United States tend to revolve around tracing the establishment and growth of disciplines and the transfer of disciplinary expertise into hardened professional structures, complete with societies, codes of ethics and accreditation rubrics, journals, and success in the marketplace. As sociologist Andrew Abbott explains, though, the existence of a recognizable profession is not always the best marker of knowledge creation. Rather, "the essence of a profession is its work, not its organization. . . . The proper unit of analysis is the jurisdiction, or more generally, the larger task area."[45] Such is certainly the case with fire expertise, where one could not rely simply on the professionalization of firefighting or the work of skilled architects in the city to rest easy that the fire problem would be solved. The interdisciplinary nature of disasters generally, and fire risk specifically, would mean that the experts who defined and met it most effectively worked across disciplines in ways that were often ad hoc and unprecedented. There is no better example of this among fire disaster experts than John Ripley Freeman.

John Ripley Freeman was the most influential student of Edward Atkinson's methods at the Factory Mutuals, and among his many works he left a detailed (unpublished) autobiography. From this document we are able to gain significant insight into the work lives of fire experts in the late nineteenth century as they developed fire safety knowledge and worked to push it out into practical usage. Freeman was born in Bridgton, Maine, in 1855, and grew up on a farm before leaving home to attend MIT in 1872. In November of Freeman's freshman year, the Boston Fire broke out—a horrifying conflagration that consumed the downtown business district. Alexander Graham Bell, teaching at the Boston School for Deaf Mutes at the time, later remembered walking the streets all night, captured by the "spectacle."[46] Freeman, along with a number of his classmates, volunteered for guard duty in the burned district. Slinging an old Springfield rifle with no ammunition, it was the young man's first encounter with the results of a major urban fire. The next year Freeman investigated the burned out hulk of the Globe Theatre in Boston, simply out of curiosity, while on his Christmas vacation.

Graduating in 1876, Freeman found the nation grappling with the aftereffects of the 1873 depression. These were tough times for the few professional engineers coming out of the nation's technical institutes. Not only was the economy slow, but it was still largely an era of "heroic" engineers, with accolades going to men like John Augustus Roebling and James Eads, but most design and construction management work still carried out by traditional practitioners without college degrees. Large-scale engineering works in the United States, going back at least to the Erie Canal project, had not relied on the expertise of college-trained engineers. In fact, the history of American engineering up to the turn of the twentieth century was more one of ad hoc and on-the-job learning than application of professional expertise to technical challenges. Some of Freeman's classmates took work in the west on the transcontinental railroad, but Freeman stayed in the east, working for a hydraulic engineering firm in Boston for the next several years.

In 1886 Freeman was offered a job at the Rhode Island office of the Factory Mutuals, through the recommendation of fellow "Technology" (MIT) man Charles Woodbury. Freeman found himself one of eight factory inspectors at the Providence Factory Mutuals office. His colleagues included a former steamship engineer, a fireman, a cotton mill worker, and a watch repairman.[47] Freeman was certainly the best educated among them in science and engineering, and his hiring reflected Atkinson's faith in adopting "a higher degree of scientific training for special problems of fire prevention than . . . older 'practical' inspectors' possessed."[48] It remains unclear whether Freeman considered Woodbury a "practical" or a "scientific" man, but when he found that he was to serve as Woodbury's assistant he bristled at the arrangement. Atkinson agreed and decided that initially Freeman should report directly to him, placing the young engineer's desk directly across the aisle from his own.[49]

The factory inspector's job involved traveling for weeks at a time, a pattern of work that Freeman would adopt and continue throughout his long career. The insurance inspector made the rounds of the Factory Mutuals' insured factories, arriving unannounced, and expected to be admitted immediately, so that the workers had no time to fill up fire pails or clean the factory. According to Freeman, the "inspector's examination extended from the top to the bottom of every building, and from end to end of every important room, looking first of all for dirt or lack of prompt removal of waste . . . noting evidence of poorly cleaned machinery." Then the inspector conducted a fire drill, with the fire pumps put into full operation and lines of hose laid out and used just as if a real fire were underway. The Factory Mutuals expected policyholders to organize their workers into fire brigades, and the inspectors graded the efficiency of the brigades as they conducted the drill. This exercise would, ideally, illustrate that workers knew where firefighting tools—hoses, pails, shovels, and axes—were kept, and how to use them. The records kept by night watchmen were also examined for thoroughness. Freeman noted that following "this routine of inspections, there was a friendly conference with the superintendent of the factory about means by which it could be made safer against fire." Finally, the inspector filled out a 3x5 "report card," inscribed with "final notes as to quality of construction for resisting fire, quality of neatness and order found throughout the premises, condition of maintenance of the fire protection appliances, and . . . his judgment upon the risk as a whole." The inspector noted on the back of the report card if he thought the conditions of the mill required an additional visit from a "Special Inspector."[50]

Freeman quickly realized that to succeed at his job he needed to develop friendly relationships with factory owners and managers while also exhorting them to stay vigilant in the face of possible fires. As the personal face of the company, he educated owners on Factory Mutuals standards and recommendations, but could also threaten them if necessary with higher premiums or recommend termination of their policies if an inspection turned up egregious dangers. Freeman carried with him a book full of product information and advertisements about fireproofing supplies the Factory Mutuals endorsed. This book gave examples of fire protection products in categories ranging from steam pumps to waste cans, and included the different parts of sprinkler systems, as well as elevators, fireproof paints, fire alarms, watchman's clocks, fire doors, and fire extinguishers.[51] In the same cotton textile-producing counties where Samuel Slater had inaugurated the American textile factory system nearly a century earlier, Freeman roamed the miles, a fire expert promoting an evolving private sector methodology of comprehensive risk and disaster mitigation.[52] When he found problems in factories that he thought "seemed to call for special or technical treatment or engineering suggestions," he conducted more detailed investigations and wrote up more detailed reports. Freeman remembered that he did his work and wrote his reports with such "zeal" that the inspector at the next desk "cautioned me that I was wasting my energy, that all this uncalled for effort would never be appreciated." Freeman disagreed; he enjoyed the challenges of working as an expert technical intermediary between the insurance company and the manufacturer, translating the factory-in-action into a catalog of risk information.[53]

Inspectors hit the road on Monday mornings and returned to their home offices for conferences on Saturdays. For "more distant localities," inspectors set out for two weeks at a time. For Freeman this was an opportunity to travel, analyze the different varieties of manufacturing in New England, and build contacts with factory managers. Freeman often scheduled his inspection trips so that he could make side trips for hiking, visiting his family, and courting his future wife.[54] On one extraordinary inspection trip Freeman was stopped at a railroad station in Exeter, Maine, waiting for the train to change engines, when the city fire alarm went off and a report came in that the cotton mill was on fire. He abandoned the train and headed to the burning mill, a Factory Mutuals customer, finding the manager "so distracted and things going so badly that he gladly welcomed my assistance." As he later recalled it, Freeman took command of the scene and raced to the top floors of the factory to assess the situation. He found the factory's fire pumps being driven by the same engine that turned the machinery-driving belts, and these leather belts were bringing firebrands from the burning upper stories down to the lower floors. After the belts were cut and the upper floors flooded with water, the factory was saved. Despite the destruction of his overcoat (which he charged to the Factory Mutuals), Freeman "had a perfectly glorious time" fighting a real fire for a change.[55] After only a few months at the Factory Mutuals, John Ripley Freeman was promoted from inspector to the rank of "Engineer and Special Inspector." His enthusiasm for the work undoubtedly played a role, but Freeman attributed his success to his "supplementing of routine reports with reports of a more distinctly engineering character."[56]

In the 1880s Edward Atkinson also wanted to expand the Factory Mutuals' abilities in the testing of fire protection devices, not out at the factories, but under controlled conditions. He tapped Freeman for the project. Freeman set to work in a small testing lab of his own design behind the company's offices in Providence. Without any models to work from, Freeman carried out tests and experiments on fire protection devices with a great deal of freedom to innovate. He conducted performance tests and experiments on fire pumps, fire hose, pipes and valves, and hydrants. Most important, Freeman turned his attention to automatic sprinklers—a technology the Factory Mutuals believed held out great promise in augmenting slow-burning construction. If the design of a slow-burning mill required fires to burn for some time before doing great damage, then the added protection of a sprinkler system promised to potentially eradicate serious factory fires altogether. Determining exactly how much water should flow from sprinkler heads, and in what pattern of distribution to optimally tamp down fires, was a question remaining to be answered. More critical to winning over consumers was preventing sprinkler deluges that happened unexpectedly when no fire was present.

Although fire sprinklers go back to the eighteenth century in England, the first successful sprinkler in the United States was patented by Henry Parmelee in 1874. A Massachusetts factory under Factory Mutuals protection adopted Parmelee's invention in 1875. Frederick Grinnell, an engineer educated at Rensselaer Polytechnic Institute and owner of the Providence Steam and Gas Pipe Company, purchased Parmelee's patents and was active in selling his revised system to cotton mills in the 1880s.[57] The technological challenges of fire safety at the time for many architects and engineers were largely found in protecting structural items such as iron and steel building columns and terra cotta beam coverings, as well as improving fireproof design more generally. The sprinkler promised to give a measure of protection to those equally concerned about what was in their buildings as with the buildings themselves. Atkinson used his typical formula in pushing Factory Mutuals members to adopt sprinklers, first by "persuading, next by coaxing, next by manipulating the rates of premium, next by conditioning renewals, and, finally, by refusing to insure any unsprinkled factory or works."[58]

Freeman started testing Grinnell's sprinklers in 1886, and he "discovered some that would not open over a test flame." Freeman performed the experiment again for Grinnell, whom he later described as "greatly upset when I demonstrated to him personally several failures of his sprinkler to open over fire in a test oven, even when the apparatus was in his own hands." Freeman later filed a patent claim for a sprinkler of his own design, a design that Grinnell wanted and purchased for $1,500 in 1888.[59] Freeman's interests in the sprinkler were undoubtedly also fed by his background in hydraulic engineering, and he found himself using skills that he had learned designing water systems for Boston. The sprinkler, to Freeman, was only one point in a larger technological system—the city water supply—that needed to work flawlessly in order to assure fire safety not only for factories and factory workers, but for the city as a whole. The type of contact that the Grinnell episode represented—with test methods and results, product designs, and money flowing between the insurance engineer and the manufacturer—would within a couple of decades come to define the informal network of innovation that the fire experts created.

Though he might at this point have branched off and opened a manufacturing business or his own fire protection engineering firm, Freeman
stayed on with the Factory Mutuals. He liked the travel and the challenges
of inspection work. He also enjoyed the intellectual freedom provided by
experimenting in his tiny fire research "laboratory" in Providence. Freeman
"resisted efforts made to draw . . . [him] into the adjustment of losses and
other features of insurance work not pertaining to engineering."[60] The next
few years found him researching and publishing technical papers on nearly
every facet of fire-safe construction, including fire hoses, structural engineering, inspection procedures, and sprinkler systems.

Like many of his colleagues, Freeman also took part in the professional
activities of American engineers, activities aimed in part at raising the status
of engineers in the eyes of building contractors, architects, and city officials—not to mention potential customers requiring technical work in the
growing electrical, chemical, and mechanical sectors of American industry.
Freeman's own specialty did not, as of yet, have a professional niche of its
own. This proved to be a benefit of sorts, as it allowed Freeman and other
fire safety experts to cross the increasingly rigid lines of demarcation
between engineering specialties. Freeman also built recognition for fire protection by taking a leadership role in the American Society of Mechanical
Engineers, later serving as its president.

Throughout his career, Freeman maintained a close relationship with
his alma mater. In 1891 he was called on to recommend fireproofing measures for the Rogers Building at MIT. In 1898, there was a fire in the architecture building. By this time, Freeman's reputation among his fellow
engineers was established. He had been made head of the Inspections
Department at the Providence office and was on his way to becoming president of the Rhode Island Factory Mutuals. He lectured widely on fire safety,
published often, and trained fire inspectors at the Providence office. So
MIT hired Freeman, the only person they knew of with his particular expertise, to investigate the causes and results of the fire. How had it started?
Why had it damaged certain parts of the structure and not others? These
were questions that under ordinary circumstances might have been investigated by a city fireman or a fire marshal. However, MIT was receptive to
the idea of Freeman's unique expertise, and he not only answered the questions posed to him, but made specific suggestions about how such a fire
might be prevented in other MIT buildings in the future. By the 1890s,
largely through the institutional framework of the Factory Mutuals,

connections had been forged between manufacturers, technical universities, and fire insurance companies.

The evolving Factory Mutuals method, a hybrid between the growing emphasis on bench science for industrial application and the old-fashioned rule-of-thumb shop methods of the factory or workshop, resulted in dramatic savings for the Factory Mutuals, and equally important, for their industrial clients. Edward Atkinson's melding of the practical and the theoretical approaches to an as of yet uncodified body of fire safety data, paved the way for future investigations along such lines. Insurance companies across the country took note, as did engineers outside of the insurance profession, architects, city building inspectors and fire service officials, and manufacturers of electrical goods and structural materials.

As the number of factories located in cities grew, so too did the Factory Mutuals' interest in urban fire risk and disasters. In this way the world of mutual insurance made a connection to the broader concerns over urban conflagrations and fire risks. In a speech delivered before Philadelphia's Franklin Institute in 1891, Charles Woodbury presented his version of the history of urban fires. Sweeping from the ancient world—the loss of the library at Alexandria, Constantinople, Rome—to modern fires in London and Paris, Woodbury found that "cities have gained much from the experience derived from conflagrations."[61] "The cities of America," he thought, "on account of the larger amount of wood in their construction and the prevalence of irresponsible methods of building, have suffered severely from fires, and it is from these fires that conclusions are to be drawn for suggesting measures that will tend to diminish their recurrence."[62] Woodbury was aware, though, of the difficulties municipal government officials often faced in using the "experience" from great fires to establish comprehensive fire safety codes. Changes came after such fires, he thought, but in "the course of such changes many acts of injustice have been perpetrated by those who did not grasp the whole force of the chain of circumstances causing these devastating fires . . . conditions too strong to be controlled by any one set of rules formulated at white heat after a conflagration."[63] The difficulties growing from attempts to control fire through building codes and zoning in Chicago after the 1871 conflagration certainly fit Woodbury's description.

The insurance underwriter had provided an example, Woodbury argued, from which cities might learn. Underwriters weighed all the factors that made a building a good risk. In addition, "underwriters went above mere consideration of physical conditions to the ethical questions relating to . . . the probity of owners, who are always possessed of every opportunity to effect the destruction of their property by fire."[64] In Woodbury's view the systematic inspection efforts and methods of private sector persuasion used by the Factory Mutuals could and should be emulated by city government officials. As he explained:

> Inspections by . . . associations of underwriters have given the most satisfactory results, but it may justly be queried whether this is the proper source for such an espionage over the community. These inspectors are . . . without any legal authority to enforce obedience to suggestions which are admittedly for the weal of all. Their requests are, for the most part, complied with; but the results are a benefit to the community, and it would appear that this service should be performed by persons clothed with authority from a municipality, as a part of the protective system which now extends protection to person and property by means of the police, the water supply, and the fire departments . . . leaving to the underwriters their legitimate work of insuring property at prices based on estimated hazard.

Woodbury was arguing for rigorous risk inspection at public expense and under municipal authority, a remaking of the largely ineffective, corrupt, and politically mired building inspection departments of American cities.

Woodbury cited the successes of urban underwriters' associations—such as Charles Hexamer's association in Philadelphia—in educating property owners and city officials about how risks should be assessed and fire safety achieved. The Inspection Department of the Boston Board of Fire Underwriters had performed 11,000 inspections per year since 1884, achieving good results, especially with buildings occupied by tenants, where owners were unaware of building conditions. In Chicago, the Inspection Department of the Fire Underwriters' Association, performed about 16,500 inspections per year, reporting about a 97 percent success rate in persuading building owners to "remedy" defects found by inspectors. To Woodbury this absolutely proved the efficacy of Factory Mutuals methods, applied to cities and carried out by fire insurance inspection bureaus. Certainly there were material differences between rural factories and the urban risks that gave rise to conflagrations. He did not mention whether the financial suasion the Factory Mutuals used with customers could be replicated in cities. But to the degree that cities would adopt the Factory Mutuals' recommendations, they would see their conflagration hazard decrease.[65] Woodbury concluded that insurance rates in cities were double what they should be and that "apathy" was the only explanation. The "hazard," he said, "can be reduced by general action on the part of any municipality to any extent that is demanded by general public opinion."[66]

Eager to build on the successful small-scale experimental work done by Freeman as a basis for technical education, Atkinson suggested in the late 1880s that a department of Insurance Engineering be established at MIT. This department would have the "double function of teaching the knowledge already acquired, and, more important, would develop through tests and experiments advanced principles to be followed in the practice of fire prevention and improved building construction."[67] MIT would not undertake the challenge without an endowment. Atkinson appealed to the Factory Mutuals, stock insurance companies, and other interested parties, but could not raise the necessary funds for such a program. Despite this setback, in 1890 the Factory Mutuals established labs in connection with their inspection department to test devices "of immediate concern to their clients." Such tests were still too limited, Atkinson thought, and in 1902 he presided over the founding of the Insurance Engineering Experiment Station. He hired Charles L. Norton, a professor at MIT, to run the experimental side of the lab, and Atkinson handled the publications. A new journal—*Insurance Engineering*—was founded, advancing what was by now a coherent body of expertise broadly applicable to fire risks and disasters, rooted in practice but more and more bolstered by experimentally derived basic science research.

Though there was no official connection with MIT, much of the Insurance Engineering Experiment Station's work was done there. According to Atkinson's biographer, the "work done by this organization covered an interesting group of subjects, most of which had a significance far beyond the immediate concern of the fire insurance companies. This was true, for example, of experiments upon 'fireproof' wood, as a result of which experiments, it was demonstrated that the claims for these materials were largely specious, and an end was put to a small industry which had been profiting by the credulity of uninformed buyers."[68] Concrete, and corrugated steel and cement roof testing also took place at the Experiment Station.[69] The

Experiment Station would later publish its own disaster investigation reports after two major fires: the Iroquois Theater Fire (1903) and the Baltimore Fire (1904).

Fire insurance underwriters were moved to innovate by the very real threat to the survival of their business in industrializing America. The results of several decades worth of risk research across the fire insurance field were measurable by the turn of the twentieth century. The insurance engineers were truly experts in fire disaster by this time, with proficiencies that included: routinized risk analysis through factory inspections, risk mitigation in design, laboratory research and product testing, codification of fire risks and massive publication of risk information, and strategies of pressure on city officials to adopt suggested fire codes and practices. Performing what he often called his "missionary work" among underwriters in St. Paul, Minnesota, in 1885, Edward Atkinson pointed out that, ultimately, "the interests of the strong and well managed Stock Companies and of the Mutuals are identical."[70] But Atkinson was not convinced that the shared mission of fire insurance experts would be enough to save the city, especially in the exciting and dangerous electrified metropolis. Edward Atkinson, Charles Woodbury, and John Ripley Freeman were well known as fire experts at the end of the nineteenth century, though their ideas and accomplishments did not fit easily into one professional or business category. They agitated for fire safety both within and outside of the boundaries of the fire insurance industry. Atkinson wrote letters to university presidents, mayors, and other executives in the insurance business, proselytizing his unflinching faith in the Factory Mutuals methods for reducing fire risk, not only for factories, but also more generally in the urban environment. "I have no personal interest in the matter," he wrote in a characteristic letter to the president of the Case Scientific School in Cleveland after a major fire had occurred there in 1886, "other than that of an anti-combustion missionary."[71]

Still, it was unclear yet whether or not the innovations of the fire insurers were adaptable to rapidly changing and seemingly ungovernable urban environments. The risks of conflagration in the industrializing city prompted a sustained effort to understand fire risks systematically in the insurance field. Laboratory research was emerging as a useful method of knowledge creation in American industry. The insurance engineers seized the moment. And yet, there was not a clear path along which the insurance industry, or any other private sector interest more broadly, might travel to force the creation of a fireproof metropolis.

White City/City of Smoke

Shadows overtook the White City and an orchestra struck up patriotic tunes. It was May 8, 1893, in Chicago the World's Columbian Exposition had been open for just over a week, and the electric light display—its most anticipated spectacle—was now at last ready for its first showing. A *Chicago Daily Tribune* reporter captured the scene as hundreds then thousands of expectant fairgoers filed in through the gates. "Suddenly a single beam of yellow light, like a falling star, flickered and grew bright on the high dome of the Administration Building."[72] Standing before the Electricity Building, a statue of "Franklin, with his kite, looked out upon the consummation of what he dreamt of when he drew lightning from the summer cloud." Then "a wide pyramid of fierce white light was thrown upon the . . . dome. Its blazonry of yellow died away, and under the new glare the delicate lace-like tracery of gold and white was brought into strong relief." The crowd erupted, the "vocabulary of adjectives in the English language was exhausted, and the hum of praise was the prolonged . . . applause of a multitude." The White City, named by its designer Daniel H. Burnham for its uniformly neoclassical and whitewashed buildings, "blossomed in new beauty," the *Tribune* enthused. Meanwhile out beyond the fairground gates a "heavy pall of smoke brooded over the city," and "the chimneys of a blast furnace belched their red flames high into the darkness." Here was a utopian White City glowing within an infernal City of Smoke.

While the White City was designed in part as a celebration of Chicago's rise from the ashes, memories of the Great Fire of 1871 were still alarmingly fresh. The rebuilt Chicago was a city where risk-taking ran well ahead of concerns over protection in the name of safety. Constructed with hardly a care for tomorrow, factories and tenement neighborhoods sprang up side by side, still often in wood and other flammable materials, with few if any restrictions. The demands on urban space forced an era of experimentation in materials and design that could prove profitable and simultaneously deadly in the hotels, apartment buildings, theaters, and high-rise office buildings that could not adequately supply water for firefighting or escape routes for tenants and workers trapped in the flames. While such fires might not rise to conflagration status by burning down whole cities, they often consumed multiple buildings and dozens, even hundreds of lives. Fire insurance companies, as we have seen thus far, were working toward making technical sense of this rapidly changing and risky urbanization. But their influence was strongly limited to individual policyholders and a limited number of municipal officials who were amenable to their fire code suggestions.

The White City was a controlled experiment in humane urbanism, constructed in the middle of the most rapid period of population and physical growth the world's cities had yet witnessed. A new urban form—the industrial metropolis—was taking shape. The rapid proliferation of urban technological systems defied the imagination, each combining invention, new forms of investment and management, and the talents of an evolving technical workforce. As the city was being remade, so were its class relations—a process fueled by the arrival of millions of wage-earning manufacturing workers and inscribed in the reorganization of urban space. The miseries of foul air and water and ramshackle tenements multiplied in factory districts, while center city commercial districts reflected in their sturdy stone and high-rise steel the profits and the confidence derived from industrialization by an emerging corporate elite. The smoke of industrial production all too often signaled that the conditions were ready for the smoke of conflagration to follow.

Daniel Burnham was at the vanguard of urban planners and architects working aggressively to revoke the "Devil's privilege" of reckless urbanization. Planners, architects, and social critics readily noted Burnham's achievements in the White City, especially his commitment to erecting a coherent urban space that was served well by the technologies of construction, transportation, power, and light that were making and remaking the real cities of industrializing America. Yet while the White City presented itself as a model of reasoned planning, it too reflected the very impulses that had built industrial Chicago. Despite its hopeful image, disasters came easily to mind in the White City—fast in construction and improvisational, it was in fact itself a disaster waiting to happen.

Over the frames of most structures in the White City workers spread a plaster and fiber material called "staff." Easy to sculpt and paint (white, of course), staff gave the structures the desired look of classical antiquity, on time and on budget. Underneath this plaster city snaked miles of electrical wires and connections, an electrical infrastructure unmatched in any real city in the world at the time. Concerns over this new and untested technological system—the electrified building—and the flammability it presented led the fire insurance companies contracted to underwrite the fair to consider denying coverage for the fairgrounds in 1892. This threat led Burnham to beef up the fire department and water delivery infrastructure at the fair, and to adopt a more rigorous inspection regimen than he had initially planned.[73]

The concerns of the fire insurers at the Columbian Exposition were not without merit, as events would show. Dozens of small fires broke out during the fair. Most were of little concern and may very well have proved more thrilling to observers than anything else. However, in the summer of 1893 a fire in the Cold Storage Building led to the death of 11 firemen, most of whom fell to their deaths as a smokestack collapsed while thousands looked on in horror. An investigation showed that the design of the smokestack was flawed, and the firemen's lives had been unnecessarily lost. While such tragedies did not escape the analysis of the insurance engineers, their real concern lay in the conflagration threat—the very real possibility that cities, composed of millions of little fire risks, might go up in flames as a whole. The Columbian Exposition grounds provided a working laboratory of a city built to scale—risks, disasters, and all.

When the White City closed to visitors after a phenomenally successful run, playing host to 27 million visitors, its ghostly buildings remained a source of fascination in Chicago, the grounds becoming a squatters' metropolis as the economic crisis of 1893 continued into 1894. In July that year a fire sprang up that quickly grew out of control. The fire department looked on helplessly as the White City was engulfed by a massive conflagration. To many who watched, it was a fantastic ending to a season of spectacle. Legend had it that the flames were visible from as far away as Milwaukee. Somewhere between the extremes of national enthusiasm for the technological metropolis and the burning of the White City sat a politically and financially acceptable level of fire risk. The inability to locate that level by 1894 signaled the magnitude of the task ahead to the experts in disaster who were wondering whether or not the conflagration hazard would prove to be an implacable threat to urban expansion. In response to the real concern of bankruptcy for the fire insurance industry, a number of skills associated with successful fire underwriting were bundled together, funded, and formed into novel institutions focused on fire safety research, policy formation, and education.

The Columbian Exposition has been eulogized, criticized, and scoured innumerable times by historians looking for ways to understand its historical importance, but little has been written about the significance of the event for experts in disaster. The arrival at the fairgrounds of fire insurance engineer William H. Merrill, brought in to investigate fire risks and report on actual fires, marked a watershed moment for the fire experts. Merrill would go on to found a laboratory for fire safety testing of electrical goods and other building materials—Underwriters Laboratories (UL)—so his arrival in Chicago symbolizes the institution-creating impulse growing from the fire insurance experts' work over the previous three decades. Harry Chase Brearley, writer and promoter of the NBFU and UL, captured the gravity of the moment as he and the fire experts saw it (and still see it):

> Like many other important influences of American life, Underwriters' Laboratories was, in a way, an outgrowth of the World's Fair of 1893. This great exposition, which gave a pronounced impetus to American architecture, which opened the eyes of the public to the coming dominance of electricity, which exerted a profound influence on manufacture, transportation, mechanics and art, and which, perhaps, first taught the American people to think in international terms, also furnished an opportunity for the germ of a protective idea to take root and begin to grow.[74]

To William Henry Merrill and the fire safety experts he represented, this model city within a city was also a city of disaster within a city of disaster. Merrill, while certainly captivated by the fair's technological environment, had not come to Chicago to join in the hymn of praise for technological progress. While the fair was a vision, the fire risks were real, and they did not bode well for the future of the electrified city.[75]

Merrill's work was funded by the Chicago Underwriters' Association and the Western Insurance Association Electrical Bureau—both local NBFU affiliate underwriters' organizations. His charge was to make some sense of the electrical fire risks that the Columbian Exposition presented. He was hired to investigate and solve problems that had surfaced with the automatic fire alarm and to inspect the electrical installations at the fair. Merrill proposed to take what he found on the fairgrounds, through building inspections and by following the fire patrol around when they responded to fires, and study them in greater detail under laboratory conditions. His efforts were highly specialized and interdisciplinary in nature, bringing together the skills of scientific bench-level analysis with an engineer's understanding of technological systems, and a businessman's attention to profit and loss. Freeman had pioneered this method of laboratory

Figure 1. "Burning of the Peristyle, with western view of the Court of Honor and Administration Building." From an illustrated poem about the World's Columbian Exposition, H. H. Van Meter, *The Vanishing Fair*, 1894. Courtesy of the Paul V. Galvin Library, Illinois Institute of Technology.

testing for the Factory Mutuals only a few years before with good results. Merrill had already evidently picked up on the idea and suggested it to the Boston Board of Underwriters. The Boston Board rejected his plan, but now, in a new city, with a pressing set of risks to investigate, Merrill tried again, and his offer was accepted.[76]

The institution Merrill founded in Chicago with insurance industry support—the Underwriter's Electrical Bureau—tested electrical products like arc lamps, sockets and switches, and wires thought to pose a threat in the flammable environment of the White City.[77] When the Exposition came to an end, the underwriters supporting Merrill were pleased with his methods and results, and transferred their hopes for a fireproof model metropolis to the vision of a fireproof Chicago. Merrill, who had attended MIT, was joined by

WORLD'S COLUMBIAN EXPOSITION

1893 marked the beginning of developments which have had profound and beneficial influence on American life. From the first Chicago Fair stemmed new ideas in the fields of manufacturing, transportation, mechanics, art, architecture and science. Not the least of these was a new idea in conservation, based on technical knowledge and the use of engineering to prevent fires and other hazards which threaten destruction of lives and property.

2

Figure 2. Fighting fires at the World's Columbian Exposition. This image shows the founding narrative of UL, as an organization with "a new idea in conservation, based on technical knowledge and the use of engineering to prevent fires and other hazards." From *UL: A Symbol of Safety, A Report of 50 Years of Continuous Service* (Chicago: Underwriters Laboratories, 1944). Courtesy of Underwriters Laboratories, Inc.

William C. Robinson, a Cornell graduate working as an automatic sprinkler inspector for the Chicago Board of Underwriters.[78] Robinson was working on acetylene gas, which had been discovered in 1892 and was being used for illumination and welding, displaying utility but also a propensity to explode.[79]

Merrill's first handwritten test report, issued in 1894, indicated a second area of interest beyond electrical risk—devices and materials that could mitigate fire loss and inhibit the spread of fire once it broke out. The new lab's first official test analyzed a type of asbestos paper, a "Noncombustible Insulation" that claimed to be both fireproof and nonabsorbent. Merrill conducted the test, and concluded that the paper was indeed fireproof, but that asbestos "cannot be considered a non-absorptive or an insulating material."[80]

With the reports on electrical fires and the success of Merrill's general approach to compiling test reports, the NBFU started contributing to the work, and the name was changed to the Electrical Bureau of the NBFU.[81] Now Merrill had access not only to local and regional fire insurance underwriters. Working within the organizational structure of the NBFU, Merrill had access to hundreds of insurance companies and cities and thousands of individual risks. Though it would take a few years for Merrill to exploit the possibilities inherent in his access to a national audience of fire safety expertise, the immediate result was a dramatic increase in testing output. In 1895 Merrill and his small staff completed 75 tests on a budget of $3,000.[82]

The first lab, at Fire Insurance Patrol Station Number One, was built in the front of the third floor, where the National Automatic Fire Alarm Company had recently resided. A hayloft took up the back part of the floor. A heavy pine floor was laid, and a bench was installed along the wall. Staff engineer William S. Boyd was responsible for making the testing apparatus, using as he later recalled "a box of tools I had used as a practical wireman in and about Chicago, and Seattle, Washington, and for several years this kit represented the sum total of equipment of this type."[83] The son of the superintendent of inspections for the Chicago Underwriters Association was hired to take care of mailing lists. These lists were maintained to build up a local network of underwriters who might be interested in the work of the lab. They also hired a photographer who took pictures of tests, photographs "which formed the basis of illustrations in connection with a Laboratories' report." It was a busy and informal place; and as William Boyd remembered, the tedious mailing list work along with the testing work often went into the night. "This was done very willingly," according to

Boyd, "especially as Mr. Merrill usually worked with us and when supper time came we would adjourn to the old Grand Pacific Hotel lunchroom. . . . We returned to the laboratory about 6:30 and worked until 9 or 9:30."

Boyd also noted the "crank ideas" with which the early lab came into contact. For example, one day a man arrived with the idea for a novel fire alarm system. Small torpedoes, placed at intervals in a building, would be attached to a hemp cord that, when it burned, would explode the torpedoes and give the alarm. Merrill early on established the policy of popularizing his work, not only with mailing lists and test reports, but also by opening the lab to visitors. Not long after the lab was underway, he decided to give a reception for prominent local fire underwriters, especially those who were funding his operation. A number of fire demonstrations were staged. Some of the demonstrations were intended to show the dangers of electricity in the home. In one, for example, the risks of incandescent light bulbs were seen when "paper shades [showed] the speed with which the incandescent lamp burned through the paper, and how likely it was to set fire, if left in that position any length of time." As to the risks of fire from electricity in more commercial settings, there were "a number of fire exhibits such as motor starting boxes which had caused fires, metal pipes with holes burned in them by the electric current, and a wooden service head which had caused the fire in the old Grand Pacific Hotel."[84]

In line with the NBFU's philosophy of creating a national network of insurance companies operating under similar business principles, and sharing similar perceptions of fire risk, Merrill soon set about creating a wider audience for his work. It was in sprinkler testing that Merrill perhaps saw the potential of a national audience for the work of his lab. He remembered working on the first sprinkler test with William Robinson, and

the fear we had that they would be shot to pieces by our learned confreres in the East. We used to sit up nights and go over them page by page to be sure that they were as nearly bombproof as we could make them. . . . When we sent them out and nothing happened except that the manufacturers of some of the then standard sprinklers we criticised came to pay their respects and began making the improvements indicated by the reports, we were immensely pleased with ourselves and decided that if we could test automatic sprinklers to the satisfaction of insurance engineers and manufacturers, there might be no limit to the extent of our activities.[85]

Merrill's lab also hosted an informal "standardization group," composed of local fire safety experts who met frequently to discuss fire prevention and automatic sprinklers with Merrill and Robinson.[86]

In 1901, Merrill's testing lab was chartered by the state of Illinois and renamed "Underwriter's Laboratories, Inc.," authorized "to establish and maintain laboratories for the examination and testing of appliances and devices and to enter into contracts with the owners and manufacturers of such appliances and devices, respecting the recommendation thereof to insurance organizations."[87] The possibilities for collaboration among fire experts were great at the turn of the century, but the work was still largely scattered and disorganized. Merrill noted a lack of uniformity of opinions and requirements, and saw these as factors hampering the growth of the industry. "A socket approved in one community would be condemned in another and factory distribution on a nation-wide scale was difficult if not impossible." This is the problem that Merrill focused on—developing safety standards that would become ubiquitous among manufacturers and in municipal government. Summarizing Merrill's approach in these years, UL engineer A. R. Small claimed that, "Generally speaking, municipal, state, or national boundaries are products of the mind or of politics. Fire is not conscious of them nor do the laws of electricity, of physics or of chemistry become modified in the slightest degree because printers of maps see fit to picture political subdivisions in contrasting colors."[88] As such, it was an industry with multiple geographies to consider, multiple business strategies and, more to the interest of UL, multiple specifications. In this uncertainty, William Merrill saw opportunity, and he jumped at it.

Fire Protection Engineering

By the end of the nineteenth century the varied skills associated with fire protection engineering had developed to the point where they could be codified into a formal, albeit nontraditional for the time, curriculum. A course of study in Fire Protection Engineering was pioneered at the Armour Institute of Technology in Chicago. Established first as a school dedicated to workers' training and social "uplift" on Chicago's South Side, the Armour Institute had emerged as a cutting-edge engineering school by the turn of the century. Chicago's fire insurance companies, in connection with national insurance associations, were actively pursuing new methods in the struggle to anticipate and control the risk of fire. In UL we saw one of these new methods—laboratory research. At the same time, the insurance companies also agitated for more expertise in the fields of electrical installation, building design and construction, and building inspection and code enforcement. Engineering professionals fit these demands by taking many of the new inspection and regulatory jobs in the city, along with jobs in the private sector that relied on elements of technical expertise obtainable primarily through higher education. These jobs frequently gave urban engineers and architects the chance to express themselves as "modern" and "professional" as opposed to tradesmen and mechanics who were competent in their specialties but generally not educated broadly in the sciences and engineering.

As the nineteenth century drew to a close, engineers in the United States were in the midst of turning their craft into a profession.[89] All the major branches of engineering—civil, mechanical, electrical, and chemical—had, by this time, established professional societies, begun to publish journals, and commenced regular conferences for the dissemination of technical and employment information. Many stimuli may be cited for the growth of the engineering profession at this time; the technical expertise demanded by the technological metropolis was undoubtedly the strongest. In the past, much of the installation work for large, integrated systems would have been performed by skilled craftsmen—inheritors of their trades through traditional shop education and promotion. Yet, with the volume and complexity of such work on the rise, degreed engineers began to actively promote themselves as the proper men for the job. Technical colleges provided foundations in scientific theory, as well as the sort of hands-on training associated with traditional training in the mechanical trades. Moreover, the technical degree became both a shorthand for "professionalism" and a shortcut to working on the most cutting-edge urban technologies. Armour, reacting to the growth of Chicago—the new electrical metropolis—began to turn out electrical engineers at a furious pace, beginning with its first graduating class in 1897.

The Columbian Exposition, as we have seen, presented a vision for an electrified city. System builders like Charles Yerkes and Samuel Insull were well on their way to transforming the vision of the fair into a real Chicago, with electric streetcars, street lights, and central station service for factories, business, and homes. It was noticed that a great deal of the machinery in the Electrical Building at the fair bore tags denoting a new owner—the Armour

Institute. Armour's first president, Victor C. Alderson, cited the fair as a landmark event in shaping an entire generation of technical schools. "As the London Exhibition of 1851," he said, "was the time in the middle of the century when technical education began, so the World's Columbian Exposition in 1893 marks the beginning of that educational technical movement of which we are now a part."[90] Starting with two full-time professors and increasing to six by 1903, Armour's Department of Electricity and Electrical Engineering enjoyed the full financial support of the young institution. The curriculum included instruction in machine tool work, power plant operations, alternating currents, central station design, operation of steam and gas engines, illuminating engineering, electric railways, telephone engineering, and laboratory work. The electrical laboratory was stocked with the latest dynamos and generators from Westinghouse and Edison, along with intricate calibration equipment for setting and testing standards. The aim of the department, by combining class work with an unusually high degree of laboratory work, was to "accomplish the most thorough training both in theory and practice, in the hopes that students may upon its completion be immediately available for commercial work."[91] To help ease the transition from the classroom to the city, engineering students also participated in inspection visits to electrical substations, local railways, telephone companies, testing laboratories, and insurance companies.[92]

In 1903, Armour responded to the call from insurance companies for specialists in the modern techniques of fire prevention by launching a degree program in Fire Protection Engineering. The first such program in the nation, it was established in partnership with the Underwriters Laboratories. Students in the new program, once finished with their core work in basic science and engineering subjects, found themselves taking a variety of specialized courses. These included fire protection lectures, laboratory work, strength of materials, heating and ventilation, electricity lectures and labs, building construction, chemistry of fires, schedule rating, special hazards, manufacturing processes, insurance practice, and engineering contracts. Inspection visits began in 1905 and included municipal pumping stations, a Chicago fire boat, on-site insurance inspection, and the Chicago Fire Alarm Telegraph Department.[93]

In the last two years of the degree students worked on-site at the Underwriters Laboratories facility. Here they witnessed safety tests, and took an active role in inspection and standard setting. Most importantly, the students came into contact with the entire range of people they might

Figure 3. The fire disaster experts. Top left: Edward Atkinson, president of the Associated Factory Mutual Fire Insurance Companies, from Harold Francis Williamson, *Edward Atkinson: The Biography of an American Liberal, 1827–1905* (Boston: Old Corner Book Store, 1934), frontispiece, courtesy of University of Pennsylvania Libraries. Top right: John Ripley Freeman, vice-president of the Associated Factory Mutual Fire Insurance Companies and investigator of the Iroquois Theater Fire of 1903 and the Baltimore Fire of 1904, courtesy of Massachusetts Institute of Technology Museum. Bottom left: William Henry Merrill, founder of Underwriters Laboratories, Inc., from *UL: A Symbol of Safety, A Report of 50 Years of Continuous Service* (Chicago: Underwriters Laboratories, 1944), 4, courtesy of Underwriters Laboratories, Inc. Bottom right: Franklin Wentworth, National Fire Protection Association, from Percy Bugbee, *Men Against Fire: The Story of the National Fire Protection Association, 1896–1971* (Boston: NFPA, 1971), 18, courtesy of Indiana University of Pennsylvania Libraries.

encounter as fire protection engineers. As the field was new and relatively undefined, opportunities ran the gamut from insurance work to local and state government safety inspection departments, along with teaching, private inspection, and consulting work. Accordingly, during this period of fluidity in the new profession, the Armour curriculum provided more breadth in its fire protection training than in any of its other engineering departments.

While it is difficult to directly map the trajectories of Armour graduates, it is possible to build a profile that suggests that the expertise generated at Armour not only fit the need for electrical professionals but also tended to stay within Chicago. Of the approximately 160 graduates of the Institute in its first ten years, 54 percent were working in the city in 1906. Among those who stayed in the city, electrical engineering graduates in these years numbered about 50, with civil engineering claiming 8, mechanical engineering 20, chemical engineering 3, and the rest attending the School of Architecture. Approximately 25 percent of these students went to work directly in engineering jobs, while another 25 percent went into business and/or management. The rest were equally divided between teaching, drafting, and insurance work.[94] These figures suggest that Armour graduates not only received training tailor-made for the new industrial metropolis, but they also often put this training to work in electrical design, manufacturing, and management of complex technological enterprises. In later years, fire protection engineers would come to represent 25 percent of Armour graduates.[95] These students, combined with the electrical engineers, staffed city and insurance inspection departments, representing a body of engineering experts unique to the demands of the Chicago economy, and the unique dangers of the city of smoke.

Victor C. Alderson summed up the new role for the urban engineer in 1902:

The Day of the Untrained Man is past; the day of the technically trained man is here. At no time have the untrained, the unfit, the poorly prepared been so ruthlessly weeded out by the professions, the arts, the trades and business callings as they are to-day. The incessant demand, heard by him who has "his ear on the ground," is for young men in the vigor of manhood, whose eyes, ears, and hands, as well as minds, are trained to do the work demanded in modern industrial pursuits.[96]

The "Day of the Untrained Man" had actually passed quite rapidly in Chicago, at least as far as fire safety experts were concerned, and they were glad of it. The Armour Institute was only one of many technical colleges that were quick to develop engineering curricula highly adaptable to the demands of the urban industrial risk environment. It was a national phenomenon. The Case School of Applied Science in Cleveland, Carnegie Institute of Technology in Pittsburgh, Drexel Institute in Philadelphia, and Stevens Institute in Hoboken were just a few of the institutions undergoing rapid transformations in line with the developing needs for technical experts in the late nineteenth century.[97] Fire protection engineering education, following in Armour's footsteps, was introduced into engineering departments, firemen's training schools, and fire insurance inspection training, as well as city and state inspection bureaus after the turn of the century. Schools like MIT and Johns Hopkins taught fire protection as a multidisciplinary subject, where it often fell between chemical, electrical, and structural engineering. The Armour Institute's fledgling fire protection program was just one of the many institutional avenues by which the experts in fire safety could advance their efforts at bringing fire protection into the mainstream of knowledge production and policy control in the industrial metropolis.

With a full generation of development at their back the fire safety experts were poised in the early twentieth century to take on government—the next frontier in pushing their standards out into the urban environment. The challenge would prove enormous, and enormously stimulative to organizational ingenuity. Their work to this point had the power of scientific authority and technical skill, of market control in fire insurance coverage practices, and in the realm of professionalization afforded by university training. An incredible era of disasters beginning with the Iroquois Theater Fire (1903) would place the fire experts in a unique position to demonstrate that their hard-won investigative skills and fire protection standards and recommendations were the only things that might finally revoke the "Devil's privilege" in the American city.

2

Reforming Fire

How can we bring the manager, the architect, and the official
guardians of public safety—the fire chiefs and public inspectors of
buildings—to understand and introduce the well-proved
safeguards, and to be critical about that perfection of detail on
which safety depends? How can we bring the public to demand
these things? . . . We cannot leave it to the underwriter.

—John Ripley Freeman

Fire in the Conflagration Era exposed a crisis in American government. Expert knowledge and techniques were increasingly available to protect citizens and their property, but government officials struggled to apply the work of the disaster experts to the challenges of reforming the governance of urban fire. The stakes of this failure in policy innovation and enforcement were raised dramatically in the opening years of the twentieth century. The year 1904 alone saw disasters unfolding one after another. Chicago buried the dead of the Iroquois Theater Fire, Baltimore's downtown harbor district and downtown Rochester both burned down, and the steamship *General Slocum* caught fire in New York City's East River resulting in 1,021 deaths, many of them children, by burns and drowning. The fires following the San Francisco earthquake in 1906 brought down 25,000 buildings, and in a time without earthquake insurance the structural damages caused by the enormous quake were mostly blamed on fire, as well. By the time of the Triangle Shirtwaist Fire in 1911, the high point of popular outrage against fire disasters in American cities, fire experts and fire reformers were finally communicating, though the outcome of their collaborations were often just as contentious as they were productive of safer cities.

The Conflagration Era overlapped the Progressive Era, a time in American political history marked by rising demand among reformers both within and outside government for expert technical, social science, and public policy solutions to the problems wrought by industrialization. Wealth and political power were rapidly accumulating in the hands of a few, while immigrants and middle-class Americans alike experienced environmental degradation and economic uncertainty. The rise of a new national economy tended by an industrial oligarchy challenged deeply cherished American beliefs in class mobility and vibrant local democratic practice.[1]

The history of reform related to disasters, fire specifically, demonstrates some of the frequently overlooked complexities of the Progressive Era. Progressive reform, for example, often took on two meanings simultaneously: (1) a rising demand for new laws protecting public safety; and (2) state regulation of large-scale corporate interests. It is important to hold these two concepts of reform in front of us as we follow the historical process in which disaster experts and government officials groped toward establishing new standards of urban fire safety. Public fear of fire disasters and disgust with decades of ineffective urban governance flowing from one direction collided with a wave of outrage against the amalgamation of monopoly power—the fire insurance industry included—coming from the other. While the fire experts and the public railed against government officials to modernize their approaches to risk mitigation, the limitations on government to enact sweeping reforms were real and substantial. The 1869 Supreme Court decision in *Paul v. Virginia* set down a precedent in which the regulation of the fire insurance industry was left to the states, and it would not be overturned until 1944. At the state level, reformers in this era were conflicted over how to at one and the same time apply the expertise generated by the fire insurance industry while also regulating the industry in the name of anti-trust reform. The political enticements of trust-busting, more often than not, offered more immediate electoral rewards to reformers than did the patient policy-making of disaster mitigation. Regulation of land use had also, by law and tradition, been jealously guarded by government at the most local levels, a fact that militated against the wholesale adoption of the fire experts' more abstract and scientifically derived principles of fire protection. At the very same time, the public was demanding answers from their elected officials with increasing urgency, answers as to why the most modern techniques of public safety were not being applied in the nation's most modern cities. Without their own labs, their own field experts, and only their overmatched fire services to draw from, municipal and state officials were increasingly persuaded to apply as much private knowledge as possible to a growing bureaucracy of urban fire control. As Brian Balogh points out, Americans of the Progressive Era were often very happy to accept pragmatism over neat and tidy ideological categories anyway. Purely public or private sector solutions to the fire disaster problem were not viable in this context, and once we throw out those possibilities we begin to see more clearly the ways fire experts brought about previously unknown applications of expertise to policy formation in the American city.[2]

The Iroquois Theater Fire presented the worst loss of life of any fire in the United States in the twentieth century. Iroquois, and the subsequent investigation by insurance engineer John Ripley Freeman, showed the chasm between what was known by the experts and what could be done by government to protect the public in the built urban environment. This dysfunction in the face of disaster compels an examination of the policy environment surrounding fire insurance in the period, as a way to understand why fire insurance companies could not more forcefully exert themselves in public policy—while at the same time looking at openings they found through research and public relations in order to extend their reach into city halls and state houses across the country. The case of the 1914 Salem Conflagration shows a key example where the expanding knowledge of fire protection could, in the right policy environment and in connection with the newly organized field of city planning, lead to tangible change.

The Iroquois Theater Fire and the Failure
of Municipal Fire Protection

The Iroquois Theater Fire in Chicago brought together the most vexing aspects of the fire problem. Flawed fire and building codes, lax government oversight of weak laws, and risk-taking by private property owners combined to result in the greatest loss of life of any fire in the twentieth-century United States. On the afternoon of December 30, 1903, an overflow crowd jammed Chicago's newest theater, the Iroquois, to take in a performance of *Mr. Bluebeard*, a traveling spectacular from London with a cast and crew of 400, famous for its elaborately painted 800-piece set and thrilling electrical lighting effects. The Iroquois, costing over a million dollars to build, had opened just over a month before to wide acclaim from architects and theater managers for its inventive combination of style and safety. It had a three-story façade, a mirrored lobby decorated in white marble, and a grand foyer. It had an orchestra level, balcony, and gallery, and a spacious stage 110 feet long and 60 feet deep. Advertised as absolutely "fireproof," the Iroquois also had multiple fire escapes, an overhead smoke vent, and an asbestos curtain to shield the audience from a fire that might break out on stage. The theater seated 1,600, but there were well over 2,000 people in the audience that day, a standing-room-only matinee crowd of mothers with their children, teachers and teenagers on break from school, and holiday visitors from out of town.

In the second act, during a number called "In the Pale Moonlight," with a bluish glow supplied by an electric arc light washing across the stage, a small puff of flame was noticed halfway up one of the stage curtains. The singing and dancing on stage continued, but the cry of "Fire!" went up in the crowd. Seeking to avoid a panic, lead actor Eddie Foy came up from backstage, walked to the edge of the stage, and announced to the crowd sitting out in the darkness that they should remain in their seats. He told the orchestra to keep playing.[3]

Joseph Peaks, a railroad commissioner in town from Maine, was sitting in the audience with his young son. Peaks was aware that the new big city theaters all had fire curtains, asbestos-reinforced shields that would drop in case of a stage fire, keeping smoke and heat from filling the auditorium. Peaks stayed in his seat next to his son, waiting for the asbestos curtain to come down. The theater's house fireman, formerly a member of the Chicago Fire Department, was trying desperately to extinguish the blaze. Unsuccessful in hoisting a pike to rip down the smoldering side-stage curtains, he had moved on to his last resort. With a metal Kilfyre brand fire extinguisher canister in his arms, the fireman again confronted the flames. When he aimed the canister, a cloud of white powder sprayed weakly from the nozzle. The vent above the stage, designed to allow smoke and heat to escape before spilling out into the auditorium, remained inexplicably closed. The fire curtain hung immobile. The lights went out, plunging the auditorium and foyer into darkness.

"The confusion was indescribable," said Peaks later. "The screams of the women, the cries of the children, and the stampede of the whole audience created a bedlam of the entire place. . . . Suddenly we thought someone had opened wide a door in the rear, the wind blew the flames out from the stage into the theater so that our faces were burned and our clothes scorched."[4] Many of the victims were later found immolated in their seats, not having anticipated that a small stage fire might release a fireball into their faces within a couple of minutes.

By this point hundreds of people were rushing down from the balconies along either side of the main auditorium, and those with floor seats crammed the aisles heading to the rear exits. The staff had not performed fire drills, and not knowing what to do, they fled with the crowd. The theater's poor design seemed to conspire with the rapidly thickening smoke and intensifying heat. The landings at the bases of the balcony sections were too small, and some people lost their footing as those descending from behind trampled over them in their rush to escape. Several of the rear exits were inexplicably blocked, even locked in some cases. Many of the functioning doors opened inward. People grasping for the doors were crushed as the crowd surged forward, the immense pressure from behind preventing them from pulling the doors open. The exhaust vent remained closed, and smoke filled the auditorium. The asbestos stage curtain had descended partially, then become stuck, billowing with smoke. Fire escapes had been installed with an unexpected drop between the doorway and the escape. People lost their balance and collapsed, falling over the side.

When the numbers were in, they were far worse than originally thought possible. At least 600 people died from burns, suffocation, or trampling, while another three hundred or so were seriously injured. In terms of lives lost it was the worst fire disaster ever to hit the United States to that time. Sympathy poured in from across the nation. Chicago, it seemed to many, was somehow marked for destruction. The *Tribune* issued a not-so-subtle reminder that the city had not been prepared, in the most fundamental way, for such an abrupt and devastating tragedy. "In all quarters of the city," the paper reported, "the undertakers say there are not hearses enough to bear the dead to the cemeteries. . . . Hearses may even be brought in from suburban and outlying cities, but the undertakers advise that, where necessary, services be postponed a day or so."[5] In Chicago, the New Year passed in silence. Analysis of the Iroquois Theater Fire provided fire disaster experts the opportunity to display their methods of analysis and make recommendations based on their expert judgments. Historical analysis of the episode today reveals the stark disconnect between the sharp forensic tools of the fire safety expert and the

Figure 4. "Inside the Iroquois Theater While the Fire Raged," The Iroquois Theater Fire, December 30, 1903. From Marshall Everett, *The Great Chicago Theater Disaster: The Complete Story Told by the Survivors* (Chicago: Publishers Union of America, 1904), 173. Courtesy of University of Pennsylvania Libraries.

blunt forces of construction and fundamental municipal government ineptitude in risk and disaster mitigation at the turn of the twentieth century.

Within a few days after the disaster Chicagoans were demanding answers. How was such a fire possible, in a modern, "fireproof" downtown building, with a crowd of innocent women and children in attendance? Why Chicago *again*? What about the building codes that ensured that public venues were safe? And, the most pressing question, who was to blame? This question of blame excited the most immediate interest among victims' families, the press, fire insurance companies, and the public at large. Allegations, lawsuits, or both were leveled at the mayor, city building inspectors, Will J. Davis, owner of the Iroquois, house manager Harry J. Powers, and other members of the Iroquois staff. Davis and Powers especially were singled out for immediate scorn, perhaps, in part, due to the faith in the Iroquois as a safe theater that they had cultivated throughout its planning and its first five weeks of operation. Theater fires were common in Chicago, and two of America's most famous and horrific fire disasters had happened in theaters—Richmond in 1811 and Brooklyn in 1876. Opening the door to future questions and lawsuits, Powers and Davis advertised the fireproof safety of their theater, writing in the souvenir program of the dedicatory performance in November that the "American public now, more than ever before, demand elegance of environment for their amusements, as well as provisions for comfort and security."[6]

Even the hand of God was invoked as a cause for the tragedy, not an uncommon invocation then, or at any time in the history of disasters. However, this view was vehemently attacked and turned against Davis and Powers, as well as the entire collection of possibly blameworthy officials, by Chicago Episcopal bishop Samuel Fallows. According to Fallows,

> He [God] did not cause the calamity. No responsibility for it can be rolled upon him. . . . his laws had been palpably broken by human negligence and incompetency. God is love; and human greed and selfishness had violated every principle of love which worketh no ill to his neighbor. . . . Mayors, architects, fire-inspectors, managers, stage carpenters, electricians, ushers and chiefs of police in every city have had their duty burned into their inmost consciousness by this consuming fire.[7]

On New Year's Eve, city coroner John Traeger impaneled a grand jury for an inquest into the causes of the disaster. Though Traeger must have known the difficulties involved in assigning legal blame for such a chaotic event, he set about doing his job and prepared to start calling witnesses. The profound loss of life and long list of injured patrons demanded a full hearing. Meanwhile, Mayor Carter Harrison, Jr., son and namesake of the mayor who had brought the Columbian Exposition to Chicago, acted quickly to reassure the public that action would be taken by City Hall, that an investigation was underway. Harrison has been aptly described as a "reform boss," a politician in tune with the rising tide of Progressive concerns who still operated within the system of urban machine politics.[8] Harrison was especially eager to improve the material environment of the city, and in this the fire safety of buildings was a key factor. He had called for a full investigation of Chicago's theaters only months before, in October, in reaction to allegations of corruption among building inspectors and severe code violations in the Cleveland

and La Salle Theaters. When Building Commissioner George Williams's report came in it appeared that nearly every theater in the city was in gross violation of the building codes. The matter was referred to the city council, the aldermen, under extreme pressure from theater owners, sat on the issue. Until a proper study could be made and amendments to the building code passed, the aldermen decided, the theaters should remain open. Now, with the Iroquois a smoking ruin, Harrison acted alone.[9]

Building inspectors moved out into the city, building and fire ordinance books in hand. Individual theaters responded quickly, trying to convince audiences that they were not in danger. There was a law on the books requiring sprinklers above and under the stage, but it turned out on quick inspection that *none* of the city's theaters were so equipped. Building Commissioner Williams also presented to the mayor a list of theaters without asbestos curtains. On New Year's Day, by "5 o'clock orders for the closing of eighteen theaters . . . were being taken to the managers of the playhouses by . . . policemen."[10] This represented half the theaters in the city, a seating capacity of twenty thousand. Such dramatic and profit-destroying action was required, according to the mayor, as he refused "to take additional responsibility for further calamities." When a plaintive group of theater managers arrived at the mayor's home and asked him to repeal his order, his response was terse: "I told them that it should not be necessary for me to tell them what they ought to do." The Grand Opera House closed voluntarily for an examination by city officials, arguing that "their playhouse is practically without defect, yet the public mind is so wrought up that nothing will reassure theater patrons except a complete official inquiry."

The city council aldermen made an investigation of the Iroquois, accompanied by the theater's architect, Benjamin H. Marshall. They toured the charred building, still littered with scraps of clothing from the victims, and expressed alarm at the scene before them. Unwilling to admit that the Iroquois was less than a marvel of modern construction, Marshall explored the theater. "I cannot understand it at all," he said, looking around the rubble. "The theater was fireproof."[11] Mayor Harrison made his own investigation, accompanied by the building commissioner and a few architects. The mayor toured the building, picking up scraps of the failed asbestos curtain and pointing out code violations as he went along. Back in his office, he said: "I could not see any explanation for the calamity except the fatality connected with the lowering of the curtain. I tried a lot of the doors and they seemed to open and shut readily. I got into the rigging loft and

Figure 5. "Measuring the Exit Where Hundreds were Killed and Burned," the Iroquois Theater Fire, December 30, 1903. From Marshall Everett, *The Great Chicago Theater Disaster: The Complete Story Told by the Survivors* (Chicago: Publishers Union of America, 1904), front section. Courtesy of University of Pennsylvania Libraries.

everywhere else except into the cellar. Harrison went a step farther to bolster his claim for an objective investigation, inviting a number of architects and builders to conduct their own investigation and report back to him as soon as possible. The *Chicago Daily Tribune* sponsored its own investigation, conducted by a prestigious "Theater Commission," with members including engineers, architects, and building contractors. On January 2 the *Tribune* published a list of city theater ordinances that had been violated by the Iroquois, as well as a list from investigations performed in October and November, identifying all the faults found in Chicago theaters by the building commissioner. The *Tribune* claimed that had "the building laws of Chicago been strictly complied with in the Iroquois Theater the loss of life should have been comparatively small, if there had been any loss at all." The list of infractions was startling, and included provisions

> That a theater must have direct fire alarm connection with fire headquarters; That all lights must be protected so adjacent material

cannot touch them; That suitable fire extinguishing apparatus be on the stage; That all exits shall be suitably marked with large signs; That all galleries shall have independent entrances and exits; That the number of auditors in a theater shall be limited by the size and number of its exits; That no auditorium seating over 1,000 persons shall be connected with any building not entirely fireproof; That automatic sprinklers shall be used over all stages; That a suitable flue be in the roofs of all stages to carry out smoke and fire; That the apparatus and fittings of all stages and rigging lofts be fireproof; That all theaters must face on three open spaces.[12]

Such an astounding list of violations called into question the integrity of the entire building and fire safety code system in Chicago and launched an argument as to who, ultimately, was responsible for enforcing the codes.

Amid this flurry of activity, it was beginning to appear that the disaster at the Iroquois might not be easily blamed on one single party. Building Commissioner Williams gave his side of the story to the *Tribune* on New Year's Day. "I was in the Iroquois Theater a whole afternoon," he recounted, "on and under the stage, in the auditorium, galleries, dressing rooms, rigging loft, and everywhere, and I thought it the best theater ever built up to that time. The sprinkler ordinance never has been enforced, and not one theater in Chicago, to my knowledge, has a system as required by law." Williams in fact questioned the wisdom of the sprinkler ordinance, one of the many ordinances the Iroquois had violated, and asserted that he had heard that sprinklers could cause more damage to property on their own than could be done by fire. This criticism was one the Factory Mutuals had contended with consistently over the years, evidence that lower premiums and even city fire codes were often not enough to force property owners to adopt design changes endorsed by fire experts.

Williams marveled at the layout of the theater, stating that the "Iroquois Theater had 45 per cent more exit space than the ordinance calls for. . . . The doors to the exits were easy to work if you knew how." Williams admitted that there were not enough men to see that overcrowding did not happen in theaters, though it was his responsibility. This he regretted, and claimed that he "shall assuredly demand an explanation from Inspector William Curran, who was in the Iroquois ten minutes before the fire and reported everything all right." Finally, Williams explained the economic rationale for systemic violation of city fire safety codes: "When the report on theaters was made up last November, it was a matter of throwing 3,000 to 5,000 persons out of employment if we closed the violators, and of reducing to want the 15,000 persons dependent on them. It was too big a thing for me to handle offhand. I took it to the mayor. He sent it to the council, which has it yet." Williams shifted responsibility away from himself and the city's building inspectors and over to the city council aldermen who were responsible for legislating the city's building codes in the first place. He pointed to a fundamental dereliction of duty on the part of the aldermen, but still made a weak plea for clemency on their behalf, noting that the council "has more to do than it can wade through."[13]

Williams's point about job losses resonated with the broader critique of fire safety in cities—that its adoption would be too costly for builders and owners, and enforcement would necessarily criminalize businessmen just trying to compete and survive in the rough-and-tumble urban economy. There is no better example of this argument over the costs of fire safety technologies than the debate surrounding the asbestos stage curtain at the Iroquois. The *Tribune* interviewed C. W. Trainer of Trainer and Company in Boston, manufacturer of the curtain. Trainer claimed that the curtain "we made for the Iroquois theater did not contain the wire insertion, but it was of a good grade of cloth. . . . Wire adds to the tensile strength of the cloth, and of course it is calculated in a degree to prevent a curtain from 'bellying' as did that in the Iroquois . . . the contract was awarded to us, presumably because we were the lowest bidders." Trainer would not discuss the quality or price of the curtain, but the *Tribune* called it "a second grade article." Gustave J. Johnson of the Western Society of Engineers, yet another interested party on the scene, reported on the curtain "there was some asbestos in it, but it was largely wood pulp, and would not have been of much avail if it had been lowered." He examined it under a microscope to determine the exact composition, pointing out that "It has been discovered that by mixing wood pulp with the asbestos fiber the life of the curtain is prolonged, the cost is cheapened, and the wire foundation can be dispensed with. It results in a curtain that can get inside the city ordinances, but is of no value in a fire."[14] But had the curtain failed because it was of poor composition, or because it had failed to drop correctly? Was this the fault of the theater owner or staff, or perhaps the building inspectors? Johnson's discourse on the asbestos curtain provided yet another possible explanation for the disaster that only seemed to lead to more questions.

On the evening of January 2, Mayor Harrison went a step beyond his original closures, shutting down the big playhouses along with smaller vaudeville and outlying theaters, 35 in all, "until they have conformed to the laws or until the council has modified the ordinances."[15] The mayor and building commissioner were prompted to take this action due to the *Tribune*'s scathing "Theater Report." Again, police served the notices, which told managers which specific sections of the ordinance they had violated. The theaters largely complied, and evenings of dark theaters and full cafes followed. The Bush Temple carried on with its performance that night, but the show was halted while underway. The manager at the Thirty-First Street Theater, F. M. Brown, voiced a common complaint. "I ordered an asbestos curtain yesterday," he protested, "but today I canceled the order until I can find what the city wants."

Chicago Fire Inspector Monroe Fulkerson weighed in next, and leveled blame at the Iroquois Theater staff. Stage manager William Carlton was to blame, Fulkerson claimed, finding that one of the stage lights swung out in such a way as to impede the proper function of the asbestos curtain. The light was "so arranged that when in use during the play it was an absolute bar to the descent of the fire shield." Fulkerson went on to say that "Whoever left that north light swung out under the curtain was immediately responsible for the failure of the fire shield to drop," supposing that an employee had fled in fright of the fire.[16] A Mr. H. Hill explained to the *Tribune* that Stage Manager Carlton "always had left these lights to the haphazard care of anyone who happened to be within call when needed." Hill saw the fire start, saw the fireman come up and shout for an alarm, and saw someone at the curtain signal. "This is a light switch, which, when pulled, turns on a light in the flies," he explained. "This light is a signal to the curtain man up there to run down the fire curtain." Clearly, the failure of these safety precautions, lack of fire drill training, and implication of the stage manager in the malfunction of the asbestos curtain warranted further investigation as factors contributing to the tragedy.[17]

On January 8 the group of outside building experts assembled by the mayor returned its *Iroquois Theater Fire Investigation Testimony Report*. This group of 32 investigators included members of the Chicago Builders Club, Chicago Architects Business Association, Builders Exchange, Mason Builders Association, and Illinois Chapter of the American Institute of Architects. There were no fire experts in the group.[18] The *Testimony Report* included transcripts of interviews with the Iroquois Theater's electrician and assistant electrician, stage carpenter, light operator, house fireman Eddie Foy, other Iroquois staff, and a number of witnesses. The *Report* reached the conclusion that the fire started due to "Sparks or heat from an electrical projector, spot or flood light, igniting draperies . . . about twelve feet above stage floor." The fire extended due to the failure of the Kilfyre extinguisher, the absence of standpipes and automatic sprinklers, and the absence of hooks to tear down the burning scenery. The fire spread out into the auditorium because of the failure of the asbestos curtain, the descent of which was "probably interfered with by some projection." The failure of the exhaust vent was also noted. On the critical question of the loss of life, the *Report* pointed to one main factor, "panic," followed by "asphyxiation" and "burning." It presented a complex picture of liability, with multiple technological failures augmented by multiple human failures, failure of the building code, and the panic of the crowd all adding to the catastrophe.[19]

On January 25, the jury returned its verdict in the coroner's inquest, and the results were stunning. Agreeing with some of the basic findings of the *Testimony Report*, the jury "found that the grand drapery of the proscenium had caught fire from an electric light, and that numerous city ordinances had been violated." Eight individuals were held over to be examined for their role in the fire: "Mayor Carter Harrison; William J. Davis, owner and manager; William H. Musham, Fire Department Chief; George Williams, Building Commissioner; Edward Laughlin, Building Inspector; William Sallers, House Fireman; James E. Cummings, Stage Carpenter and William McMullen, the operator of the floodlight." All eight were arrested and posted bail. It would take time to assemble a jury and continue the legal investigation.[20]

In the wake of this unexpected outcome, a final expert weighed in: William Clendenin, editor of *Fireproof Magazine*. *Fireproof* consistently promoted steel fireproofing above all other methods. In fact, Clendenin was outspoken against the Factory Mutuals, Edward Atkinson specifically. Clendenin held that slow-burning mill construction was not a good model for urban structures, and he frequently let his view on the matter be known in the pages of *Fireproof*. However, Clendenin had found an enemy stronger than Atkinson in the Chicago city government, which he blasted soundly after the fire. Clendenin investigated the theater himself in the summer of 1903 and condemned it on four points: "The absence of an intake or stage draft shaft; the exposed reinforcement of the concrete arch; the presence of wood trim on everything; the inadequate provision of exits." He said that the poor curtain made the Iroquois a "terrible trap." The flame destroyed the concrete, which "crumbled away, exposing the twisted mass of steel reinforcement girders, and fell on the audience. . . . Looking from below, the bewildered, choking, and maddened crowd thought it was the result of a panic above. They believed the galleries were falling," and as a result of this panic many more were killed. Unfortunately, the Iroquois was held up as the best of modern fireproofing. According to Clendenin, his investigation revealed that it was, in fact, one of the worst buildings in the city.[21] As a fire expert Clendenin was more willing than the mayor's "builder's group" to find fault with the overall approach to construction at the Iroquois than with piecemeal failures inside or human negligence.

Clendenin proceeded to develop his model of blame for the disaster, hinging on the key question of whether the structure was indeed fireproof, and ultimately settling blame for the deaths on the city government. Clendenin's technical expertise, combined with his understanding of the Byzantine structure of Chicago's city bureaucracy, rendered his voice unique among investigators to that point, and is worth quoting at length:

> The story of the Iroquois, in all its appalling, overwhelming detail, will never be written. The whole truth has been buried in the agony of the death of those who suffered martyrdom within it. Who is responsible? A legally constituted authority has involved the mayor for wretched, feeble enforcement, and, collaterally, nonenforcement of the building ordinances. The building department of the city of Chicago, whose commissioner has also been bound to the grand jury, has been criticised for years. Not only has the department been utterly incompetent, but there have been repeated and proven charges of corruption and bribery. . . . The spectacle of the mayor of Chicago censured by one of his own officials, proceeding with a plea for release under a writ of habeas corpus, immediately and complimentarily issued, followed by a jollification and a session of high glee at the city hall, is enough to make the plainest citizen of the western metropolis ashamed of his city and his citizenship. . . . the Iroquois disaster is not only primarily, but directly, attributable to lax executive methods of those who stood for election to the executive offices. . . . The Chicago city council can be safely relied upon at all times to do the worst thing possible.[22]

Clendenin's tirade, while stirring, left the most critical question unan-
swered: if builders, architects, private businessmen, and most especially the
city government cannot be trusted to look after the safety of the technological metropolis, who could be trusted? Naturally, the disaster experts had an
opinion on this question. The most thorough investigation of the Iroquois
Theater Fire was conducted by one of the nation's foremost authorities on
fireproof construction and fire safety engineering, Factory Mutuals insurance engineer John Ripley Freeman.

The Iroquois Theater Fire and Expert Investigation

John Ripley Freeman's investigation of the Iroquois Theater Fire built on a
lifetime of experience in the field as an insurance inspector, in the lab as a
fire protection engineering researcher, and in the boardroom as a fire insurance executive. Examination of Freeman's investigation shows us the fire
expert fully engaged, limited by his lack of legal authority but emboldened
by the increasingly relevant niche of expertise he and his colleagues claimed
for themselves. His Iroquois Theater investigation, especially, offers us
through close examination a prime case where private sector fire expertise
met and understood a major risk but failed to convert the findings into
effective policy reform.

Freeman, whom we met in Chapter 1, spent most of his career as an
inspector and an executive for the Factory Mutual fire insurance companies
in New England. He was an expert in fireproof construction, having
inspected factories for decades. An early advocate of sprinkler systems, he
also innovated in hydraulics, fireproof construction, and assessment of
structural risks. Wealthy and prominent Chicagoan Charles Crane wrote to
Freeman asking him to come and investigate the Iroquois Theater Fire.
Socially connected and active in reform politics, Crane had lost two nieces
in the fire.[23] Moved by the tragedy, and also seeing an opportunity to
expand the work of the Factory Mutuals Inspection Department into a
direct examination of urban structural risks, Freeman agreed. He arrived
via the 20th Century Limited the first week of January 1904 and immediately set to work. Continuing the Factory Mutuals tradition, Freeman spoke
freely and at great length of his concerns over fire safety in America in both
the popular and the technical press and expressed unbridled enthusiasm

for the investigation ahead. In the disaster lay an opportunity, morbid perhaps, but a chance to show the value of private fire expertise to a large and anxious audience, both of citizens, and government officials. At the same time, Freeman wrote privately back to his assistant E. V. French about his shock on witnessing such an unprecedented scene of carnage in the Iroquois Theater, or as he took to calling it, the "chamber of horrors."

Freeman met Mayor Harrison, an event covered eagerly by the press. Harrison granted Freeman an unrestricted pass to enter and move undisturbed through any part of any theater in the city. The press greeted Freeman warmly, eager to cover the story of an "outside" opinion of the disaster— an opinion potentially free from the corruptive influence of Chicago politics. This story line fit in with the broader narrative of negligence and government malfeasance that had been building since the fire. Though it might have had the virtue of being true, such a narrative was also a well-known and profitable one for newspapers in the Progressive Era, stretching back well before the tragedy.

"The City Club of Chicago," reported the *Chicago Record-Herald*, "has secured the services of John R. Freeman . . . to make an exhaustive examination of the existing conditions of the Chicago theaters and to report on the proper requirements for fire protection, and also the proper methods of enforcing these requirements. Mr. Freeman is probably the best qualified man in the United States for this purpose, and will, of course, be entirely unaffected by local influence or personal considerations."[24] Though his entire career had been devoted to avoiding fires, ostensibly for the profit of insurance companies, the reform-minded City Club gambled that Freeman's professional status as an engineer and accomplished fire safety expert might remove him from the arguments between city officials and their detractors. His investigation would be different primarily because of his ability to translate the disaster out of the language of urban politics and into the language of technological risk and failure. Ultimately, Freeman would lament the fact that he could not translate it back again into enforceable law.

Freeman's first steps were much like those before him, a tour of the theater's wreckage, interviews with the staff, a review of the relevant building codes, and consultation with city authorities. But this is where his investigation ceased to be like the others. Working outward geographically from the Iroquois stage, Freeman designed an easily reproducible inspection form, much like those used by Factory Mutual inspectors, and set out to evaluate as many of Chicago's theaters as possible. To this time-consuming task Freeman put his Mutuals inspection assistant E. V. French. Freeman himself traveled back and forth to the east coast to carry out his other duties for the Factory Mutuals as the Iroquois examination went forward.[25]

E. V. French's Chicago theater inspections put the mind of a New England factory inspector to work in America's fastest growing and riskiest city. The degree to which a theater adhered to city building codes—the handbook of fire safety requirements followed by the city's building inspectors—was not French's concern. The Iroquois, after all, had passed city inspection and was considered "fireproof" by its architect, builder, owner, manager, and staff. Freeman and French agreed that quite obviously a higher level of scrutiny was required before the fireproof denotation was applied to a building. Therefore, French evaluated theaters based on his notions of what constituted a safe and fireproof environment, ideas developed through years of Mutuals inspection work. French and Freeman had the fire expert standard in mind, not the municipal fire standard.

In each theater French first noted the seating capacity and the overall constitution of the structure. "Quick burning" theaters were those of joist construction, with hollows in floors and walls. "Semi slow-burning" theaters were joist or plank construction, with fire stops. "Incombustible" theaters were ones that conformed to the Factory Mutuals model of slow-burning construction—with heavy plank floors, no hollow spaces for fire to hide, brick fire stops, and partitions that would limit the ability of a fire to race through a theater quickly. French broke his evaluations down into "auditorium," "stage," and "general" sections. In the auditorium he looked at the basic structural features: walls, roofs, floors, attics, and basements. Then he noted the exits, aisles, exit doors, and fire escapes. On stage he again surveyed structural features, and added a look at fire curtains, vents, dressing rooms, and scenery. In the general category, French looked over boiler rooms, electrical fittings, gas, and water delivery. In line with the slow-burning mill construction philosophy, he paid close attention also to the presence (or general absence as it turned out) of fire mitigation technologies: automatic sprinklers, hoses and pumps, fire alarm boxes, fire axes and pole hooks, water pails, and fire extinguishers. The competence of watchmen and the theater fire brigade was also taken into account. French spent one to two hours in every theater he visited, judging the theater in each category, and compiled a list of suggestions by which the theater might be brought up to the fireproof standard of the Factory Mutuals. In most cases he also obtained copies of blueprint plans for the theaters, which he attached to his reports.

French judged that most of Chicago's theaters were built and maintained at a very low standard of fire safety. Mirroring Freeman's early assessment of the key failures at the Iroquois—the asbestos fire curtain, overhead smoke vent, and lack of sprinklers—French paid careful attention to these features in his inspections. In his grading, he "considered the fire curtain and the vent as belonging to construction, and when these were not satisfactory, have rated the construction low, as without them loss of life and large fire damage in the auditorium may easily occur."[26] The issue of sprinklers was practically moot, as none of the theaters French inspected had them, and only one was in the process of installing a system. None of the theaters passed with flying colors. Some stood up moderately well to scrutiny, such as the Illinois Theater. French commended its "brick and stone . . . fireproof construction throughout." He found a good fire curtain and vents, and that "the general plan is simple and clear, the exits are direct, and the currents of people coming from gallery, balcony, and floor are well separated. . . . it is, I think, the best example in Chicago of what location, general plan and construction should be for the safest result." Despite this praise, French still had 13 suggestions for making the theater even safer, including relatively inexpensive fixes like the addition of a small fire hose and fire pails, and an organized fire brigade. He also suggested that the Illinois needed a rebuilt orchestra pit, rearrangement of fire escapes, and of course a sprinkler system, all very costly and time-consuming changes.[27] Such suggestions reflect the fire expert's mindset: there is no perfectly safe building, only buildings evolving toward safety. It also demonstrates why builders and owners often showed resentment toward fire experts. From their perspective the fire experts—either insurance engineers or reform-minded municipal officials—were always dissatisifed, and satisfying them always cost time and money.

Most of the theaters came in for serious criticism. The Academy of Music, French wrote, was "a great barn-like structure, thoroughly quick-burning, joisted and hollow, and with much fuel in its structure. . . . Nothing short of practical rebuilding would entirely remove the objectionable features."[28] The Trocadero was singled out for particular censure. French found it "a theater of very low order," going on to suggest "it would probably be for the good of the general public if it were closed up entirely. Even a very mild theology would probably indicate that the regular frequenters of this theater would be burned up in the next world even if we find a way to save them in this."[29] Moralizing aside, French's reports presented a damning picture of Chicago's theaters. Unfettered by the prevailing standards of the building code, French took a blue sky approach to his inspections, imagining each structure as a completely fireproof, completely safe environment for the public. French captured this view in his assessment of the Bijou, a theater where "the general character of the whole property make[s] it difficult to suggest any changes short of complete rebuilding." Strong medicine for a major theater that seated more than 1,200 people, but such was necessary in order to achieve "absolute safety." And, even if absolute safety was improbable, French reasoned that his 17-point plan for improvements would "very much reduce the danger and make the chance of a serious catastrophe small."[30]

Other fire experts volunteered to help in the investigation, including members of the City Club, F. J. T. Stewart of the Chicago Underwriters Association, and Professor Charles Mayer, a chemist with the Chicago Fireproof Covering Company. Chicago architect G. F. Shaffer compiled a comparative study of stage scenery used in Chicago theaters. Shaffer also recorded "times to exit" at theaters by noting how long it took for patrons to leave after performances. At the Grand Opera House production of *The Darling of the Gods*, Shaffer found 25,000 square feet of sheeting used in the scenery, 6,000 board feet of braces, and 16,000 feet of hemp rope.[31] In talking with a stage carpenter at the Iroquois, Shaffer discovered the incredible amount of scenery used in staging *Mr. Bluebeard*: 100,000 square feet of sheeting, 26,000 square feet of gauze, 8,000 board feet of braces and battens, and 11 miles of hemp rope. At the Garrick Theater, Shaffer attended a performance of *Erminie* and timed the audience as it left. People started moving before the curtain was down, coats were on within 40 seconds, the balcony was cleared in two minutes, auditorium cleared in two minutes, and every person was out of the building within four minutes. Shaffer added to his statistics that it was a fashionable audience, and "slow moving." Shaffer sent his observations to Freeman, who used them to develop a context for the rapid acceleration of the fire on the Iroquois stage, and the dynamics of the crowd's escape movements.

French and Shaffer did not receive unqualified support from theater managers and staff. While noting that most of the people he encountered in his inspections were helpful, French also found cases where return visits were refused or blueprints not provided. At one theater he found a confusing ventilation system for which "the mechanic could not give a satisfactory explanation."[32] Shaffer wrote to Freeman about the trouble he had with the manager of the Garrick Theater, who "was present at the City Club to hear your [Freeman's] report and left shortly after you had finished your talk on sprinklers. I judged at the time that he was rather sour on the questions of theater betterment." Shaffer found this to be true when he went to time the audience's exodus at the Garrick and the manager "said his house could be emptied in about 2 minutes but did not seem to care to have me prove it." Shaffer, sniffed that "I shall do so," and then apparently sneaked into the crowd to accomplish his objective.[33]

With his inspectors in the field, Freemen widened the investigation by writing letters to city building inspectors across the nation and Europe. Gathering facts about building codes for comparison was not a new practice among insurance engineers—in fact, such cross-listings and tabulated lists of risks nationwide were instrumental in helping the NBFU and the Factory Mutuals standardize their premiums and standards of coverage. Now Freeman adopted it as a way to shine light on the comparative danger of Chicago theaters. Next, identifying himself as someone "making an impartial investigation of theater fire protection on behalf of a committee of leading citizens," Freeman sent out a questionnaire to about 70 theater owners, in Chicago and across the country, trying to gauge the use and effectiveness of automatic sprinklers in theaters. Operating under the dual authority of the fire expert community and the Chicago municipal government, Freeman planned to gather as much information as he could while the memory of the disaster was fresh.

In the sprinkler questionnaire, Freeman asked theater owners about the location of their sprinklers, how long the systems had been in use, and overall impressions of the automatic sprinkler as an effective fire mitigation tool. Responses came in from Boston, Philadelphia, Providence, and New York and indicated a general satisfaction with sprinklers; there were cases in which sprinkler heads had accidentally opened and caused damage, but when called on in case of fire, sprinklers had performed well. Answers to the "sprinkler questionnaire" undoubtedly bolstered Freeman's already substantial faith in the sprinkler as an element in an overall strategy of structural fireproofing.[34]

Freeman moved on to a series of studies in which he isolated the key technological parts that had failed during the Iroquois fire. First, the stage scenery had been troublesome—why had it caught fire so readily? Also, the fire extinguisher had performed poorly when put to the test. The fire vent never opened, and the asbestos curtain did not come down completely. The painted scenery caught fire too rapidly to be extinguished. He questioned the exits, the paucity of fire escapes, and the poor design of the inward-opening doors, which had refused exit to the victims. Freeman wrote letters to the top manufacturers of each of the above products, stating plainly his fears that there had been flaws in design, installation, and use of each at the Iroquois. Asking manufacturers to submit samples for examination, he threw down the gauntlet to the entire fire protection supply industry, one he clearly knew quite a bit about from his days as a roving factory inspector, when he had systematically noted and compared the efficacy of such technologies in operation. Many manufacturers responded, and even a few unsolicited products came in from companies eager to gain Freeman's seal of approval.

Freeman took the specimens he received from manufacturers, as well as those that could be salvaged from the Iroquois wreckage, and parceled them out to an informal network of fire safety experts for analysis. Asbestos cloth from the ruined fire curtain was dug out of the frozen wreckage of the Iroquois, and samples were sent away for laboratory composition analysis. Freeman's own Factory Mutuals laboratories performed part of this work, as did his friends in engineering labs at MIT. For small-scale tests such arrangements were fine, but for the kind of extensive testing Freeman wanted to do he needed a different venue. He found it close by, in Chicago, at the largest fire safety research laboratory in the nation: Underwriters Laboratories. As UL received its funding from the NBFU, it may have seemed unlikely that director William Henry Merrill would be willing to cooperate with Freeman, an agent of the rival Factory Mutuals. It was proof, perhaps of Edward Atkinson's claim that the NBFU and the Factory Mutuals were, ultimately, engaged in the same work: the development and application of fire safety expertise. Merrill expressed early interest in Freeman's investigation, at first apparently due to the role of the electric stage lamp in igniting the draperies and stage scenery. Soon UL assumed the role as the primary testing lab for the Freeman investigation, embarking on a comprehensive set of tests of asbestos cloth. Writing to John Howard Appleton, city engineer of Rochester, New York, Freeman explained his decision:

> I have not yet found any satisfactory tests of fire curtains designed for use on theaters. It has been quite common to simply apply a

flame from a plumber's gasoline torch to one or two points on [the] curtain and to conclude that it was fire proof if it did not burn up. Such a test is totally inadequate to indicate what the action of a curtain is likely to be when subjected all over to the fierce heat of a general stage fire. . . . To get better information on this curtain question, I have arranged with the Underwriters' Laboratories here to make under our direction tests of ten or a dozen sample curtains in their large gas furnace, samples about six by eight feet in size and heated completely and I am planning to test several curtains of asbestos . . . both with and without wire reinforcing. . . . There is considerable reason to believe that a curtain of thin sheet steel . . . and fireproofed on the stage side, will give good results . . . our tests here will throw light on all these matters.[35]

William Henry Merrill saw in Freeman's investigation a fruitful collaboration not only with a famous engineer but by extension with the Factory Mutuals. Such publicity could only be good for the fledgling UL, in business only ten years at the time.

Not waiting for the results of his asbestos tests, Freeman began to agitate for the most ambitious aspect of his investigation program—reenactment. He proposed to build a fire on the Iroquois stage, to re-create as closely as possible the conditions of the actual fire. The press and many engineers were enthusiastic. One newspaper reported that

the sole object in desiring to make the experiments is to gain scientific and accurate information . . . NOT FOR AMUSEMENT [capitalization original] It is not proposed to amuse or gratify the idle curiosity of spectators. . . . This is no scheme of a hare-braned (sic) enthusiast, but the sober-minded suggestion of an eminent engineer . . . an expert fire inspector of many years' experience.[36]

Such "experiments" would offer a tremendous spectacle, but also a serious chance to expand the horizons of the epistemology of fire disasters.[37] Freeman was fascinated with a live fire test performed in Vienna after the 1881 Ring Fire there killed over 600 attendees. Nevertheless, the plan was blocked—rather ironically considering whom Freeman represented—by an insurance company. In a letter outlining his company's objections, Henry Evans of the Continental wrote that, "as an official of this Company, responsible to the stockholders who put me here to make money for them, I could not justify myself in saying to you that you could start a fire on the stage of the Iroquois Theater and the Continental would pay its share of any resulting loss, either to the theater or adjoining buildings."[38] There were limits to the zeal for safety, and for investigation. The UL facilities at that time did not permit reenactment on that scale.

Despite the clamor of the parade of investigators, and despite Freeman's strong lobbying efforts, the tragedy at the Iroquois was seemingly forgotten by the summer of 1904. Those charged with responsibility for the fire by Coroner Traeger, and investigated by the grand jury, were exonerated. And though legal action would stretch out to 1909, only one of the many lawsuits—against the city of Chicago, the theater company, or the producers of *Mr. Bluebeard*—resulted in a damages award.[39] The George H. Fuller construction company was found guilty of violating city building ordinances, and rather than appeal they settled with claimants for a total of about $30,000.[40] This outcome was not at all surprising for the time. First of all, the legal concept of "contributory negligence" was commonly applied in such cases. The concept held that if a person contributed in any way to his or her own injury or death, then another party (such as a theater owner) could not be held responsible. Contribution might mean something as simple as running rather than "calmly" proceeding toward the exits. The most common impediment to victims' families receiving compensation was the absence of strong tort law protections for consumers. Second, in the case of Iroquois owner Will J. Davis, his lawyer Levy Mayer challenged the basic legal authority of the Chicago municipal government to pass and enforce building ordinances as specific as those that governed the Iroquois. In cases where the city ordinances seemed to go beyond those allowed by the state, Mayer argued that the city had no authority. Additionally, on the sprinkler requirement specifically, the defense alleged that the city had looked to outside experts in the fire insurance industry for specifications and assistance in writing the law. The judge hearing the case ruled that the ordinances were indeed invalid in the way they were written, and Davis was acquitted.[41]

The Chicago City Council now faced a challenge to its authority over writing specific building and fire ordinances. Even had the Council sorted out the legal issues, they were looking at the politically unpopular prospect of forcing Chicago theater owners to install expensive sprinkler systems over their stages and rigging lofts. In the end, City Council balked and removed the requirement from the building code. These types of difficulties would show up time and again in the first decade of the twentieth century as municipal governments attempted to systematically address fire risk through new and more stringent laws. From state to state laws were different as to how much power city governments had along these lines. In some states, cities were given more freedom to tailor laws to their local conditions —but as the Iroquois case shows, courts might also rule such enhanced ordinances invalid if they seemed to preempt state laws. The Iroquois case also shows that a court might look skeptically at the involvement of fire insurance experts in helping to draft building and fire ordinances. Though they might have the most knowledge, the perception of private gain at public expense could be very damaging, especially in the Progressive Era context of increasing scrutiny of big business. With no federal regulations on building ordinances at the time, fire experts were left trying to decide where to focus their time and money in the hopes of getting more stringent, enforceable laws on the books.

The rapid evolution of urban fire safety analysis was epitomized by Freeman's investigation and subsequent report, in which he combined the collaborative work of E. V. French and many other various inspectors; UL, MIT, and the Factory Mutuals labs; fire safety experts around the world from insurance, city inspection departments, and universities; and manufacturers of fireproofing technologies all together into one coordinated, multi-disciplinary attack on the problem of fire safety in theaters. After an exhaustive survey of each material and human component of the disaster, Freeman's technical solution to the problem of theater fires was a surprisingly simple three-part formula: installation of automatic sprinklers above the stage, provision of adequate smoke vents, and an incombustible fire curtain. Bringing simple recommendations from such a tangled web of risks bolstered Freeman's claim for having pioneered a powerful new method in the ongoing formation of fire expertise. He delivered his report on the fire, *On the Safeguarding of Life in Theaters*, to the American Society of Mechanical Engineers in 1905. In the report, Freeman stated flatly that the theaters and public buildings of the United States were ten to twenty years behind factories in their level of fire safety. *On the Safeguarding of Life in Theaters* was printed and reprinted, widely cited (and is still cited) in newspapers and technical journals, and established Freeman's credentials as a fire safety expert with interests far broader than simply inspecting New England factories for insurance companies.

When the smoke cleared, Chicago went on much as it had before. Freeman visited the Iroquois a year later, by then doing business as the Colonial

Theater. He found that new automatic smoke vents were in place, but had been designed so badly that "it surely could cause a repetition of the terrible loss of life . . . should a similar fire again occur."[42] The expert technical solutions were, if not meaningless, ineffective in forcing policy change toward public safety. In the end, Freeman presented the problem as a search for responsibility, asking:

> How can we transfer the care and precautions of the modern factory to the modern theater? How can we bring the manager, the architect, and the official guardians of public safety—the fire chiefs and public inspectors of buildings—to understand and introduce the well-proved safeguards, and to be critical about that perfection of detail on which safety depends? How can we bring the public to demand these things? . . . We cannot leave it to the underwriter. . . . We cannot leave it with the framing of a good building law.[43]

How, then, would the problem be solved? Through "*a full study of a few of the notable examples*" (emphasis original) of disasters like the Iroquois fire, Freeman argued, fire experts might come to understand such problems in their full complexity, and then suggest answers. The growth of interdisciplinary knowledge—and new ways to create that knowledge and disseminate it—was a key feature in the insurance industry's awareness of the urban conflagration crisis. Enormous impediments, as witnessed by the Iroquois tragedy, lay in the way of applying the knowledge, particularly in the reform of urban governance to enforce existing fire laws, or the emergence of private-sector fire experts in the absence of such a government function. Though the public demanded investigation and reform in the wake of fire disasters, and though the fire experts like Freeman had the techniques to understand fire disasters at an extremely high level of specificity, the experts did not yet in 1904 have the ability to force meaningful laws onto the books, laws that would apply those life-saving techniques toward mitigating the real risks of the urban fire environment.

Fire Insurance Reform

Americans in the Progressive Era expressed concern over increasing economic concentration in the hands of fewer and fewer large corporations.[44]

The fire insurance industry came under intense public scrutiny in these years, with public officials called to ensure that what was becoming an indispensible public good was affordable, equitably available across geographical and class divides, and managed without corruption. A reform wave aimed at the fire insurance industry swept across the nation, resulting in significant government regulation and oversight. Add to this what was demonstrated previously, heightened fire risk in industrializing cities forcing commitments across the fire insurance industry toward developing both theoretical and applied risk and disaster knowledge—knowledge that could be usefully applied to meeting the need for fire protection in the cities.[45] Taken together, a rather counterintuitive situation resulted: fire insurance business practices were increasingly called out for regulation, even sanction, while at the same time the industry's research practices were creating a critical mass of knowledge that could be readily applied to the real and rising threats of urban fire.

Traditionally, studies looking at the emergence of public safety have characterized it as a natural outgrowth of the state becoming more attuned to the rising expectations of citizens in the Progressive Era. The classic formulation along these lines would cite Upton Sinclair's muckraking exposé of the meat industry, *The Jungle*, as a spur to the government to take the safety of the food system seriously—the result being the Meat Inspection and Pure Food and Drug Acts (1906). Struggles for safety played out on the factory floor as well, and these made headlines more and more frequently as labor union power expanded, especially in urban centers. Progressive Era limitations on child labor, for example, or efforts to hold employers responsible for injuries on the job show examples where safety and risk became front page concerns.[46] However, Progressive Era public safety reforms were often extremely local in nature and rarely showed a comprehensive effort to reform government functions along the lines of significant risk mitigation efforts. When they were found, Progressive gains in public safety usually affected types of people—child laborers, for example—rather than types of environmental risks. Exceptions to this premise might be found in uneven efforts to enhance water and air quality, but more often than not these were also class-based appeals, focused on beautifying cities for the benefit of middle class city-dwellers.[47] Jane Addams spent her life working to assist immigrants in Chicago, for example, but assimilation and class mobility were far more critical to her than were the larger-scale risks of untrammeled urban growth. It was, after all, industrialization that was bringing the immigrants in the first place, and to most Progressives this process was to be studied and civilized, democratized. Limiting urban industrial expansion itself was not on the Progressive agenda.

Progressive Era reformers also focused on trust-busting, but this focus could sometimes return unanticipated effects. For example, at just the moment when fire safety experts were poised to push their knowledge into the public realm they faced a major threat to their legitimacy in the form of a Progressive Era pushback against monopolistic corporations. Consumer-led control over fire insurance companies and their rate-making powers emerged strongly in the 1880s to 1890s and were highly politicized, tying into populist animus against Wall Street and big business. The fire insurance industry, especially through organizations like the NBFU, Factory Mutuals, and local insurance organizations, was very eager after the Civil War to meet the rising threats to their business through information sharing. Without any federal oversight of the industry, each state regulated fire insurance individually. In some states this meant close scrutiny of rate-making processes, business practices, and pay-outs on claims. In other states it meant a complete lack of oversight.

Hoping to reduce the inefficiencies (and the high costs of lobbying) of such a situation, the industry sought to force regulatory oversight by the federal government. A test case was brought in 1869, and in *Paul v. Virginia*, the U.S. Supreme Court found that "issuing of a policy of insurance is not a transaction of commerce . . . but is a simple contract of indemnity against loss."[48] The court perhaps did not understand, and certainly could not foresee, the highly profitable nature of an industry that became more and more crucial as capital investments in the built environment increased. *Paul v. Virginia* placed the insurance business in a class of activity outside of the constitutional reach of congress, a place it would remain until the 1944 *United States v. South-Eastern Underwriters* decision redefined insurance as commerce. Throughout the entire Conflagration Era the government control of fire insurance—and by extension the ability to not only regulate the business but also learn lessons from it that could inform public policy—was controlled by the states.

As significant state level anti-trust anxiety began to build in the 1880s, fire insurance companies were the subjects of scrutiny. This is not surprising considering the ubiquity of the industry; most property-owners in both rural and urban settings dealt with fire insurers. Major issues included high rates, companies frequently refusing to pay out the full value of policies, and discrimination against certain classes of risks. The NBFU established a "rating bureau" after the Civil War, and 37 companies entered a "Chicago compact," pledging to charge rates established by the board. The Chicago and Boston fires of the 1870s, and the difficulties in policing such an arrangement, moved the NBFU to abandon centralized rate-making in 1877, and from then on local and regional underwriters associations took on this work. The NBFU focused more on collecting fire statistics, promoting uniformity in business practices, and promoting fire mitigation efforts as we saw in Chapter 1. Underwriters associations or boards were organized from the regional level down to the level of specific cities. For example, the Western Union covered companies throughout the Midwest, while New York City, Boston, Baltimore, and Philadelphia had their own local boards. From the perspective of the insurance industry in the Conflagration Era the underwriters association was a crucial tool of business, allowing companies set rates and standards of coverage that would limit cut-throat price competition while also sharing information about risks that could help standardize policies. Additionally, the underwriters associations were on the front lines of advocacy for insurance-friendly legislation, plugged as they were into local and regional business and political circles. And, of course, we have seen the crucial relationship that local agents and boards might play in building up from the local to a national picture of expanding fire risk across the nation.

From the perspective of many reformers, however, underwriters associations were just more local iterations of monopoly, and as such they were marked as the subject of anti-trust action.[49] The central choice for reformers hinged on whether to break apart large firms and trusts through legal action or to regulate big business through bureaucratic means. Keeping in mind that the federal Interstate Commerce Act (1887) and the Sherman Anti-Trust Act (1890) did not apply to the insurance industry, regulation at the state level was a way forward—and it was a politically advantageous way forward for public officials who could successfully channel populist enthusiasm for regulation.

States had difficulty using the common law to bring anti-trust cases against underwriters associations, primarily because it was difficult to show fire insurance as an indispensible product or service. State-level anti-trust laws faced the difficulty presented by the Supreme Court's *Paul v. Virginia* decision, trying to decide whether or not insurance was "commerce." In the midst of this legal uncertainty, but with public sentiment rising for "busting" the trusts, state legislatures found that the best way to gain control over insurance companies was to pass "anti-compact" laws, specifically prohibiting companies from combining to fix prices for fire insurance premiums.[50] Though they pushed back, anti-compact cases against insurance companies were successful at the state level. Ultimately, it became clear though that with the importance of fire insurance—particularly in states like New York, Illinois, and Pennsylvania with rapidly growing cities and industrial sectors—there needed to be some sort of compromise that would allow stock insurance companies to prosper within a regulatory framework that would build public confidence in the fairness of insurance rates and coverage. Neither the companies nor the states wanted to be spending their time in court.

The first legislative results were seen in states where strong feelings against trusts were shaping local and state politics, particularly in the Midwest and southern states. In some states the effort was focused on establishing independent insurance rate-making bureaus, and in others it was in enforcing competition. Stock fire insurance companies often reacted angrily, in the case of Missouri, for example, the Western Union body of insurers refused to write policies altogether as a means to influence the mood against state rate-making authority. Wisconsin went so far as to establish a public insurance company. Mutual insurance companies received favorable reviews in such contexts because they were usually operating locally or regionally, and were not focused on investing the premiums they collected. A very common trend was for states to pass rate-making acts, giving a state official, usually an insurance commissioner, the responsibility over the rates. While the commissioners' offices served in a de facto way the function of the underwriters associations, the friction between companies and commissioners was perhaps predictable.

Solomon Huebner was one of the first social scientists to promote risk and insurance as an important interdisciplinary subject area within which to study public policy in the midst of American industrialization. Huebner taught courses in the subject, published a journal and wrote textbooks, and established the insurance department at the Wharton School at the University of Pennsylvania in 1913. Among Huebner's students and colleagues were analysts of the major problem for the Progressive Era: finding and maintaining the right balance between effective state regulation and private sector success in the midst of rapidly changing conditions in both areas. In 1906 Huebner published a major study in which he found that 25 states had insurance commissioners, answerable directly to governors. These tended to be very powerful officials. In Pennsylvania, for example, the commissioner could: enforce all insurance laws on companies and agents, certify that all companies were solvent, provide permits for foreign insurance companies doing business in the state, collect the annual reports of companies, examine companies and agents under oath and examine their papers, including out of state firms, and he could suspend and revoke licenses.[51] Huebner estimated that since 1852 there had been 420 state insurance commissioners, serving an average term of 3.5 years. Of course there was also nothing to keep governors from using patronage posts, like an insurance commissioner's position, to reward political allies. To Huebner this suggested a real mismatch between the knowledge and experience of those working in the industry and those regulating them. Huebner also surveyed three-dozen presidents of the nation's largest insurance companies to get their perspectives on the regulatory environment. The presidents cited several complaints in common, the most serious having to do with the preparation of reports and statements in different formats for every state in which they did business, as well as the lack of uniformity in laws, guidance, and supervision over insurance business from state to state. In two-thirds of the respondents federal control was favored—but it was stressed that federal control should come instead of state control, not in addition to state control.

Huebner expanded his research to include a survey conducted by New Jersey Senator John Fairfield Dryden, the founder of Prudential Insurance Company, who sent letters out for opinion to 8000 organizations and people connected to the insurance industry. Of the 700 commercial bodies that responded a staggering 96 percent favored federal supervision, and 80 percent believed that insurance constituted "commerce."[52] In analyzing Dryden's obviously skewed yet still revealing survey, Huebner was surprised at how many of the insurance presidents he surveyed felt that federal control was "constitutionally impossible." It was also feared that state intervention would not be avoided, compounding the level of oversight if federal oversight were ever achieved. States were generating rather large revenues in charging fees for out-of-state firms to hold licenses and submit reports, and as such it was lucrative for states to be in the insurance regulation business. With this in mind, even if the Supreme Court were to overturn *Paul v. Virginia*, why would congressional delegations (especially at a time when Senators were elected by state legislatures) work to override the interests of their states?

From the national insurance industry's perspective the implications of uneven state control were great. For example, in New York in 1903 the 17 largest companies did only 25 percent of their business in state, and in Pennsylvania that amount dropped to 10.5 percent. Of the 18 companies outside Pennsylvania and New York only 5.3 percent of new business was in state. Additionally, it was estimated that one-third of fire insurance policies in the United States were written by British companies and an additional 7 percent by other foreign-owned companies. This was a snapshot of an industry doing business at a national and international scale, but regulated piecemeal at the state and local level. To Professor Huebner, the "commerce" issue was "mere semantics," and "federal supervision of insurance . . . should be regarded as a part of that larger movement for federal control over industry and commerce which has been going on ever since the Constitution was framed."[53]

The issue came to a head in New York State in 1910–11, when a committee was convened by Governor Charles Evans Hughes to investigate claims of insurance industry corruption. The result was the Merritt Committee, named after state representative Edwin A. Merritt, Jr., from Potsdam. A regulatory era in New York was taking shape, with public utility regulation on the books since 1907, and the Merritt Committee was its high-water mark. The Merritt Committee report laid out the questions and the conclusions of state legislators as they sought to understand how fire insurance worked from the boardroom all the way out to the inspector's notebook. The results would give them knowledge on which to create a regulatory structure for the fire insurance industry in New York. The business of fire insurance, it was concluded, required the hand of government as an honest broker between customers and companies, especially to ensure that all potential customers would be offered coverage, and that rates of coverage would not be overly discriminatory against one class of buildings.

In the investigation the committee members came to know about the work of insurance engineers and how they did their risk analyses and made their recommendations, within the larger institutional framework of the industry. The efforts of fire experts to control urban conflagrations came in for praise, as did the model building code, a suggested "best practices" code formulated at an abstract level and provided free to interested cities by the National Fire Protection Association (NFPA). The NBFU's sponsorship of NFPA and UL was pointed out, and NBFU was cited in this regard as "in the highest degree public spirited and its activities are to be highly commended."[54] In the final report UL was described as a place where "all men are placed upon equality," at least in terms of evaluation of their products for testing.[55] The work of the NFPA was likewise explained; it was pointed out that they had in the previous year produced 400,000 copies of pamphlets on fire protection—evidence cited as public-spirited action. The Merritt Committee was curious to know more about the exact connection between the interindustry advocate NBFU and its fire expert spin-offs, and called witnesses from NBFU, NFPA, and UL.[56] In his testimony, Willis O. Robb of Underwriters Laboratories was asked to explain the process whereby fire insurance rates were set. Robb gave UL's perspective, explaining that a new device or product that might affect insurance rates for a customer—a fire door, for example—would have been tested by Underwriters Laboratories, and its results would be known to New York underwriters who would then take this as one of the main factors in assessing risk and setting premiums. "It is judgment," Robb asserted to the Committee, "largely controlled by that of experts who have made the primary examination." Robb's response distills the essence of the fire experts' argument in the early twentieth century: risk expertise was neutral, scientific, and even public-spirited, even if it was at the same time serving the profit interests of large insurance companies.

The Merritt Committee's in-depth study—42 sessions and thousands of pages of published testimony—resulted in a rate-making association law for New York in 1911. The state would not set actual rates, but it would require four regional rate-making bodies to submit to state oversight, including disclosure of membership, methods, and public examination of records. A state insurance superintendent would exert oversight, with the right to intervene on behalf of consumers suffering rate discrimination.[57] With New York as the nation's largest fire insurance market, the Merritt Committee's work was bound to be influential, and it was—ultimately 34 states would enact similar legislation.[58] Regulation would take different forms in different states. Texas had a three-member rating board, whereas Kansas required companies to set rates and place them on file in a public office. Insurance commissioners became established keepers of the public trust and objects of scorn for the industry. It was a victory for consumers and was seen as such by political Progressives.

An effort was made to continue the trend to federal control, but this was ended by the Supreme Court decision in *New York Life Insurance Company v. Deer Lodge County* (1913), upholding the precedent established by

Paul v. Virginia. After this case and the Merritt Committee report the fire insurance industry would be forced to accept state interference in its work, but, as was seen in Merritt Committee testimony, the door was also open for government to acknowledge the work of fire experts, especially those working in affiliated nonprofit institutions like NFPA and UL. The role of risk experts within the industry was now afforded respect. The Merritt Committee accepted the concept of a separation of the profit-making from the public service sides of the insurance industry. This was perhaps the greatest possible victory for the industry in the context of the times.

Not surprisingly, and extremely significant for the development of fire safety standards as discussed in Chapter 3, the industry's response to regulation was to put more emphasis on its role as a protector of public safety, particularly through the development of nonprofit institutions that could derive safety standards to the benefit of, but at arm's length from, the insurance industry's profit-making functions. Reformers argued that the industry was large and restricted small companies from entering, that it gouged consumers with high premiums, and that it gambled with customers' trust. On the other hand, the insurers argued that public safety demanded a strong insurance industry, and a strong insurance industry required good fire protection laws, laws based on knowledge derived from research and information sharing. In the wave of reform and regulation of the fire insurance industry in the Progressive Era we see, therefore, an innovative way by which disaster experts could make their voices heard. Through the growth of state oversight government officials and by extension the public gained more knowledge about how the industry worked, and certain facets of the industry—particularly safety-focused research—came in for accolades. The effect was broader and more important than a disaster investigation here or there. The industry was now becoming a sort of public utility, controlled by government and thus almost a de facto arm of government, at least to the extent that government could begin to look for public safety remedies in the work of private fire experts. The door was now open for the expert-led institutions founded by the fire insurance industry in the 1890s—like the NFPA and UL—to compete for a place in the urban risk and disaster policy process. And, likewise, the conditions were right for municipal and state governments to rethink traditional limits to their powers in shaping the growth of the urban risk environment itself.

The National Fire Protection Association

The National Fire Protection Association (NFPA) is a nonprofit institution that played (and plays) a key role in connecting fire experts and policy makers.[59] Growing out of the tradition of the underwriters' associations, the NFPA was organized during a meeting of the Underwriters Bureau of New England in 1895 in Boston. Sprinkler manufacturers and insurance professionals met to discuss the difficulties of standardization in automatic sprinklers. Present were Everett U. Crosby, Umberto C. Crosby (Everett's father), chairman of the Factory Improvement Committee of the New England Insurance Exchange, W. H. Stratton of the Factory Insurance Association, John Ripley Freeman of the Factory Mutuals, Frederick Grinnell of the Providence Steam and Gas Pipe Company, and F. Eliot Cabot of the Boston Board of Underwriters. NFPA historian Percy Bugbee reports of the early meeting that Grinnell was impressive in his sales pitch for the reliable performance of sprinklers, and that John Ripley Freeman presented a report that demonstrated the Factory Mutuals' success insuring sprinklered buildings under strict installation guidelines. Umberto Crosby suggested that the "proper recognition" of sprinklers get underway. According to Bugbee, the "message was clear; unite in a sensible approach to the sprinkler problem or face substantial loss of business."[60] In 1896 the association was founded. The NBFU, much as it did with Underwriters Laboratories, served as a patron.

NFPA president Umberto Crosby emphasized the role of the new organization in assisting stock insurance companies as they sought to match the Factory Mutuals in their skill with sprinklers and industrial risks overall. Crosby was unwilling to admit any superiority in the Factory Mutuals business model, but when it came to "intelligent consideration of hazards and protection" it was clear that the Factory Mutuals had an edge.[61] From the very beginning the NFPA was recording and describing fires and presenting technical papers. By 1899 it had worked successfully to achieve some standardization in sprinkler requirements across the United States and Canada.[62] NFPA also established a Committee on Devices and Materials, headed by W. C. Robinson, later of UL. In its early days, UL looked to NFPA for advice. The key difference between the two institutions was that where UL was focused on actual testing of electrical goods and other fire safety devices, NFPA focused its attention on inter-industry cooperation, and, most important, on pushing the standards derived by fire experts into public discussion and the policy arena. In 1900 NFPA also began to reach out to other experts in fire disasters: the Fire Chiefs Association, National Association of Architects, American Society of Mechanical Engineers, and American Water Works Association. The first non-insurance members were railroads, along with Marshall Field and the Armour Company.[63]

The NFPA presented itself as an honest broker of information relevant to public safety from fire. Considering its close ties to insurance, construction, and engineering in the midst of the Progressive Era, it was critical that NFPA position itself carefully in order not to seem biased, and potentially working only for the insurers and against the public interest. Its nonprofit status was helpful in this regard, as was its style of governance by committees of fire experts. The NFPA provided a place where fire industry professionals were welcome, but where they were not entirely in control. Two of the NFPA's major initiatives in its first decades were focused on bringing fire expertise directly into the creation and enforcement of public policy. Though the Factory Mutuals had seen some success directly persuading consumers, the majority of the fire insurance industry, and other fire experts from the fire service, fire science, and fire protection engineering had not been successful in persuading builders or consumers to adopt costly fire mitigation methods like sprinklers or nonflammable construction materials, or even to make them care much about less costly methods like removing flammable garbage or performing fire drills. NFPA's consistent sponsorship of public-focused fire safety education efforts was aimed at making manufacturers, builders, and consumers alike aware of the larger risks they were taking by not adopting fire mitigation techniques. NFPA also actively promoted robust fire safety policy in municipal and state government. In this last area, NFPA lobbied hard for reform of corrupt fire departments, and the growth of a fire safety bureaucracy in city halls and state houses across the country that would act to enforce its suggested standards of safety.

In 1909 Franklin Wentworth took over the NFPA presidency. Wentworth had gone to work at UL early on, in 1894, and then moved to Boston in 1909 to expand the NFPA work. Wentworth was not a college-educated engineer, but he was an amateur actor, a background that was noted to give him "a dramatic platform flair that enthralled his audiences" as he traveled the nation making the case for the application of fire expertise to the nation's conflagration risks.[64] In the tradition of Edward Atkinson, Wentworth saw his role as a spokesman for fire safety, translating technical

arguments over standards into plain language that citizens could understand and get behind, pressuring their elected leaders for fire safety reforms.
As he assumed NFPA leadership, Wentworth explained that "the Association had through its first decade been painstakingly and laboriously compiling fire prevention standards, the observance of which would eliminate
common hazards and hazardous conditions, [but] the members now found
themselves with the results of their unselfish labors in their hands, facing
fire losses greater than those of all the world and facing a public almost
wholly indifferent to them."[65]

In seventy different cities NFPA representatives started sending letters
to newspaper editors on fire hazards, often receiving skepticism toward
their intentions due to their insurance connections. In 1910 Wentworth
went on a barnstorming trip across the country, holding "fire prevention
meetings" in conjunction with the National Association of Credit Men. In
his "stump speech," Wentworth made the comparison between the U.S.
and Europe on "fire waste." Describing it as a tax, Wentworth argued that
the public "do not realize that when they buy a hat, or a pair of shoes, or a
suit of clothes, or anything which goes through the regular channels of
industry—production distribution, and exchange—they pay this tax. Not
realizing it, they are indifferent to fire. They think fire does not affect
them."[66] Proving how much the NFPA had started to focus on consumer
behavior, *Bulletin No. 2* was titled "The Menace of the Match." A suggested
state law and municipal ordinance followed.[67] It was in education first that
Wentworth found (modest) success. In 1908 a law was passed in Ohio
requiring teachers to spend 30 minutes a month on fire education. State
fire prevention associations were also established about this time, and in
1912 NFPA published its *Syllabus for Public Instruction in Fire Prevention*.[68]

The full extent of NFPA's fire education efforts were on display every
year during "Fire Prevention Week," usually held in October around the
anniversary of the 1871 Chicago Fire. The NFPA partnered with the NBFU
and U.S. Chamber of Commerce on the effort, then expanded to working
with "men of public affairs" including the National Association of Manufacturers, Rotary, Kiwanis, Lions, and other "luncheon clubs."[69] Fire marshals offices and municipal fire prevention bureaus were used as conduits
for reaching the public, particularly schoolchildren. In Atlanta, for example,
the local insurance board printed 40,000 pamphlets on fire protection for
use in the schools. The NBFU prepared a play titled "The Trial of Fire,"
which was put on in hundreds of schools across the country; in some

instances, according to the *NFPA Quarterly*, "this performance was staged at the leading theatre of the city, accompanied by the unusually large community interest which follows such a school entertainment." Insurance agents delivered fire safety lectures by the thousands, while 238 radio stations broadcast speeches and special programs on fire prevention, and films were apparently in such great demand that NFPA's supply was "hopelessly inadequate." Wilmington, Delaware, was held up as a model for its 1922 Fire Prevention Week campaign, assigning different key tasks to every major leader in the city. The mayor, for example, was asked to make a "suitable proclamation," while the city council made "improvement to fire ordinances." Labor union officials were charged with "teaching fire prevention to workmen," while the fire department would carry out a full inspection of the downtown business district. The ultimate goal for the NFPA was that the "spasmodic activity of the week's celebration" would ultimately lead to a "continuous campaign" of fire safety awareness. The effort to accomplish something on the scale of Fire Prevention Week resembled nothing less than a full-out advertising campaign, and clearly the multimedia and multi-stakeholder approach used by the NFPA indicated a modern sensibility and facility with the tools of shaping public opinion.[70] Woodrow Wilson proclaimed Fire Prevention Day for October 9, 1920, and Warren G. Harding declared Fire Prevention Week October 2–9, 1922.

The NFPA was one of the loudest and most consistent institutional voices crying for the reform of municipal and state government in regard to fire risk. This was, in the main, a call for the creation of new fire protection bureaucracies, involving the fire service but also inspectors, commissioners, and fire marshals who would be granted legal authority and responsibility for enforcing fire codes and building standards. They placed special emphasis on outreach to the fire service. By valorizing the work of heroic firemen and casting them in opposition to unscrupulous builders and inspectors, NFPA started to gain traction in building and life safety standards by the 1920s. A model State Fire Marshal law and a model inspection ordinance were adopted at the NFPA 1912 meeting.[71] In this way, NFPA was suggesting that not only did the standards need reform, but so did the inspection service in cities. Coming at exactly the moment of fire insurance reform and the founding of state fire bureaucracies to enforce the new regulations, NFPA found success in leveraging state power against corrupt urban inspection departments. NFPA did not work closely with the building industry in the 1910s but spent the decade instead focused heavily on promoting fire safety broadly as a new area of responsibility. In NFPA's formulation, the fire experts could provide the knowledge, and it was up to reform-minded municipal officials to revoke the "fire tax" and pay serious attention to protecting the lives of city dwellers from fire disasters.

In the case of fire marshals and inspection bureaus NFPA's efforts paid off handsomely. Only a few states had fire marshals at the turn of the twentieth century. In 1905 the Fire Marshals Association of North America was founded, and by 1912 there were 25 states with fire marshal's offices. In that year the Fire Marshals Association published a model fire marshal law, outlining six duties for fire marshals, including "installation and maintenance of . . . fire alarm systems and fire extinguishing equipment," as well as "construction, maintenance and regulation of fire escapes," and at the broadest level "the prevention of fires."[72] Fire marshals were given the role of collecting statistics on fire, and they were also encouraged to promulgate their own technical standards and techniques for use in their individual states. The suggested law, which was adopted in large part by most states, spelled out a hierarchy whereby fire marshals answered directly to governors, and municipal fire chiefs should serve as assistants to "provide information as to the cause, origin and circumstances of fire occurring in their districts." Most important, fire marshals were given the power to inspect buildings anywhere in the state, and to summon witnesses and obtain testimony under oath. In 1927 the Fire Marshals Association merged with the NFPA, and afterward held its annual meetings in conjunction with NFPA meetings. By 1932 fire marshal's offices existed in 35 states.

In the case of fire inspection, this was a task that had traditionally been carried out by firemen, but with the rapid growth of cities it became more efficient to develop dedicated inspection bureaus as part of the fire service. The NFPA published a suggested municipal ordinance that city councils could adopt to create the office and was a major lobbyist on behalf of the creation and professionalization of such bureaus. By the 1930s only three cities (St. Louis, Buffalo, and Pittsburgh) with more than 500,000 people were without inspection bureaus, and in many cities they were huge, led by New York with 169 inspectors.[73] In these ways direct links were established between the knowledge of the private experts and the officers of public safety, brokered through a "neutral" nonprofit organization.

By the 1930s the NFPA was a well-established and influential hub for technical information, public safety advocacy, and fire protection policy advice and lobbying. Looking to other countries such functions fell squarely within the purview of government. However, the Conflagration Era in the United States found government at every level slow to move from a reactive to a proactive stance on fire risk and disaster mitigation. This slowness was compounded by public mistrust in the Progressive Era in purely private sector solutions (or nonsolutions) to public safety demands. The result was a novel creation, a voluntary system of fire protection, where government played a restrained regulatory role, the private sector played an innovative knowledge-creation role, and nonprofit groups like the NFPA grew rapidly into powerful arbiters of public trust, almost serving as de facto arms of government.

Planning for Fire

Dedicated institutions focused specifically on risk and disaster knowledge-creation did not exist in the United States before the late nineteenth century. At times ad hoc commissions were convened by government officials looking to address specific safety concerns; examples include public health commissions dedicated to controlling cholera epidemics and federal studies of steam boilers focused on reducing the extraordinary loss of life resulting from steamship explosions.[74] The most common efforts in this regard were coroners' inquests, grand juries, and executive-decreed investigations of specific disasters, such as those following the Iroquois Theater Fire. These investigations could be democratic, involving the entire community, and they were certainly part of the process of finding and fixing blame in the wake of disasters, but they rarely if ever led to deepening knowledge or critical policy changes in regard to risks and disasters. The outcry for such knowledge-based risk response intensified when disasters captured the public mind, blame was meted out, and investigations grabbed headlines. But low expectations of public safety among citizens and the rapidly shifting contours of the urban immigrant population generally muted the cries for expert-led reforms. A key issue raised here is the fact that urbanites, native-born and immigrant alike—and by extension their elected officials—had much lower expectations of fire safety than the fire insurance industry could profitably allow.

In terms of American political development, the risk of fire and the broader concern over disasters presented a true challenge to governance in a federalist system. The city is a useful site within which to trace the development of American political institutions more broadly. Of particular interest are the power and efficacy of urban political machines, and the evolving relationships among cities, states, and the federal government as industrialization played out in the late nineteenth century.[75] Fire risk and disaster threw multiple actors into competition around the formation of standards and norms for safety. City officials could develop safety-conscious building codes, but conflict of local interests and difficulties in assigning credit and blame for public safety presented real challenges to reformers, as did the ambiguous nature of code writing and enforcement as constitutionally valid municipal prerogatives—challenges all shown again in detail by the Iroquois Theater Fire study.

Cities grew steadily throughout the Jacksonian and antebellum period, with very low taxes and numerous functions of public safety handled on a volunteer basis. State oversight of urban governance developed in these years, but state governments found it difficult to usefully regulate risks that were diverse by geography, economy, and urban political cultures. Both city and state legislative bodies were often quite effective at passing "nuisance" laws that courts typically upheld. Nuisance laws were the predecessors to more modern zoning laws. As William J. Novak points, out nuisance laws were "neither trivial nor timid" in nineteenth-century American cities. "Along with every unneighborly hogsty or spite fence abated as a nuisance came dozens of ships, hospitals, steam engines, furnaces, dairies, sewers, slaughterhouses, stables, pumping stations, foundries, manufactories, and saloons." An inheritance from colonial common law precepts, nuisance law made sense to city-dwellers who accepted some abridgment of property rights based on the necessity of keeping an ordered society.[76] Such traditional legal concepts, however, were fitted to the smaller-scale cities of the pre-industrialization era.

The Fifth Amendment to the Constitution guarantees that private property must not be "taken for public use, without just compensation." The concept of eminent domain was most frequently employed by government officials to satisfy this "Takings Clause" of the Constitution, by designating certain properties as necessary for the benefit of the community, and compensating the owner. Going beyond the nuisance law and eminent domain traditions in the 1851 case of *Commonwealth v. Alger*, the Massachusetts Supreme Court upheld the right of the state to establish limits beyond which private property holders could not build wharves into Boston Harbor. The court's decision emphasized regulation of private property as a police power, a power of "harm prevention" rightfully belonging to the government as a necessity of community order and protection. *Commonwealth v. Alger* established a precedent for state and municipal regulation of private property—a power construed by city officials to extend to fire ordinances. As we have seen, however, the knowledge required to draft good fire ordinances was slow and difficult in the making. And when ordinances were passed their coherence and authority were frequently challenged, as evidenced by the Iroquois Theater fire cases.

While fires like the Iroquois, Slocum, or Triangle were horrific, they were perhaps limited by their lack of breadth—they were not conflagrations. In this way we return to the conflagration hazard as a motivator for real environmental change in the risky city—and a possible catalyst to government reform. Galveston's complete annihilation by flood in 1900, taking as many as 8,000 lives, provoked a complete reassessment of the city's exposure to floods, and the subsequent raising of the entire city by the U.S. Army Corps of Engineers. Baltimore undertook this after its 1904 conflagration, using the opportunity to completely rebuild and modernize its dangerous and inadequate water supply and sewer systems. As Christine Meisner Rosen has argued, disaster recovery could provide a moment of reform that, although it might benefit business interests in the city, could also result in broader mitigation and public safety efforts.[77] In such extraordinary post-disaster moments it was sometimes possible for real sweeping change that defied normal objections by private developers to land use restrictions or the prerogatives of slow democratic deliberations. The ability of fire experts to be ready with suggestions in such moments was critical to the expansion of their reach. John Ripley Freeman, building on his successful Iroquois Theater Fire investigation, also examined Baltimore after the 1904 conflagration and San Francisco after the 1906 earthquake and fire. It was still the case, though, that such efforts were extraordinary and local, and though Freeman's knowledge was abstract, it was not necessarily easy to adopt directly to public policy without robust local debate. Such debates, taking place as they were in a time of profound national debate over the power of business elites versus working people in the city, could easily overwhelm the more technical debates over building and zoning codes. Was Freeman serving business or the public? That depended on whom you asked, and this was precisely the place the insurance engineer, and the insurance industry more generally found itself in this era.

Urban planners entered this conversation in the late nineteenth century. Planning in its earliest years provided a crossover disciplinary space between architecture, engineering, and public administration. Frederick Law Olmsted, Daniel Burnham, Lewis Mumford, and Ebenezer Howard— coming from different intellectual and professional backgrounds— occupied major roles in the founding of a discipline that could include experts in landscape, economics, urban history, architecture, finance, and construction. In the United States one of the earliest areas of focus for urban planners had to do with public safety. Safety was the purview of physicians and of engineers, but it could also be the realm of planners who sought to meet the challenges of the rapidly industrialized city with techniques of forethought in design that would avoid rancid water, polluted air, overcrowding, and economic stagnation caused by the rapidly populated and degraded industrial city.[78]

Using disaster as an opportunity to bring more order, light, air, clean water, and transportation into the city was a common goal for urban planners. As Rosen has argued, this practice proceeded unevenly in the nineteenth century, usually under the leadership of business interests looking to modernize their cities. A conflagration that caught the attention of planners and proved to be a textbook case of planned urban renewal postdisaster was that in Salem, Massachusetts, after a major conflagration in 1914. On June 25 that year a series of explosions occurred in the city's leather tanning district. The fire began at the Korn leather factory, a maker of "tip finish" for patent leather, where a series of explosions were caused by chemicals including alcohol, amalacitate, acetone, and celluloid.[79] The fire destroyed the industrial district of the city, burning 256 acres and destroying over 1,300 buildings, and leaving 10,000 people unemployed. The fire losses paid out by insurance companies totaled 11 million dollars.

The Salem City Council met in emergency session on June 29 and immediately passed an ordinance requiring slate or other incombustible materials on roofs, and metal gutters. A former member of the council and a prominent local citizen, Franklin Wentworth, president of the NFPA, played a key role at this stage.[80] The NFPA and NBFU had both by this time developed model codes for cities that directed municipal officials on how best to regulate construction for maximum protection from fire. The model codes could be applied piecemeal, though, of course, the fire experts preferred they be imposed all at once—a possibility really only if an entire city or whole section of a city was leveled at the same time, and if public sentiment for reform was high in the aftermath of conflagration. In Salem, this was the case.

The NBFU published its model code in 1905, urging municipal governments to adopt it in pieces, or ideally as a complete code. The construction industry pushed back, but strong reaction was not really necessary. As we saw in the Iroquois Theater case, builders and inspection departments worked very closely together, and codes on the books did not necessarily spell code compliance. Nevertheless, NFPA picked up the NBFU code and promoted it broadly, working to pit municipal authorities against one another.

The Salem Council put forward an idea that five men should be appointed to a rebuilding commission, a commission that would need extraordinary legal authority in order to see that the city was not rebuilt in a way that would allow future conflagrations. The idea was drafted and sent to the governor, and in the post-disaster climate of strong action a bill to authorize the commission passed the legislature and was before the governor for signing on July 7. Serving for three years, without pay, the commissioners were granted planning powers not common to public bodies in the United States up to this time, including power to site public buildings and exert eminent domain, and sole construction permitting authority including location, size, and materials for structures. They could define the boundaries of parks, streets, ways, squares, and even sidewalks in the burnt district, and do the same outside the burnt district if it could be argued to be necessary. Cheap housing was outlawed, as were inexpensive factory construction methods. The commissioners hired an architect for a three-year contract, and the first meeting of the Salem Rebuilding Commission was held as a public hearing. Though there was robust community debate about allowing wooden structures and heights of buildings, the commissioners made it clear that new methods of fire protection would be applied in the reconstruction effort. As we have seen, the post-disaster zeal for investigation and "never again" political promise-making was no different in Salem from that in Chicago of 1871 or 1904. Few cities in the United States had, however, created an ad hoc commission with such sweeping powers.[81] What was perhaps not known about fire safety in 1871, and what restrictions on reconstruction were politically impossible in 1904, were by 1914 redefined in a reconstruction effort witnessing the fusion of strong state power and fire disaster expertise.

The effect of the Salem fire was felt in Boston as well, creating a ground-swell of support for robust new laws authorizing government to assume greater oversight of fire protection.[82] The Boston fire law was less focused on establishing building standards, and more directed toward supervising maintenance of buildings. It created the office of a fire prevention commissioner, as well as requiring sprinklers in wood working factories and basements, trash removal, and public education about fire protection. The metropolitan fire prevention commissioner was named by the governor, and among other duties the commissioner took over authority of regulating explosives including fireworks. He could also order fire drills in theaters and schools. He could direct fire chiefs to investigate and report to him on fire hazards. He was to keep complete fire records.[83] The Boston fire law was adopted across the metropolitan region, an area that included roughly one third of the population of the state.

The Massachusetts Supreme Court heard a case in 1916 brought as a challenge to the authority of the Salem Rebuilding Commission. The court notes that the law allowing the commission was "unlike any heretofore enacted in the commonwealth. . . . Unusual powers were conferred upon the defendants in order to enable them to meet unwonted conditions." In this case the plaintiff had sought and was granted permission by the Salem Board of Health to build a two-story brick stable with no windows. He filed for it with the Rebuilding Commission in 1916, and after not hearing back for nine days filed suit, not waiting for (and perhaps not actually desiring) a decision from the commissioners.[84] The court pointed out that the building in question met state and Salem building codes, but that the case had been brought before the Rebuilding Commission to pass its judgment. For its part the Rebuilding Commission contended that though it had not gotten to the stage of making recommendations on this building, it intended to do so, under its authority granted by law. The court ruled that the law creating the Rebuilding Commission and outlining its powers was valid. "The commission," according to the court, "reserves the right to prescribe additional requirements for any buildings to be erected within the burnt district where the safety of life or property is involved, or public health." The court concluded that the "commission is clothed by the legislature with unusual powers in order to deal with the extraordinary conditions following the Salem conflagration."

Salem was perhaps an exceptional case, considering the dramatic conditions under which the Rebuilding Commission did its work. However, at just this time cities across the country were asserting for the first time in American history powers to aggressively regulate land use and building construction in the name of public safety, and courts were siding against developers. The 1916 Zoning Resolution in New York was the first major example of a city applying height and building mass limits, establishing the "set back" formula where building heights were regulated by ratios intended to force the building further back from the street the higher it rose. This more comprehensive approach also included exercise of powers to designate certain types of uses—industrial, commercial, residential—that would guide city planning across entire cities and regions. The 1916 New York zoning law became the template for two Standard Zoning Enabling Acts promoted by the U.S. Department of Commerce in the 1920s. These acts laid the legal framework for the establishment of city and regional planning bodies, and the power of those and similar government bodies to regulate development through tools like zoning and height restrictions, master plans, and oversight of public land development. A major Supreme Court case followed: *Village of Euclid v. Ambler Realty Co.* (1926), in which the court upheld the power of a municipal government, using its police powers to protect public health and safety, to restrict private development through zoning and other urban planning methods. With *Euclid v. Ambler* urban planners joined the fire experts in celebrating a radical expansion of their authority in the development of a rational, planned, and fireproof American urban environment.

The NFPA promoted zoning and building height restrictions extensively, and carried out a war of sorts against skyscrapers, or what it saw as a form of "abnormality, which has its genesis partly in human vanity and the desire to dazzle and surprise, and partly in the desire to realize as much rental as possible on an extravagantly valued plot of ground." This "monster" was "menacing to comfort and safety."[85] The canyons of lower Manhattan and the Chicago loop were exhilarating spaces for developers and real estate agents, but they presented fearsome risks to firefighters and disaster experts. In an era before comprehensive zoning laws, Chicago's city council was first with a height restriction ordinance of 150 feet in 1892, on the eve of the Columbian Exposition, but it was vetoed by the mayor. Other cities did establish height limits around this time, mostly in the range between 100 and 200 feet.

The NFPA advocated height restrictions of 2.5 stories for wooden frame buildings. "If it were possible to secure ideal conditions," mused "City Planning Engineer" Jacob Crane in the pages of the *NFPA Quarterly* in

1925, "fire-resistive buildings might be allowed to go to any feasible height." Crane judged that it was, however, virtually impossible for fire protection to be guaranteed in buildings above 10 stories, or 125 feet.[86] High-rise construction was a place where fire experts watched in awe and concern, as suggested limits like 125 feet would be rendered null and void through the rise of the American skyline in the 1920s. New York City saw new height records established almost every year in the '20s, with the Empire State Building topping them all at 1,250 feet in 1930. Breathtaking innovations in building construction and skyscraper design kept the fire experts busy throughout this era, a time when technological enthusiasm, just as it had in the era of electrification, seemed to outrun caution and concern over public safety.

With the establishment of zoning as a valid role for government, and the accompanying growth of the urban planning profession, it seemed by the late 1920s possible to imagine public safety as achievable not through the reactivity of firefighting and investigation, or only through middle ground associations like NFPA, but also through vigorous public action. Fire experts were gaining ground in their attempts to find more venues through which to push their knowledge into practice. Pointing to the rebuilding of Salem as a success story for planners, in 1927 Harvard professor and urban planning expert James Ford in the journal *City Planning* argued: "The essential fact to be kept forcibly in mind on the occasion of comprehensive urban disasters is that they offer an opportunity for a city to undo its mistakes of the past, to protect or guard against recurrence of similar or other disasters in the future, and to facilitate or promote a general leveling up of civic standards."[87] This sentiment perfectly mirrored NFPA president Franklin Worthington's 1926 speculation that the "science of fire extinguishment has seemingly nearly reached its high limit, but only concentrations of values in cities and large factories are affected by that. It is the slower process of replacement by a better kind of construction that will help the most."[88] Ford reminded his readership, urban planners across the country, that the NFPA has made ample information available to "eliminate the conflagration risk in every American city within a generation or less without unduly overburdening the city governments or property owners with expenditure or tenants with increased rents." He also cited the NBFU, U.S. Department of Commerce, and National Housing Association for their efforts in providing information about fire protection to municipal governments. Ford recommended similar planning for floods and earthquakes,

Ford and Wentworth—the fire protection expert and the planner—
promoted ideas shared broadly by urban reformers of the Progressive Era,
namely that municipal governments needed to rebuild and renew the
nineteenth-century city and bring it into a modern age where experts
understood how to marry design and development with public safety. Such
a view put planners in the central role as interdisciplinary experts on laying
out streets, locations or public buildings, parks and playgrounds, transportation, and zoning for air and open space. Fire experts like Worthington
also served as intermediaries, bringing together the technical knowledge of
fire protection and the willing, or at least not hostile, public official.[89]

The rebuilt Salem of the 1920s presented a test for what the city of the
fire experts and the urban planners might look like. The major effect of the
changes dictated by the Rebuilding Commission were that more than 50
percent of the manufacturers who had been making leather and other goods
in the city at the time of the fire, had left Salem by the late 1920s. James
Ford viewed this as remarkable, and a very positive outcome. It was the
readiness of Salem's government to roll out a comprehensive plan that
allowed such radical change, in his view, and as such he recommended
similar preparations in other cities. "Upon the occasion of a disaster," Ford
argued, "the city plan commission, building department, and civic improvement committee should immediately take in hand the problem of rebuilding
the city." In disaster lay opportunity, but only if the disaster experts were
empowered in the aftermath. "By these means" Ford concluded, " any city
in ruins may emerge a model city, distinctive in its plan and architecture
and its plan for community welfare."

Public investigations of fire risks in the aftermath of disasters took on new
urgency after the Iroquois Theater Fire in 1903. Callous and rampant disregard for fire safety laws as they existed was found throughout the private
sector, including construction, transportation, manufacturing, and entertainment. Corruption and simple neglect of the law in the fire service and
building inspection departments, not to mention in city halls and state-
houses from coast to coast, enabled such flagrant disregard. John Ripley
Freeman's investigation of the Iroquois Theater Fire and his report *On the
Safeguarding of Life in Theaters* demonstrated the skills of the fire insurance
engineer in action. In the contrast between the bickering and clamorous
parade of investigators and the more methodical approach taken by Freeman we see what was to fire experts of the time a maddening situation.

Their work could save lives (and profits for fire insurance companies), but the structure of municipal government and conflicts inherent in its approach to public safety made the application of expert knowledge to construction and enforcement of fire safety ordinances unreliable at best and criminally negligent at worst. Insurance engineers had the knowhow, but knowhow in risk and disaster was not enough to effect broad safety reform, especially for experts so closely tied to the fire insurance industry.

In the latter years of the nineteenth and first decade of the twentieth centuries, state legislatures took up the process of investigating the insurance industry in the broad cause of reform. The results varied state by state, but overall a decidedly new and active government stance emerged toward regulating the industry's practices, in favor of greater transparency, access for all consumers, and cost control measures. It was in this atmosphere that the claims to objectivity and public service put forward by fire experts started to gather an audience. In the realm of urban planning cities started by the 1910s and 1920s to take into hand the wholesale reform of the urban environment in the name of public safety—fire control played the deciding role here in launching an era of reform handing more power to experts who wanted to use strong city and state authority to meaningfully regulate development for the first time. In sum, a consensus over fire safety in twentieth-century America was building, and while government had been late to the conversation, the Progressive Era did reveal a growing interest among reformers in controlling fire, learning from private experts, and using regulatory powers to remake cities along more sustainable lines. Government though, would not, just as the insurance industry could not, completely capture the role of ultimate fire expert. The maturation of fire expertise into a realm both of technique and policy would not be driven by predominantly private or public sector actors.

3

The Invisible Screen of Safety

If you drive to work in the morning, these engineers stop worrying about you for a while . . . because all makes and models of passenger cars have been checked by U.L. for the fire hazard. When you get to the plant they begin to worry a little bit . . . many, but not all, of the fire extinguishers, the fire doors, the sprinklers and the explosion-proof switches have been tested by U.L. After dinner, when you take your family to the movies, they relax again . . . they feel pretty certain about the . . . switchboard, the projection booth, the aisle lights and the panic bolts on the exit doors. Thus do these engineers follow you about at home, at work and at play, trying to throw around you an invisible screen of safety.

—*Saturday Evening Post*, April 28, 1945

By World War II, American fire experts would comprise a powerful network, capable of conducting costly risk research and quickly implementing knowledge into the realms of manufacturing, the built environment, and public policy directed at preventing fire disasters. Their "invisible screen of safety" was composed of interlocking techniques, codes, and standards, the results of a half-century's worth of institution-building and policy advocacy. Invisibility was success for the disaster experts. What had begun as a raucous set of debates in the midst of an urban crisis would die down to a quiet consensus among experts on acceptable levels of fire risk, and best practices for keeping those levels tuned to maximum profitability and public safety.

Fire experts by this time held influential positions; they were insurance commissioners, fire marshals and building inspectors, fire protection engineers, urban planners and architects. They also worked in interdisciplinary teams in major institutions like the United States National Bureau of Standards, the National Fire Protection Association, and Underwriters Laboratories. Across these diverse settings the experts eagerly participated in a standard-setting process enjoying both de facto and in many cases real legal authority over fire protection across the United States. Their standards informed municipal and state building codes and code enforcement. Their standards decided the winners and the losers in manufacturers' arguments over the safety and reliability of their products. Their standards succeeded in lowering the urban conflagration hazard significantly, and lowering the overall annual fire loss by the end of World War II, achieving a brief moment when the pace of risk-taking and the knowledge and power to control risks were in rough equilibrium—a rare condition in the modern United States.

The most notable features of fire expertise in its mature form at mid-century were that it was not the purview of one single discipline or profession, nor was it controlled by government or by the private sector. Fire experts worked across disciplines, in both public and private settings, with claims to authority that stretched across state and municipal boundaries. Additionally, fire experts had achieved, and would continue to achieve, their greatest success in both knowledge creation and control over the built environment not through capturing one industry or through regulation or public policy, but instead through the refinement of a "consensus code" system, or "voluntary standard-setting system." No single organization better exemplifies the rising power of fire experts in the overlap of technical, business, and policy realms than Underwriters Laboratories.

A Day in the Life of Underwriters Laboratories

In the spring of 1920, a 300-member assembly of National Fire Protection Association members made a trip to Chicago to tour the headquarters of Underwriters Laboratories. Founded in 1894, but no longer confined to its garret "over the horses," UL was by this time the largest fire-testing laboratory in the world. The NFPA visitors—a varied group of fire officials, manufacturers, and fire protection engineers from across the country—had come to see the results of UL's efforts. William Henry Merrill, the engineer who founded and managed the labs from the early days of electrical fire troubleshooting at the Columbian Exposition, still directed the work, and his testing engineers were quite accustomed to hosting visitors. Merrill relished the opportunity to show off his so-called "City Unburnable" lab complex and to demonstrate the striking variety of work carried on by the staff of more than 100 engineers.[1] Underwriters Laboratories—more than any other fire expert institution—promoted an idea that acceptable levels of safety from fire could be achieved through scientific experiment and testing. The work at the labs often focused on replicating real world conditions in controlled settings; but by the 1920s engineers and scientists worked together at UL pursuing both applied and basic research. Not everyone agreed that this method reflected an appropriate epistemological approach —and even more critics were found arguing that though the method was sound, UL's close connection to the insurance industry rendered its claims to objectivity null and void. In analyzing these very critiques we may explain the evolution of UL's institutional form over the early twentieth century. From a small-scale testing lab working in an ad hoc fashion and funded directly by the insurance industry, UL grew rapidly into a nonprofit institution at arm's length from the insurance industry, practicing intensive laboratory analysis for specific products but also for the creation of basic, abstract information about fire and materials.

Visitors were treated to a sort of Dante's Inferno tour of the labs. Moving from room to room, they were invited to see the engineers at work, testing products submitted by manufacturers who hoped to receive a listing among the thousands of "approved" products. With this listing and its accompanying "UL Label," manufacturers were in a position to sell a guarantee of product safety to customers, with the additional promise of lower insurance premiums for property owners.

One of the more popular stops along any tour of the labs was the Hydraulic Department. Here, visitors might see, according to business writer and UL's enthusiastic promoter Harry Chase Brearley, "a typical testing engineer with a frown of concentration between his eyebrows, [a] smooth-faced, spectacled, youngish-looking man" at work on a fire hose-testing machine, a device that stretched hose out until the rubber interior snapped.[2] Sulfur content in the rubber itself was measured. Hoses were heated to see how long they would operate before being consumed by fire; then they were filled to the bursting point. Each of these stress tests was conducted before a hose could pass inspection and earn a UL listing, and, Merrill was looking to add further dimensions to the hose-testing operation. It was rumored that he had a standing offer of $25,000 for anyone who could produce a scientifically accurate fire hose "chewer."[3] This was, in fact, just one of the many fire-fighting technologies tested by UL; others included water cannons, hose couplings, hydrants, standpipes, pumps, and fire engine boilers. The Hydraulic Lab also had the ability to test different types of water: fresh, salt, clear, muddy, alkaline, soft. "A valve or pump might work perfectly with the clear Lake Michigan water of Chicago," Brearley observed, "but give trouble with the more substantial fluid used by St. Louis or Cincinnati. . . . The hydraulic laboratory . . . has facilities for producing imitation Mississippi River water or any other kind that has to be reckoned with."[4]

In another room, a "miniature device like a tiny pile-driver" dropped a weight on the heads of matches. If the match ignited, it failed the test.[5] The next stop revealed roofing tests, involving a large burner hanging down over a composition shingle roof built on a sloping framework. This "radiation test" was followed by the "conflagration test." Here, the roof was pushed into the opening of a blower-duct, a burner was lighted, and a wind machine supplied a forty-five mile-per-hour gust, to simulate the conditions a roof might face in the midst of a rapidly advancing urban firestorm.[6] The NFPA assembly witnessed oxy-acetylene blow-pipe tests, fire extinguisher tests, the combustion of motion picture film, and a fire sprinkler distribution test, a demonstration that illustrated and compared the amount of water coverage provided by a range of the different models of sprinklers on the commercial market.

Finally, the tour ended out in the testing yard.[7] Here the guests were treated to the "drop test" of a burning safe. UL engineers frequently tested safes, sometimes filling them with papers and magazines to simulate a cache of important documents, then setting them on fire in an open field "lab" outside the city, trying to precipitate an explosion caused by gases building up inside the safe. Safes that received the UL listing had to stand up to such treatment, leaving the documents inside undamaged. Similarly, the drop test was a destructive test, and by virtue of this fact it was a true crowd-pleaser, a meeting of science and spectacle. The safe had been heating up in one of the furnaces for some time, and the visitors now gathered around to watch as UL engineers and technicians assessed whether the time was right, if the safe was "done." Once they verified the temperature inside the furnace, several technicians in coveralls wheeled the safe out into the yard. White hot by this point, the safe was about to go through what the engineers reasoned was a close approximation of the conditions it might face if it were to tumble through the buckling floor of a burning office building. The crowd closed in, jostling for a good view, the safe was attached to cables and secured for lifting, and it was finally time for the test:

> The hoist motor hums, the steel cables tighten, the pulley creaks and the safe rises into the air. . . . Down comes the safe whizzing from the height of a fourth floor-window and landing with a crash on . . . [a] pile of bricks. The bricks being purposely uneven to represent the chaotic debris of a real fire. . . . When the safe has cooled, examinations are made as to its stability and strength. . . . Then an autopsy is performed; workmen take the safe apart, dissecting it as a coroner would a corpse.[8]

The scene, captured on film by a motion picture cameraman, reveals what almost certainly qualified as the most unorthodox scientific research experiment conducted in all of Chicago that day. Here we find an expectant crowd of diverse fire safety experts, the crash landing of a superheated safe, the eager and smiling inspections after the fact, of safe, of contents, of furnace, and the work of the note-taking testing engineers transforming a dramatic, and planned, failure into a replicable standard. In this specialized and interdisciplinary setting multiple methods came to bear on the creation of the standard: laboratory testing by technical experts, certification of commercial products according to predetermined standards, and finally dissemination of "fire-risk information" ranging from the published lists of "approved" products to the sensational showmanship of the "drop test."

As UL's horizons were expanding, the Chicago headquarters, the various regional offices, and the testing equipment inside were funded largely by the stock insurance companies, totaling up to an investment of $250,000 by 1916, the year before UL stopped taking money from the insurers and began to generate all of its revenues from testing fees.[9] Day to day operating expenses were paid by the manufacturers who submitted their appliances for testing. Merrill maintained that this arrangement was ultimately the best for the testing client, offering "a greater and more valuable return in proportion to the money expended than is obtained from any other outfit undertaking engineering work with which I am acquainted."[10] Most of UL's

Figure 6. Drop test of a burning safe, Underwriters Laboratories, 1923. From *The Truth About Testing Safes* (New York: Brearley Service Organization), 1923. Courtesy of Underwriters Laboratories, Inc.

product tests took place at the Chicago headquarters. Manufacturers were required to pay a deposit, and pay the balance for the testing at the completion of the tests. A limit of expense was fixed, and the cost of testing was the same whether the device was judged "superior" or "inferior," or anywhere in between. The applicant's obligation to pay the charge was not, therefore, "contingent upon the nature of the opinion rendered—whether favorable or otherwise." Tests were divided into five classes. Groups A, B, C, D had preliminary fees of $100, $50, $25, $15; Group F was also $100, and included "experimental" work on subjects with which UL was less familiar. Tests were usually begun within ten days following payment of the preliminary fee.[11]

Upon request manufacturers were informed exactly when their product would be tested and could attend the tests, which sometimes had a positive outcome, sometimes led to conflict, and sometimes provided rather comic episodes. We know of the interactions between UL and manufacturers primarily from the UL viewpoint, and from this view we find that UL engineers often found a manufacturer's faith in his product not only unfounded but also quite humorous. Describing one test, Brearley explained:

> Sometimes the manufacturers are mightily surprised. One of them felt such confidence in the non-explosive properties of his particular preparation that he offered to stand by the generator with a lighted cigar. The inspector, wise with the experience of many tests, firmly vetoed the cigar, but finally permitted the enthusiast to stand by the machine. To his consternation, the bell of the generator presently soared to the ceiling with a bang, and he was covered from head to foot with the sludge. A sadder and wiser manufacturer retired to clean his clothes and observed that apparently there was "only one way in which a d———— fool could learn anything."[12]

Brearley also described a test of a connecting "thimble" used to join a stovepipe with a chimney. The thimble failed to protect the woodwork behind it after being heated. "The inventor has been standing by; he looks disappointed, but says that the showing is better than the last time. It develops that he has made considerable changes in the device within the past few weeks because repeated tests, here made for him, have shown him its defects."[13] In this case, the manufacturer used UL as a research and development lab of sorts, because he probably lacked the resources to perform such tests at his own factory. Another manufacturer was so pleased with the positive outcome of his test that he gave each of the four testing engineers a watch as a token of his appreciation—gifts that were refused on Merrill's direction.

Manufacturers would apply for a test and file a description of the device for test, and UL would then say how many and what sizes should be submitted. For large devices, usually one test device was sufficient. For smaller devices, often many would be tested. In some cases, with extremely large machines, like industrial steam boilers or generators, UL inspectors would go on-site for tests, with manufacturers paying the cost of travel. Time for tests ranged from ten days to six months. In 1916, the average time was one month. When finished, if the results were favorable, they were sent out to the UL branches and the insurance organizations subscribing to UL's bulletins. The bulletin and the complete report were given to the applicant. About half of products submitted passed, and UL took pride that they did not serve as consulting engineers for failed products. The manufacturers could consult the safety standards related to their class of goods, and in many cases minor changes to a product might gain UL approval and a follow-up test. Of course, the manufacturer had to be willing to pay, pass or fail.[14]

Tests could, as we have seen, take a variety of forms, in a variety of locations within the UL complex. In describing their methods, UL engineers boasted that some "things we test by explosion, some by corrosion, some by weathering; some by flame and artificial hurricane, as in the case of roofing; some by collision, as with automobile bumpers; some by heating and dropping, as with safes."[15] Another UL engineer stated his philosophy of testing a bit more simply: "we give it hell."[16] As the NFPA visitors found in 1920, in many cases several of the different divisions within UL were called upon to conduct tests. On fire hose, for example, chemical testing was necessary to find out the exact composition: gum and sulfur, oils, asphalts, and substitutes. Mechanical testing was needed to take the hose to the stretched breaking point, the strength and elasticity of the rubber. In the hydraulic lab, a pressure test determined the bursting point, elongation, and twist.[17] Much of the testing apparatus was "specialty equipment," especially with sprinkler testing, for example, having no duplicates elsewhere. Such equipment served as another factor UL used to set itself apart from other testing labs.

Standardization was critical to the recording of test results. For example, in a 1911 *Manual of Instructions for Preparation of Reports,* a standard terminology was proposed for the work of the Lab. The subject of the report was to be termed "The Device." Other "appropriate" terms included "Material, Apparatus, Equipment, Product, Machine, Article, System, Appliance." The client was the "Submittor"; if the device was to be seen regularly the client could be listed as a "Manufacturer."[18] The report featured a number of key sections, including an introduction, a description of the device, the claims made for the device, the object of the investigation, the general plan of investigation, the examination and test record, the record in service, improvements, and conclusions.[19] At the end, the testing engineer noted his recommendation on the product. Finally a guide card was printed. Such regimentation in recording tests and results was deemed necessary considering that many products would be tested multiple times. It was also, perhaps, yet another method of demonstrating to UL's patrons the thorough work done by the testing engineers. The guide cards were kept at UL offices, as well as at the "Principal Boards of Underwriters and Inspection Bureaus . . . many of the general offices of insurance companies, . . . [and] certain federal, state, and municipal departments."[20] Lists of Inspected Mechanical Appliances and Inspected Electrical Appliances were similarly distributed.

Through its massive outpouring of technical listings and publications, and through use of an open-door policy at its many nationwide offices, UL worked to cultivate good relations with commercial clients and the broader community of fire safety experts. But, what about average consumers, who by the 1920s were filling up their homes, apartments, and driveways with hazardous products: electric irons and lamps, radios and room heaters, automobiles? Beginning in the 1920s, and with the coming of the Great Depression, consumers in the United States began to demand both economy and safety in their purchases. The UL label was already firmly established by this time, alongside the *Good Housekeeping* seal and soon to be joined by the Consumers Union rating, as a marker that consumers turned to for reassurance. Beyond the label, though, UL also took part in the cause of "consumer education" using the new media of radio and the movies. In this activity they frequently made common cause in their publications and education efforts with the NFPA.

We have already seen the importance UL placed on guest visits to the "city unburnable" as a tool by which to impress safety experts and manufacturers. By the 1920s visitors were arriving at the Chicago office in droves, touring the labs, watching "drop-tests," and viewing the charred metal beams that were kept in the testing yard, evidence from the "Fire Test of Building Columns" project. Sometimes visitors virtually took over the labs, as with the NFPA assembly in 1920, or when 160 members of the Western Association of Electrical Inspectors visited in 1922. This group saw an elevator door test, the hydraulic lab, a fire in a portable moving picture booth, a fire stream test on a door, and the automatic sprinkler test.[21] In 1925, 100 members of the Chicago section of the Society of Automotive Engineers toured the labs; and the same year a 500-member assembly of the National Fire Protection Association made an inspection visit. Though UL engineers were touted as rarely noticing visitors, one must assume that the more exotic or powerful visitors excited some interest in the labs. International visitors hailed from Belgium, China, Czechoslovakia, England, Germany, Holland, India, Japan, Norway, and Sweden. The fire chief of Berlin, for example, turned up in 1925, as did Senator Exnard from California, and W. E. Mallalieu, president of the National Board of Underwriters.[22] In 1926, two actors, one from Al Jolson's company, came by to tour the hydraulic lab.[23] In 1929 fire sprinkler magnate Russell Grinnell took the tour with nine directors and members of his staff.[24] Visits from the press were common, with editors of *Popular Mechanics*, *Engineering News-Record*, and *Electrical World* stopping by, among others. And, of course, engineering and architecture students were common sights, especially the Armour Institute students, some of whom worked at the labs as part of their degree programs.

The Symbol of Safety

After a favorable test at UL, three types of follow-up service were possible: "Reexamination," "Inspection," and "Label Service." Reexamination service occurred when the manufacturer paid an annual fee and UL either bought a sample on the open market or received one from the manufacturer, retesting the device at least once per year. If any "sub-standard features" were found, the manufacturer would be compelled to correct the problem or lose his "listing." Manufacturers were also graded against each other, with UL calculating test failures of total tests for three-, six-, and twelve-month periods. They were then sent a grade, letting them know if their products were gaining or losing in overall "safety."[25] The second form of follow-up was the Inspection Service. This involved specially trained UL inspectors visiting factories in order to determine if the products tested at UL were actually being manufactured up to standard. This was done in conjunction with reexamination in many cases, and the Inspection Service was billed monthly to manufacturers. In one case, regular inspection turned up a situation where a factory owner's instructions to his foremen were evidently being disregarded. He found out about the problems on the shop floor from UL inspectors. In this way, some manufacturers successfully used UL's Inspection Service as a managerial tool, as well as a way to keep their UL listing.[26]

Joseph Forsyth, chief electrical inspector at the New York office, made a strong argument for the efficacy of electrical inspection. In 1925, for example, he noted that more than "ninety percent of the loss caused last year by fire from electrical causes in New York . . . was either directly chargeable to improper maintenance of electrical apparatus or to alterations and extensions made without the knowledge or approval of the underwriters' inspection department." To Forsyth, and to UL's inspectors in general, consistent reinspection was the only solution.[27] Regular reinspection would tend, he claimed, "to discourage owners from trying to do their own electrical work or from hiring incompetent, unauthorized persons." In 1924 the New York office reinspected 4,042 buildings and 13,974 individual pieces of electrical equipment. The inspections found a startling 60 percent rate of defective equipment, but on the bright side many owners were willing to correct the defects that the inspectors found. Forsyth noted that when "the owner does not correct the fault our only recourse is to bulletin the building so that the fire insurance companies will know the condition of the risk." In explaining the methods of the inspectors, Forsyth claimed that it was actually quite simple: "We take a map of the city, mark off the high valued risk sections and go over them first. The high valued risks are usually in office building zones, loft and storehouse sections, large apartment houses. . . . Department stores and churches are also carefully inspected." The kinds of problems the inspectors found fell into a few main categories and were often blamed on inexperienced, nonexpert installation or repair of electrical appliances. "Janitors, housewives and even school boys seem to think that the only thing to be careful of in wiring is that two bare wires do not touch, and when my men find poor work that is unsafe and want to have it rectified, a debate sometimes follows."[28] Flexible cord caused problems, as it was often "carried around base boards, stretched across ceilings, sunk in door jams and even hidden under carpets where

everyone walking across it will damage it so that trouble is inevitable."[29]
Even if Forsyth's inspectors had to engage in "debate" over their findings,
the threat of an electrical fire risk being communicated to the insurance
companies often pushed the owners into submission.

The UL inspector's official duty was to see that every appliance and
material that bore the label was made in accordance with the rules and
specifications outlined by UL. What qualities were needed? Technical training or practical experience in manufacturing were favored, in either case
stressing electrical and mechanical expertise. Also, as E. F. Reisenberger of
the New York inspection office noted, the inspector needed "integrity, tact,
and a goodly amount of common sense."[30] Such qualities were especially
useful as the inspector worked on his own; there was no set amount of time
allotted inspections, though he was expected to take as little time as possible. Traveling was time-consuming for the inspector, but he was expected
to manage this travel time efficiently by good planning and to use "reasonable economy" in his expenses. Reisenberger reasoned that the inspector's
tact made the difference between his being welcome or a nuisance at the
factory. He thought that the toughest part of the job was to "distinguish
whether, through some oversight or error in the manufacturing process,
material is sub-standard or whether there was an intent to 'get away with
something'." Sometimes it was necessary to send a telegram back to the
home office for clarification on a technical point or a listing. Inspection
forms were to be filled out at the time of inspection whenever time permitted, with the first page used for criticisms and points of interest related to
the factory and the product. The rest of the inspector's report served as a
"written manifest" of test details and a guarantee that the necessary features
and methods of construction had been thoroughly checked. "The inspector
in this way goes on record as having fulfilled his duty and made the
required inspection."[31] Every three months inspectors in the larger regions,
such as New York or Boston were changed from one route to another to
avoid "unconscious carelessness."[32]

UL's most highly regarded and influential follow-up service was the
label service. The UL label, the "symbol of safety," might take a number
of different forms, but was generally a small metal tag stamped with
"Underwriters' Laboratories, Inc.," the type and class of the product, and
a serial number. The label might also be stamped directly onto a product if
there was fear that it might fall off in use. Only devices already in commercial production were allowed to be "Listed." But the Laboratories were

prepared to "receive, examine and test devices in the model stage, and to render to the submittor only, a report for his information and guidance in their future development."[33]

The Label Service began in 1906; by 1915 it was turning out fifty million labels per year, and by 1922 the number had skyrocketed to five hundred million per year.[34] In this increase we can envision the rapid growth of not only UL as an institution, but also the American economy more broadly, with urban construction taking place at a fever pitch, and the filling of American homes with consumer products.

For firemen, fire marshals, and inspectors across the United States, the Underwriters Laboratories label served as an immediate guarantee of the device's success under examination. For manufacturers the label served as a sales tool, allowing them to argue to prospective buyers that products with the label were less likely to burn and more likely to result in lower insurance premiums. Brearley relates a story of how the label might influence the price of electrical products, using the example of an auction of electrical goods in Brooklyn in 1922. Apparently, as the auction got underway, the question "Are these goods approved?" went up in the crowd. The auctioneer, not knowing the answer, answered in the affirmative. The final price was ten dollars for a hundred. Later it was found that the goods were not on the UL inspected list. "You should have heard the storm of complaint," said a witness. "Most of those present were the cheapest kind of dealers, but even they knew the value of Laboratories' listing; the dumbfounded auctioneer took back the box, put it up again, and the highest he could get was four dollars a hundred." When the auctioneer was later caught in another lie regarding the UL label, the entire auction was called off.[35]

Vice President A. R. Small voiced the role of the UL Label Service in its relationship to industry in 1920. He stressed the need to convince manufacturers to label a greater percentage of their output. Yet, he worried about the ways manufacturers might use the label for their own gain, with little concern for the larger goal of universal fire safety. Many manufacturers were "selfish," he said, and used the label service for "maintenance of the policy of the company covering the products of the company." Another problem was preventing factory inspection in places where the label would serve only as a means of "advertising," and the cost of inspection was not justified by benefits to manufacturers or insurers. One interesting development, Small noted, was that 50 percent or more of UL's tests were being conducted for manufacturers who were compelled to submit to testing by the trade associations or inter-industry organizations to which they belonged. These collaborative inter-industry organizations were setting standards for their entire industries, and UL functioned as a means by which to hold individual manufacturers up to the standards of these organizations. One example was in oxy-acetylene and oxy-hydrogen cutting and welding work, using compressed oxygen and hydrogen. The industry, after many bad accidents, apparently considered barring any company from membership if it did not seek the advice of UL.[36] Deceptions did sometimes occur. One manufacturer submitted some goods for test, then when they passed and were labeled he removed the labels and put them on lesser quality goods at his factory. He returned the first lot to UL for another "test," and the process was repeated. Inspectors became skeptical, secretly initialed the samples to identify them later, and caught the manufacturer at his game. Approval was withdrawn, and when the manufacturer again sought the label, he was told he would have to keep two UL inspectors in his factory full time to ascertain that he was using the label in good faith.[37] In another case a railroad company took bids for fire extinguishers, specifying that the UL label be a qualification, and one manufacturer came in with an exceptionally low bid. An inspector went to the factory, saw a few made, then was told that the factory was closing down for boiler repairs. The inspector refused to leave, and after several weeks, having never left, the manufacturer gave up the bid, exposing the deception.

These inspectors, and the adventures they had in the field, fall directly into the lineage of the factory inspector established by the Factory Mutual inspectors, like John Ripley Freeman, in the nineteenth century. The tenacity of the Label Service inspector, in conjunction with the skill of the testing engineer back at the lab, comprised a combination of skills taken for granted at UL as a signal part of its early success.

As UL's founding was closely related to the testing of electrical appliances, it followed that the first major testing department at UL involved electrical goods. It was UL dogma that electricity, the universal servant, was safer than gas or open flames for light and heat. The engineers still recognized that electricity, improperly managed and unsupervised, could also cause a disaster. As one observer put it, "energy is energy; heat is heat, whether made electrically or not, and it is [the] failure to appreciate this fact that is responsible for many electrical fires."[38] As we saw in Chapter 1, UL was practically founded on the mantra that the use of electricity in the city required supervision, standardization, and an educated public to be rendered safe.

The first way that UL spread its influence in electrical safety research involved borrowing the information gathering and dissemination tactics of the National Board of Fire Underwriters. The NFPA, NBFU, and other insurance organizations like the New York Board of Fire Underwriters had long made a habit of publishing lists of electrical products on the market and publishing lists and descriptions of electrical fires. UL soon started to get involved in publishing its own lists of electrical failures. This was a genre of writing unique to the insurance industry, now adapted to the safety inspector. In August 1916, for example, UL's journal *Electrical Data* published 19 different categories of "causes and losses due to fires attributed to electricity."[39]

Underwriters Laboratories made information about electrical fires available to those who subscribed to *Electrical Data* and later its second publication, *Laboratories' Data*. What kinds of fires were reported? The reports included everything from small home fires to large industrial losses, with the amount of loss indicated in many cases, from $2.00 to $30,000.[40] Alongside such statistics, collected by the Actuarial Bureau of the National Board of Fire Underwriters, UL also published narratives of electrical risks and failures. In *Electrical Data*, UL published "characteristic" tales of fires. Though details were left out, upon application UL would supply localities and details with a reference number. UL also implored "disaster reporters" to include "all available information," including photographs.[41]

Certainly the editor of *Electrical Data* chose the most outrageous, and perhaps therefore the most effective stories to relate. Case 3486 unfolded in a manner reminiscent of the Iroquois Theater disaster: "Electric Lamp Ignites Curtain. In a theatre filled with guests assembled to witness a carnival performance, fire was discovered by the watchman in making his rounds." A plush curtain had been thrown up over an electric lamp because it was obstructing the view of the stage. Rather than causing a melee similar to the Iroquois fire, nothing more than damage to the curtain resulted.[42] In Case 4209, "Fire Escape Carries Street Railway Current into Building," we find that street railway electric feeders were built before the fire escape, and the two came into contact when the wooden feeder sleeve, damaged, allowed an arc to pass between the escape and the feeder.[43] In Case 4194, "Drills into a 13,800-Volt Cable," we find an electric lighting employee badly burned on the hand upon drilling through a manhole and hitting a live electric wire. In Case 4195, "Received Severe Shock Through Metal Handle of Umbrella," we learn about a newsboy who carried an umbrella after a violent thunderstorm and came in contact with a 2,300-volt downed power line. Though burned, the boy lived. Case 4248, "$200,000.00 Loss Due to Careless Use of Electric Iron," details a comedy of errors, beginning with an iron left on in the alterations department of a large clothing establishment. No watchman was on site. Downed electric wires charged up the metal fire escapes, and with no city fire alarm system, great time was lost in getting the alarm sounded.

Other listed fire narratives included losses caused by careless consumers, such as "Dish Washing Machine Short Circuited," loss $10.00; "Amateur Wiring Starts Fire," loss $71.50; "Electric Iron Burns Hole Through Board," an iron burned through the board and set fire to a basket of clothes; and "$1,200 Loss Due to Forgotten Iron."[44] Case 4199, "Accepted a Dare," relates the tale of a returning World War I veteran who challenged a 250-volt mercury arc rectifier, grabbing both electrodes just after boasting that he had taken 150 volts before. The soldier died, and it was reported that he had recently been under a doctor's care for a nervous breakdown.[45] Case 4238, "Death Follows Taking of Electric Iron into Bath Tub," tells of a thirty-four-year-old man who stepped into his bath, bringing with him a six-pound electric iron.

The electrical "risk narratives" offer us some insight into the range of risks that UL was working on by the time of World War I. Manufacturers and consumers were to blame, as the fire experts saw it, along with "careless workmen."[46] Manufacturers and workmen would be educated and influenced, presumably, through UL's testing, examination, inspection, and label services. Consumers posed a whole different type of problem. UL worried that "The fool will never be eliminated from society; safety can be found only in 'fool-proof' devices. Appliances in endless variety are being manufactured, bought and inexpertly used by people who are intelligent or stupid, careful or careless as the case may be. The intelligent, careful man may at any time be endangered by the carelessness or stupidity of a neighbor."[47]

The UL staff in the years since the Columbian Exposition had increased steadily, from just a handful in 1894 to well over one hundred by 1920. UL employees apparently earned less than they might have in comparable jobs elsewhere. To compensate for this fact, UL employee G. T. Bunker claimed that "There is no monotony here. Great variety in work is a constant stimulus. . . . The fact that we are working for a common end, and that this end is to benefit humanity, not to enrich a class or an individual, is in itself an inspiration."[48] It is, again, the hyperbolic reform language of the Progressive Era, and yet a language we cannot easily dismiss considering that engineers were in demand in those years. Engineers who ended up at UL stayed, as Bunker and others claimed, because the work was interesting, and there was a culture of corporate pride in the larger goals of fire safety that filtered down to the testing bench and out to the factory inspector.

The fact that UL's strongest patron in its first two decades, the National Board of Fire Underwriters, was at the time the largest fire insurance inter-industry body in the United States ultimately gave UL the reach it desired in promulgating product standards and risk information nationwide. The NBFU shifted its focus in the 1890s to electrical hazards, thus its sponsor-ship of William Henry Merrill's lab. But, with the wave of tremendous urban fires that swept the United States between 1904 and 1906, the NBFU enlarged its fire prevention work to include what it called the "conflagra-tion hazard."

After the Baltimore Fire in 1904 exposed the weaknesses in so-called "fireproof" construction, the NBFU established a Committee on Fire Pre-vention and Engineering Standards for the purpose of "examining, report-ing on, and advising as to the fire protection facilities and the structural conditions and hazards of cities." The Committee on Fire Prevention main-tained a staff of engineers, "including those trained in waterworks practice, mechanical and electrical engineers to report on fire departments and fire alarm systems, and structural engineers to examine into the character of buildings and the degree of congestion."[49] To make the reports it was neces-sary to rely on city records and the word of city officials, but whenever possible they tried "to secure information at first hand and by actual exami-nation or test." Committee on Fire Prevention staff engineers examined fire hydrants and gate valves, fire engines and fire boats, and all buildings in central business districts, in order to see "the likelihood of a fire getting beyond control in a single building or group of buildings, and if beyond control, of extending to involve a considerable section of the city, especially in a high-value district." After the inspections, "fire hazard diagnosis" reports were issued with maps and suggestions for correcting defects. The reports were supplied to affiliated insurance companies, city officials, and civic organizations. By 1928 the Committee on Fire Prevention had reported on 397 cities, some two or three times. In 1905, the NBFU also started publishing, based on similar research and inspections, a Model Building Code, which went through three editions by 1928.

Underwriters Laboratories was central to the NBFU's attempts to control the conflagration hazard. By continuing to test electrical and chemical hazards, UL's influence in these industries grew at a time when the industries themselves were reaching maturity. So, UL continued to focus on a core set of fire hazards after 1904. It is also important, though, to note that UL expanded its influence by eagerly responding to the NBFU's anxiety over the urban built environment and the financial losses inherent in runaway downtown fires such as those seen in Baltimore, Rochester, and San Francisco. This meant not only electrical testing but also elaborate and expensive testing of building materials, especially structural columns and fireproofing materials. By claiming this role as the materials lab for the NBFU, UL grew into a truly national laboratory in these years—not in the meaning of the term as a laboratory operating under federal control, but as a lab with a national audience, a network of labs spread nationwide, and a range of interests and research focused on problems in more than one city or region.

The first electrical work in New York involved reexamination and label service by engineers working out of the offices of local civic authorities and local insurance underwriters. With increase in volume and variety of products to review, though, the work increased and grew to encompass Trenton, New Jersey, Bridgeport, Connecticut, Syracuse, and Buffalo. In New York, UL engineers did inspection and labeling of rubber-covered wire as part of an organization called the Wire Inspection Bureau, starting in 1905.[50] In 1912, a branch office was opened in New York City, strongly directed toward electrical testing. Electrical testing was now done in both Chicago and New York. This makes sense, due to the fact that a great share of electrical manufacturing in the United States took place on the East Coast. The New York Testing Station was in lower Manhattan, and the New York staff was pleased by their new location, "in a building adjoining a substation of the New York Edison Company." This location made "available for test purposes supply circuits of a range of voltage and current capacities which it would be difficult to obtain elsewhere . . . it is seldom necessary to go outside to secure the needed facilities for conducting tests."[51] Aside from private testing and inspection work, the New York Testing Station sometimes served the City of New York. In 1918, the Station tested fire alarm telegraph cable for the city, along with electrical insulation for thousands of terminal bases and street fire alarm boxes.[52]

A brief look at the New York staff reveals that many of the engineers were from the area and had been locally educated. Four were graduates of the Pratt Institute in Brooklyn, three were graduates of Stevens Institute in Hoboken, others had attended Cooper Union and MIT. One graduated from Union College and came to the New York UL office after a stint in the General Electric labs. The field inspectors did not all have college degrees, but experience in some aspect of fire protection was preferred; one of the field inspectors, for example, had previously worked for a fire hose manufacturer.

A review from 1928 reveals the remarkable reach of the inspection work emanating from the New York office. In that year alone, 92 cities were visited, stitching together a network of regional contacts. Engineer C. J. Peacock summarized his activities for the year:

> On account of the distance between the various cities in this section, the municipal people do not get in touch with each other as frequently, hence they welcome contacts from outside sources. . . . Besides contacts established with municipal and rating authorities, there has been opportunity to get in touch with jobbers, electrical contractors, clients, state officials, power men, secretaries of electric leagues, members of the staff of the Bureau of Standards, as well as the engineers and inspectors of Underwriters' Laboratories. The total number of interviews in these various contacts has been well over 800 this year.[53]

Despite all the travel and hard work, the stories inspectors collected were often quite amusing. Sometimes, for example, manufacturers demanded immediate label service and were annoyed by UL's refusal to speed through the testing ritual. One manufacturer sent a boy running into the office with a tin-clad door under his arm wanting on-the-spot labeling, only to be disappointed. Another tale engineers clearly relished telling involved a manufacturer who wanted his architect to use UL-labeled fire doors for a new structure. The "architect said he'd see him in————first." The manufacturer replied that since the architect was headed there anyway, he had better get some fire doors.[54]

A network of manufacturers, insurance companies, and civic fire authorities similar to those on the East Coast and in Chicago existed on the West Coast as well. Yet, manufacturers were reluctant to send their products cast to Chicago for testing, considering that it was a five-day train ride away, even longer for freight shipments. Seeing the opportunity that this isolation presented, William Henry Merrill hired an electrical engineer named R. J. Larrabee with a plan to open up a San Francisco office of the Underwriters Laboratories. A graduate of the University of California, Larrabee had worked with fire underwriters and inspectors in Michigan and at the Board of Fire Underwriters of the Pacific doing reexamination, label service, and electrical testing. In 1923 a UL electrical testing lab was established on Commercial Street in San Francisco under Larrabee's direction. Work on the West Coast quickly picked up speed. Products were submitted for testing from Vancouver all the way to Tijuana, with the lab developing special expertise in electrical heating equipment, elevator equipment, and gas tube electric signs. In fact, within a few years, both Portland and Los Angeles adopted "sales control ordinances," which required that all electrical products sold in these cities be listed by Underwriters Laboratories.[55] In sum, by the 1920s, UL had established a nationwide network of clients, with regional labs to serve them. The lab had around 200 engineers and "inside" employees, 250 outside inspectors, 55,000 square feet in Chicago, labs on both coasts, a Canadian organization, offices in 141 cities, and a "connection in London."[56]

Testing for Consensus

As described previously, government at all levels had traditionally backed away from vigorous control over land development and construction. Private entities like insurance companies were unable, due to public mistrust and to increasingly vigorous government oversight in the Progressive Era, merely to dictate to manufacturers, consumers, or government officials that a new type of building material be used or sprinklers be installed. As such the collaborations among fire experts, organized into councils and committees, was a central factor in their ascendance to authority over American fire protection. The work of the code councils and oversight committees helped establish a "voluntary" fire standard-setting process in the United States, also known as the "consensus code" system. It was a voluntary system in the sense that the NFPA, UL, and their peer institutions did not possess legal authority to mandate adoption of their suggested standards and codes into law. They likewise did not have the authority to mandate the behavior of their closest allies, like fire insurance companies, or even to regulate one another, except through refusal to participate. Instead, the power of the councils and committees derived from the accumulated strength that their collaborations provided.

Wrapped in their constantly repeated mantras of science and "testing for public safety," the fire experts of one organization lent their credibility to their peers by serving on their councils. The experts at UL wrote articles for the *NFPA Quarterly*, and NFPA representatives appeared in the pages of UL's *Laboratories Data*. By the 1920s it is likely that every person in a given room full of fire experts had attended a major American engineering school—perhaps even fire protection engineering at the Armour Institute—and/or had worked either in the fire service or the fire insurance field, and was serving on one of the committees or councils of a local fire insurance association, the National Fire Protection Association, Underwriters Laboratories, National Bureau of Standards, Associated Factory Mutuals, National Board of Fire Underwriters, or even several of these at once. Charles Hexamer, for example, was at one time or another president of the Philadelphia Underwriters Association and the NFPA. UL founder William Henry Merrill also served as NFPA's president for two years. Though UL worked to establish a separate, independent identity for itself, its connection to the NFPA and NBFU was formalized in 1914 with a memorandum of understanding, directing that the three would "continue to co-operate in preparing regulations for the installation of devices and apparatus having a bearing on the fire hazard." Among the three, a division of work was decided, with UL alone determining the technical "suitability" of "devices and apparatus."[57]

Product testing for manufacturers was the central focus of UL's work. This was, after its financial separation from the NBFU in 1917, how the labs brought in revenue. However, when testing similar products year in and year out it was possible over time to develop minimum standards that every product of a certain type—from electric irons to roofing materials—needed to meet to earn the label. Technical standards, once established through repeated testing, were sent to oversight councils, with one council for each engineering department at the labs. In 1928 this consisted of 7: casualty and automotive, burglary protection, hydraulic, gases and oils, protection, chemical, and electrical. The councils were a key linkage mechanism between the technical, knowledge-creation side of the labs, and the application side through the insurance industry. Council members were, according to UL's W.D.A. Peaslee "prominent men in the insurance and inspection fields," insurance representatives who could determine the impact of UL standards on insurance rates. "In this way," Peaslee explained, "the field experience of the insurance organizations and the knowledge of what is required from a rate-making point of view is applied to the technical findings of the Laboratories while the Laboratories itself still remains a separate distinct organization entirely separate from the technique and practice of rate making."[58] The councils were composed, most important from UL's stated point of view, of "men without commercial interest in the devices covered in reports submitted for their review."[59] The goal of such oversight was to receive unanimous approval for the test results, because, as one UL engineer put it, "we do not believe that in matters of technical opinion, majorities are necessarily right."[60]

Additionally, UL established "industry conferences," through which leading manufacturers could work directly with UL engineers to establish minimum standards. Through the industry conferences manufacturers had a voice in the testing process, yet another way UL could simultaneously enrich its technical abilities while also presenting itself as an honest broker. As Peaslee explained, the industry conferences helped establish requirements "mutually agreed upon that enable the Laboratories to equably discharge their obligations to the insurance organizations . . . that may be used by them in rate making, and at the same time insure a reasonable protection to the public . . . and not impose upon the manufacturers an undue economic burden in requiring greater refinement than necessary."[61] In addition to its councils and the industry conferences, three other fire expert organizations shared supervisory responsibilities over UL's activities: the Underwriters' National Electric Association, the consulting engineers of the National Board of Fire Underwriters, and the National Fire Protection Association.[62]

Through the establishment of oversight councils like those at UL, or the over 100 committees of the NFPA in place by World War II, and by sitting on one another's committees, the experts created an inter-connected network through which they could establish by consensus the standards, codes, and suggested policies that made most sense to them. Likewise, these committees always included representatives of the fire service, and state and municipal fire bureaucracy, as well as representatives from the building trades and industry groups, academic researchers, and of course fire protection and fire insurance engineers like John Ripley Freeman. There could be disagreement in the councils and committees, but in the end they, by necessity and design, always reached a consensus. Through this process the fire experts began to speak with one voice in the 1920s, though it emanated from several inter-connected institutions.

"It must be borne in mind there is no legal authority back of the findings of the Laboratories," UL's W.D.A. Peaslee reminded his readers in 1928. But, rather than limiting their reach, this was a strength, as it had necessitated that the fire disaster experts develop something entirely new in American political economy:

> a democratic method of standardization giving each of the parties interested a representation in the establishment of the minimum requirements and sufficiently flexible to keep pace with the changes and developments in our industrial life. It is opposite to the autocratic and sometimes despotic system resulting from standardization by governmental authorities and is also free from that inertia liable to result from any governmental standardization. . . . The democracy of this method extends even to the follow-up service which is an inspection controlled entirely by consent of the governed.[63]

In his enthusiastic rendering of UL's business methods as a new model of democracy for American industry, Peaslee might as well have been speaking for the NFPA, and for all of the nation's expanding collection of industrial standard setting associations. In standardization, derived voluntarily and through the consensus-code system, technical experts had arrived at a way to achieve authority for their technical directives outside, or parallel perhaps, to the public policymaking process. It was lawmaking by collaboration among experts.

Inter-industry cooperation was the larger business context within which the fire experts thrived. Here was a developing method of industry-wide "best practice" and standard sharing that had grown in part out of federal demands on industry in World War I, and included all major sectors of American industry by the 1920s. Commerce secretary and future President Herbert Hoover was an enthusiastic proponent of this form of partnering, also referred to as "associationalism," especially when it worked to alleviate tensions between industry and government, or when it created partnerships across the public/private divide.[64] In the case of fire risk we find institutions, some of them a generation old by this point, without the power to make law at any level of government. Nevertheless, by the 1920s manufacturers and public officials alike mostly agreed that the suggestions of these code councils were the closest thing to "objective" fire risk information that could be found. To manufacturers there was a cost, but for public officials the services of code councils were free. By this point we know why—the fire insurance industry had founded these institutions in large part to shape public policy and they had evolved over time into nonprofit institutions that filled a niche where private sector influence ran out and public sector ability was limited. In the realm of fire risk and disaster the United States had given rise to a novel system of knowledge creation and application. The challenge that lay ahead for the fire experts was in deepening the research, continuing to build credibility, and working steadily to bring down the fire losses of cities, still high in the 1920s.

The NFPA itself—in addition to its education and public policy-focused discussed in Chapter 2, was also focused on technical standards work. For example, just after its founding, the NFPA was focused on sprinklers and electrical technologies. In 1896 the organization convened a conference on electricity, in which European and the five existing American electric codes were reviewed. In 1897 the NFPA published its first "National Electric Code" (known as NFPA 70). This was, like all of NFPA's technical codes a "consensus code"—without any force of law, but written by electrical experts who had reach into the fire insurance industry. As such, the NBFU adopted the NEC as its recommended code. NFPA 70 became a big seller, as municipalities and states adopted it for use in their own laws. The NFPA updated its codes to reflect changes in technical consensus, and as the code changed, consumers of the code bought (and still buy) the revisions. This was a "profit model" for NFPA that could help underwrite its costs.

The Triangle Shirtwaist Fire in New York City (1911) was yet another horrific moment in an era full of fire disasters. Like Iroquois the human tragedy was the most intense part of the Triangle Fire—145 garment workers, many of them immigrant women, were burned, suffocated, fell from shoddy fire escapes, or jumped to their deaths in full view of a multitude gathered on the Manhattan streets. Triangle was a media sensation, and led to court cases (and outcomes) also very similar to the Iroquois fire. A state Triangle Commission used the opportunity to investigate the working conditions of industrial laborers across the state, with repercussions across the country. Labor activist Frances Perkins addressed the NFPA in 1913, calling for enhanced safety measures for workers and others caught in burning buildings. The NFPA established a new committee, the "Committee on Safety to Life," which produced in short order a "Life Safety Code" (NFPA 101). This code was focused on all design features and technologies related to helping people escape from burning buildings, particularly public facilities. This included recommendations for stairways, fire escapes, and stairways as well as human behavior preparations like fire drills.[65] This code, like all NFPA suggested codes, was updated every three years; this one is still in use, and has been adopted as law in many states and municipalities. For both the NFPA and UL a tipping-point of success was reached in the 1920s. By this point both had succeeded in building a base of knowledge and technical experience. Through public relations and lobbying efforts they had filled a need amidst the rising risks of the Conflagration Era. With ever-growing numbers of cities, buildings, machines, and consumer goods marked with the UL label or encompassed by an NFPA standard, the fire experts now had an established position without having to justify their claims either to technical or policy mastery.[66]

During World War I, William Henry Merrill served as section committee chairman of the Fire Prevention Section of the War Industries Board. His responsibilities included assessing fire risks in munitions plants and other plants doing war work. This effort enlisted not only Merrill but also the insurance industry, along with state fire marshals and municipal fire prevention officials.[67] This war work, though, was not the first time UL had come into contact with the federal government. For, at the same time that UL was growing geographically into a national laboratory, its scientific testing work, and its network of collaborative institutions similarly broadened in scope. An indication of this expansion involves its connection with the United States National Bureau of Standards (NBS). The NBS was created in 1901 and took over the work of establishing the national standards of weight and measurement from the Treasury Department. Under the authority of the United States Department of Commerce, the NBS analyzed industrial standards and served as a center for information on technical standardization work through its serial publications, the *Technologic Papers* and the *Journal of Research*.[68] Soon, however, the NBS was called upon to advise on government purchases, which led it into product and materials performance testing not unlike that conducted at UL. Seeing perhaps a way to gain outside endorsement of its methods of testing and standards, and to receive outside consultation on technical matters, UL approached the NBS on a number of occasions to give opinions. Connections were established between NBS director S. W. Stratton and William Henry Merrill, and at times inspection visits were arranged where UL engineers could see what their government counterparts were doing, and vice versa.[69] In 1911 William Henry Merrrill (on behalf of the NFPA) testified before the House Committee on Public Buildings and Grounds. He asserted that the federal government was in a position to set an example through the fire protection measures it applied to its own buildings. Merrill even enjoyed an opportunity to speak with President Taft on this trip. More formal connections were forged as both the NBS and UL sent representatives to serve on the voluntary standard-setting code councils, such as the National Electrical Code Committee. Here, for example, UL engineer (and future president of the labs) Merwin Brandon met Morton G. Lloyd of the Safety Standards Section of the Bureau of Standards, and the two shared information about the work and the history of their institutions. The Bureau was also known to use UL for factory inspections and label service as a means to make sure that the equipment the government was buying matched up with the specifications of the NBS—exactly the same use to which many private manufacturers put UL field inspectors.[70]

Collaborative testing was a way for fire experts to establish consensus, as well as learn from one another, and display their technical acumen. In 1903, the British Fire Prevention Committee released its "Standards for Fire Tests." These standards were intended to set guidelines for the relationship between the time and temperature variables used in fire tests, primarily fire tests of structural materials such as iron and steel beams. In 1913, Ira Woolson, a consulting engineer with the NBFU, was named chairman of the Committee for Fireproof Construction with the National Fire Protection Association; he also served with the American Society for Testing and Materials (ASTM). Though the British standards were considered a good pattern, it was found that these classifications were not in line with the temperatures used in tests conducted at Underwriters Laboratories. Woolson therefore called for a joint effort between the ASTM and UL to study the subject of "Standard Specifications for Fire Tests." ASTM was founded in 1898 by a coalition of businessmen and testing engineers in Philadelphia; its work included collection and distribution of standards for nearly all industrial materials. Like UL, it was an attempt to focus the time-consuming, geographically dispersed, and multidisciplinary work of industrial materials standardization in one institution.[71] A roll call of the organizations taking part in the time and temperature tests gives insight into the diversity of the fire expert community:

Committee on Fire-resistive Construction, NFPA
Committee on Fireproofing, ASTM
National Bureau of Standards
Underwriters Laboratories
Associated Factory Mutual Fire Insurance Companies
American Institute of Architects
American Society of Mechanical Engineers
American Society of Chemical Engineers
Canadian Society of Civil Engineers
American Concrete Institute

The result of the conferences held in 1916 and 1917, composed of these organizations, included primarily an agreement to adhere to a Standard Time Temperature Curve in fire tests. The standards adopted were broken down into different classifications, according to different levels of fire resistance offered by structural materials, and included four-, two-, and one-hour protection. Such standards were in keeping with those already in place at UL and the ASTM, and now stood as the dominant standards across most of the building trades and the engineering professions.[72]

While the Standard Time and Temperature Curve tests were taking place, UL was also in the midst of one of the most ambitious and most influential standard setting ventures it would ever undertake: the "Fire Tests of Building Columns" project. The Factory Mutuals were growing increasingly anxious, just as the NBFU was, about the conflagration hazard in American cities. In 1910 the Factory Mutuals proposed that a series of tests be conducted on building columns, and it sought out and received cooperation from the NBFU, in conjunction with UL. The motive for first conducting the tests was the lack of authoritative information on the ways that building columns would stand up to fires. Because there was uncertainty on safe methods of construction, there were "wide variations in building code requirements." This seemed particularly troubling as, of course, the first three decades of the twentieth century saw a remarkable growth and elaboration of the urban skyscraper as a signal feature of the cityscape. It was an era of great experimentation and one-upsmanship for architects, which delighted corporate patrons eager to fill offices while simultaneously showing off their corporate power in majestic downtown structures. From Daniel Burnham's Montauk Building (1882) in Chicago and Flatiron Building (1903) in New York, to Cass Gilbert's Woolworth Building (1913), to William Van Alen's Chrysler Building (1930), the sky-scraper defined the modern urban landscape. This landscape, just as the electrical landscape developing at the same time, presented both opportunities and terrors for insurance companies and fire safety experts. Preparatory work for the building columns tests, including the construction of a large testing furnace and a testing machine to compress the heated beams, began in 1912.[73]

The purpose of the Fire Tests of Building Columns project was to find out first "the ultimate resistance against fire of protected and unprotected columns as used in the interior of buildings," and second "their resistance against impact and sudden cooling from hose streams when in a highly heated condition."[74] Engineers noted that "columns form the most impor-tant element in the strength of a building, [yet] few representative tests have been made to determine their ability to support load when exposed to fire, and fire experience has only a limited value, due to the many unknown variables involved."[75]

UL engineers designed the testing equipment and finished it in 1917, with a cost estimated at $35,000, shared by UL, the Factory Mutuals, and a third institutional player, the NBS. At UL's Chicago lab a testing room was constructed, seven feet square and twelve feet high, built of heavy masonry and topped by a hydraulic ram that Brearley described as a sort of animal force. The ram, he said, "rears itself forty-five feet . . . a ram of such enor-mous power that it might have pulled the building from its foundations, had not special foundations been constructed to support it." In the room heat was built up to simulate a conflagration, while "The ram . . . [exerts] a downward thrust equal to the weight of many stories."[76]

The actual testing took place in 1917–1918. The tests included 106 types of columns, each type subjected to heat, compression, and water tests. The columns were also tested and compared as to the level of protection offered by a range of different types of fire-protective coverings, such as concrete, gypsum, and terra cotta tile. According to "accepted formulas" the columns were designed to hold 100,000 pounds. The load was maintained on the column constantly, "the efficiency of the column or its covering being determined by the length of time it withstood the combined load and fire exposure." Using the time-temperature curve, the column was heated and measurements were made of the furnace and the column. Deformations in the column were noted and photographed. Fire and water tests followed with similar heating and compression, but after a predetermined period the furnace doors were thrown open and the column was sprayed with a hose.[77] At UL, William Robinson was in charge of the tests, assisted by several engineers, including Fitzhugh Taylor, who was also a professor in the Armour Institute's fire protection engineering department.[78] Temperature and deformation testing equipment was supplied by the NBS. Further physical and chemical tests of the columns and the protective coverings were made at the Pittsburgh and Washington labs of the NBS.[79] Concrete analysis was done by the Department of Geology at the University of Chicago.

The structural materials used in the tests—the steel, iron, and timber columns and the protective materials—were largely donated by industrial manufacturers. These manufacturers stood to gain the goodwill of the fire experts, while at the same time gathering valuable data about their products, data available only from research and development of a type too technical and too expensive for most companies to pursue. In this sense, UL was again functioning as a sort of research and development lab to industrial clients. The results of these tests were studied by a wide range of fire experts—they were published in the NBS *Technologic Papers* series, also in the *Engineering News-Record*, and as a book by UL. These results imposed a consensus-driven set of standards on a complex technology that demanded (and demands today) a wide range of expert opinion for its success: the American high-rise building. Considering the wide range of institutions involved—manufacturers, government researchers, university scientists, fire safety experts, and fire insurance professionals—the *Fire Tests of Building Columns* illustrates the strongest evidence one might find in its day of the growing maturity and complexity of the American fire expert network. Fire experts were by then working across disciplines and jurisdictions, conducting original research in nonprofit institutional settings, and using their results to influence both public and private sector clients. A follow-up to this test was conducted by the NBS in conjunction with the NFPA in 1928 when two entire buildings were allowed to burn completely, in order to test the "actual fire behavior of brick joisted buildings as compared with the assumed fire conditions of the standard time-temperature curve." Such an expensive test was possible in this case because of government purchase of a plot of land and the need to remove existing buildings from it. From these tests flowed influential standards written and applied by the NBS for federal buildings, and UL, ASTM, and NFPA all focused on commercial builders.[80]

In the 1920s the growth of inter-industry groups came to a high point, and the interactivity of these groups was productive of a blizzard of new standards and codes. The different national engineering societies banded together with the U.S. War Department, the Navy, and the National Bureau of Standards in 1918 to form the American Engineering Standards Committee. This group grew from the interaction of engineers and the military in World War I, and was focused on promoting standard-setting as a collaborative process involving both private and governmental bodies in the "consensus" model. Ten years later, this organization evolved into the American Standards Association. This group put itself forward as a meta-level standards clearinghouse, standardization and consensus-code facilitator, and promoter of United States standards worldwide. Though the fire protection experts participated in ASA activities and sat on ASA committees, the leadership of the group was composed of presidents of some of the country's largest corporations. The outlook of the ASA was decidedly production oriented, not necessarily risk-oriented, with the group looking to achieve standardization in industries like steel and electrical goods. This kind of inter-industry cooperation was the hallmark of 1920s associationalism, and showed the aspirations of corporate leaders and business enthusiasts for a modern economy in which corporate capitalism would function best with limited oversight and maximum cross-industry collaboration. Standard-setting was technical work, but it demonstrated the ways that firms could police themselves, a fundamental argument against government regulation. Of course the Great Depression and the coming of FDR's National Recovery Administration would dampen the mood of the standard-setters somewhat, but during World War II their networks of collaboration were mobilized by the government itself in the war effort.

Of particular importance was the introduction of the building code groups into this process. As has been discussed, the United States had no tradition of centralized land use law, and the path to zoning, height restrictions, and building codes was a long and uneven one. The NBFU and NFPA had both promoted model building codes—paying special attention to the conflagration hazard—since 1905. And while the construction industry may not have agreed with the fire experts on every point, they did envy their methods of persuasion enough to copy them. In 1915 building officials from 9 states and Canada convened to establish the Building Officials Code Administrators International (BOCA) in Illinois. The International Conference of Building Officials (ICBO) convened, and published its first Uniform Building Code in 1927 in California. The Southern Building Code Congress International, Inc. (SBCCI) was founded in 1940 in Birmingham, Alabama.[81]

These groups created a loosely organized national network of code writers covering the nation, functioning precisely as had the fire code groups, employing a sort of "democracy of experts" idea to achieve technical consensus, and to also forestall federal intervention into their work. Like the fire experts the building code experts served as intermediaries between state and municipal government and the private sector. The building code groups also worked closely with the NFPA, UL, and other inter-industry groups to understand and apply the fire protection techniques that fire experts were establishing, but naturally with greater representation and focus on the construction industry and details of construction going beyond fire safety. In this way, the consensus code process extended directly into the construction industry, in part bridging a divide between fire insurers and builders that had a very long history.

From what we have seen thus far the fire experts were almost entirely focused on building environments and setting standards for safety that would prevent consumers from causing fires and/or injuring themselves and others. It is clear, for example, from the ways that UL engineers structured their consumer product tests—irons left on for weeks at a time in contact with flammable materials, simulated broom handle whackings of television picture tubes—that their model of a consumer was the harried housewife or her clumsy husband. And, judging from the bounty of fire narratives that UL collected featuring hapless and forgetful consumers, and from the advice they gave to consumers through their films, lectures, and publications, UL saw the consumer and the engineer as two quite different types of people. One would not imagine a UL testing engineer needing a reminder not to use "electrical equipment for playful experimenting or practical joking." Likewise, advisories not to "use lamps, irons or toasters to warm beds in the winter," might seem unnecessary to the engineer, or to the manufacturers of lamps, irons, and toasters—the producers. At the end of the day, UL saw producers and consumers as separate sorts of people, a view that informed UL's commitments to "casualty work." As William Henry Merrill explained in 1916, it was this consumer-focused work that had won goodwill with government, and thus it was and remained a central focus for the labs. However, consumers were also beginning to look at the possibilities of establishing institutions answerable to their specific interests.

By the time of the Great Depression consumers were asking serious questions about the failures of the mass-production/mass-consumption economy. What *is* in the products we buy? Am I getting a good price? How safe is it? Under what labor conditions are these goods produced? Such questions, exacerbated by the deprivations of the era, gave rise to a variegated movement of consumer advocacy organizations in the United States, the most influential among them being Consumers Research, Incorporated (CR), and its spin-off organization, Consumers Union (CU). These institutions gathered information about consumer risks and consumer products from whatever sources they could find—newspaper articles, popular magazines like *Good Housekeeping*, the Bureau of Standards, Underwriters Laboratories, and the American Standards Association, for example—and began to spread the call for informed buying of safe and reliable products. Manufacturers, and the advertising agencies they hired, came under attack for filling the nation's homes with, among all manner of products, dangerous medicines, impure foods, and shoddy electrical goods.

CR and CU also sought, whenever possible, to perform their own comparative product tests, along with tests for safety and performance. These two testing functions were related but served two different needs. Comparative testing gave consumers a sense of what products were in the stores, and how they fared against each other. Few consumers could afford to sample widely from their supermarket shelves in order to compare taste, quality, and value. Safety and performance testing pushed products to their failure points, something that consumers rarely ever did, at least on purpose. Such tests revealed hidden weaknesses and dangers, and by extension revealed rip-offs and fraudulent advertising claims about product durability. Taken together, comparative testing and safety testing were technically demanding, expensive, and time-consuming, three factors often at odds with the impetus of consumer advocates to rapidly build a body of evidence on which to achieve a "consumer consensus" and drive the movement forward.

Consumers Research, Inc. (CR) was the first institution in the consumer movement devoted entirely to spreading and articulating a consumer-centered ideology focused on product testing and the free flow of product performance and safety specifications. Known around Greenwich Village in 1927 simply as the consumer's club, this organization formed around the work of American Standards Association (ASA) engineer Frederick J. Schlink, and noted social activist Stuart Chase. Before joining the ASA, in fact, Schlink had held positions at the Bureau of Standards and Bell Laboratories. He was, therefore, perfectly familiar with the early efforts of R&D engineers and safety experts trying to standardize products across multiple lines of expertise, geographical barriers, and methods of manufacture.[82]

Suspicious of many of the common household products on the market, CR's serial publication, the *Consumers' Research Bulletin*, often exhorted readers to "make their own," rather than buying products of a suspect quality. Recipes appeared in the *Bulletin* for many everyday items, including breakfast cereal, toothpaste preparations, paint and varnish. By this time there were 2000 CR members, who paid $2.00 each year in dues, and in return received CR's publications. By 1932 CR had 42,000 subscribers, and Schlink expanded the operation, moving out of New York City to Washington, New Jersey.[83]

In its early years CR tested few products at its headquarters. When it did perform tests, on shock hazards of electrical products for example, Schlink was clear that CR's goals were different from other testing labs. "Our tests do not agree in all respects with those made by the Underwriters' Laboratories," he explained. While UL was concerned with a broad range of fire hazards, Schlink was more interested in tests that analyzed the specific risks presented by individual appliances, as they were used in the home. He felt that "appliances tested at Consumers' Research are tested under circumstances closely paralleling those in which they will be used by the consumer."[84] CR's base of cooperative labs and investigators was wide, including established private laboratories like the Electrical Testing Laboratory in New York City. Spelling out CR's approach to "contracting out" its testing work, Schlink wrote that "Tests and examination of large or elaborate appliances are done under our direction in outside laboratories adequately equipped for such work, and normally we undertake such tests only when we are arranging for the examination of a number of different brands of a given commodity at the same time, for comparative purposes."[85]

Many of the outside tests were done on a volunteer basis under more informal arrangements. CR had about 200 "volunteer consultants," many of them home economists and sympathetic academics and scientists. Many of these tests were made at university and college labs or at small, private testing labs. Most of this testing was done "as a labor of love," in many cases at "outrageously low prices." R. C. Emmons, for example, tested refrigerators and air conditioners for CR at the University of Wisconsin. Dewey Palmer, a former physics teacher, and early CR employee remembered that such people "from the university and even from private laboratories . . . had seen some of the reports, knew about the efforts to publish this information, and liked the idea and wanted to help." In cases where they could not perform a test asked of them, CR referred people to institutions like the American Standards Association and the American Society for Testing Materials.[86] Rather than having to cast about too much for help, though, CR's staff soon found themselves inundated with information, too much even to effectively publish.[87] With the publication of Schlink and Arthur Kallet's *100,000,000 Guinea Pigs: Dangers in Everyday Foods, Drugs, and Cosmetics* in 1933, CR gained an even greater level of publicity.[88] The book sold extremely well, and brought intense scrutiny on everyday consumer items like Kellogg's All-Bran breakfast cereal, Pepsodent toothpaste, Crisco, and Listerine. Kallet was an MIT-educated engineer, served on CR's board, and like Schlink also had worked for the American Standards Association. With the success of *100,000,000 Guinea Pigs* CR continued its expansion, with a staff of more than 50 by 1935.

Consumers Union Reports acted just as its name implied: it was an instrument by which consumers could act as a union, and receive information not only about the safety and reliability of products, but also about the labor conditions under which a product was made. Consumers Union established early and lasting contacts with sympathetic scientists and academics, much as CR had done. But, CU also worked to build a stronger public identity than CR had managed to create. Thus, publicity, image and presentation were important to CU. Where *Consumers Research Bulletin* often appeared to be slapped together, jammed with lists of test results, Consumers Union intentionally designed *Consumer Reports* magazine to grab attention, with photographs and graphics inside, and photographs on the cover. CU gained wide public attention, positive and negative, when it published a report on contraceptives in 1937. Despite the left-leaning politics of many of CU's managers and staff, the magazine remained politically neutral in its pages. Investigation by the Dies Committee into CU's connections with communists in 1938 went nowhere, and the organization pressed on with its formula of supplying technical information to consumers, while at the same time holding to the earlier CR-style "everybody is a consumer" ethos. The formula worked. Starting with 3000 charter members, the number shot up to 40,000 the next year, and by 1939 *Consumer Reports* circulation was up to 85,000.[89]

The consumer movement was about more than criticizing industry and advertisers, more than product comparisons and testing. Consumer advocates were promoting an antidote for the exclusions and inefficiencies of industrialized democracy, they were calling for what historian Lizabeth Cohen has termed a "consumer's republic." At one level this transformation—embracing and often directly borrowing the tools of fire safety developed by the NBFU, the Factory Mutuals, safety investigators like John Ripley Freeman, and UL—grew naturally from the desire to test products independently. At another level, the move to scientific safety and performance testing insulated the consumer advocates from charges of political radicalism, while preserving their relevance to generations of consumers who did not see consuming as a political act. Like the fire safety experts that preceded them, the consumer safety experts used multi-disciplinary investigations, information sharing among a network of testing and standard-setting bodies, and laboratory research as means by which to capture authority over a specific body of knowledge—the efficiency, value, and safety of consumer products.

Speaking to the convention of the International Electric Protective Association in Chicago in 1922, UL Casualty Department engineer C. R. Alling asserted that his company was the first "national laboratory" devoted to fire protection. He developed for the audience a hypothetical case to illustrate the extreme need that had prevailed among manufacturers for fire protection, fire prevention, and electrical appliances before the days of UL. He asked the audience to suppose that a wired-glass window manufacturer submitted his window for testing at an insurance testing lab in Atlanta and the window was accepted. The same manufacturer might then submit the same window in Chicago, only to be rejected. Suppose that the manufacturer then makes a bid to install his windows on a skyscraper in Cincinnati. His window wins the contract, and at the same time ten or twelve fire insurance companies bid to insure the building. A problem erupts: insurance companies that privileged the Atlanta agency would insure and give a discount for the window, but those from other parts of the country would

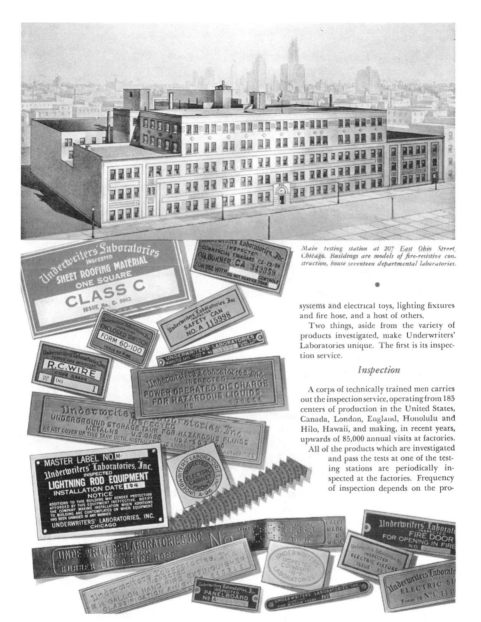

Main testing station at 207 East Ohio Street, Chicago. Buildings are models of fire-resistive construction, house seventeen departmental laboratories.

•

systems and electrical toys, lighting fixtures and fire hose, and a host of others.

Two things, aside from the variety of products investigated, make Underwriters' Laboratories unique. The first is its inspection service.

Inspection

A corps of technically trained men carries out the inspection service, operating from 185 centers of production in the United States, Canada, London, England, Honolulu and Hilo, Hawaii, and making, in recent years, upwards of 85,000 annual visits at factories.

All of the products which are investigated and pass the tests at one of the testing stations are periodically inspected at the factories. Frequency of inspection depends on the pro-

Figure 7. Underwriters Laboratories labels and the Chicago UL headquarters. From *UL: A Symbol of Safety, A Report of 50 Years of Continuous Service* (Chicago: Underwriters Laboratories, 1944), 10. Courtesy of Underwriters Laboratories, Inc.

Figure 8. Automatic fire sprinkler test at Underwriters Laboratories. "The distribution of water by an automatic sprinkler is carefully determined in this Laboratory with cross-sectioned walls and ceiling and floor covered with buckets each one square-foot in area." From *UL: A Symbol of Safety, A Report of 50 Years of Continuous Service* (Chicago: Underwriters Laboratories, 1944), 27. Courtesy of Underwriters Laboratories, Inc.

not. This was only one type of complication that was typical in the age before UL's dominance in product testing and listing. The result of many thousands of manufacturers submitting their products to hundreds of different testing labs nationwide, Alling suggested, could only be chaos. "Mr. Merrill . . . conceived the idea of a really national laboratory and with this in mind," Alling said, "and placed his proposition before the National Board of Fire Underwriters, an organization comprising over one hundred and eighty stock fire insurance companies operating in this country and Canada."[90] Whether or not UL's mission as a national laboratory was democratic, whether or not it considered the risks of the homeowner and the factory worker, and whether or not UL's standards might begin to lose their rigor and quality when the institution no longer had any competition for its authority were questions left unasked.

Revolt Against the Fire Experts

A great deal of the fire experts' success was dependent on their ability to work among highly competitive commercial interests while maintaining an aura of detachment from the considerations of profit. Research and development labs like Bell Labs and General Electric often had this problem in winning young scientists away from academia in favor of the corporate lab. Though corporate R&D promised greater remuneration for scientists and engineers, it threatened to tie them to the greater good of the corporation rather than the greater good of knowledge creation for society. In response to this concern, many labs developed strict lines between the commercial and the scientific realms of their business. This could dispel worries about squandering technical talent in the commercial rat race. Framing their R&D activities in this way—as university-oriented and public-spirited— also helped high-tech firms like AT&T and General Electric to avoid antitrust action, as they successfully argued to the Justice Department that they were "public monopolies," turning out scientific research and complex technologies that also served the public interest.[91]

Underwriters Laboratories, as a nonprofit testing lab, was understandably touchy about its close connections to the fire insurance industry. It was a conundrum that many engineers and scientists faced at the time (and today), wishing to turn their time and attention to the betterment of society while at the same time advancing their careers. One UL commentator addressed the concern frankly, stating that "Public service may indeed be tied up with purely business motives, and, if this were the case at . . . [UL], or its branches, no apology need be offered, since the making of money is a legitimate and necessary human activity. By the choice of its founders, however, Underwriters' Laboratories has no commercial character. It makes no profits. It pays no dividends."[92] Additionally, the commentator reasoned that "It is the fashion on the part of some narrow-minded . . . people to deprecate the interest of fire insurance people in fire prevention as a sordid matter of larger profits. . . . No human motive in this complicated world of ours may be considered 100 percent altruistic, but it is not improbable" that the stock insurance companies support work that is as "near to pure altruism as can be found in any business field."[93] According to this view, fire insurance was an inherently public-spirited enterprise, and could not be fairly considered as simply one among the pack of profit-driven industries. Furthermore, UL's nonprofit character promised to save it from any of the criticism one might level at comparable R&D labs as selling science for cash.

William Henry Merrill, writing in 1916, articulated the unique place he saw in the American political economy for UL. "I like to compare this situation," he explained, "to Mr. Rockefeller's act in establishing a hospital for medical research and to other foundations made by public-spirited men, who, of course, probably had a partly selfish motive in having some of their pet theories adequately and intelligently advanced." Railroads, utilities, life insurance—none of these industries had established a nonprofit lab quite like UL, he argued. "The "Laboratories' work is not an absolute necessity to an insurance company."[94] To Merrill that fact proved that UL's identity veered much closer to charity than it did to commerce. "I know of no other business that has contributed a quarter of a million dollars to any enterprise having the public welfare chiefly in mind."[95] William Henry Merrill was also expert in defining the activities of the institution he had built, working constantly to allay public fears that UL was out only to generate money for insurers. The credibility of UL's standards did not stand on the scientific merits of its research alone—authority over risk was also connected to the success or failure of the institution's efforts to define itself as serving public over purely private interests. The same could be said for the many other inter-industry and nonprofit standard setting groups working on fire disasters and material standards in this era.

A further concern, especially as the fire insurance industry was frequently accused of monopolistic activity, involved the issue of how UL's opinions influenced the writing of fire insurance policies. If it was demonstrated that UL exercised direct control over policy-writing, then its claims to authority based on the neutrality of its scientific mission might be substantially tarnished. One UL commentator, speaking directly to this issue in 1922, remarked that, "It can be appreciated that [anything] other than voluntary recognition of our work by . . . regulatory bodies, particularly underwriting bodies, would result in the establishment of a monopoly . . . and probably also in lessening the sense of responsibility and the inspiration to strive for this voluntary recognition, which, in our effort, takes the place of active competition in commercial pursuits."[96] This viewpoint sheds light on UL's intense efforts to publicize its activities and publish its test results and standards. In a sense, UL viewed publication and its "open door" policy of visits to the labs as the best mechanisms through which to maintain its reputation and simultaneously compete for business.[97] As one UL advocate put it, "It may chance that some of you have heard the Underwriters' Laboratories characterized . . . as an institution that restricts competition, boosts prices for favored products, and generally helps to betray the public . . . . please now be assured that . . . our detractors may easily obtain all desired data by addressing the Laboratories or any of its branches."[98]

In another way, though, UL's managers were happy to argue that their work did represent a monopoly of sorts. This line of reasoning fell right into line with UL's carefully cultivated identity as an organization that walked a thin and virtuous line between the competitive world of commerce and the dispassionate realm of science. "A claim to a monopoly in our work can be justified," they intoned, "so long as none other is equally competent in technique, in experience, in facilities, and in sincerity of our motives. Our goal, the complete elimination of fire waste, will be the sooner reached if loyal competent co-workers join in the fight." The key word here was "competent." For, there certainly were many manufacturers of fireproofing products in the United States at the time who might plausibly argue that their motives were directed toward the eradication of fire and the safety of the public. That such companies sought to achieve these ends through direct manufacturing and competition in the marketplace could reasonably present them as champions in the war on fire, and many advertised themselves in just this way. Moreover, we have already come across some of the vast number of local and state level institutions that worked to mitigate fire risk, such as underwriters' organizations, fire service officials and firefighters, and urban safety councils. So, in fact, UL did have a great number of competitors. UL responded, perhaps predictably, that they had "an obligation to state our earnest opposition to the activities of individuals, organizations, commissions, or similar bodies engaged in the classification of fire fighting equipment except that the motives, the ability, facilities and other most necessary equipment is available and skillfully employed.

Good intentions may be useful as paving brick in a well known place. They do not replace knowledge and skill in the preservation of life or of property from loss by fire."[99] In short, in their view UL had a monopoly on expertise and the responsibility to use this monopoly to influence both manufacturers and government officials.

Another criticism, leveled in 1922 by the burglary protection industry, involved the fact that UL was, in effect, one laboratory testing products that required multiple types of installation, without having any experience in installation. The accusation painted UL's testing engineers as too far removed from the specifics of on-the-job improvisation and the realities of fire safety on the ground to have the real expertise possessed by the burglar-alarm technician, or by extension the builder, the electrician, and the fireman. The UL response to this criticism was to build a case for the power of UL's generalized approach to fire safety, willing to apply standard setting and laboratory practice on all facets of manufacturing and installation:

> We have the same answer for this industry that we have had in the rubber-covered wire industry, the automatic sprinkler industry and some ten thousand others with which we have an intimate point of contact; that is, that we do not assume to know all details of the manufacture and installing end of the game as well as those who have been in the business for years, but our staff is composed of technically trained engineers, and the fundamental principles involved in the proper performance of burglary protection appliances are the same as those of any other industry. It is only natural to assume that where an engineer has had opportunity of examining a large number of systems of any particular class and has the engineer's perspective, he can readily perceive the good and bad qualities of any individual system.[100]

UL was also sensitive to problems that might arise when listed products were improperly installed or architects and building contractors misunderstood the UL listings. In a theoretical case presented in *Laboratories' Data* involving fire doors, we learn about UL's notion of responsibility for using the label. In this example, an architect specified tin-clad fire doors with the UL label for a building; the building contractor ordered "and [placed] in position on openings in a 'fire wall' six tin-clad fire doors" with the UL label "for opening in corridor or room partition." That is, the contractor used labeled doors, but the wrong kind. The property owner paid for the doors, but the fire insurance inspector refused to pass them as he would have had they been labeled "for opening in fire wall." The article seeks to answer the question of who is at fault in this type of mix-up.[101] The article reasoned that it can be generally assumed that the property owner is unfamiliar with fire safety requirements and thought he had covered himself well by hiring an architect. A "conscientious contractor would point out to the owner or the architect that certain types of doors were not suitable for the situation in which they were placed." The contractor should know the difference between a fire wall and a corridor or room partition. But the architect came off worse. According to UL, "the architect did not specify exactly what type doors were required in the opening. . . . it is part of his business to familiarize himself with such requirements. If he does not have the information at hand he may very easily obtain it by consulting his local rating bureau."[102] In conclusion, UL held that the architect was primarily responsible for the error, and the contractor can be criticized if he failed to call the situation to the attention of the architect. The owner is excusable. Not surprisingly, the "person connected with the matter who appeared to know his job was the insurance inspector, who very properly refused to pass doors which were not labeled as suitable for the openings in which they were used."[103] The proposed solution to such problems was to educate architects about fire protection and UL-listed materials.

In an actual case from the field, UL New York agent C. J. Krieger addressed the sort of problem that might arise when the sanctity of the label came into question. A town of 30,000 people decided to purchase UL-listed 2-inch hose for its fire department. The city officials had never used labeled hose, and so were skeptical, watching a test of the hose closely. The city lodged an "indignant protest" as a length of the hose failed at low pressure, 180 pounds. Krieger ran up to the town to investigate. He found that cotton threads surrounding the rupture points had been burned. "A casual mention of the fact by the writer," Krieger recalled, "nearly caused a riot. How could the hose burn? It had never been near a fire or spark." Chemical tests indicated that it had indeed burned. The fire chief was asked to repeat his test so that Krieger and the city officials might observe. Water was pumped out of a canal and discharged back into the canal, but to avoid stretching the hose over a railroad track it was stretched over the top of a heavy fence, topped by rough timbers. The hose touched the wooden beams in three places. And, at each, smoke was seen once the pumping was underway. Krieger was vindicated, arguing that "The evidence was complete; all the city officials who had witnessed the test agreed that an abnormal and abusive test condition had ruined the hose, and that there was consequently no justifiable criticism of labeled hose under the circumstances." The writer took two morals from this episode: a fire chief is not a testing engineer; and, criticisms of labeled hose, and by extension any criticism of the UL label, should always be thoroughly investigated.[104]

One type of potentially damaging threat to UL's reputation was that coming from manufacturers who challenged test results. If a manufacturer could demonstrate negligence, lack of professionalism, or worst of all bias on the part of UL's testing engineers, the dependability of the label might come into question. A case erupted in 1915 that threatened to do just that: a disagreement between the Economy Fuse and Manufacturing Company and UL. The Economy Company had won the UL label for its fuse in 1912. Since that time, UL contended, the design of the fuse had changed in such a way as to render it unsafe—the major problems being that it had not seen adequate testing and that it could easily be tampered with by users. Economy refused to accept UL's judgment on the primary basis that thousands of Economy fuse customers were pleased with the safe operation of the present model of their fuse. Neither side willing to back down, the dispute received a unique public arbitration hearing at the NBS headquarters in Washington, D.C., in 1915.

The first matter discussed at the hearing involved NBS qualifications and authority to pass judgment on such a case. NBS director S. W. Stratton discussed the fact that UL had asked for technical advice in many cases, and UL had also sought to establish an arrangement whereby the NBS would adjudicate disputes that might arise between itself and its clients. Stratton endorsed this plan, in part because it seemed to mark "an important period in the Bureau's history." As a government lab the NBS could claim impartiality, a claim UL itself usually made successfully, but not in this instance. In one way, Stratton's assuming the role as an industrial mediator fit in with the role the Progressive Era federal government was establishing as a mediator in anti-trust and labor disputes, banking, and the conservation movement. In another sense, he was reacting to the broader desire previously discussed among technical experts to seize control of debates on technical matters. Stratton voiced this desire, finding the proceedings a "break away from . . . exceedingly expensive and senseless legal fights regarding technical matters, nine-tenths of which can be settled if scientific men and engineers will get together and honestly endeavor to find out the facts and settle the question upon those facts and the facts alone."[105] In his opening remarks for UL, after effusively praising the NBS, William Henry Merrill seconded Stratton's remarks, adding that, "In certain of the courts you have to face juries, not of intelligent, educated men versed in the science of the particular thing that may be under consideration, but such men as are picked up in the street or chosen by raffle of some kind."[106]

The Economy Company's attorney, R. J. Foote, posed what appeared to be a simple question, one on which he intended to make his case for the utility and the safety of the Economy fuse. The question was "Has it been shown that the use of the fuses manufactured by the Economy Fuse & Manufacturing Co., results in no greater fire or accident hazard than the use of other . . . fuses at present approved by the Underwriters' Laboratories (Inc.)?"[107]

To begin to answer this question, Foote stated that Economy had 7,080 customers in the United States, Europe, Canada, and South America, a full list of which had been turned over to the NBS. He argued that the popularity and wide usage of Economy fuses was the key point in favor of the company. Foote then complained that Economy had received great opposition from "certain insurance organizations of nation-wide activity and from competitors who have left no stone unturned to stop the growth of the company's business." But, he reasoned, if the Economy fuse were such an inferior and dangerous product it could never have gained so many customers, especially in the face of opposition from powerful industrial and insurance interests. Then he leveled a serious accusation: "The making and selling of cartridge-inclosed (sic) fuses has been a large, profitable business, controlled for years by a few . . . companies. . . . It is, to those who know the real facts of the fuse situation, not surprising that the [Economy Company's] entrance into this . . . field . . . should provoke a storm of criticism and engender opposition from every possible quarter."[108] The NBFU and UL were clearly implicated here in using their network of fire safety experts to restrain trade. Foote continued, claiming that even "expert opinion" had been wrongfully turned against the Economy fuse, and therefore "the answer to the question submitted is not to be determined by the announcement of opinion, expert or otherwise, when not based on the facts of experience."[109] Clearly, to Economy, the "facts of experience" went against UL's opinion, an opinion that needlessly "discriminated" against their product. With thousands of satisfied customers, Economy rested its case on the experience of the user over the engineer.

In William Henry Merrill's testimony he developed a history of the Economy fuse, arguing "several radical changes had been made in its construction since its advent three years ago." He admitted that the first Economy fuse had proved up to UL standards, but that it had been through several iterations since and was now completely unlike the original model. Whereas the first model contained a powdered filler, a second model had a shredded asbestos filler and a third no filler whatsoever. Merrill stated flatly that he did "not understand . . . [how] the manufacturer contends that the shredded asbestos fuse was in any way successful . . . under experimental laboratory conditions . . . or that it was a successful fuse in service."[110] Furthermore, Merrill claimed, most of the affidavits from industrial users of Economy fuses and technical experts who had found the fuse acceptable, including the city electrician of Chicago, were in fact thinking of the older Economy model and not the current design. And, as to the opinions of actual users, Merrill was unreserved in his scorn. He related the case of a dry-powder fire extinguisher that had won wide approval of industrial users in Chicago, joking that the UL staff had stopped counting the endorsements they received for the extinguisher but had taken to measuring them by the foot. In the end, it was this same extinguisher that had been found useless at the horrific Iroquois fire in 1903. Only those who "have given it study for a number of years, who have made tests from year to year" were qualified to assess the Economy fuse, and this required more time and much more study.[111] On a purely technical level, the primary objection UL had to the present model Economy fuse was that it allowed the user to easily refill the fuse element himself, rather than a trained technician; this was seen to be a potential hazard.

The NBS, in addition to holding the hearing, conducted a number of tests on Economy and competitor fuses in its labs and in power plants. These tests were done according to UL standards, as well as NBS standards, and those suggested by manufacturers. In sum, NBS inspectors found that Economy fuses could indeed easily be refilled by users despite all the favorable testimony submitted on their behalf. This design invited disaster if unqualified users tampered with the fuse.[112] The NBS conducted three types of tests under short-circuit conditions: the first at its labs, the second at one of the Boston Edison power plants, and the third at a Commonwealth Edison plant in Chicago. Economy fuses were compared to six other makes of UL-approved cartridge fuses. Economy was found inferior to the other six in one test and to five in the other. In the third test, Economy was satisfactory. These tests were done according to UL testing specifications. The NBS noted that this sort of degradation in quality could happen with a device after UL approval. UL, they noted, generally demanded that the device be brought up to standard or lose its approval. The NBS engineers concluded that a new line of fuses that performed as these did would not be approved, and that they would have their approval removed if they were not improved in due time.

What could be said for Economy? The NBS found that there was no direct evidence that more fires or accidents had occurred due to the use of Economy fuses rather than approved fuses. The testimony of Economy users was favorable. And there were, of course, compensating advantages for a lower quality product, namely, reduced cost to the user.[113] Finally, the NBS issued its finding: though the evidence did not show that Economy fuses had resulted in greater fire or accident hazard, they recommended that Economy fuses *not* be approved for general use like those listed by UL. Continuation and extension of use could be permitted by "municipal and underwriters' inspection departments under conditions where their performance can be observed by each inspection department until sufficient experience . . . can be obtained to justify an unqualified approval or refusal to approve."[114] UL's argument had prevailed against damning criticism of its methods and its claims to the moral high ground of objective, scientific safety testing. The Economy fuse was not the top of the line article, but appeared to pose no great threat. It worked fine in most cases, was popular, and was inexpensive. But it had not been submitted patiently to the UL testing regimen, and it allowed the unskilled individual user too much leeway to alter its function. Therefore, Economy could not bear the "symbol of safety."

The consensus code system did not escape criticism from disgruntled manufacturers who wanted remedy not through expert arbitration, like the Economy company, but in the courts. In 1917, UL and the NBFU were ending their close financial relationship; the labs were established and able to earn enough income to continue expansion. Still, Merrill worried intensely about the perception among critics that the connection between the fire insurance industry and the labs was too close. This concern went all the way to a consideration of how UL described itself in the letterhead on its promotional materials. Merrill corresponded with NBFU officials frequently in 1917, wanting to change the language describing the labs from "Under the direction of" the National Board of Fire Underwriters to "Established by" the underwriters. In his letters to the underwriters, Merrill explained the reasons for his level of diligence over appearances of independence for the labs. First, he thought a political shift could cause "severance of our friendly relations with the authorities at Washington." In such an instance, "an ably or even intelligently presented case against us" might arouse the attention of the Attorney General. Having the Justice Department merely begin an anti-trust suit against UL could, he worried, cause the loss of millions of dollars in "injury to our goodwill." And he had an additional concern: the danger of a firm hostile to UL or the NBFU bringing a lawsuit simply for the "advertising value" it presented.[115]

Merrill's concerns were not paranoid. In 1912 the Gutta Percha and Rubber Manufacturing Company—representing about 30 makers of rubber fire and factory hose—brought a lawsuit against the National Board of Fire Underwriters for restraint of trade. News coverage cited the hose manufacturers' claim that the National Board and its "adjunct corporations"—the NFPA and UL—have "maliciously required that this plaintiff and other members of the manufacturers' committee before they could manufacture and sell their respective fire and factory hose must conform their product" to UL specifications and pay the cost of the UL Label.[116] It seemed that UL also "exercises the right to inspect from time to time all the processes . . . including secret processes" of the manufacturers. The hose manufacturers not participating in the suit were alleged "to have been approved" and "now have practically a monopoly of the business because of this approval." The complaint specifically cited the costs of the UL labels, 25 cents each, and that they were "wrongfully required" to purchase the labels. Also, the hose manufacturers cited the "thousands of circulars to the authorities having charge of the purchase of fire hose in cities of the United States, containing names of only" the companies bearing the UL label. The suit had broader implications, as the complaint directed attention to the roughly 100 other "appliances and commodities" going into buildings for which fire insurers required the UL label, a fact supposed to have caused 30,500,000 UL labels to have been sold in the previous year.

The Gutta Percha Case became a frequently cited precedent, but not for anything related to its content. The case was dismissed by the New York State Supreme Court, in essence because of the poor quality of the complaint, and it has become a textbook example of how not to write a complaint. The court found that that the number and the breadth of the accusations forced the judge and defendants to themselves sort out the plaintiff's charges, placing an undue hardship on the defendants. Still, the seed of real concern was planted. The Gutta Percha case actually showed the possibility for a manufacturer, or the public, or a court (most important) to look at the consensus code system and draw an entirely different set of conclusions from those promoted by UL, the NFPA, and their partners. In the testing process the plaintiffs found reason to complain: it was onerous and it potentially caused the revelation of trade secrets. The cost was unreasonable for the tests and for the labels certifying the quality of the product. In the promotions—the core business of the NFPA—the plaintiffs described an unfair advantage granted by the "thousands of circulars" and the fact that they were eagerly consulted by people, public officials in this case, who made purchasing decisions. The hose manufacturers had described in detail the entire consensus code system, and found in it the opposite of public service, testing for public safety, scientific neutrality, or any of the other merits fire experts had argued for so long and so strenuously. And despite the failure of this case, from 1912 forward the fire experts paid careful attention to every word they and others used in describing their motivations and their methods. Additional cases would follow, none strong enough to disrupt the successful workings of the consensus code system. But such criticisms would always remind the fire experts that they sat in a precarious position, with the specter of anti-trust prosecution and a return to their formerly limited status seemingly just one court decision away.

The End of the Conflagration Era

Though it had always operated under a nonprofit model, in 1936 UL applied for and formally chartered itself as a nonprofit corporation in Delaware. Despite the formal status, the IRS did not accept UL's claims to being a nonprofit company, leading to a case in tax court decided against UL, and finally an appeal brought by UL to the U.S. Seventh Circuit Court of Appeals in 1943. The issue before the court was whether UL could claim tax-exempt status as a 501(c)(3) organization, based on claims to its status as a "charitable, educational or scientific" organization, or whether it was an exempt "business league."

The court characterized UL as an organization conducting "research and investigations as to insurance risks and hazards for the National Board

[of Fire Underwriters]." It "conducts tests, experiments and investigations," mostly for insurance companies, but "data are also made available
to a wider group of the general public through publications, movies, and
the radio, all of which agencies of publicity extol the work and services of
the petitioner." The following facts were worthy of note by the court. At
the time of UL's application for nonprofit status it had $1.15 million in
assets. Seventeen regular members controlled its governance. The National
Board of Fire Underwriters carried as many votes as it had member companies, whereas other members had one vote each; UL had 15 trustees elected
by members, all but two of them officers of stock insurance companies.
Though UL operated in a nonprofit manner, and never paid dividends, in
1937 it earned a profit of $183,000. This was the amount in dispute, the
amount UL claimed should be tax exempt.

The court found against UL, and in its decision it called into question
the core claims to authority of fire experts across the board, even by extension those working in government, so long as what they did benefitted fire
insurance companies. The decision is worth quoting at length:

> This does not sound like charity to us. . . . It was not the public
> interest that prompted the establishment of the petitioner. It was
> financial gain and business advantage. The primary concern of the
> petitioner was that of its membership, made up almost entirely of
> insurance companies, and the manufacturers who paid its ample
> fees. Whatever benefit inured to the public was only incidental to
> the primary concern. . . . [UL did] enable someone to sell something
> to the public by giving to the public something better than it other-
> wise would have received. That may be good business, but it is not
> charity. . . . It did not operate on the basis of science for the sake of
> science. It was science for the sake of business . . . Most business
> today uses some kind of scientific process or methods. . . . The
> petitioner's business and not the public's education is primarily the
> purpose of the films, bulletins, and other literature circulated by
> the petitioner. . . . We know judicially that many business concerns
> conduct commercial testing laboratories for profit. The business in
> which the petitioner was engaged was a commercial testing labora-
> tory, and of a kind usually conducted for profit, and is not
> exempt.[117]

The very next year the Supreme Court overturned the longstanding precedent set by *Paul v. Virginia* in 1869 barring federal oversight of the insurance industry. In *United States v. South-Eastern Underwriters Association* the court found the insurance business to constitute "commerce," therefore falling under congressional oversight. The end of an era seemed to be at hand. A long period of evolution through which fire experts had gained authority in a novel realm of public-private governance was halted by a new way of conceptualizing insurance and a rejection of "nonprofit" as a fair description of UL, and by extension its peer institutions.

In fact, though, very little changed. Congress passed the McCarran-Ferguson Act in 1945, exempting insurance companies from the Sherman Anti-Trust Act so long as they were under state regulation, as all of them were by that time. Fire insurance remained under the control of states, leaving intact the power of the state fire bureaucracies that had emerged in the Progressive Era.[118] No federal fire insurance regulatory agency was created, and no sweeping federal land use restrictions were set in motion— actions that would have created a radically new way of imagining the relationship between disaster experts, the built environment, and the law. This is not to say, of course, that fire experts would have receded into history—the stakes of property loss and public safety were too high for that—but their institutional arrangements would have changed dramatically had the power of the federal government grown to encompass responsibility and authority over the risk of American fire disasters.

In the case of UL, the Seventh Circuit Court decision expressed the exact view UL and NFPA's critics had been voicing throughout their rise to prominence in fire protection—these were tools of monopoly, "information launderers" for insurance companies, out there creating standards for profit under the guise of "testing for public safety." Looking back over its 50 years in business at the time of the court's decision, UL estimated it had tested 375,000 products. With a failure rate of 50 percent, this still meant that every year 5,000 manufacturers in 5,500 factories were producing half a billion UL "approved" goods across the country.[119] Not science, not education, not charity, but what? What was UL? It was an admixture of these things, defying easy categorization, as did all the most powerful fire disaster experts and expert institutions in the United States by 1945. The opinion of the IRS and one court decision, albeit from a powerful federal court, were not enough to turn back the momentum of the fire experts.

History might have unfolded differently had *Paul v. Virginia* been decided differently, if municipal officials had taken on the conflagration hazard vigorously, or if a single powerful fire disaster profession— protective and effective like medicine or law—had arisen and taken control of fire research and legislation across the country. But history had not unfolded differently, and the result was something unique to the industrializing United States, a field of disaster experts coming from many (sometimes vastly) different disciplines, working with variable authority both legal and advisory across jurisdictional boundaries, embedded in the private sector, and in government, and in the nonprofit sector, and largely by the 1940s trusted by the public. By mid-century the experts proved themselves to be no longer politically feeble, either. In 1954, Congress formally amended section 501(c)(3) of the tax code to explicitly include "testing for public safety" among the list of exemptions; UL's nonprofit status was upheld in that year and has not been overturned since.

Fire risk and fire disasters in the United States did not end by World War II, but they were strongly curtailed in certain types of products and certain urban geographies—and the fire experts' role in this process was crucial. UL's standards and its labels, what it termed its "symbols of safety," grew from obscurity to wide acceptance by fire experts and the general public alike as evidence that risk expertise and public service could come together to end conflagrations and manage fire risk in industrializing America. UL today remains the largest and most influential fire risk testing lab in the United States. Fire risk did not go away through the processes of risk research and education, political reform, voluntary standard setting, and consensus code work, but it was decisively shaped to fit norms acceptable to the broad range of interdisciplinary experts invited to the standard-setting table. Center city business districts stopped burning, and unsafe electrical products claimed fewer lives, marking the end of the American Conflagration Era by World War II. Of perhaps greater importance, the experts in fire risk and disaster established their methods of research, knowledge dissemination, and standard setting as a successful compromise between industrial control and government regulation. It provides us one crucial model for understanding how disaster knowledge and disaster policy coalesced over time into an effective system for risk and disaster control, in this instance for fire.

By the 1940s urban conflagrations were mostly a memory of an era receding from American life, the great wave of urbanization and industrialization. By this time it was the automobile and the airplane—not the railroad—that defined technological progress. The fire experts had made it through the Conflagration Era far stronger than they might have imagined—powerful in terms of their knowledge base, and also in the system they had established to use their knowledge to shape building and fire codes, city plans, and product specifications.

On July 28, 1945, a B-25 Mitchell bomber lost in the fog and attempting to land at LaGuardia airport crashed into the north side of the Empire State Building in New York. The impact left a hole in the side of the building between the 78th and 80th floors and ignited a fire that shot 15-foot flames into the air. The disaster killed 14 people, but the fire was out in 40 minutes —the highest building fire ever extinguished in American history. Perhaps the firemen got lucky that their equipment worked right or that the plane was not full of fuel, but to the public this was a symbol of safety. The tallest buildings could be built, the greatest cities could innovate, and disaster could be defeated through expertise and wise governance.[120]

Nine days later an atomic bomb destroyed Hiroshima.

4

Ten to Twenty Million Killed, Tops

Mr. President, I'm not saying we wouldn't get our hair mussed,
but I do say no more than ten to twenty million killed, tops, that
is, depending on the breaks.

—General Buck Turgidson

George C. Scott's performance as General Buck Turgidson in the 1964 film
Dr. Strangelove or: How I Learned to Stop Worrying and Love the Bomb is
notable, hilarious even, for the utter sincerity and optimism with which he
rationalizes the mass civilian deaths that will result from a nuclear exchange
with the Soviet Union. Of course, it may have been slightly funnier had
Americans not just come right to the brink of such a horror in the Cuban
Missile Crisis, though certainly less poignant. The use of nuclear weapons
in Japan in 1945 by the United States launched the world into the nuclear
age, and the successful Soviet detonation of an atomic bomb in 1949 signaled that a starkly new global political reality was at hand. The next major
conflict, it was presumed, would feature the use of nuclear weapons, and
this meant without a doubt that cities would be meeting the same fates they
met in World War II—they would be annihilated. Unless—unless expert
knowledge could be created and applied in the nation's urban centers
quickly enough to gird them for the coming battle.

The farce of General Turgidson's proposal for victory—"ten to twenty
million killed, tops"—was the reality of American civil defense experts in
the Cold War. If they could keep the body count that low in the face of
thermonuclear war they would have succeeded in developing and applying

a new type expertise to a radically new type of problem. As General Turgidson thumbs through his briefing book for the hair mussing but nevertheless winning "Plan R" strategy (presumably there were at least 17 preceding it), he is relying on expert research into nuclear war scenarios. Though most of it was classified at the time, director Stanley Kubrick was not too far off the mark—civil defense was the purview of Cold War era risk and disaster experts, and they produced study after study, plan after plan, designed to prepare the nation to survive, rebuild, and "prevail" in the face of a nuclear attack.

The Civil Defense Era marked a new chapter in the history of American disaster experts. The broad historical dynamic was very similar to the Conflagration Era: changed technological conditions gave rise to a new urban threat, a threat serious enough to bring urban life and urban growth to an end. And like the urban conflagration threat the nuclear threat prompted innovations among experts whose areas of knowledge seemed best suited to the problem. Also echoing the earlier era, the nuclear threat prompted technical innovations that redrew disciplinary lines, and public policy innovation that challenged the traditions of American federalism. For example, a broad sampling of problems posed by the nuclear threat demanded new knowledge in physics, fire science, urban planning, psychology, organizational sociology, law and public policy. A final central challenge hearkened back to the prewar struggle against fire, namely the thorny political problems that emerged from the desire to create one-size solutions rooted in abstract knowledge, and then implementing that knowledge through plans and policies that were effective in every unique city and town across the country.[1]

There were also serious differences, differences that allow for useful historical comparison between the two eras. The threat of urban conflagration had led over a 75-year period to a steady evolution of fire expertise, rooted not only in the science of fires but also in the implementation of fire safety in engineering practice, public policy, and public relations. In contrast, the Civil Defense Era arrived with the culmination of the Manhattan Project's three dedicated years (based on a half century of research in physics) of scientific output, resulting in the atomic bombs used on Japan. In 1949 the Soviet Union emerged as a nuclear competitor and the lines of the Cold War were drawn. In 1950 President Truman called for a coordinated civil defense and created the Federal Civil Defense Administration; Congress passed a sweeping Federal Civil Defense Act, charging the newly created

Federal Civil Defense Administration with preparing the nation's localities for shelter and evacuation, as well as training state and municipal government officials and the general public for nuclear attack readiness. This left a great deal of the organizational work to the states, who were expected to establish a system of interstate compacts in order to coordinate relief efforts with one another. With the outbreak of war on the Korean Peninsula in 1950 and the Soviet Union and the U.S. launching headlong into an arms race, by the time the nuclear experts had started their work in earnest in 1950 they were already behind.

Another key historical departure, the potential losses from a nuclear exchange were infinitely greater than the world had ever before seen. The fires caused by nuclear attacks in Hiroshima and Nagasaki were horrific, not to mention the damage from the blasts, and of course the lingering effects of radiation—and those two bombs were just the prototypes of far more powerful weapons to come. Finally, the nuclear war experts drew their authority from government, from the most serious promise of government, to protect its citizens from attack. From this the rest of the development of nuclear disaster expertise flowed, pure command and control: top down, and from Washington out. Though there were real difficulties to forcing the will of Washington, D.C., into localities, federal leadership was the essence of the claim to civil defense legitimacy. Without central control it is unlikely many states or cities would have done even what they did by way of preparation for nuclear attack.

Last, time was of the essence in a world on the edge of return to war. This may be the most critical distinction to bear in mind from the Conflagration Era, a time when the private insurance industry (for its own survival) led the initial attempts to understand and manage the dominant risk to cities of the time. The Civil Defense Era unfolded entirely within a wartime context, with military leaders and a military culture exerting the dominant influence over creating and implementing solutions to the nuclear disaster threat.

Analysis of the Civil Defense Era provides a new context for the two main trends outlined in this book: the interdisciplinary history of disaster expertise creation and the process by which it shapes normative judgments of acceptable risk inherent in safety standards and public policy. The resources pumped into civil defense research and preparations dwarfed previous urban risk and disaster preparations, even the extraordinary efforts of the insurance industry in the Conflagration Era. Civil defense experts concluded very quickly that nuclear attack would mimic the types of all-inclusive disasters common to American cities of the early twentieth city: conflagrations, earthquakes, floods, and pandemics. The most desirable kinds of preparations would be based on research—interdisciplinary research bringing together the various strands of knowledge necessary to understand the city as a system—and spot the vulnerabilities in the system before a disaster occurred. And, under the rubric of nuclear disaster research, several types of disaster experts developed tools of analysis that would outlive the nuclear threat, particularly disaster sociology and emergency management. The most devoutly "command and control-minded" civil defenders carried on their work throughout the period, but never developed much interest in the sociological and ecological research they were funding; nor did they expand their power base into municipal or state disaster policy in meaningful ways, as did the fire safety experts earlier in the century. We consider the reasons for that outcome in this chapter. By the late 1960s, though the Cold War carried on, mayors and governors began to vocally criticize the federal expenditures going to fallout shelters and civil defense training films as their cities dealt with floods, earthquakes, industrial accidents, and mounting losses from household fires.

The key concepts and attempts to implement a federally managed command and control model of nuclear disaster expertise are demonstrated particularly well by the case of Philadelphia. As the third largest city in the United States during much of the Cold War, and situated near the top of the manufacturing hierarchy, Philadelphia's civil defense concerns were those of every major city across the country. The plans were mostly on paper and never aroused public spirit or commitment. Only Washington displayed a deviation from the pattern exemplified by Philadelphia, and in Washington civil defense saw its only true success. Successful or not—and the metrics of success of course bear examination—the Civil Defense Era saw an army of disaster researchers spread out across the land dreaming and preparing for the worst, regardless of cost or public opinion.

Unlike the fire disaster consensus—growing from private knowledge creation efforts and ultimately including city and state government—disaster knowledge of the Civil Defense Era was created under secrecy and funneled from Washington out into the geographies of nuclear risk, the American cities that were expected to apply it. The process never worked in the sense of accomplishing meaningful preparedness or public trust, but the experts retained their power nevertheless, a puzzle worth examining. From the civil defender's point of view, the control of nuclear risk was too wrapped up in national security to be left to states and municipalities. The core of civil defense knowledge was so rooted in war planning and perpetuation of a federal defense bureaucracy that it would never be meaningfully integrated into planning for the more tangible risks and disasters that did affect American cities in the era. Nevertheless, the Civil Defense Era left a lasting mark on the history of American disaster research and disaster preparedness, a mindset of preparedness rooted in the professional imagination of nightmarish attack scenarios and military-style preparations for survival.

A Well-Planned Apocalypse

At 5:30 A.M. on February 13, 1951, Philadelphia mayor Bernard Samuel received a telephone call from Pennsylvania governor John Fine, informing him that "enemy planes were being tracked in the general direction of the Philadelphia-Camden area and that appropriate segments of the armed forces had been alerted and were actively defending that area."[2] Between 5:35 and 5:40 A.M., news broadcasters broke through regular programming and announced that three American cities had just been attacked with atomic weapons. Minutes later, two 80-kiloton atomic bombs exploded within 3 seconds of each other over the city. Almost six years after the bombings of Hiroshima and Nagasaki, two years after the Soviet Union's first atomic detonation, Philadelphia joined the atomic age.

The first blast occurred in the industrial northeast section of the city, the second in densely populated West Philadelphia. The damage pushed out in concentric rings of destruction. Total chaos and death ranged more than three-quarters of a mile in every direction from each ground zero, with nearly every structure destroyed at this range and every person killed; structures were damaged beyond repair and deaths and injuries were widespread more than a mile and a half from each blast. Total damage spread out in a radius of four miles from each bomb, blanketing an enormous swath of the city in death, fire, debris, and misery. By 7:50 A.M., the mayor—as civil defense coordinator for Philadelphia County—had received a preliminary briefing on the situation and sent a message to President Truman with the grim news: thousands were dead, and as many as 150,000 were seriously injured. Enormous fires were raging out of control, with one threatening to leap the Schuylkill River and destroy the central business district and City Hall.[3] Though downtown would be saved, the final death toll in Philadelphia would rise to 164,100 by the end of the first day, and the total injured to 293,000. In a city with more than 2 million citizens, 22 percent had been killed or hurt.

The attack on Philadelphia followed a bone-chilling pattern—it was not the first American city to be hit by nuclear weapons. Following a late night warning, at 5:30 A.M. on September 18, 1950, the mayor of Chicago received "a yellow alert" from civil defense authorities. At 6:26 there was an atomic burst 2,500 feet in the air near North Kedzie Street and Irving Park. A second burst followed a few seconds later at W. 107th Street and Prospect Avenue. At 7:30 there was a third burst on the ground at the railroad yard near W. Sixteenth Street and Ashland Avenue, leaving a 50-foot crater 1,000 feet in diameter. Total deaths from the Soviet nuclear attack on Chicago was estimated at 129,440 with 129,500 injured, among them 114,825 hospitalized.[4] Seattle suffered a very similar attack as well. And, the first attack on the United States, if anyone could remember it amid the repeated horrors, had leveled Washington, D.C., on June 29, 1950, when 2 nuclear bombs exploded, the first close to the Capitol Building, killing 80,000 and leaving 64,000 injured.[5] World War III was underway and the American city was marked for destruction.

American cities were, of course, never attacked with nuclear weapons in the Cold War. Scenarios like the ones just described seem to issue from some lost *War of the Worlds* panic, or perhaps a nightmarish figment of the Cold War imagination. However, these "hypothetical test exercises" were devised by disaster experts—federal civil defense experts—and used in the early Civil Defense Era as real instruments to evaluate American cities for their atomic attack readiness and stimulate planning for attack. And, they were based on the realities of nuclear destruction visited on Hiroshima and Nagasaki in 1945. In the earliest days of the Cold War, as cities, states, and the federal government went about planning for nuclear attack, it was not yet clear exactly what skills were necessary to master the problem of civil defense in the face of nuclear attack. To note that the creation and application of civil defense expertise called forward a diverse set of disciplines and actors is an understatement.

In Washington, defense professionals with military and intelligence backgrounds were often at the forefront of the planning. Out in the states and cities civil defense fell to elected officials, the fire service and police,

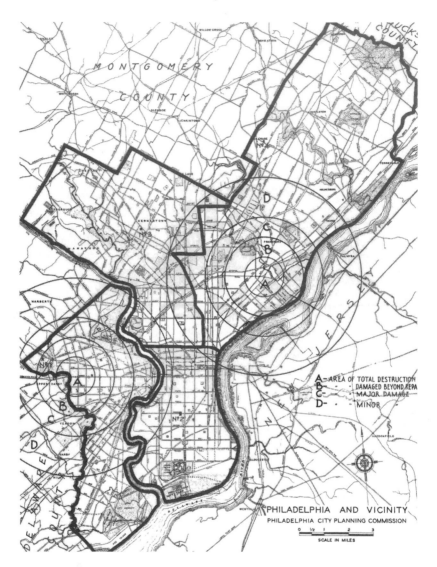

civic leaders in business and industry, doctors and nurses, teachers, and volunteer organizations. In the sciences, particularly physics and fire protection, as well as urban planning, civil defense created opportunities for research and policy advocacy. Just like the fire experts before them, but with substantially more existential pressure, the civil defense experts set to work on a problem that was almost impossible to define, not to mention

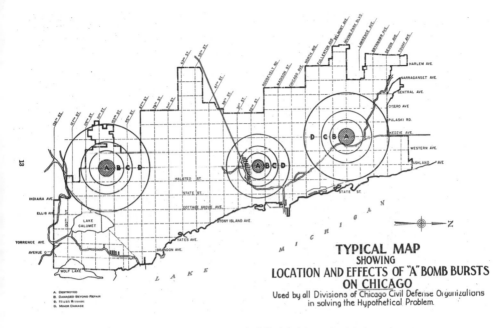

TYPICAL MAP
SHOWING
**LOCATION AND EFFECTS OF "A" BOMB BURSTS
ON CHICAGO**
Used by all Divisions of Chicago Civil Defense Organizations
in solving the Hypothetical Problem.

A. DESTROYED
B. DAMAGED BEYOND REPAIR
C. MAJOR DAMAGE
D. MINOR DAMAGE

Figure 9. Left: Destruction Zone Map of Philadelphia and Vicinity After Two Atomic Bombs, February 13, 1951. "Hypothetical Test Exercise," Office of Civil Defense, 1951. Courtesy of City of Philadelphia, Department of Records, City Archives, Mayor's Correspondence, 1950–1951, Box A-5311. Right: Destruction Zone Map of Chicago and Vicinity After Three Atomic Bombs, 1950. "General Outline: Civil Defense Plan for the City and County of Philadelphia." Courtesy of City of Philadelphia, Department of Records, City Archives, Mayor's Correspondence, 1950–1951, Box A-5311, folder "Chicago Test, 1951."

solve. Though engineering and physical science research were crucial to civil defense as an overall area of expertise, civil defense departed from fire expertise in the added human dimension of its work. While fire experts imagined, tested, and controlled for human factors in fire, they did not conduct research directly on humans—the civil defense experts did. The civil defense experts overall task was to anticipate nuclear attack, but this broke out into several discrete areas of research, thinking about how nuclear attack would affect the built and natural environment, and how American institutions and citizens might react. In cities across America disaster experts were imagining the worst, then getting to work.

As early as 1946, the United States Strategic Bombing Survey, in its study of the Hiroshima and Nagasaki bombings, concluded that civilians could be protected from atomic warfare, especially if planning for urban evacuation was coupled with planning for shelters.[6] In 1948, President Truman established the Office of Civil Defense Planning (OCDP), under the leadership of former Northwestern Bell Telephone Company president Russell J. Hopley. The result was the report *Civil Defense for National Security*, known as the Hopley Report, a document that comprehensively spelled out the organizational requirements of a workable civil defense, down to the state and local levels.[7] The Hopley Report recommended that ultimate control over civil defense be located in the executive branch of the federal government but insisted that state and local governments would bear most of the responsibility in actual practice, an idea that would prove influential. Still, there was lack of consensus over the extent to which preparations should be extended.

International tensions escalated rapidly: the Berlin blockade and airlift unfolded in 1948–1949, Mao Zedong's communist China emerged in 1949, the Soviet Union successfully tested a nuclear weapon in 1949, and Truman announced early in 1950 that the United States (and presumably the Soviets as well) was working on a hydrogen weapon that would dwarf the fission bombs used on Japan. The National Security Resources Board (NSRB) was given authority over civil defense in 1949. Truman signed Executive Order 10186, creating the Federal Civil Defense Administration within the Executive Office of the President, and weeks later signed the Federal Civil Defense Act of 1950, moving federal responsibility for civil defense again, this time under the auspices of the FCDA, and formally codifying the role for technical planning and leadership within the federal government and actual operations under the state and local governments.[8] The Act stipulated that the FCDA would undertake research "as to the best methods of treating the effects of attacks," and that it would conduct training in a civil defense college and in technical training schools. Responsibility for dissemination of civil defense information also fell to the new agency. Additionally, states were encouraged to begin the process of establishing "civil defense compacts" that would bring states into uniformity with one another and with federal civil defense plans. As to funding, the federal government would match state expenditures on civil defense (within the limits of congressional appropriation) and would allocate funds according to a formula that would prioritize high-population "critical target areas."[9]

At this time governors across the nation started developing civil defense plans for their individual states, a process Pennsylvania governor James Duff had already begun in December 1949 by naming eight members to a defense committee chaired by Judge Vincent A. Carroll. Carroll established an office in Philadelphia in April 1950; its first goals were to help the Air Force build observation posts and air raid warning stations and recruit volunteers.[10] The city of Philadelphia's political boundaries are the same as its county boundaries, and as the governor left local planning to the county level, this made Mayor Samuel de facto first director of the Philadelphia County Civil Defense Council. The expected planning and leadership demands of such a job were enormous, far beyond what a big city mayor could accomplish while still governing effectively, so Samuel established a council to take on the job, starting to staff it in the early summer. In a call for readiness and for a $500,000 emergency appropriation from City Council, Samuel described the situation as he saw it. "Realizing the great scale and spread of disasters that could happen here if a Third World War occurs," he argued, "immediate plans are being developed for the coordination and pooling of all the Defense resources of the Philadelphia metropolitan region. . . . A single atomic bomb exploded over the Philadelphia area would overtax all of the present combined disaster resources of this great and prosperous region."[11]

Appointing the council was a positive step, but clearly much planning remained to be done. What followed was a long, fearful summer in Philadelphia, full of chatter about nuclear war, especially with the outbreak of the Korean War in June. Philadelphia County Civil Defense Council members, for example, were among a crowd of 300 who took in a public lecture at the Franklin Institute on June 12, in which they heard Lieutenant Colonel Marcus R. King of the air force describe scenes of atomic destruction— 20,000 killed and 50,000 injured, City Hall's clock tower collapsing, thousands of fires, debris hurled like missiles through the city streets. "If City Hall were 'ground zero,'" King mused, "winds of 1000 miles an hour would rage briefly within 1000 feet, and up to 85 miles an hour two miles from the center of the blast."[12] The Red Cross designated six regional relief centers, warning that an atomic attack would necessitate a full city evacuation and speculating that a hydrogen bomb attack "would probably destroy the entire area."[13] Colonel King's scenario was not an improvised fancy but a theoretical exercise based on classified data drawn from Hiroshima, Nagasaki, and atomic tests taking place in the United States. Much like the

Manhattan Project, civil defense would operate under a cloak of secrecy
based on a claim of military necessity and national defense.

Military bases and industrial plants began renewing World War II-style
anti-sabotage protocols.[14] Ships arriving at the Port of Philadelphia from
"communist-held ports" or flying the flag of a "communist-dominated
nation" were searched for atomic bombs. Geiger counters would be used,
according to the collector of customs, though he ominously noted to the
press, "Nobody's been able to tell me how to detect an A-bomb."[15] Calls
were made to implement background checks and fingerprinting, to catch
communists who might try to infiltrate the new civil defense organization.[16]
The *Philadelphia Evening Bulletin* published an article describing steps for
personal protection in the event of nuclear attack, based on federal civil
defense publications, instructing readers to "drop to the ground instantly
with back to the light. . . . Keep in a knot at least ten seconds. After that get
up and look around."[17] Philadelphians were encouraged to be anxious, and
while impulses to organize were present, the mayor waited for further
instructions and leadership from federal and state authorities. Tired of
waiting, and signaling to the press that he was looking for the right military
officer to lead civil defense, he decided to "forge ahead" at summer's end.[18]

With his council in place, Mayor Samuel asked retired army major general Norman D. "Dutch" Cota to assume the position of executive director
of the Philadelphia Civil Defense Council. It was common for cities and
states to seek out retired military officers and law enforcement officers for
civil defense leadership in the Cold War. This fact reveals the shared belief
among policy-makers such as Mayor Samuel that disaster planning was best
practiced in a military mindset, under the assumption that citizens would
react badly in chaotic situations and would need the discipline, order, and
motivation only a military officer might provide.[19] With the war over and
the prestige of the military as high as it had ever been in the nation's history, it made sense to hire a war hero for the job. General Cota was well
known for his exploits as assistant division commander of the 29th Infantry
Division at Normandy on D-Day. Fifty-one-year-old Cota had landed on
Omaha Beach, and realizing the suicidal nature of remaining so exposed,
he organized the scattered landing units he encountered and got them moving to safety. According to lore, in finding the Fifth Army Ranger Battalion,
Cota cried out "Rangers, lead the way!" This slogan was adopted as the
motto of the Army Rangers, and Cota's actions on D-Day were later
immortalized in the 1962 film *The Longest Day*.[20]

Here was a decorated officer, a bona fide warrior, tested and calm under fire. Heroics aside, an irregular heartbeat and diabetes had brought Cota to Valley Forge Hospital in Pennsylvania at war's end, and in 1946 he retired from the army at the rank of major general. Cota and his wife Connie liked the Philadelphia area and were encouraged by Republican governor Edward Martin—a military colleague when Cota had commanded the 28th Infantry Division, a unit from Pennsylvania—to settle in the area, which they did in the Philadelphia suburb of Ardmore. Most likely with Governor Martin's assistance, the general was named director of the Philadelphia office of the War Assets Administration (WAA), a federal agency in charge of disposing of the enormous stockpile of postwar military surplus. At the height of the effort, Cota oversaw as many as 3,000 employees, but by late 1948 the work was mostly complete. Now, a few years after the war's end, he would return to government service, given the daunting task of preparing the nation's third most populous city for the unthinkable.[21]

On assuming the role of executive director for civil defense in Philadelphia, Cota made a few demands of the mayor. First, he was to be on "equal footing with his cabinet officers." He also requested "the necessary clerical help, and at the proper time . . . a full time staff." The mayor was to remain the responsible officer as coordinator, and Cota would act more or less as his chief of staff; his duties "were to be confined to planning, submitting recommendations and carrying out the policies and decisions made by the Coordinator."[22] Last, Cota wanted a robust public relations operation, and he requested that it be handled by the mayor's office, feeling that he was not experienced enough to succeed in this critical function.[23] With these assurances from Mayor Samuel, General Cota assumed the post on September 1, 1950.

Municipal civil defense planners across the nation faced a thorny situation in the early Cold War. They were charged with long-range planning, hardening the city against attack over the long term, but were often given only abstract civil defense guidelines from Washington that they needed to tailor to local circumstances. They also needed to anticipate the immediate hour-by-hour and day-to-day demands of an actual attack, if it were to happen. Which was more important: establishing a disaster response plan to meet the medical, fire, security, and leadership needs of an unfolding disaster or investing in physical infrastructures of warning, shelter, and escape? Ideally, Cota would not have to choose, but when City Council's first appropriation came in at $250,000, half the mayor's request, the ideal was nullified. It was time to prioritize the risks, but on what basis? Compli-cating the matter was the expanse and diversity of the city itself, with more than 2 million residents, and its infrastructure, spread over 135 square miles with dense residential neighborhoods, vast industrial sectors, and a down-town with modern high-rise buildings. Crisscrossed by rivers, roads, rail-ways, wires, pipes, with an original grid dating to William Penn's days, Philadelphia presented a puzzle of exposed citizens and vulnerable infra-structural pieces. Was it worthwhile to protect one type of infrastructure over another, the water system over the electric grid, for example? Was it possible, or ethical, to protect some neighborhoods over others?

Making it even worse was the realization that atomic blasts and radioac-tive fallout would pay little attention to city or county lines. From the beginning, in fact, Cota thought of civil defense as a regional problem and worked to involve the surrounding counties in his planning. But on what legal basis would a region be defined and governed, what compacts would be necessary to insure that authority and coordination would easily cross county and even state lines? From the beginning federal civil defense placed strong emphasis on municipal-state and state-state cooperation, but work-ing out such compacts was of course contingent on state laws.

The legal issues were mind-boggling and were never solved by civil defense planners. A 1955 article in *Columbia Law Review* suggested some helpful steps that could be taken to prepare a city for the disruptions to its legal system that a nuclear attack would bring.[24] Maintaining the legal force of mortgages and lease contracts would be highly problematic and probably defunct in "cities, where partially damaged, windowless, deserted houses and apartments would be many." It was possible, the article suggested, to plan for such an unhappy real estate contingency ahead of time, thinking about how "lessors and lessees might now provide, keeping in mind that inflation might render the rent reserved in a long-term lease an extremely economic arrangement for the tenant who survived the war period." Con-tracts of all types would be difficult to maintain after a nuclear war. Price contracts, distributorships, employment contracts, and regulated contracts like utilities would all be challenged by the realities of missing documents, missing funds, and missing persons. Nuclear war would also bring major corporate managerial problems, for which executives needed to plan now "to facilitate the continued operation of headless corporations."[25] The work of the courts would also undoubtedly be interrupted, so planners needed to be thinking about how handling estates, for instance, and the daily work of courts and judges—trials, appeals, sentencing, even executions—might all be continued after attack.[26]

Unfortunately, direction from Washington was missing or confusing on these and most of the other difficult questions about how society would regain its functionality after attack. Planners in Truman's FCDA mulled over the possibilities of dispersing urban populations, evacuating them in advance of a suspected attack, or sheltering them in blast and fallout shelters. Shelters seemed the most realistic option but still posed serious problems, potentially trapping and suffocating people underground as firestorms raged above. Location and equity of shelter protection, post-attack radiation, and cost—estimated at $300 million by FCDA director Millard Caldwell—added up to an FCDA policy that Truman only lightly pushed and Congress refused to fund.[27]

In other words, the FCDA had ideas, it had pamphlets and organizational charts and hypothetical test narratives based on hard research-driven data, but when it came down to nuanced local planning, Philadelphia would have to stand largely on its own. Rejecting theoretical debates over dispersal, evacuation, and shelter, General Cota first moved to establish a command and control structure—a means of sending orders from a central commander to designated subcommanders, then out to functional units, with appropriate channels of feedback—that would seek to integrate long-range planning and day-to-day disaster response functions. He set into motion a civil defense plan that proved straightforward and was, in a word, military. Cota would later recall his early agenda for Philadelphia civil defense:

> Now, here in Philadelphia we had to act, we couldn't wait for the formulation of an overall planning by the Government nor by the State. We had to do first things first, or at least we had to begin to do first things first, and we had to establish an efficient Air Raid Warning System. Certainly if you cannot get the warning, all your other problems don't amount to very much. Secondly, we had to organize a sound Civil Defense organization with necessary control and communication facilities. . . . Third, we had to put in effect a thorough and sound training program based on sound warden organization, and number four, we had to introduce a modest training program . . . [with] the . . . auxiliary police and auxiliary fire organization, trained to control traffic and fight fires, and also to

guard against the destruction of vital property, and lastly, we had to
have a foresighted plan for the future.[28]

Advance warning, command and control, training and organization, firefighting and security, and advance planning, if you ever got to it—these
were the critical elements of the Cota plan for the defense of Philadelphia.
The city was divided into four regions, roughly corresponding to the northeast, northwest, southeast, and southwest sections of the city. Every region
was assigned a headquarters, and an additional command center was placed
in City Hall. Command resided in the mayor, but Cota was the true organizational chief. He named four staff officers, all military men retired from
service, to manage the four zones: Colonel Beeson Hunt, army; Rear Admiral Robert Lee Porter, navy; Lieutenant Colonel Murl Corbett, marine
corps; and Harold V. Murdock, air force.[29] Planning was broken into eight
operational units, supervised by city officials and local businessmen: (a)
education and training, Dr. Louis Hoyer, schools superintendent; (b) security, Samuel Rosenberg, director, Philadelphia Department of Public Safety;
(c) communications, Arthur Williams, Bell Telephone Company; (d) engineering, utilities, and public works, Lawrence Costello, Department of City
Transit; (e) medical and health services, Dr. Rufus S. Reeves, Department
of Public Health; (f) evacuation, transportation, and emergency welfare, N.
Newlin Bailey, executive assistant, Reading Company; (g) technical, Dr.
Henry B. Allen, executive vice president and secretary, Franklin Institute;
and (h) auxiliaries, Ralph W. Pitman, vice president, Central Penn National
Bank.[30]

Each division would have a representative assigned to each of the four
regions. In this way, if one, two, or even three quadrants of the city were
destroyed, the remaining quadrant or quadrants could function independently, able to carry out all critical functions, with a clear line of authority
from the officer in command to the officers under his control. Filling out
the roster of the organization included Thomas Buckley, director of the
Philadelphia Department of Public Works. Mrs. E. A. Van Valkenberg was
made representative of women's organizations and placed in charge of reg-
istering volunteers. Public relations fell to Clement V. Conole of the Philadelphia Chamber of Commerce. Finally, Cota established a Mutual Aid,
Regional Civil Defense Advisory Commission to integrate Philadelphia's
planning with that of surrounding counties and municipalities. This list
included judges and mayors from Doylestown, Media, Norristown, and

Phoenixville, Pennsylvania; and Burlington and Mercer Counties, Atlantic City, Burlington City, Camden, Trenton, and Woodbury, New Jersey.[31]

In September 1950, in the midst of implementing his plan, General Cota took a delegation from Philadelphia to witness the hypothetical test exercise "critique" in Chicago. Washington, Chicago, and Seattle had been chosen by the federal officials as the first three cities to test (destroy), based on their differences in "geography, forms of municipal government, density of population," and the results of these tests were intended to serve as models to help other cities plan.[32] Civil defense experts in Washington wrote the test exercises, they were presented to the cities to play out, and a major conference or "critique" was scheduled where federal civil defense experts could meet with their local counterparts to review the lessons learned, and tailor the results into comprehensive local and metropolitan civil defense planning.[33] The hope of the federal officials was that a "pattern of civil defense arrangements among local authorities, between cities and their state authorities, and between the States and the Federal Government thus will develop naturally, and not according to a rigid pattern imposed from above."[34] Chicago's civil defense planners had spent two weeks on their test by the time 700 civil defense officials from 20 states and 200 cities across the nation, as well as Canada and London, descended on the Field Museum for the critique. By the time of this impressive gathering the NSRB had already hosted 24 state representatives and 175 municipal representatives at its test exercise critiques.[35]

The author of both the Philadelphia and Chicago test exercises was army lieutenant colonel Irl D. Brent. A University of Michigan economics graduate with a master's degree in industrial relations, Brent epitomized the federal civil defense experts of the early Cold War. A Bronze Star-decorated veteran and an officer with great experience in logistics, he had a facility with high-level military planning culture. On retiring from active duty he took an interest in nuclear defense planning, was recruited by the CIA, and served as a science advisor in the 1950s to James B. Conant's Office of Scientific Intelligence.[36] Brent brought together battlefield military logistics experience, a social science educational background, and a strong interest in the technical issues of nuclear weapons. And he seemed to take delight in researching and writing about hypothetical conditions under which American cities would face nuclear war.

Brent described the goals and methods of his text exercise for Chicago as "a cooperative effort," with a "narrative . . . sufficiently realistic to accomplish . . . getting an interim civil defense plan for Chicago that will enable your city to make a practical start toward a more complete plan later. It will greatly reduce your casualties in the event of attack whenever it may come."[37] Brent asserted his position as an expert in writing such exercises, stressing his hope that local officials would "accept this narrative for what it is; that you will not 'fight the problem' but constructively solve it as given as best you can do now." The city's civil defense officials took on the added restriction of not changing any of their preparedness plans once the exercise was underway, and only addressing the hypothetical case with the tools they had at the time, not projecting what might be available down the line. This was the best way to start, Brent believed, to get a real sense of "the grass roots problems of civil defense planning," and how well the city was prepared for nuclear attack. "Later on," he suggested, "you can pose your own similar attacks to test your more permanent plans and organization."[38]

The research and details that went into the test exercises were quite elaborate. The bombs dropped on Chicago were not to be understood as the same as those used in Japan: "because more powerful bombs are or may be in existence," more powerful bombs were imagined. Brent noted that most bombs were expected to explode in the air, as those do the most damage. He wrote a ground burst into his narrative for Chicago, though, to stimulate planners' thinking about subsoil conditions (which he researched for the test narrative) and earthquake-like effects on buildings. The first burst was in a high population density area, the second close to the city line to enable thinking about "mutual aid and mobile support."[39] The bombs were hypothetically dropped early in the morning, while people were home. "This was done to point up the need for research in your population densities, and habits, as well as in the field of building density, use and types of construction. Much of such information may now be available in the records of your planning commission, local public utilities and various departments of your city government." The structure of the test narrative was a guide to the local research the federal civil defense planners felt was necessary and unique to every city and metropolitan region. By suggesting complexities in the narrative, the federal civil defenders could ensure that at least for the purpose of this first major planning exercise, federal and local experts would be working on the same problems. Besides, as Brent chillingly reminded his audience, this was the type of research that was "part of any enemy's target analyses." Local schools (of which 71 were destroyed or badly damaged) would be in demand for shelter, as would hospitals, where 21.5 percent of emergency beds had also been destroyed. In a flourish that might be more appropriate to a novelist or screenwriter, Brent closed his introduction by pointing out that "to add another touch of realism we used some old advertising information to determine roughly the number of . . . commercial or retail establishments affected by this attack." There had not been time, unfortunately, to assess or write imagined effects on industrial facilities into the narrative.[40]

Addressing the assembled experts, newly appointed Chicago civil defense director and chief fire marshal Anthony J. Mullaney boasted that "we, in Chicago, have always taken the position that any type of disaster within our territorial limits was our problem and ours alone. We dealt with it with our own forces and put our own house once again in order without calling for Federal or Military help."[41] Such a notion seemed far-fetched in the face of nuclear attack, and was certainly not the idea promoted by federal officials. Still, Mullaney stressed that municipal independence shaped Chicago's planning in response to the hypothetical test.

The range of federal agency involvement in the critique was extensive, including of course civil defense officials, but also the Department of Defense, Atomic Energy Commission, Federal Security Agency, Government Services Agency, and Bureau of Public Roads. Illinois state civil defense director Major Lennox R. Lohr was on hand as well. Lohr was president of Chicago's Museum of Science and Industry and had served as general manager for the 1933 Chicago World's Fair. From the state perspective the priorities of planning were to keep the highways open and prepare and coordinate relief groups that would then be turned over to the jurisdiction of a stricken area. "Panic is certain to cause disruption," Lohr imagined, a point that "emphasizes the importance of the rescue work that may be performed by teams from the outside, who will be spared at least some of the anguish of those in a stricken community."[42]

Speaking on "Civic Participation," Daniel A. Sullivan, assistant vice-president of Commonwealth Edison, reported that on finishing the hypothetical test, the news was, in fact, quite cheerful:

Chicago survived this ordeal with a minimum loss of life and property damage as a result of very thorough pre-arranged plans. Within a week or two after the bombs exploded, the large percentage of the City's great industries were in full production, its transportation systems restored to service, the homeless and casualties provided for and in spite of the damage inflicted, the city still remained a very important factor in the very life of our country.[43]

Mayor Martin Kennelly was confident that Chicago's citizens "will feel more secure and safer when they read of the work that is being done by this Committee." It would fall to the local civil defense committee "to advise the citizens of what is expected of them."[44]

Civil defense director Mullaney had been in the Chicago fire service since 1914, a World War I veteran later named to the U.S. Strategic Bombing Survey Civilian Defense Division research team in Germany, one of only two American fire department experts in the group. On returning from Germany he reported his impressions to the 50th Annual Meeting of the National Fire Protection Association, and subsequently published his findings on "German Fire Departments Under Air Attack" in a volume published by NFPA titled *Fire and the Air War*. Mullaney was particularly impressed with the effects of the allied 1943 fire bombing of Hamburg, a series of attacks that trapped thousands of civilians in basement shelters where they died of lack of oxygen, heat inhalation, or coal and gas asphyxiation. An estimated 55,000 died in Hamburg, 10,000 of them were never recovered, and a 5.9 square mile area was completely destroyed.[45]

Obviously, Mullaney's experiences in Germany gave him familiarity with the types of conditions civil defense planners thought they might encounter in Chicago. He pointed out that Europeans did not use wood frame construction and that they enforced height restrictions—both factors that might make fires after nuclear attack in the Unites States even worse than the European firestorms. He concluded that "most weapons of warfare are eventually directed against civilian populations . . . in an effort to break civilian morale or destroy civilians themselves." He recommended that a national institution be created to conduct fire research and train the civilian fire service as well as the military in "combating the thought-staggering fire problems of a future war."[46] Fire research was carried out throughout the early Cold War, bringing together institutions we know from the first half of the book, like the NFPA, and war planners around how to cause, and if necessary react to mass fires. Mass fires were conflagrations that destroyed entire cities, leaving ruins like those Mullaney had witnessed in Hamburg.

In fact, as historian Lynn Eden has very effectively demonstrated, nuclear weapons experts in various arms of the United States defense structure misguidedly focused more on nuclear bomb blast than they did on fire, a reality she argues led experts to radically underestimate the potential damage of nuclear war.[47] Blast was, to the "nuclear weapons effects community," more predictable than fire, so it was studied more completely. Nevertheless, research money flowed into all aspects of the fire problem in ways unmatched since the threat of fire to cities had given rise to expert institutions like NFPA and UL. Academic researchers like mechanical engineer Howard Emmons from Harvard and fire protection engineers at the National Bureau of Standards (NBS) took up the research—and fire protection engineering saw a second wave of interest rivaling that of the Conflagration Era—with a major degree program founded at the University of Maryland (just down the road from the NBS fire research labs). The Society of Fire Protection Engineers was founded in 1950.[48]

Reporting back on his visit to the Chicago test critique, Philadelphia civil defense director Cota noted that the Chicago test required a city inventory in a way "never contemplated," and that it required government departments to solve a common problem, brought government in contact with industry, showed it to be an "area" problem, and showed state government to be "far behind local governments in defense planning." He reassured the mayor that "few, if any city, is as far advanced in Civil Defense planning as the City of Philadelphia."[49]

By February 1951, Cota had staffed his command and control structure. All his regional and divisional directors had submitted their individual plans, air raid posts and wardens were selected, and volunteer recruiting and training was underway.[50] When federal planners asked whether Philadelphia was ready for a test early in 1951, the governor, mayor, and Cota agreed it was time.[51] As we saw earlier, a hypothetical atomic attack on Philadelphia was played out on February 13. A month later, the Philadelphia County Civil Defense Council hosted a three-day test critique at Convention Hall. Hundreds of local and state civil defense officials were invited. Colonel Brent was in attendance. Although the test critique was not open to the public, the press covered it, and in this way Philadelphians received a comprehensive vision of what an attack on their city might look like and how well they were expected to fare. The critique's first day started with a prayer, followed by a speech from the mayor, who pointed out that the Civil Defense Council had developed plans to meet a hypothetical atomic

attack: "Although these plans are only on paper, they are the result of practical, measured thinking. . . .They represent the combined voluntary efforts
of men and women from administrative, business and professional fields,
as well as the physical facilities of the organizations they represent."[52]

The governor spoke, followed by a representative of the U.S. Civil
Defense Commission. Recently named director of the Pennsylvania Civil
Defense Commission Dr. Theodore Distler spoke next, followed by the
Chamber of Commerce president's speech on the nation's "stake" in Philadelphia. Next, Colonel Brent read the chilling and detailed hypothetical test
narrative to the audience. Armed with sober details of mass murder, precise
destruction radii, and blast heat predictions that drew whistles, Brent's narrative captured the imagination of the crowd. His challenge was followed
by Cota, who was to present the civil defense plan for the city and his
solution to the city's proposed obliteration.[53]

General Cota related in detail how the hypothetical attack had wreaked
havoc on the city. The Control Center in Region 3 was completely
destroyed. Key personnel had great difficulty getting from their homes to
their assigned posts. Many were injured, and many others determined to
stay home with loved ones rather than report for duty. Two hours after the
attack, the Command Center was operating at only 50 percent effectiveness,
and it would take another day before the extent of the damage was known.
The all-clear air raid signal was disseminated with great difficulty because of
downed power lines and destroyed telephone communications. The public,
therefore, had no idea whether the attack was over. An "overwhelming
panic" was rampant in Regions 1 and 2.

Then Cota turned to the positive, the actionable elements of his command and control plan that had survived the bombing. The mayor and
executive director were presumed to have survived the attack and would
be spending the next days and weeks allocating aid, issuing bulletins, and
communicating with the public on the radio. These commanders would be
talking with advisors about the legality of requisitioning food, medicine,
and supplies. They would be closing off neighborhoods, preventing looting
and issuing "shoot to kill" orders, directing auxiliary firemen and police,
checking on industrial plants, locating burial grounds, and raising funds
from City Council for the homeless and wounded. "By the end of five
days," Cota asserted, "Philadelphia was beginning to dig itself out of the
ruins. This was made possible by prior civil defense planning by local, state,
and federal Governments." The plan was solid; the city would survive.[54]

Here the hypotheticals ended, both on the attack and on the response. Cota proceeded to honestly state the facts on the ground, and they bear quoting at length:

> Ladies and gentlemen you must remember that this hypothetical problem was solved by the application of PLANS only. Plans are only plans. They become effective only when the tools are made available to carry them out. On February 13, 1951, many of the tools used in this solution were not in existence. . . . Civil Defense, like Military Defense, is a waste of money and resources unless it is organized and trained before an enemy attacks. Does anyone know when an enemy will attack? Think of the lives that will be saved by intelligent Civil Defense preparations ahead of time. Why does this condition exist? The answer is simple. Lack of funds, equipment, and directives from higher civil defense authorities.[55]

Despite this devastating assessment, Cota remained optimistic that with time to plan, financial resources, and political support from above he could whip civil defense in Philadelphia into shape. Though City Council had appropriated only $250,000 the previous year, the mayor had only days before hopefully asking the governor for $9 million.[56] There was talk of real federal funding finally materializing. Now, with these new nightmares made public, the city would leap to its responsibility, volunteers would stream into civil defense recruiting stations, and Philadelphia's paper plans would become real.

A similar process was playing out across the country, as civil defense planners in Washington rolled out their plans, expecting cities to enact them, test for them, and fund them. The 1950 Federal Civil Defense Act had neglected one key thing, funding, and this was becoming a serious impediment to sustaining the "wartime" preparedness mindset. States and cities like New York, Chicago, and Philadelphia were hard pressed to come up with the funds, though the call for patriotism and war service harking back to World War II provided strong sentimental and political reasons to do so. As the realities of sustaining the plans became clear in the early 1950s, a dynamic opened up in which civil defense planning existed more on paper than in reality. This did not, however, slow the proliferation of paper plans.

Figure 10. Elwood P. Smith, "Independence Hall is Lighted by Flames," October 7, 1953. This nuclear attack "demonstration" in Philadelphia was one of many held throughout the United States in the early Cold War, designed by civil defense experts to enhance public awareness of and preparedness for nuclear attack. Courtesy of Urban Archives, Temple University.

Although horrifying to imagine, civil defense director Cota confidently concluded that Philadelphia would dust itself off and be functioning again as the workshop of the world five days after a nuclear attack. Such optimism reflects the will of many U.S. defense strategists of the era to "win" a nuclear war—thought possible in part through fostering the willingness of civilians to rationally (or irrationally) face down the nuclear threat and prepare to live in its aftermath.

Federal civil defense experts also took heart in the results of a survey of public attitudes to civil defense conducted in the nation's 11 largest metropolitan areas (cities and suburbs) in 1951, run by the Survey Research Center at the University of Michigan. According to the results of this elaborate survey, 65 percent of Americans believed cities would be hit with atomic bombs, and 64 percent believed their own city would be hit. The survey found that 65 percent of respondents had an accurate idea of civil defense measures underway, 91 percent believed children should be educated on civil defense; asked if such education should be done even though it might scare children, 80 percent said yes. A healthy 87 percent had heard about safety measures, including shelters and "duck and cover" techniques.

From here, though, the experts saw they had their work cut out for them. While 67 percent of those responding knew about civil defense preparedness in their cities, only 33 percent believed their city could do a good job. When asked why progress had not been faster, 42 percent cited "apathy." Pushing on this point, the survey asked about volunteerism, and 77 percent said they would volunteer if asked; but when asked to give up a few hours a week for 6 months, only 13 percent said yes, 58 percent said yes with qualifications, and 24 percent said no outright. Among the conclusions were that people accept "sustained international tension," but fluctuations in public mood did not seem to affect support of civil defense. Most people seemed to take it seriously, and information had reached a large audience. Though most metropolitan residents said they would participate in civil defense activities, "a sizeable part of the population was not aware of local civil defense in their cities."

Civil defense experts undoubtedly took caution from this survey, but most important to them was their success and dynamism in early efforts toward staffing civil defense organizations and starting planning, a palpable confidence that "victory" was at hand. The remarkable hypothetical attack narratives and critiques allowed civil defense experts to begin building networks across geographical and intergovernmental boundaries. In the planning committees they assembled they undertook the creation of cities within cities, imagining the variety of skills and disciplinary experts required to rebuild a shattered metropolis from top to bottom. The civil defenders needed now to charge ahead, keep up public education efforts, and stoke positive community participation, in order to make civil defense "real," a successful means of applying expert knowledge to preparation for warfare that could, literally, end the American city.[57]

Command and Control Versus Urban Realities

While national civil defense planners moved ahead with their plans, the realities of urban economics and politics dictated that nuclear preparedness would ultimately reflect local realities. And while civil defense planning rolled on in Philadelphia, so did the wheels of political change.

Federal civil defenders could continue to advise on planning, but had nothing to say about local politics. Corruption, not particularly new to Philadelphia politics, was a major campaign issue in the 1951 mayoral race. Philadelphia had a long tradition of Republican control, a situation that put the city in line with the national electorate in the immediate postwar years, when Congress in 1946 and the presidency in 1952 flipped from New Deal Democratic to Republican. In 1947, Richardson Dilworth—a decorated World War II veteran and attorney—ran for mayor against Samuel with the slogan "Sweep the rascals out!" Dilworth accused 128 city officials of receiving bribes and payoffs—accusations that led City Council to create a "Committee of Fifteen" to investigate. Though Dilworth lost the election, the resulting investigation turned up a staggering $40 million missing from city coffers. A grand jury followed up, and scandal after scandal came to light during the next four years. The Philadelphia Republican machine was against the ropes.[58]

In 1949 Dilworth ran for city treasurer, and his fellow Democrat and friend, retired army air force colonel and lawyer Joseph S. Clark, ran for city controller. Elected, they turned their energies to advocating for a new city charter for Philadelphia. This home-rule charter changed city government in several key ways. Most important, it created a city more independent of the state legislature, with a "strong mayor" form of government. It also required a Civil Service Commission to review government appointments, taking this form of patronage and potential cronyism away from the mayor. Important new advisory boards and commissions like the Philadelphia City Planning Commission were also created.[59] The voters approved the home-rule charter in May 1951, and later in the year elected Clark mayor, Dilworth district attorney, and Democrats for 15 of the 17 city council seats. Reform was the word of the day; Bernard Samuel and his administration were a memory. Civil defense remained, but it too was not immune to reform and the political mood. When the new mayor began to examine the bureaucracy he inherited, he was naturally interested to find out what civil defense organization was in place. Cota and his team had been busy indeed, but busy doing what was difficult for Clark to know, as Cota had yet to make a public report or even a detailed written report to the mayor or City Council.

The test critique in 1951 provided the most public exploration of Cota's ideas, but almost a year had elapsed since then. Even before taking office, Clark and some members of Council had volunteered in one or another capacity in civil defense duty. They were, in short, unimpressed with what they had seen thus far. Constituents were writing letters; complaints were coming in: "I volunteered but no one has contacted me. . . . How do I get information? . . . I don't hear the air raid sirens at my house. . . . What can I do to protect my family?" In an effort to get General Cota on the record and gain a fuller understanding of his civil defense objectives and strategies, City Council— at Mayor Clark's request—summoned him and his top aides for public hearings in February and March 1952. In three separate hearings over two weeks, Cota and his top staff testified before the Special Committee to Investigate the Civil Defense Program, chaired by Councilman Paul D'Ortona. Cota appeared first with a recitation of the history of civil defense going back to the 1948 Hopley Report, quoting from it to emphasize a point he would frequently return to, that to have civil defense, the demand for civil defense had to come from the people. In other words, it had to come from the community, from the ground up, the way the citizens of Philadelphia—or any American city for that matter—wanted it.[60] In this argument Cota found himself in a tough spot as a municipal civil defense director. Ultimate authority over civil defense was at the federal level, but without meaningful municipal government and citizen buy-in this authority and the expertise it represented was ineffectual.

Cota went on to explain how civil defense had been established at the federal, state, and ultimately local levels, symbolized by his appointment in 1950. He impressed on the committee his feeling that atomic attack was a regional problem not confined to city limits. He reiterated his belief that federal and state guidance and financial commitments had been entirely insufficient. He decried lack of public interest. Still, it was all worthwhile according to Cota, as he spelled out his pressing concern that civil defense will "some day in the future be called on to function under fire, and I mean under fire, under actual bombing. . . . To wait for another Pearl Harbor before organizing, training and equipping Civil Defense forces will be too late."[61]

The committee explored two primary concerns in the hearings: a full understanding of Cota's command and control structure and the degree to

which the civil defense plan had been enacted to date. It is painfully clear
from the transcripts that the examining council members never fully
grasped the intricacies of Cota's plan. It is likewise clear that the general
himself knew the outlines but had delegated the details to subordinates.
The first difficulty arose in trying to understand the relationship between
Cota as executive director and the mayor. Cota explained the division of
power, emphasizing his role as making plans and recommendations and
the mayor's role as acting on this advice. The Civil Defense Council met
every Wednesday at 10:00 A.M.; division directors would report on progress,
Cota would make a report, and he and the mayor would meet for a private
briefing in the mayor's office. The committee began to ask specifically about
how this relationship worked, for example, what actions the mayor had
taken after reports in August and September calling for more public relations activities. The mayor, they learned, had told Cota to hold the status
quo with elections coming up, to "sit tight." This caught their interest:

Council [C]: These reports of August 1951 and September 1951 were
detailed reports making recommendations primarily for the purpose of
alerting the public to the real danger?

Cota [CO]:Yes.

C: You got no reply to either report from the Mayor?

CO: No.

C: And the Mayor suggested to you that the matter be in status quo due
to the coming in of the new administration?

CO: Yes.

C: What was the enemy doing during that period, or even during the
next five minutes while you are sitting here?

C: Is it not your duty as the head of this organization, if you make
recommendations, to see if they are carried out, or if they are not carried out, why they were not carried out?

CO: I'd like to make one thing very clear, the responsible officer in
Civilian Defense is the Mayor, he is the Director of the Civilian Defense
setup, appointed by the Governor . . . after I made my recommendations I felt I had done my duty.[62]

Further questioning revealed that information in the Civil Defense Council
was highly compartmentalized. Specific knowledge on communications or

education, for example, resided only with the officer in charge of that division. Cota was unable to address a great number of specific questions about the actual functioning of his regions and divisions. It turned out on questioning that meetings between Cota and top aides were often informal; issues were "thrashed out" but no written records were kept. This was, he went on, the way he had always worked.

> CO: You are asking how I run my staff, and by God, I run a lot and I think I know how to run it.
> C: We are not criticizing you, General, on that score. I don't think it is necessary, however, for vital information as far as the safety of the people of Philadelphia is concerned . . . [to] be kept locked in some one's head.
> CO: I think you will find the division directors have the information. . . .
> C: If all the reports are made orally and at staff meetings, it seems to me the information is locked in someone's head.[63]

With an executive director relying on staff officers to advise him, what might happen if these advisors were killed? More damaging, what good was such a command and control arrangement if the top commander—the mayor—was unwilling to command during election season? The committee was decidedly unimpressed. It was even more unimpressed when it learned about the command structure at the volunteer "warden" level. The wardens were organized geographically, with several zone wardens for every region, a smaller number of post wardens below them for 4 to 6 block areas, and block wardens for every block in the city. This might have seemed unimportant, until the responsibilities of the wardens were explained. The list was daunting, including

> [to oversee] the Civilian Defense organization's self-protection program, to assemble data . . . on occupants of buildings . . . facilities and equipment, and to make and require reports of actual damage, and call for all needed assistance from the next higher headquarters, to cooperate with the officials responsible for equipment and police and firemen, communications and transportation, and medical and health and welfare and rescue service . . . to be a leader and keep calm and still rumors and know his neighborhood.[64]

The warden, it seemed, was the real lifeblood of the city's civil defense effort. With a chain of experts that began in the Pentagon and passed through the White House, state house, and city hall, the warden was a vulnerable link in the system, meant to be in the street applying civil defense knowledge. In the wardens, presumably well-known local figures, resided the detailed knowledge of the neighborhoods. The warden knew the buildings and the people, and wielded local control in the midst of disaster. Therefore, it came as an unpleasant surprise to learn how dismally the warden recruiting and training was proceeding. In Region 1, Admiral Porter admitted that 12,000 wardens were needed, and 417 were signed on, with no way to be sure whether any of these had completed the required training. Furthermore, the training program consisted of a 6-hour course, much of it taken up with watching federal civil defense films.

Moving on, the committee turned to an evaluation of the progress in enacting the civil defense plan, flawed as it might be. How much equipment was in place? Was critical infrastructure protected? How many staff had been selected and trained? What about volunteers and public education? The picture was bleak. In addition to the bad news about warden recruit-ment, it seemed that a similar picture existed for all volunteer positions. In Region 3, for example, Colonel Hunt reported that he had recruited 790 air raid wardens to spot enemy aircraft. When asked whether this was a full staff, he replied that 15,000 were actually required. An auxiliary police force of 3,000 was needed, with 68 signed up, and for auxiliary firefighting he had 8 men for a region with a population of half a million.[65]

The report on infrastructure was not much better. Schools were desig-nated as "improvised" hospitals, but only 79 had been established and medical supplies were nonexistent. Emergency vehicles were needed, 2,580 of them to be exact, but none existed. Most pieces of heavy equipment were limited to those owned by city departments, and these had not been marked or identified. Private taxis and "volunteer" cars were hoped to be available in the event of an attack, but no solid numbers were known. Industrial plants were asked to organize themselves, but it was unknown how many had done so. The same was true of office buildings and retail establishments in the downtown business district. Even the regional command centers were problematic, all with exposed windows, one on an upper floor of a school, and none underground. It was reasonable to assume that a couple of well-placed bombs would actually knock out every command center. Put to the test, none of the regional officers were willing to state that their region was ready for an atomic attack. In sum, the likelihood of success for Cota's command and control plan was highly questionable, and his other civil defense objectives—a warning system, a volunteer-based warden system, and trained auxiliaries—were grossly unfulfilled.

Asked by the committee how much money he needed, General Cota answered $12 million, but he had spent just less than $300,000 to date. Volunteers were impossible to find. City organizations were uninterested. Merchants such as Wanamaker's were reluctant to post civil defense placards so as not to arouse customers' fears. Industrial plants were quiet on preparations and not required to report. The state was no help, federal authorities even less. Only Cota and his staff knew the risks and civil defense plans, and apparently even they were a bit hazy on the plans.

The committee chairman concluded that Philadelphia civil defense was a wreck, noting that "we have all generals and no soldiers."[66] Having "generals" in the first place seemed to be causing some problems, as revealed in a pointed exchange between Cota and City Council.

> C: I'd like to ask you this, General, whether or not . . . operation of the Civilian Defense Council . . . has not been attended with friction because you and the regional directors are military men and the personnel of the office are volunteers, unsalaried volunteer civilians?
> CO: I have had no friction . . . I believe we have gotten along very agreeably with the regional commanders and the directors . . . however, I assume you will have each one in and they will be able to enlighten you on that score.
> C: It is a serious question, and it is a rather difficult question, and it has come to our attention that the cooperation was rather difficult, that the men at the top, including yourself, and the regional directors were military men, retired, some of them on the payroll, and these men and women that were asked to serve as volunteers . . . they got no compensation for their efforts.[67]

Thus, even the effectiveness of placing military leaders in the ranks of the civil defense leadership was brought into question.

This strategy promised to be one of the real strengths of civil defense, building on the shared national experience of World War II, so fresh in national memory, and so particularly sharp to Philadelphians who had seen their city transformed by industrial production and high rates of military service throughout the war. The broadly shared experience of military service in that time meant, as well, that by the 1950s it was a city (and a nation) full of veterans, a time when military service was revered, required through Selective Service, and expected among political and civic leaders. The apathy of citizens and bitterness among volunteers reported by City Council undoubtedly perplexed Cota, considering the extremely strong record of civil defense in Philadelphia during World War II. At the start of 1943 the city had 75,000 air raid wardens; 30,000 turned out for the army show "Action Overhead" at Memorial Stadium that year. It was reported that 155,000 Philadelphians participated in wartime civil defense.[68] Now, with nuclear weapons, the risks were far greater and volunteers were nowhere to be found.

In its postmortem on the hearings, the *Philadelphia Inquirer* reported that "Philadelphia's defense setup was depicted as a virtual failure," pointing out in a damning headline: "Gen. Cota Is Uncertain on Setup."[69] Cota resigned within the year, no doubt finding that Omaha Beach was easier to manage than Cold War Philadelphia's civil defense. Similar problems beset preparations in other major cities, while in Washington the federal structure went through name change after name change, plan after plan— sending confused, often contradictory messages to states and cities.

In truth, Philadelphia's proposed survival of atomic attack was just as hypothetical as its destruction in 1951 and throughout the Cold War. Mayor Samuel lamented after the test exercise that his city had only "paper plans," not real resources and infrastructures with which to defend itself from atomic annihilation.[70] Still, faced with little choice but to defy federal directives and consign their city to doom, Samuel, Cota, and the mayors and local civil defense officials who would follow them attempted to convert Philadelphia's paper plans to real protection. In examining the founding, functioning, and challenges presented to experts in their attempts to establish a workable civil defense regime for early Cold War Philadelphia, we see the abrupt creation of a new realm of risk and disaster expertise focused on the American city. The overwhelming consensus among policymakers, journalists, and scholars who study civil defense is that it failed, unequivocally, to provide anything approaching realistic protection from nuclear war for average citizens and their property. Proceeding from this general premise, however, it is imperative to note that this was a failure with a very long history, stretching from the early Cold War years into the Reagan era. It bears considering how local politics, infrastructure, urban geography, and culture—especially in cities like Philadelphia, considered critical to the national economy—shaped the growth and implementation of civil defense expertise.[71] Planning for civil defense was hard enough, considering the interdisciplinary nature of the nuclear attack problem. Once the nation got past the first rush of planning in the midst of the Korean War crisis, implementing the plans seemed almost impossible.

It is likewise important to consider the role of federalism in allowing civil defense experts to continue their work long after state and municipal governments, as well as average citizens, ceased to pay much attention. The lasting power of federal preemption over more contextually realistic risks and disaster concerns in the Cold War demonstrates yet another way relationships between expertise and standards or policy implementation are not straightforward. Whereas fire experts pushed their knowledge up and out from private sector concerns into public policy and voluntary standard setting, federal civil defense experts pushed their knowledge out of Washington down into local urban contexts—with strong legal powers and the political imprimatur of the president of the United States. Nevertheless, just as the fire experts before them, the civil defenders found that local politics, federalism, cultural factors, and economic cycles mattered tremendously and raised significant barriers to a simple transformation of knowledge into universally authoritative standards and policies for nuclear war preparedness and "survival."

Civil defense in Philadelphia failed to achieve its goals not solely because of lack of funding or an apathetic citizenry, the two explanations most frequently cited by its frustrated promoters and many historians. A close look at Philadelphia's civil defense initiatives in the early years of the Cold War reveals a critical and underexamined barrier to success. The top down command and control orientation of civil defense plans came into conflict with the realities of Philadelphia politics and governance, urban infrastructure, and cultural contours, resulting in critical lapses of trust, authority, and efficacy for civil defense officials. More critically, the expertise in disaster scenarios developed by the civil defenders became national policy by direct order of the president. Where the fire experts worked for over half a century to push their knowledge out into the policy realm, the civil defenders were placed in very powerful positions before they had developed much core disaster knowledge. They were learning as they went on very serious issues, from blast and fire impacts of nuclear attack to the legal, economic, and human behavior aspects of life in the post-attack city.

Writing plans turned out to be the easy part; coordinating plans through intergovernmental action was harder, but still easy compared to motivating the public to rally to the civil defense banner. Not that city-dwellers found civil defense an unworthy enterprise—especially as great majorities believed nuclear attack imminent in the early Cold War—it was just that many were uninterested in taking steps toward preparedness. In this sense civil defenders had succeeded in a way they might have rather not—the public trusted them enough to leave the job to the "experts." Clearly this outcome was fine when plans were being drafted and tested, but would not be very good in the event of an actual attack.

Civil Defense Marches On

The problems of local civil defense were not limited to Philadelphia. Across the country city and state civil defense officials worked to keep connected to the new information and policy directives coming out of Washington while simultaneously trying to keep planning going and engage the public at home. Writing in the *Bulletin of the Atomic Scientists* in 1950, Milwaukee mayor Frank P. Zeidler discussed the plans for his city. He had called together a Milwaukee Civil Defense and Disaster Committee in 1948, but very soon became a critic of the federal civil defense attitude toward cities. In the Federal Civil Defense Act he saw a "passive defense" strategy, where cities would be expected to pay the price in the event that nuclear deterrence failed. Zeidler saw a civil defense structure where cities were cut out of the conversation, with the federal government dealing most directly with states. In assessing the prospects for the city against nuclear weapons, he concluded "the circular-form city densely packed, is doomed as a place of future living."[72] Zeidler promoted an idea for a ribbon-shaped urban dispersal pattern, with cities spreading out into the countryside, narrowly compacted and carrying on for miles, making them exceedingly hard to destroy with a few nuclear bombs. The open spaces between these urban ribbons could be used for parks, playgrounds, airports, and farming.[73]

This was a far-fetched idea that in just a few years time would actually move into the mainstream of civil defense urban planning discussions. Sheltering meant certain death if there were not enough shelters or if firestorms starved a city of oxygen. Evacuation meant death by the roadside, or at least radiation exposure by the roadside, from fallout that could encompass an entire region. The projected effects of hydrogen weapons from 1953 on added urgency to the idea that it might make sense simply to evacuate the cities for new, more defensible, less densely populated and built forms. In 1953 federal civil defense experts teamed with the Department of Defense on a top to bottom study of civil defense issues, and their 10-volume report concluded that dispersal was the optimal approach to protecting urban populations.[74] As historian Jennifer Light has demonstrated, the conversation around urban relocation as a realistic civil defense measure attracted an "astonishingly long list of city planners and urban scholars." Well-known city planning experts such as Tracy Augur, Robert Moses, Catherine Bauer, and Burnham Kelly flocked to the idea of dispersal.[75]

As Robert Kargon and Arthur Molella have argued, the enthusiasm for dispersal broke into two camps. Planners like Tracy Augur at the Tennessee Valley Authority found in dispersal a way to connect civil defense necessity to the regional planning movement and luminaries like Lewis Mumford, and therefore drew intellectual sustenance from nineteenth-century planning innovators like Patrick Geddes and Garden Cities pioneer Ebenezer Howard.[76] A second group of dispersal enthusiasts were more fascinated with the process as part of a desirable postwar suburbanization, and movement of population from the northeast to the south and west. The 1956 Federal Highway Act connected the dots between dispersal planning and federal policies geared toward suburban development. The reality was that suburbanization did more to decentralize the American city than any civil defense dictates by the experts. Suburbanization was as close as the civil defense experts ever got to achieving their most far-reaching plans for war readiness, and this process was entirely beyond their command.

Like the fire experts before them, the civil defense planners had a zest for completely remaking the nation's cities—this was of course the only way to achieve their ends. The fireproof city was not possible when its buildings were built of wood. The nuclear attack-proof city was not possible when its buildings were so closely built and its people so tightly packed. Despite the creativity of the dispersal plans, they raised serious concerns not only of cost, but also of the radical shift away from local and state prerogatives in land use planning to the command and control of federal civil defense planners. Entailed in such a shake-up was government intrusion into the booming suburban land market, as the pattern of civil defense suburbanization would undoubtedly create winners and losers. The winners would be the ones holding land marked for development (though what if they wanted to hold out for a higher price?); the losers would be those whose land was marked for open space, to remain undeveloped. Of course the most difficult problem would be convincing political leaders and citizens in major metropolitan areas to dilute their power and diminish their populations, and therefore, utterly remake the political economy and culture of the American city.[77]

To return for a moment to Milwaukee, Mayor Zeidler also expounded on a very important concept that would more and more arise in discussions of civil defense's national utility: "dual use." Zeidler described dual use in a very straightforward way: any planning for nuclear civil defense in Milwaukee also had to "enable our present organization to cope, at least theoretically, with a flash flood or a major conflagration."[78] Civil defense was now taking an important turn toward expanding its mission and responsibilities. Federal involvement in disaster relief has a long history in the United States, dating back to a congressional appropriation to assist Portsmouth, New Hampshire, after a major fire in 1803. Rather than establish a permanent agency for disaster response, however, the federal government made funds available on a disaster by disaster basis; and the American Red Cross was chartered by Congress in 1905 to serve as a permanent disaster relief organization. The Great Depression and New Deal changed the context, opening the opportunity for more aggressive federal involvement in disaster relief.[79] In 1950, the same year that Congress passed the Federal Civil Defense Act, it also passed the Federal Disaster Relief Act, which for the first time allowed the president to declare a disaster in a state or locality and send relief funds and support services without going to Congress for an appropriation. As with the Defense Act the federal patron was not assuming control, leaving initiation of the relief request and long-term mitigation and recovery costs to the states. Still, the pieces of legislation considered together demonstrate a major shift in federal orientation toward creating a permanent structure of both disaster research and disaster aid to the states. Federal civil defense reports from early on charted not only their planning efforts for nuclear attack, but also their efforts in providing disaster assistance.

The Office of Defense Mobilization (ODM) was created in 1950, tasked with controlling industrial production as well as economic oversight of wages and prices during wartime. Both FCDA and ODM took a vital interest in supplying relief from natural disasters. As "natural disaster may have both a negative and a positive impact on our mobilization readiness," explained ODM director Arthur S. Flemming in 1955. "The impact is negative in the extent to which parts of our mobilization base are destroyed. The impact may be positive to the extent that the experience of fighting the disaster helps us to create the organizations and learn the techniques needed to fight the much greater disaster of war."[80] Flemming cited the quick response of ODM to the Mid-Atlantic and New England in the aftermath of Hurricane Diane in 1955, including directing "the Department of Defense, the Atomic Energy Commission, and the Maritime Administration to do what they could to channel procurement contracts to disaster areas," pumping millions of dollars in federal contracts into these areas. Tax write-offs and equipment leases were other ways ODM could help restore the economy in disaster zones. In the midst of the disaster response, ODM had learned that it was not really prepared for this role. Hurricane Diane had prompted the preparation of a "Disaster Readiness Plan," tailored toward assuring coordination of government agencies around the resource mobilization role, and also for assessing damage. On this point the ODM was hard at work, cataloguing information on 20,000 industrial plants in target areas, and the 400 largest power-generating plants across the country. Damage assessment, using cutting-edge magnetic tape recording technology and electronic calculators, could rapidly compute projected impacts of nuclear attack—so why could the same not be done for natural disasters?

Flemming was hopeful that "dealing with natural disasters and with simulated attack disasters is increasing our competence and capacity to handle the problems of a surprise attack upon us. And by the same token, our ability to handle the problems of an attack will stand us in good stead in responding quickly and effectively to the lesser problems of any future natural disasters."[81] When DCPA and ODM merged in 1958 into the Office of Civil and Defense Mobilization, the dual use function was fused into one agency. At this time civil defense was made a "joint responsibility" of the federal government and the states.[82] The disaster experts were experimenting with the notion that nuclear attack and natural disaster might be more alike than they had thought, and helping communities with real disasters rather than always planning for apocalypse might be a more politically realistic approach to bureaucratic longevity.

According to disaster researcher Gary Kreps, this concept held that "participation of civil defense organizations in natural disasters would increase their ability to cope following a nuclear attack," while at the same time "linkages FCDA had already established with state and local governments for civil defense purposes . . . would be very useful for responding to peacetime disasters."[83] What occurred over the next three decades was an increasingly unmanageable task for civil defenders, as weapons became more and more powerful and budgets remained flat. At the same time, peacetime demands on civil defense grew rapidly. As Kreps explains, "during the 1964–1980 period, in particular, federal natural disaster assistance programs expanded to the point where they represented hundreds of millions of dollars or more annually."[84]

One of the great successes of civil defense at all government levels was in public relations. In fact citizen education was one of the most consistent and effective things civil defense spent money on throughout the early Cold War. Pamphlets, films, speakers, and public events tended to create a constant hum about civil defense, going back to that early opinion survey laying emphasis on this need. It was a task General Cota always pushed for in Philadelphia.

It is not a surprise, when one studies the dismal state of civil defense across early Cold War America, to see that General Cota failed to reach his goals—he was certainly not alone among municipal and state officials attempting to bring abstract civil defense knowledge into realistic use on the ground. It is worth lingering, though, over the ways he imagined the challenge of defending Philadelphia from atomic attack, and even more to understand the factors he saw as crucial to his failure. As the historical literature on civil defense makes clear, Congress and President Truman were confused and sent confusing messages to the states and cities during the early Cold War. President Eisenhower's civil defense team was perhaps even more problematic for local officials. Eisenhower rejected shelters—on the basis of expense—and endorsed evacuation as national civil defense policy. However, this policy was shown to be farcical once the fallout effects of hydrogen weapons were made public in the mid-1950s. And appropriations from Washington continued to be absent or minimal throughout the Eisenhower years. Eisenhower placed his trust in nuclear weapons themselves to deter the enemy and in local missile defenses to shoot down enemy planes. These ideas seemed logical, too, until Sputnik, intercontinental ballistic missiles (ICBMs), and a growing Soviet nuclear stockpile invalidated them in the late 1950s. Nevertheless, it is still instructive to study General

Cota's disaster plans and the assumptions he made about the city he was trying so earnestly to save. In doing so, it is best to remember that he saw his real enemy as a public that lacked the "will to win" on one side and an unwieldy collection of studies and suggestions from federal civil defense experts on the other. As he stated in the 1952 City Council hearings, Cota believed that for civil defense to work, the citizens of Philadelphia must rally around the effort. However, this was not a vision of grassroots community organizing or even a neighborhood-based preparedness model.

Instead, General Cota saw Philadelphia as a volunteer army, an army of 2 million soldiers waiting to be inducted, trained, authorized, organized, and commanded. Why was this military model the dominant model? For Cota, there was probably no other way to conceptualize the problem. His disaster imagination had been trained in war, and he carried the war metaphor over to postwar Philadelphia. Command and control, at least on paper, offered maximum assurance that the city could be simultaneously hardened against future attacks and managed in the horrible midst of atomic attack. Centralization of command and strict compartmentalization of information would keep things simple and efficient, allowing the commander to act quickly and unilaterally in emergency. His was the opposite of a bureaucratic model, with interlocking institutions exercising checks and balances over one another, or a community-based model, with preparedness aggregating up from local units. Furthermore, with World War II so fresh in public memory and military expertise so highly regarded and easy to locate, we can see why Mayor Samuel might have recruited a military man to solve the civil defense problems of Philadelphia.

However, Cota had been away for a while. In fact, he did not even live in the city he was defending but in the suburb of Ardmore—a point that caused some public comment when he was appointed. Cota was not a native Philadelphian, had never lived in the city, and thus had never been integrated into the city's local ward-based political culture or ethnic- and race-based neighborhood cultures. The military chain of command operates the same in occupied Germany as it does on Omaha Beach, portable and absolutely impervious to local conditions—this is the planning mindset Cota brought to his adopted city. Had he known a bit more about how Philadelphia was already organized before his arrival, Cota might have concluded that it was a city of churches, a city of neighborhoods, a city of factories and union halls, a city of businessmen, a city of African American and immigrant ethnic populations, a city of wards and ward-heelers, a city of police and firemen and civil servants. It was just about anything but a city of soldiers waiting for their general. Local organization in the form of "block and post wardens" or "plant protection," organization based on identities and local knowledge, was, however, left to last on Cota's list, and in fact it never happened throughout the history of Philadelphia civil defense.

Asked in City Council hearings whether he had conferred frequently with the city's influential labor leaders, Cota mentioned that a couple had been named as advisors, but he could not remember ever talking to them. This is a remarkable admission, considering the overwhelming blue-collar orientation of the workshop of the world. A recognition that the city had racial, ethnic, and income differences also never surfaced in his writings or his final disaster plan. He did recognize women and school children as special populations and actively recruited both. However, it is not clear what role children could really serve beyond dutifully performing "duck and cover" drills; organizing the city's wives and mothers was left to the only woman on his executive staff, and he knew little about the effort. Local constituencies were perhaps interesting, the existing organizational structures of the city worth noting, but both proved ultimately unimportant in the military model of defense. Command and control was seen to be the way to react to a war, despite the fact that the citizens of Philadelphia did not see themselves at war.

This imposition of a wartime command structure on a vibrant, living, peacetime city was Cota's fatal move, among the many fatal moves made by planners like him throughout the Cold War. It did not help that he was caught up in the greatest twentieth-century overthrow of political entrenchment in Philadelphia. Appointed by a Republican, Cota was a marked man when the reform Democrats came to town. So fearful of charges of corruption that he spent even less than he was appropriated, Cota still represented an authoritarian cronyism that Philadelphians voted to throw out in 1951. Cota himself was never accused—nor should he have been—of profiting by civil defense. Still, a command and control organization with little oversight, an enormous appointed staff, and a constantly growing budget requirement did not sit well with the reform-minded Democrats of the Clark-Dilworth era. Lesson: local politics matter, even in the face of Armageddon.

Cota's replacement, Paul Hartenstein, would prove a far more politically savvy civil defense coordinator. Public relations moved front and center during the next few years, with long lists of accomplishments offered to the press and published in reports to the mayor every year. Public evacuations, such as the 1954 "Operation SCRAM" exercise, gave the public a tangible product for their civil defense dollars, as did the millions of brochures sent out through schools, supermarkets, and local organizations. Operation SCRAM—Survival of our Citizens depends on Cooperation, Response, Alertness, and Mobility—brought thousands into the streets, but more in a parade-like atmosphere than that of a sober rehearsal for crisis. Operation SCRAM was staged at a national level in summer 1955, when 13 cities simultaneously ran evacuation drills. The results were disappointing to civil defenders, with the public participating without enthusiasm. The civil defenders were facing difficulty across the country translating the logic of their plans into drills and activities that could be tested and measured for effectiveness.

In Philadelphia, Paul Hartenstein ran up against new problems that were reflected in other cities as well, such as the unwillingness of property owners to turn over their private building basements to use for bomb shelters. General Cota might have predicted such a problem based on the unwillingness of factory or department store owners to let him anywhere near their property. Why risk public encroachment on your property when you are not required to accept it? Though shelters were built in public spaces such as subways, it would not be until 1969 that the city would boast enough fallout shelter space for every citizen, and this was helped by the rapidly declining population.

When it was revealed in 1958 that an exercise such as the 1951 "hypothetical test" had taken place—this time with a 2 megaton hydrogen weapon dropped on the city—the conclusion was that very little of the city would be left, perhaps only a third of the population uninjured. Rather than a public outcry for more civil defense, budgets continued to decrease, and public engagement continued to decline until the Cuban Missile Crisis in 1962. General Cota's vision of a garrison city—by extension the entire civil defense expert mindset—was not in step with the dreams of prosperity and reform, of mobility, of work and home, of community that Philadelphians were developing in the 1950s. Each of these ideas would be challenged thoroughly in the 1960s, as the deindustrializing city tore itself into pieces.

Despite their inability ever to substantially overcome these difficulties, the civil defenders continued planning for Armageddon throughout the Cold

War, in Philadelphia and across the nation. That they retained the authority to do so raises deeper questions about the powerful role of nuclear disaster experts in the postwar era. How did experts with so few concrete results to show for their efforts keep their mandates to keep planning throughout these years? The rhetorical and technocratic tools disaster experts were developing to help retain their standing were many, even when they lacked meaningful empirical proof to show that they were providing safety and security from disaster. Their main weapon was authority granted directly from the Commander in Chief in the midst of a generations-long war. At the federal level, especially, Cold War planning experts wrapped themselves in secrecy and claims to technical mastery of nuclear attack scenarios that proved unassailable for local officials and average citizens.

The technological frontiers of nuclear war expanded rapidly in the early Cold War as well. In the 1950s, fission bombs gave way to fusion bombs and bombers to ICBMs. This uncertainty placed special emphasis on federal experts who had the president's ear and could influence federal civil defense policy based on shifting technological realities, even if this meant a confusing mishmash of orders trickling down to the states and cities. The rapid pace of technological change, a central feature of the offensive capabilities of the American nuclear arsenal, was a consistent obstacle to local civil defense attempts to create coherent plans for nuclear attack preparedness.

General Cota may have resigned his post in disgust, but not before leaving a permanent imprint on the city's Cold War civil defense. His mantra that citizens lacked the will to win and bureaucrats lacked the will to fund proved to be a fairly insightful analysis, proven more and more true with every passing year. Though he was held up to public scrutiny in 1952, Cota's command and control plan was never substantially altered, a fact applicable to civil defense across the nation. Failures notwithstanding, alternative modes of preparedness—community-based, private sector-based, or entirely run by the federal government, to name a few—were never seriously explored; why? The federal government, to take on the intergovernmental issue for example, could have followed from 1950 a method of straightforward command and control from Washington, dictating policy, implementing knowledge created through federally funded research, all paid for by the federal government. That did not happen, and here we find more evidence (as in the Conflagration Era) of the strong pushback by states and municipalities—even at the expense of putting themselves perhaps at greater risk—against federal encroachment into decisions traditionally reserved to state and local levels. These traditionally have included land use regulation, police powers, economic and urban planning, and, most important, civil defense.

As to the roads not taken in knowledge creation and implementation, it is good to note that command and control as a managerial ideology had a powerful psychological hold on civil defense planners who saw the pre-Vietnam era military as the paragon of efficiency and order in the face of chaotic conditions. This factor was critical to the ongoing authority of civil defense experts in an era when perhaps their greatest achievement was the longevity of their authority rather than the utility of their plans. Nuclear war is not "winnable," but the battle over how to learn and what to apply in risk and disaster control is, and in this regard civil defense experts proved masterful.

In the early Cold War, civil defense experts had considerable authority and resources and a well-defined research area, but negligible real support in the private sector, municipal government, or the public at large. It is in many ways a complete inversion of the fire case. Whereas the fire experts worked against government disinterest for more than fifty years before erecting their own system of authority, the nuclear experts were granted authority almost overnight, but were unable to translate it into workable contextual disaster knowledge and application tools on the ground. The civil defense mission within a few years of its founding lost its clarity, and civil defense settled into a predictable pattern of low-impact activities through the mid- to late 1950s. The Cuban Missile Crisis found an external threat shining light again on a public demand for meaningful civil defense. For almost two weeks the world watched in jittery awe as the United States and the Soviet Union came to the brink of a nuclear showdown over the placement of Soviet missiles in Cuba. Aside from the very early days of nuclear civil defense in the 1950–1951 Korean War crisis, this was the only time civil defense experts really succeeded in convincing Americans to take their plans seriously. Fallout shelters and supply stockpiling, volunteering and wearing the CD armband became fashionable, temporarily.[85]

Among the advocates of civil defense, the most outspoken was former Manhattan Project physicist Edward Teller. "The United States today is not properly defended," Teller argued in 1962. "We literally invite attack because our potential enemies know that the United States today could not survive a big thermonuclear attack."[86] Teller isolated a "defeatist" attitude at the heart of American reluctance to implement civil defense, an attitude fostered by fears that civil defense shelters would be inadequate to survive a nuclear attack, and that for those who might survive, the post-attack United States would be an uninhabitable hell on earth. He insisted that with proper civil defense "we can dig out of the ruins; we can recover from the catastrophe. . . . If we are adequately prepared . . . then the main motivation for a nuclear attack upon our nation will have vanished."[87] Teller's view lived on throughout the Cold War, put forward time and again by civil defense officials and politicians who tied their careers most closely to a hawkish posture against the Soviet Union.

Civil defense experts had to agree, however, that civil defense as they imagined it was a massive undertaking, involving nationwide dispersal of the population away from key urban centers, a system of early warning technologies, blast and fallout shelters for the entire population, relocation plans, and post-attack plans for continuity of government and business. Only a fraction of this work was undertaken in major cities like Philadelphia, with less than impressive results. While Teller argued that civil defense could be the secret to remaining "an optimist in the nuclear age," as he professed to be, it was going to be tremendously disruptive and costly. Teller's view—lampooned in Kubrick's 1964 film *Dr. Strangelove*—met powerful resistance among other high-profile experts pondering the effects of nuclear weapons.

While most Americans remained favorably inclined toward civil defense but disengaged from it, a vocal contingent worked throughout the early Cold War, and particularly after the Cuban Missile Crisis, to expose civil defense as a sham, an elaborate ruse through which the defense establishment could lull the public into a dream of safety while nuclear stockpiling and "mutually assured destruction" strategies were paving the way to world war. Scientists like Linus Pauling, Ralph E. Lapp, and Eugene Rabinowitch, publications like the *Bulletin of the Atomic Scientists*, and groups like Physicians for Social Responsibility and the National Committee for a Sane Nuclear Policy (SANE) organized, wrote books, made speeches, and directly challenged the claims of civil defense experts in these years. Psychologist and anti-nuclear activist Robert Jay Lifton—who had closely studied the survivors of the nuclear attacks on Japan—developed the concept of "psychic numbing" to explain how survivors could press on with their lives in the face of so much misery and psychological trauma. The concept was not limited to the Japanese—Lifton saw in American culture of the 1960s evidence of "psychic numbing" as well. As he saw it, the realistic prospects of nuclear war were just too great to bear on a day-to-day basis, so people denied them and went ahead with their lives. Lifton's analysis provides another way to understand how civil defenders had overall public approval but not public participation in their programs.[88]

While in the weeks leading up to and after the final tense resolution of the Cuban Missile Crisis the costs of civil defense may have seemed reasonable to many Americans, the nation soon returned to skepticism about civil defense as a sustainable approach to the looming nuclear risk. This skepticism was not, as Teller would argue to the end of his life, based on irrational fears of being entombed in a fallout shelter or scavenging for food in a post-attack wasteland (though undoubtedly these were not rosy thoughts). Reluctance to buy into the vision of the civil defense experts had much more to do with community level assessments of the trade-offs required in preparation for and response to the risks in everyday life. If a nuclear attack came, that was largely out of the control of average Americans and average cities—more pressing were the disasters on a seasonal basis like hurricanes, floods, and fires, or on an intermittent basis like earthquakes and industrial accidents. The rejection of civil defense was, in other words, really an embrace of the reality that a full range of hazards faced Americans that could perhaps be effectively planned for and responded to through expert study and action. Civil defense officials continued to commission research studies in the 1960s focused on two main areas: preparedness for nuclear attack, and public opinion of civil defense measures. They wanted to know, time and again, that they were popular—which the surveys always showed. They wondered, time and again, how they could transform that popularity into more money from Congress, more authority to take on coordinated planning and dual-use preparedness work, and more tangible support in volunteerism.

A 1966 retrospective review of twenty years of civil defense public opinion polling captured the situation well. The review pointed out a longstanding consensus that civil defense, shelters, and evacuation measures were worthwhile, and were an appropriate government responsibility. At the same time the public did not think about civil defense except in crisis moments, like 1950 or 1962, and undoubtedly in years to come, considering the view in 1966 that the end to the Cold War was not in sight. When it came to taking action in favor of civil defense, that was less certain. "The general tendency," the report concluded, "is to feel that there is very little one can do in the face of a nuclear threat."[89] In the end Americans in the Cold War did "not think that civil defense systems will make war more probable. Nor do they believe that war will become less likely." In a time when Americans generally trusted government to do the right thing, it is unsurprising that the public left civil defense to the experts and went on with their lives. Civil defense, in other words, was something government did to prepare for a threat so grave and so complex that real citizen involvement (rather than symbolic volunteerism) was more or less impossible.[90]

Sociologist Lee Clarke has seriously considered the paradox of Cold War civil defense authority—a situation in which the experts planned away, never really expanding their authority, never really losing it. "Shelter wasn't possible and evacuation was improbable," Clarke notes. "'Could we evacuate the evacuation centers?' 'Would there be anything to return to?' By their own logic the answer would be 'No.' If that were so, however, and if the overall society had been leveled in nuclear warfare what, finally, would be the point of trying to defend against nuclear attack? Such questions were never addressed. To admit them openly would have been to admit the very strong possibility that nuclear civil defense wouldn't work. As important, to admit them openly would have said that the 'experts' had no idea of whether their plans would in fact work. That would be like saying, 'Let us spend millions, even billions of your dollars on something whose effectiveness we can't even fathom.' "[91] In this case Clarke provocatively asserts the power of planning, the existential organizational necessity of planning that disaster experts who have succeeded over long periods of time have always mastered, through control of technical standards or control through governmental decree as with civil defense. The plans don't have to be rational, make sense, or be applied in the real world to inspire research and shape public policy.

Americans never seriously considered retreating deep into mine shafts to happily wait 100 years for the radiation of their bombed cities to dissipate —another dark joke on the civil defenders portrayed in *Dr. Strangelove*. The fact that their plans were never tested, very much unlike those of the fire experts, was not detrimental to them; in fact, Clarke suggests, it is most likely what kept them viable. Their strengths resided in claims to authority shrouded in secrecy and fear, but also based on hard interdisciplinary research aimed toward understanding every aspect of nuclear risk and nuclear disaster. The legacy of the civil defenders was twofold. First, command and control approaches to disaster management would persevere long after the Cold War ended—as a managerial tool closely wedded to "fighting" disasters the way one fights crime or a war, command and control is a method of applying disaster expertise that is difficult to question and harder to unseat, especially from the local level, and most especially in times of war. Their knowledge gains were impressive, their status was secure so long as nuclear war was an American defense strategy, but they never succeeded in connecting their knowledge to their dreams of preparedness through workable public policy, particularly at the state and municipal levels. If paper plans were what they could do, then they would keep doing that, and so they did.

In closing, a few points should be stressed. First, Cold War civil defense research was interdisciplinary and the experts could rightfully claim to truly know more about the threat of nuclear attack than any other single profession—even nuclear physicists or air force generals. Second, their reach was intergovernmental, with civil defense experts turning up daily to work at the Pentagon, Executive Office building, state house, and city hall. This chapter has shown the ways civil defense experts stationed at different levels of government often disagreed and sometimes openly confronted each other, but in the end theirs was a fairly streamlined chain of authority running from the president's desk out to the municipal command center and even the air raid warden's post (if anyone showed up). This combination of interdisciplinary and intergovernmental efficacy built the power of the civil defense expert. Third, with this power they enabled the nation to continue racing toward the day when it could reliably "win" a nuclear war, whatever that win might look like. Perhaps it would be won by scaring the Soviets into never attacking, or maybe it was a win by degrees, only getting our hair mussed, losing only ten or twenty million Americans in a morning.

These three points—the defining analytical points that run through the book in terms of assessing disaster experts—are matched by a fourth, that their work was focused almost entirely on the nation's urban centers. Even today it is almost impossible to walk through a subway station, or past a school or government building, and not see a weathered but unmistakable fall-out shelter sign. Nuclear civil defense planning may have been hypothetical, but the stakes for cities were high, making it even more important that we note the distance between civil defense fantasies and urban realities of the early Cold War. What could the citizens who did volunteer have been doing with their time instead—what could those planners have been trying to plan instead—what shared goals might cities have aspired to other than defense? Considering the civil rights movement(s), and the medical and technological revolutions of that era all were launched in cities, it *is* possible to speculate.

5

What Is a Disaster?

Disasters provide a realistic laboratory for testing the integration,
stamina, and recuperative power of large-scale social systems.
They are the sociological equivalent of engineering experiments
that test the capacity of machines to withstand extreme physical
stress. The social scientist, unlike the engineer, cannot produce
destructive experiments at will. Sociologists and psychologists can
experimentally expose human subjects to frightening experiences,
but fortunately they must stop short of inducing experiences that
constitute a real threat . . . Disasters do not "stop short."
                    —Charles Fritz, Disaster Research Group,
                        National Academy of Sciences, 1961

In 1951 the U.S. Federal Civil Defense Administration (FCDA) released a
film based on its widely circulated publication *Survival Under Atomic
Attack*.[1] The eight-minute film advises its viewers—Americans facing the
first hot moment of the Cold War, with fighting underway on the Korean
Peninsula—as to exactly how they can save their lives and protect their
families and homes should their city come under nuclear bombardment.
In one extended sequence, the narrator explains in detail how a typical
family should behave once the air raid alert sounds. "The alert will be a
warbling siren blast lasting three minutes," a calm and confident voice
intones. For the next minute we watch mother and father, son and daugh-
ter, act out the necessary ritual of civilian preparation for an atomic war.

Once you hear this act fast: pull down shades or blinds and close the drapes against flying glass, turn off the burners of your gas or electric stove, disconnect any heating elements such as electric irons, hot plates, or bathroom heaters, close all outside doors but leave them unlocked, turn off the gas or oil burners. Taking shelter may be a race against time, even when you have some advance warning. . . . Civil Defense radiological teams, equipped with radiation survey meters, will check on contamination in any bombed area. Stay under cover until you hear officially that it is safe outside. . . . If the people of Hiroshima and Nagasaki had known what we know about civil defense thousands of lives would have been saved. Yes, the knowledge is ours, and preparation can mean survival for you, so act now, someday your life may depend on it.

Survival Under Atomic Attack exemplifies the American civil defense public education campaign, but it reveals a great deal more about civil defense planners than it does about the citizens who watched it. Consider the assumptions implicit in the film: the groups that mattered were civil defense experts and the nuclear family. Authority over preparedness and response flowed down a chain of command from Washington, D.C., through state and local officials, and finally to the average family at home. Information was vital, and with clear instructions from civil defense experts families would react rationally and predictably, waiting for official confirmation of the nuclear threat, and if they survived, for official confirmation that the threat had passed. Last, nuclear war was survivable, even winnable, with a prepared and protected citizenry. The further implication was a dark one. Without a rigid system of command and control, thorough expert-led preparation, rationality, and optimism in the face of disaster, the results would be chaos, panic, defeat, and death. These were the civil defense experts' assumptions about human behavior in disaster, and they would not change substantially throughout the Cold War era.[2] Yet, to another group of disaster experts in the Cold War era—social science disaster researchers—*Survival Under Atomic Attack* and the civil defense mindset it represented held out little hope of genuinely preparing Americans for disaster.

The civil defense experts felt that they had a sense of what the American public thought about the possibility of nuclear destruction, from their many surveys and from the consistent support for civil defense among municipal and state elected officials and members of Congress. They did not, however, really know how people would react in the lead up to and in the midst of a real attack, and in the murky and terrifying realm of a post-attack America. For that type of planning the civil defense experts had two choices. First, they could study the actual victims of nuclear attack—the survivors of Hiroshima and Nagasaki. Or they could find events that approximated the anticipated social disruptions of nuclear attack, and study those. They did both.

While federal civil defense officials prepared for the coming nuclear war and state and local civil defenders like General Norman Cota struggled with realities on the ground, a diverse collection of experts began to shape a new discipline, loosely organized under the rubric of civil defense. Physicians, nurses, public health researchers, legal scholars, and social scientists from psychology, geography, political science, and economics contributed research and practical observations from their perspectives. These disciplines contributed analysis of the ways nuclear attack would affect the nation's health system, ecology, legal and political system, economy, and the mental health of individual Americans. The discipline of sociology saw the greatest ferment in what came to be called simply "disaster research," an interdisciplinary social science research area that used both field studies and laboratory experiments to observe, model, and predict disaster response, studying a wide range of natural and technological disasters, both in themselves and as proxies for nuclear war.

With the creation and evolution of disaster research came a powerful deepening of the overall civil defense knowledge base, and with that a crisis of sorts over its direction. While civil defense officials in Washington were often funding disaster research, there was a distance between them and the disaster researchers, a distance borne out of differences in professional backgrounds, levels of authority, and willingness to accept new findings that challenged "tried and true" procedures and philosophies. It is worth noting that though the disaster researchers were in many cases working in academic settings, they were not working in opposition to America's nuclear civil defense initiative. It is more accurate to say that they found in the federal government a willing and eager patron to support research that had intellectual merit of its own, and also potentially pointed toward a more robust, more scientifically based set of preparedness procedures. It is also worth noting that, as explored in Chapter 4, the nation was in the 1950s quite used to a close relationship between military and civilians, and this was true in the realms of research. Starting with the New Deal and through World War

II, Korea, and the Cold War more generally, defense officials throughout the country were ubiquitous. Likewise, most people had first-hand experience with military culture, and in fact several among the most important first generation disaster researchers were World War II veterans whose military experiences gave them familiarity with the underlying culture of the military men who became the civil defense experts.

In March 1952 a massive tornado slashed through rural White County, Arkansas, killing 46 and injuring 615 people. White County's losses were just part of a massive tornado outbreak that would kill more than 200 people across five southern states.[3] Researchers working for the National Opinion Research Center (NORC) and funded by the Army Chemical Center arrived in the immediate aftermath of the tornado and set to work assessing its impact by interviewing residents. One man described the moments leading up to the tornado in this way:

> After I knew there was going to be a storm I told her [wife] to get under the bed quick . . . I told her to get the kids and crawl under the bed quick . . . the littlest one when I first mentioned get under the bed, he got under there like a squirrel in a knot hole. Right under there he went. But my wife and the biggest boy they wouldn't get under the bed. I crawled on under the bed and I said "Come on, get under the bed quick." She kept running from the window to the door, looking you know. By that time it had already turned dark you know, it was very dark. Then she got close to the bed and I sneaked up and give her a push, a kick knocked her off balance and she fell down to the floor and started crawling under.[4]

Unlike the model behavior of the rational American family featured in *Survival Under Atomic Attack*, the field researchers found in Arkansas a disaster situation that was, for lack of a better word, real.

After two years of study, the White County tornado research resulted in a 960-page report, *Human Reactions in Disaster Situations*. The report, perhaps the most complete disaster study of its era, reveals a field interview methodology and core of findings that disaster researchers would replicate and elaborate in hundreds of studies over the next five decades to the current day. Among these findings, most significantly, people tend not to panic or become hysterical in a disaster, disasters bring out prosocial and innovative behaviors in communities, people do not wait for help and routinely do not understand instructions from outside disaster experts or readily conform to command and control preparedness regimes. The researchers, in sum, discovered that behavior in disaster scenarios was socially constructed, contextual, and variable from community to community, while still conforming to discernible and predictable patterns. Discovering these patterns set the research agendas for the following two generations of disaster researchers, who worked largely in academic settings and offered their results in academic journals, books, and conferences. Such results, it would turn out, proved very interesting to civil defense officials at all levels, not to mention fire and police, military, and mental and public health officials. *Human Reactions in Disaster Situations* revealed a hidden set of social relationships— between individuals and within families, among social organizations, and between government agencies and other experts—that promised a new way of understanding and perhaps limiting human losses in American disasters. Whether and how civil defense and other disaster experts would interact with social science disaster researchers depended on larger professional and political agendas and relative amounts of available funding.

Survival Under Atomic Attack is merely the tip of the iceberg in revealing a persistent civil defense mentality that with few exceptions never inspired public confidence or adequately prepared the nation for the realities of a nuclear war. In large part, this was due to its fantastic hopes and claims, its assessments of human nature in disaster, assessments based on wishful thinking and command and control fantasies rather than solid research findings. As will be described, civil defense experts supported a great deal of social science disaster research, but never seemed to integrate disaster research findings into civil defense nuclear disaster plans. Since the mainland had never come under attack, civil defense displayed a mode of thought based largely on military experience and refined by the technocratic secrecy-minded experts who defined Cold War era U.S. defense policies. In Chapter 4 I examined the claims to authority and work of civil defense experts during the Cold War, in an attempt to understand how a body of disaster experts could be so unsuccessful in creating a sound research tradition or building public trust, yet remain so powerful over decades in addressing the only truly existential threat the United States has ever faced. This chapter is focused on the disaster researchers, particularly sociologists, who conducted hundreds of studies throughout the Cold War on the ways communities react to, understand, and rebuild from disasters. While they often received their funding from government sources, their conclusions rarely corroborated civil defense views on disaster preparedness and response.

How did social science research methods evolve in postwar America in efforts to study and predict disaster behavior? In what institutional settings did the research prosper, and how did different funding patrons shape the development of disaster studies? In its maturity, how did disaster studies affect public disaster policy? By way of addressing these questions, I examine the founding institutional aspects of disaster research. I look at the key theorists and core debates and discuss the professional orientation of the discipline. This lays the groundwork for further consideration in the next chapter of the role disaster research played in shaping Cold War era public disaster policy.

Disaster research served as a parallel track to the civil defense approach for understanding and predicting human behavior in disasters throughout much of the Cold War. While never moving to the center of the nation's nuclear war policy elite during the Cold War, disaster researchers did create an interdisciplinary research field that thrives today, informing activities as varied as economic risk analysis for private organizations like insurance companies to first responder training to building design. In the first twenty years disaster researchers received much of their funding from agencies interested in understanding and managing collective behavior during and after a nuclear war. Though this support allowed the field to grow, it also led to a narrow definition of "disaster" and hindered the influence of the field on public policy. As new sources of funding emerged and the field became more mature in the 1970s, researchers broadened the disaster concept and found their levels of policy influence increasing. By the 1970s disaster research had proved critical in local, state, and federal disaster preparedness, and, more important, it played a key role in the federal shift away from nuclear-centric Cold War preparedness to a more research-based and inclusive "all-hazards" mindset.

The Origins of American Disaster Research

Before World War II there was very little research or literature on disasters that treated them critically. The publishing market for instant disaster histories produced (and produces) scores of tributes, survivors' accounts, photographic books, and light histories of disasters, going back at least to the 1871 Chicago Fire.[5] Examining them critically can certainly illuminate the fears, and imaginations of disaster in their time, but they were rarely self-consciously critical works. One outstanding work to the contrary was Samuel Prince's study of the 1917 Halifax, Nova Scotia, explosion. A French ship loaded with munitions collided with another ship and touched off an explosion that killed 2,000 people and injured another 9,000. Prince, a graduate student at the time, conducted a full study of the disaster and the social changes it wrought in the aftermath. *Catastrophe and Social Change: Based on a Sociological Study of the Halifax Disaster* is generally considered the first analytical work of disaster research produced in the United States.[6]

In 1932 sociologist Lowell Juilliard Carr at the University of Michigan published "Disaster and the Sequence-Pattern Concept of Social Change." This would also prove later to be an influential work, primarily because Carr was the first to articulate a series of phases that sketch the life cycle of a disaster.[7] Examining articles on disasters, including among others the 1900 Galveston flood and the 1906 San Francisco earthquake, in sources ranging from the *New York Times* to the *Journal of the U.S. Infantry Association* to *McClure's* magazine, and also including Prince's Halifax study, Carr proposed a synthetic view of disasters based on what he saw as shared sociological features.

Carr was particularly interested in the chronological unfolding of a disaster, and was the first scholar to propose a scheme for dividing a disaster into phases. The "preliminary or prodromal period" is the time the "forces that are to cause the ultimate collapse are getting underway." This is followed by the "actual onset of the catastrophic forces," in the "dislocation and disorganization" phase; finally there is the "readjustment and reorganization" phase. Carr notes that community reaction to disaster is shaped by several factors, including "its culture, its morale, its leadership," and the severity of the disaster agent itself.[8] He observes that "absolute catastrophes" like a Pompeii in which the entire community is destroyed are very rare, and even in horrific cases like Halifax or Galveston there is usually some segment of society "on its feet fighting back." Along these lines, it is evident that the first efforts of "readjustment" are spontaneous—people collect the dead and aid the injured without formal organizational assistance. Carr makes a critical observation here as well, that "for dealing with the disorganization of community services caused by disaster no community has any plan or pre-arranged organization." The interval of time from the onset of the disaster until emergency plans can take effect he terms a "confusion-delay," a feature common to all major disasters.[9] Carr arrives at a prescient conclusion that anticipated disaster research to follow a generation later: "Social change in disaster is catastrophe, plus cultural collapse, plus peril and perhaps death, plus disorganization, plus reorganization . . . it is not a single event or a single kind of event: it is a series of events linked one with another. . . . it is a series, a cycle of events no one of which is competent to represent the whole."[10] This formulation of disaster as a process rather than a discrete event, an explosion or a body count, marked a decisively new way of thinking about the social impacts of disaster. Elaborating on some of Carr's hypotheses would take a significant research effort.

At mid-century social scientists were first called on to study and advise government experts about disasters, particularly in regard to the social effects of the new tools of modern war such as air power and nuclear weapons. Federal dollars for defense-related research had become by this time part of the lifeblood of the American university—particularly in the sciences, a situation predicted by science policy expert Vannevar Bush in 1945. With the Cold War underway and civil defenders charged with understanding how American society would hold up under the collective stress of nuclear attack, social science researchers held out attractive methods for assessing public opinion, shaping it, and modeling public reactions to nuclear attack through the use of proxy events, like natural disasters. It was a mutually beneficial arrangement: university researchers needed dollars to conduct ambitious studies (even if nuclear attack was not their real concern) and the civil defense establishment needed data.

Even before World War II, U.S. army air forces officials sought outside advice on the efficacy of air power not only to destroy enemy industrial warmaking facilities, but also to affect the psychological state of the enemy population, to crush morale and the will to resist.[11] In late 1942, for example, a Committee of Operations Analysts was convened to assess the rate at which strategic bombing would destroy the German war effort and permit a land invasion. This group included industrial experts such as Elihu Root, Jr., and also a banker, a historian, and an economist. Their studies emphasized industrial damage, not morale, but did show an interdisciplinary orientation, a departure from relying on purely military analyses.[12]

A Committee of Historians, including Carl Becker and Henry Steele Commager among others, was assembled in 1943, again to evaluate the results of heavy bombing of German cities. In their final report, focused on the relationship between aerial bombardment and German morale, the historians were not convinced by the simple "bombing leads directly to surrender" causality proposed by the army air forces, and concluded that a land invasion would probably still be necessary to end the war. The historians' cautious and contextual approach frustrated army air forces General Henry "Hap" Arnold, who had commissioned the report hoping to document the likelihood that air power would break the will of the German people and preclude a land invasion. Arnold amended the report's conclusions, leaving open the option of a victory without land invasion before forwarding it to President Franklin Roosevelt.[13]

In 1944, secretary of war Henry Stimson assembled an organization—composed of civilians—to study and evaluate the effectiveness of strategic bombing in the war with Germany, and also with Japan. The resulting United States Strategic Bombing Survey, conducted between 1944 and 1947, resulted in more than 330 separate subreports. Historian Gian Gentile argues that because the Survey's parameters, organization, and questions were produced by air force officers, a "truly impartial and unbiased report . . . was never really a possibility."[14] In effect, the Survey concluded that strategic bombing had been critical in winning the war. However, there were nuances, especially in the three volumes devoted to the relationship between enemy morale and bombing.

Historians were left out of the work this time, but economists, notably John Kenneth Galbraith, and social science savvy policy analysts Paul Nitze and George Ball were part of the effort, their job being to measure the effects of strategic bombing on the industrial capacity and morale, of Germany and then of Japan in a second study. Rensis Lickert, a psychologist and head of the Division of Program Surveys for the USDA Bureau of Agricultural Economics, was named to head the Survey Morale Division. Using interviews with German and Japanese military leaders, thousands of interviews with average men and women, and review of German and Japanese official documents and captured mail, the morale studies came to conclusions that ran counter to the overall Survey. For example, in the German study, the authors concluded that while "bombing was the major means by which the Allies were able to strike a direct blow at the morale of German civilians. . . . heavy bombing of the same communities did not produce decreases in morale proportional to the amount of bombing."[15]

In the case of Japan, research on bombing and the ways it affected morale indicated that while strategic bombing had depressed public enthusiasm, it had not destroyed the Japanese will to fight.[16] Air forces commander Haywood Hansell later came to the same conclusion, and was relieved of command before the war's end in part for this reason. Hansell pointed out that the longstanding American doctrine of precision—industrial, noncivilian—bombing went by the wayside at the end of the war, especially under the auspices of Curtis LeMay, his replacement in the Pacific. The strategy shift was seen as having worked by top air force analysts, and from then on bombing of population centers was seen again and again, in Korea and later in Vietnam, not to mention the entire doctrine of massive retaliation with nuclear weapons that threatened the world throughout the Cold War. Hansell concluded that area bombing might not have become received wisdom had analysts learned the lesson from World War II that heavy bombing does not necessarily destroy morale.[17] In sum, social science research on the effects of bombing was consulted during World War II but was relied upon only selectively, especially as it did not tend to yield definitive results in such short time periods and did not hold up well under the withering political pressure applied by military officials.

The most important figure in establishing disaster research as a social science initiative useful for civil defense purposes was Charles Fritz. Originally from Sedalia, Missouri, Fritz was trained as a photographer, and earned his living taking portraits and teaching photography until World War II broke out. In 1942 Fritz attended a four-month aerial photography course at Lowry Air Force Base in Denver. He made his way to army air forces cadet training, before being stationed in an administrative post in Britain as the war wound down. When the Strategic Bombing Survey work began in 1944, he was offered the opportunity to apply his photographic training and join the research team, and jumped at the chance. He found himself at the end of the war in Europe supervising more than 400 photographers, and eventually helping publish 75 volumes of aerial photography.[18]

It was here that Fritz first developed his interest in the effects of disasters. His job was to document the vast devastation the Allied air war had brought to German cities. But, did his pictures accurately tell the tale of German defeat? When the Survey came out, Fritz was deeply impressed with the conclusions of the social science researchers in the *Morale* volumes and the attendant problem of military analysts seeing the data selectively. "One of the significant things that they found," he later recalled, "was that the . . . heavier the bombing the higher the morale. And as a matter of fact the lowest morale was either in the unbombed cities or the very lightly bombed cities, which immediately brought into focus the whole morale producing characteristics of especially externally induced kinds of disasters." Here Fritz had observed a detail that would later come to form a fundamental theoretical observation of disaster research, that disasters can bind communities together rather than tear them apart: "That morale survey was very, very important. . . . The more you bomb the higher the production. As a matter of fact the end of the war production of military aircraft and so on was higher despite all this bombing. . . . you should never count on bombing alone to try to get surrender." Echoing Haywood Hansell, the Committee of Historians, and the researchers involved in the morale studies, Fritz came to see from this experience that you can never win wars just with air power. More critically, he learned that to reach such a conclusion required research and careful attention to cause and effect, not merely the war-technological enthusiasm so common at the height of World War II and into the Cold War.[19]

With the war over and his work on the Survey complete, Fritz attended the University of Chicago, and studied toward a Ph.D. in sociology. He encountered Chicago at the beginning of what has been called the era of the "Second Chicago School of Sociology." For half a century the University of Chicago had reigned as the center of sociology in the United States—the discipline in its American iteration having practically been created there by Robert Park with his pioneering urban ethnographic and collective behavior studies in the 1910s. The era around the end of World War II was a highly creative one in American sociology overall, with structural-functionalism flourishing at Harvard under Talcott Parsons and sociology of science taking shape at Columbia University with Robert Merton. Chicago's program at the time was defined by Everett Hughes and Herbert Blumer, who building on Park's tradition pioneered a "symbolic interactionist"— individuals act based on their interpretations of their social interactions in the world—perspective and also applied themselves to the problems of collective behavior.[20] Blumer, particularly, "saw the study of collective behavior as a way of examining new social orders [such as] . . . movements, crowds, mobs, panics, manias, mass behavior, fads, and fashions."[21] The overall orientation of the Second Chicago School, in continuation with the patterns set down by scholars like Park and urbanism theorist Louis Wirth, featured "a strong emphasis on the importance of going out and getting data—an important continuity with prewar tradition—and a relative lack of interest in more abstract theoretical issues."[22]

The University of Chicago, when Fritz arrived, was also host to the National Opinion Research Center (NORC), a nationwide polling organization founded in 1941. Begun by commercial pollster and Gallup veteran Harry Hubert Field, NORC set out to turn the "science" of public opinion polling into a nonprofit research engine for the public sector and for researchers.[23] Throughout the war NORC did surveys of public opinion on subjects ranging from African American attitudes toward the war to grocers' ideas about the Office of Price Administration.[24]

After a sulfur dioxide "smog incident" in Donora, Pennsylvania, in 1948 killed 25 and made almost half the town sick, the Army Chemical Center's Medical Laboratories sent in a team of psychiatrists to conduct a study.[25] One of the things they picked up on was that some people in Donora, though not physically ill, displayed a "sympathetic reaction" to the poisoning without exposure. "Immediately lights began lighting in the Army Chemical Center," Charles Fritz recalled later. "Aha, this is one way of disrupting society . . . disrupting the enemy . . . by imposing frightful things that would not actually harm them but would cause them to be disorganized, disrupted."[26] The Chemical Center wanted a full study of the phenomenon, but lacked a research team. After months of negotiation between the Center and NORC it was decided that it was far too late to do a study at Donora to get valid data on the true degree of psychological trauma caused by the "smog." However, NORC senior researcher and sociologist Shirley Starr countered by proposing "a disaster research team [that] would be trained and ready to move quickly into . . . [a] disaster area and do interviews of a sample population . . . as well as a special sample of emergency management officials, red cross, [and] police." The Chemical Center agreed and NORC set up a team, with an initial Chemical Center investment of $1,000.[27] Starr produced a master questionnaire, heavily focused on panic and hysteria, "the usual stereotypes that people have about disaster." The questionnaire was readied, the teams assembled, and Charles Fritz, having heard about the research and finding himself very interested, was among the first to be hired.[28]

Shirley Starr worked to get an interdisciplinary group together for her "disaster research team," including sociologists, psychologists, and anthropologists, to get a broad spectrum of the social sciences. Fritz quickly rose to a leadership role and spent a year locating and training people on how to approach and interview disaster victims. Most of the twenty or so recruited in the first year were graduate students. Around Chicago they did several hundred practice interviews around fires, porch collapses, and an incident of carbon monoxide poisoning in a local factory. At this point they were getting background experience and testing using tape recorders. Fritz remembered that

> a lot of people we talked to thought this was ridiculous. First of all at that time tape recorders were sort of bulky kinds of things . . . people were knocking around disaster areas with these heavy things. Secondly there was a feeling that particularly disaster-struck populations, one they would be so preoccupied with their problems or they would be so antagonistic to the idea of your coming in to exploit them, get information from them when actually you ought to be helping them in some way. But here you are a scientist coming in to get information rather than to provide any kind of assistance.[29]

In fact, though, few people seem to have refused to participate in the disaster team's interviews. Not all interviews were transcribed; some were just for training with the tape recorder, followed by single or small group critiques of the interviewer's method and results. Starr and Fritz would get together with three or four interviewers and play the tapes, stopping and offering critique as they went along. Also, they began an exhaustive literature search and abstracting process, to collect and process everything that had been published in the social sciences on individual and collective behavior in disaster situations. New researchers who came on were hired for twenty to twenty-five hours per month, and they all started by doing literature searches, reading, and abstracting articles.

In January 1952 NORC held a two-day conference in Chicago to discuss early findings and the prospects for future research. On hand were representatives from the Army Chemical Center, as well as the National Research Council, DCPA, Project East River (the first major civil defense study, underway at the time), Marine Corps, and University of Maryland and University of Illinois medical schools. Shirley Starr discussed the fact that her group had worked on more than 70 disasters to that point but had yet to take on a really big study. She outlined for the group the reasons for the disaster team's existence:

the ultimate objective of this social-psychological research into disasters was to obtain sufficient understanding of human reactions . . . during the disaster, to be able ultimately to make recommendations to be useful in the control of the civilian populations during disasters . . . maintaining community efficiency of operation in the face of the kinds of civilian disasters you have to anticipate in event of another war. . . . We felt that probably the most important sorts of findings that bear on the social control of disasters could only be derived from comparative studies of a number of different kinds of disasters so you could see how much difference it made if one thing went one way one time, or one way another time. . . . First of all, we found we had to try to define more and more precisely what it was we meant by a disaster.[30]

In her discussion, Starr captured the essence of the early social science research into disasters in the United States. The work was performed for a military patron, and as such it had to be explicitly aimed at understanding the intricacies of collective behavior that would plague military leaders in the event of a war reaching the U.S. homeland. Since a war had not broken out in the country since the nineteenth century, the research would require finding suitable substitute events that could be imagined as realistic approximations of wartime stresses on the population. The best way to go about such an enterprise, Starr unsurprisingly argued, was to conduct studies of different types of disasters in a longitudinal way, over long periods of time. Last, combined with the field studies of behavior in disaster, the researchers would have to keep reading up on the multiple disciplines that impinged on the work: psychology, medicine, anthropology, sociology, history, journalism. She pointed out to the assembled group that Charles Fritz was doing just that, having collected more than 2,000 titles to that point.

Furthermore, and more pressing, the researchers would have to develop a theoretical structure adequate to take in disaster behavior data from the field and develop meaningful observations and hopefully predictive tools. The first task here, Starr pointed out, was in defining terms, specifically, what is a disaster? Answering this deceptively simple question had already proven problematic for the researchers, but their preliminary take was that a disaster affects a community, and that a community exists in a specific place with a discernible form or organization.[31] That is to say, disasters are a form of community disruption that occur and then are over, leaving remnants of information that can be studied through interviews by researchers who know the right questions to ask. Such a conclusion brings together the last key element of early disaster research: it was grounded in the sociological traditions of the mid-century Second Chicago School. The participants in the conference were clearly impressed with the ambition of Starr and her team. Dwight C. Chapman of Project East River—charged with advising on national strategy for civil defense by summer of that year—had to admit that his group did not even plan on field research. The Chemical Center extended the NORC contract a second year and upped the budget to $30,000.

Just a few months later the NORC disaster researchers got their chance to take on a large-scale disaster. On March 21, several large tornadoes hit nine states, killing 231 and injuring 1,829. The damage to White County, Arkansas, as previously mentioned, was severe. With their team staffed, trained, and funded, the NORC researchers moved immediately into the area and began conducting interviews. By this time another sociology graduate student at Chicago had joined the team, E. L. (Henry) Quarantelli. Originally from New York and a World War II army veteran, Quarantelli had stumbled into sociology at Chicago and fallen under the spell of Herbert Blumer. Quarantelli was working on a dissertation on panic behavior, and in his literature searching Fritz discovered him.[32] Altogether the White County study involved 342 interviews and was conducted over 23 days by 26 NORC researchers, working 12 to 15 hours per day. The questionnaire used for the general public had 44 general questions, with 18 "census type" questions. A second questionnaire was used to gauge the behavior of leaders of organizations. All interviews were recorded and transcribed, taking about 1,500 hours to complete. When coding was complete the information was transferred to punch cards and analyzed.[33]

The results, published as *Human Reactions in Disaster Situations* in 1954, exposed that certain assumptions of the early studies had been incorrect. For example, the focus on panic and hysterical behavior was not substantiated by observations in the field. The White County population had not flown into hysterics but had in fact tended to assess the situation quickly and react by taking shelter, helping families and neighbors without waiting for outside instruction. The military assumption, expressed by civil defense experts throughout the Cold War, was that outside leadership and support converging on a disaster scene would bring order out of chaos. In White County the researchers found the opposite, noting that traffic coming into the area caused more problems. Additionally, looting—always an assumption and fear of police and military leaders—was not widespread. On the whole, the NORC study of White County depicted a community that reacted to disaster by exhibiting high self-sufficiency and significant resilience. Building on these conclusions reached by way of these methods would animate disaster research for the next generation.[34]

In 1954 the National Academy of Sciences Division of Anthropology and Psychology launched a Committee on Disaster Studies, bringing Charles Fritz on staff. Through the mid- and late 1950s this committee supported field research along the lines pioneered by NORC and published its results in a series of Disaster Studies and in its *Disaster Research Newsletter*. The first major study conducted for the Academy, by anthropologist Anthony F. C. Wallace, was titled *Human Behavior in Extreme Situations*.[35] Wallace reviewed about 10,000 items, cataloguing them on 5x8 cards to be collected and made available for researchers. Wallace found mostly items from newspapers, magazines, and trade books. "These journalistic accounts of fires, floods, earthquakes, epidemics, explosions, and other distressing events," he explained, "vary in quality, some containing only a few photographs, or a brief but sensational statement of impact agent, location, casualties, and freakish happenings, and others approaching scholarship in their scope and incisiveness of observation." Despite being a journalistic account, John Hersey's *Hiroshima* (1946) was lauded for "describing many significant aspects of the first atomic bombing which are slighted in the more systematic reports of the U.S. Strategic Bombing Survey."[36] Wallace also found "technical journalism" in periodicals produced by organizations like the Red Cross, and some "scholarly" works, many of them histories of particular disasters, ranging from John Powell's study of the 1793 yellow fever epidemic in Philadelphia to Edward Gibbon's *Decline and Fall of the Roman Empire*.[37] More "scientific" studies, sociological and psychological in orientation and produced by expert researchers, were hard to come by, and synthesis was tricky, considering "the coverage is composed of the reports of several independent investigators, working with different interests, techniques, and assumptions." Of importance among these kinds of works were recent studies of the World War II Japanese internment in the United States, British wartime evacuations, social science studies of the Great Depression, and German concentration camp experiences.

From here the disaster researcher was faced with nosing around in "psychiatry, general medicine, psychology, sociology, anthropology, economics, and political science," where "such matters as perceptive processes, panic, morale, leadership, informal small-group organization, rumor, communications, social disorganization, [and] psychopathology" were all relevant, though they had rarely been investigated with disasters specifically as part of the study.[38] The disaster research, in short, had to be wildly interdisciplinary, and pretty aggressive about reading widely across genres if the researcher wished to start deriving theory. Writing about disasters went back as far as recorded history, but analyzing those accounts for insights into human society and psychology was a brand new inquiry.

Under Fritz's leadership, the National Academy of Sciences would continue to provide seed money for disaster research into the 1960s. By this time, federal budgets for civil defense had shrunk radically, and public opinion of nuclear war preparedness was bleak. In Philadelphia, for example, it was announced in the late 1950s that a single hydrogen bomb would wipe out a good portion of the city's residents. In response, rather than rally to stock shelters or devise evacuation plans as had been true in the early 1950s, the city's civil defense leaders shrugged their shoulders, and the city council slashed the preparedness budgets.[39] Meanwhile, of course, civil defense agencies continued to print pamphlets, release films, promote "duck and cover" drills, and make plans on paper for an organized national victory in the event of nuclear war. The nation also continued to stockpile nuclear weapons. But, while civil defense preparedness regimes were stagnant, social science disaster research was thriving. Quarantelli graduated from Chicago in the late 1950s, kept in touch with Fritz, and took a job at Ohio State University, where disaster research would enter a new phase.

The first ten years of American disaster research were summarized in an influential 1961 essay Charles Fritz published, simply titled "Disaster," in *Contemporary Social Problems*, a volume edited by Columbia University sociologist Robert K. Merton. This volume situated disaster research as part of a tradition of research including crime and juvenile delinquency, mental disorders, drug addiction, suicide, the population crisis, race and ethnic relations, family disorganization, and community disorganization. It also demonstrated the practical orientation of disaster research, with field study-derived data building to broader sociological findings that could be used to direct civil defense (nuclear and otherwise) policy.

Fritz opens the essay with a discussion of the 1952 White County, Arkansas, tornadoes, placing that story alongside the Dutch floods of 1953 that destroyed the dike system and killed 1835 people. And in the same descriptive vein he invokes Hiroshima, citing 75,000 dead and another 75,000 injured in a population of 245,000. A natural disaster, a technological failure, and an act of war—disaster researchers approach them all the same way—the hallmark of the sociological approach to risk and disasters, with this definition of "disasters" in mind:

> Disaster . . . an event, concentrated in time and space, in which a society, or a relatively self-sufficient subdivision of a society, undergoes severe danger and incurs such losses to its members and physical appurtenances that the social structure is disrupted and the fulfillment of all or some of the essential functions of the society is prevented.

In this rendering of the concept a disaster is a specific disruption to normal functions. Taxonomies of disasters were possible—accident or emergency, disaster, and catastrophe—for example, might provide three different scales on which to rank the characteristics of a disaster, but ultimately the real focus was on the social disruption, not body counts, buildings burned, or dollars consumed in economic impact—and not on failure of command and control or other functional measures of civil defense planning.

As of 1959, Fritz's National Academy of Sciences-National Research Council, Disaster Research Group had conducted 161 field studies, and collected 20,850 interviews and questionnaires. These included work by the research group, as well as the U.S. Strategic Bombing Survey, and additional direct research by civil defense experts. Field studies had been performed necessarily as opportunities arose, by field teams ready to leave at once for disaster sites. Studies were provocatively diverse, and included airplane accidents (4), earthquake (1), epidemics (5), explosions and fires (13, it's unknown if they were ever shoulder to shoulder with NFPA fire researchers at such scenes), floods (14), hurricanes (6), mine disasters (2), snowstorms (3), tornadoes (19), toxicological events (5), miscellaneous accidents (72), and civil defense exercises and "accidental air raid alerts" (13).

Fritz asserts two key reasons for the importance of the work, "first, to secure more adequate protection of the nation from the destructive and disruptive consequences of potential atomic, biological, and chemical attack," and second "to produce the maximal amount of disruption to the enemy in the event of a war." Disaster research was useful, and that's why the public was funding it, not only for defensive reasons, but also potentially for defense officials to create research-based strategic uses for social disruption. This was a strategy for developing "weapons" of psychological warfare, and a reminder of the lessons learned in the Donora "smog incident," where even people who suffered no bodily harm suffered psychological trauma. In the service of civil defense, Fritz also cited that the "findings of disaster research are being utilized by national, state, and local agencies to develop more effective preparation for disaster warning, control, relief, and rehabilitation in peacetime." In this way disaster research proved its utility as one element in an integrated knowledge creation and implementation effort of a "dual-use" character.

From the standpoint of sociology and other social sciences, the research "provided an exceptionally valuable opportunity to study some basic and enduring scientific problems about the nature of human nature and group life." Fritz then explained the misconceptions commonly ascribed to human behavior under stress, a misguided "popular image of how people behave in disasters . . . filled with lurid scenes of society and human nature in the process of disintegration." The research proved otherwise. More commonly found were people living their lives, not fixated on the risks surrounding them, and reacting to disasters according to the social norms dominant in their own social contexts. The issue of disaster preparedness came in for scrutiny. In White County, Arkansas, for example, only 7 percent of the population had storm cellars and 40 percent knew about appropriate precautions for tornadoes, despite its being in tornado alley. In the Netherlands, though the dikes insured their safety, only 5 percent of 880 people sampled realized the dangers they faced before they were warned on the night of the floods. The same pattern was evident in American civil defense efforts. A 1950 survey found 90 percent accepting the need for civil defense preparedness, and in 1956, 80 percent believed they would be attacked, but only 2 percent engaged in training or service and only 6 percent had done anything to prepare. Even among federal employees in D.C., only 2 percent had bomb shelters and 13 percent had stockpiled food and necessities. Fritz concluded from these numbers that "it is extremely difficult to establish an adequate state of preparation under ordinary conditions, especially when there has been no previous experience with disaster and the threat therefore seems highly indefinite or uncertain." In short, disaster preparedness competes with earning a living, protection from day to day dangers, and working to get ahead in life.

The implications from this area of the research for civil defense were clear: discussions of preparedness for disaster were "inherently unfavorable to communications and activities oriented to the uncertain future rather than the present." Such was found especially true in cases like nuclear war, "when the future conditions are painful to contemplate," when there are no rewards for the sacrifice and "no way of realistically testing whether the preparedness measures are effective." To Fritz this did not nullify the need to plan for disasters, but it did signal that individual preparedness was unrealistic. His recommendation was for civil defense experts to train for organized, concerted action at a broad community or national level, with every person knowing his or her role in a coordinated plan, and with frequent rehearsals. In this method of "system planning," leaders sustain the effort, but "preparedness . . . becomes an accepted part of the normal patterns of social life . . . a socially approved and rewarding form of behavior . . . rather than an individual sacrifice which competes with the achievement of the normal objectives in the society." Of course this had serious implications for civil defense, where civil defense directors were paid or at least rewarded through recognition for their work, but citizens were expected to volunteer time, especially around times of international crisis, not necessarily as part of normal daily life.

Fritz went on to propose thinking of disasters not as discrete moments in time, but as social processes playing out in three broad phases: threat, impact, and post-impact. In the threat phase people "interpret disaster cues within a framework of normal expectations," an assertion which helped to understand why people often did not rush to take cover from a storm, for example. People who lived in tornado alley experienced harsh storms all the time; only a rare one required hiding the family under the bed. In the impact phase, research showed that people acted rationally to protect themselves and others. Studies of Hiroshima and Nagasaki did not find mass panic or anti-social behavior in the midst of the nuclear bomb attacks. In the post-impact phase "many of the immediate and pressing tasks of rescue and relief are accomplished by the survivors themselves," and if isolated, a community will "develop forms of emergency organization to cope." In White County, for example, within half an hour of the tornadoes 32 percent of those surveyed went searching for missing persons, 11 percent were involved in rescue efforts, and 35 percent performed acts of emergency relief. Within the next 6 hours those involved in rescue doubled and those providing relief increased by 11 percent.

There were consistent problems observed across disasters. Role conflict, for one, created anxiety when those with official duties in a disaster had to choose between fulfilling an official role and protecting family. "Convergence" also presented a huge and consistently observed problem. In a reversal of intuition, flight toward a disaster area was usually found to be more significant than evacuation. Convergence came in three forms: personal (people showing up to help or watch), informational (people calling to get information), and materiel (relief supplies). Each type of convergence created its own special challenges, often overtaxing communications and management abilities in a stricken community.

Finally, disasters were noted to have positive effects on society, first in unifying people. Fritz argued that disasters had the potential to allow for social innovation, with new social roles emerging while "there is a temporary breakdown in social class, ethnic group, and other hierarchical status distinctions and a general democratization of the social structure." The "amplified rebound" effect was evident in the ways communities often rebuilt themselves, bigger, changed, and perhaps stronger than before.[40] Fritz's summary and synthesis of the Disaster Research Group's work offers a comprehensive view of an extremely rapidly growing field for risk and disaster knowledge creation. It was remarkable how many fundamental precepts had already been established, many of which would go on to further and further elaboration without challenge, like convergence behavior or the "panic myth." Other areas would be investigated more deeply, particularly those having to do with the ability of disasters to remake communities in ways that overrode traditional prejudices and vulnerabilities.

By combining the key behavioral findings with the phase analysis, Fritz brought together two key dimensions of the total disaster environment. Future work would look to elaborate within this structure, mapping changes in individual and organizational behavior at different moments in the total disaster phase cycle. With the achievements of the National Academy of Sciences Disaster Studies Group, civil defense knowledge had found "dual use" not just in terms of material preparedness for nuclear and natural disasters. By fostering the research of social scientists toward founding a new interdisciplinary research area, civil defense now had knowledge about human behavior under stress that could apply to disasters of war, and disasters of peacetime. In other words, if a bullhorn or badge could be used equally well in nuclear attack and a flood response, so, too, could insights into human behavior under stress. The question is whether or not the civil defenders would use the research—considering that it indicated communities did pretty well on their own in disasters, without meddling outside experts converging on the scene.

The Disaster Research Center

In 1962, Henry Quarantelli and two fellow sociologists at Ohio State University—Russell Dynes and Eugene Haas—sent a grant application to the National Science Foundation requesting funding to conduct disaster research. The NSF rejected the proposal, but not long afterward a federal civil defense representative called Quarantelli, wondering whether the three sociologists could come to Washington, D.C., for a visit. As it turned out, both civil defense and the Air Force Office of Scientific Research were interested in their proposal. In the meeting, Jim Kerr in civil defense noted that their original proposal was for an 18-month period, funded at $50,000. Kerr suggested that it might make more sense to extend the period to five years and raise the funding request to $200,000 *per year* to establish a Disaster Research Center (DRC) at Ohio State. Civil defense officials wanted to fund field studies that the researchers could publish as they saw fit, but which would also result in quarterly reports of the center's research, and an annual report that would explain the applicability of the work to national civil defense preparedness. The Air Force, on the other hand, did not want to fund field research, and instead was interested in DRC founding a laboratory to conduct "blue sky" social science disaster research under controlled conditions. The timing of their application could not have been better, as it turned out. Though the nation had grown blasé about civil defense in the waning days of the Eisenhower administration, President Kennedy vowed to bring new life to civil defense. The very real precipice of nuclear war the nation ascended in 1962 during the Cuban Missile Crisis put civil defense back in the headlines. Quarantelli, Dynes, and Haas accepted the offer, and the Disaster Research Center was founded.[41]

According to Henry Quarantelli, the co-founders "learned later . . . [civil defense and Air Force] officials saw the proposal as something . . . to show they were doing something to meet the new threat to American society." This was ironic considering "this was at a time when the US Strategic

Bombing Studies were circulating, and which at least the disaster researchers on the NORC project knew showed that the civilian populations in Germany and Japan had reacted very well to massive air raid bombings."[42]

It was decided early on that Dynes and Quarantelli would focus their efforts on the field work. Russell Dynes was from Tennessee, and like Quarantelli had served in World War II, and then gone on for a Ph.D. in sociology. Haas would establish and run the laboratory. Much as in the early NORC work, an open-ended questionnaire was developed, graduate students were recruited and trained with the questionnaire and tape recorders, and practice trips were taken to gain experience with multiple geographies and types of disasters. In 1963 and early 1964 DRC researchers studied a dam failure in Los Angeles, a chemical plant explosion in Massachusetts, a hurricane in Texas, a nursing home fire in Ohio, the Vaiont Dam flood in Italy, an explosion in Indianapolis, and floods in Cincinnati.[43]

When on March 28, 1964, a magnitude 9.2 earthquake hit Alaska, the three DRC founders and two graduate students left Columbus immediately to conduct a study. They arrived the next day in Anchorage, checked in with the local civil defense office to get an idea of conditions statewide, and set to work on interviews. In their "Preliminary Observations" of the Alaska Earthquake, the researchers noted that "there are both advantages and disadvantages in getting to a disaster area rapidly . . . organizations are literally just starting up operations . . . [and] systematic interviews are clearly out of the question. . . . On the other hand, early entry . . . permits a field worker to observe directly what develops and what goes on, and makes him less dependent on what participants may later report of their activities."[44]

The issue of whether and how much to trust an interviewee went back to NORC days, and was generally overcome by doing a high volume of interviews. Where this became tricky was in interviews with key organizational leaders, where one failed memory or covert agenda could skew the results badly. In Alaska, and in the studies to follow, rapid response allowed DRC researchers more accurately to assess the performance of an organizational leader outside the context of his or her interview. In a subtle way, the researchers were now also inserting themselves into evolving disaster situations. As Fritz had earlier noted, people tended not to shy away from the researchers being on-site and asking questions. "Preliminary Observations" further explains that "early entry into organizations under stress makes field workers well known to organizational personnel. Cooperation is maximized."[45] Dynes recalled that at times this even led to situations

Figure 11. A Disaster Research Center field team on the site of the 1963 Cincinnati, Ohio, flood. Researchers in the photo are (from left to right) Dan Yutzy, John Quaid, and Bill Anderson. Courtesy of the Disaster Research Center, University of Delaware.

where local disaster responders trusted the researchers to the point of asking their advice. Though they were there to conduct studies, DRC researchers were also in many cases in the 1960s becoming experts on the ground as well.[46]

"Preliminary Observations" pays special attention to the performance of civil defense officials in the aftermath of the disaster, as might be expected considering the DRC's funding arrangement. According to Russell Dynes, "one could I suppose argue . . . that to a certain extent the Anchorage Earthquake sort of made the center in the sense of it was a good opportunity . . . we developed somewhat of a national reputation for work up there."[47] However, as time went on it became clear to Dynes and Quarantelli that civil defense officials were not paying attention to the details of their reports, or if they were, it was not being reflected in civil defense procedures. Despite pointing out, as they did in Alaska and in other disaster reports, severe problems in communications, coordination, and inter-organizational authority involving civil defense and other local response organizations, civil defense policies did not change markedly.

This was a problem inherent in the overlapping authority structures of the American federalist political structure. Top civil defense leadership remained fixated on the nuclear threat and on centralized command and control from Washington, while DRC research indicated that locally organized disaster response was preferable. The civil defense "dual use" concept remained mostly that, a concept—useful for rationalizing organizational time and effort, and continued expenditure, but without showing much by way of material results in natural disasters. The farther from the disaster on the ground, it seemed, the more likely civil defense officials were to see only nuclear threat. Meanwhile, local responders in police and fire departments, for example, who served as the true hands of civil defense, needed guidance on how to deal with other types of disasters. Nominally the federal civil defense network was responsible for all disaster response in the nation. In reality, state and local governments paid for and organized most of the training, supplies, and relief necessary after a disaster.

Research by William Anderson and Russell Dynes at the Disaster Research Center evaluated the viability of "dual use" in practice, looking at the ways civil defense offices really functioned in the 1960s. In the aftermath of the 1964 Alaska earthquake, DRC researchers started work on a major study, including attention to the effectiveness of civil defense measures. They found a very mixed picture. In Kodiak, for example, the civil defense director told a hair-raising story about the tidal wave that hit the town, and his fears that his wife had been swept away (she survived). He ended up coordinating a relief effort that fed and sheltered 700 people in the town. He was arrested at one point while driving a police car because the police did not recognize him. He felt that in general civil defense was "a fussy affair. . . . it consisted of mostly paper work that was worthless. The speeches that this man makes in various towns are worthless to you, and you get literature by the tons." In his view it was better to save the speeches, "take that god damn money and put it into blankets."[48]

An official from the Anchorage civil defense office stated that he had not heard of any significant criticism of civil defense throughout the earthquake, and that in fact civil defense's effectiveness in the disaster might very well have saved it from being shut down by the state of Alaska altogether.[49] Fairbanks had a million-dollar command facility, and the city manager explained to the researchers that after 18 years in government and serving as a civil defense director, he "had developed the opinion that a paper structure is absolutely worthless . . . the best thing you could do in a municipality is develop a simplified structure based on what you have." He put his focus on police, fire, and public works. His interview gave some texture to the personalities involved in civil defense at the state and local level. He joked that people "laugh sometimes that our regional civil defense director happens to own and operate a bar," but to him it made no difference "what a person is, or what he does in his normal activities," the real question was: "how well does he respond in a disaster?"[50] Here was more evidence from the field that disaster researchers were correct in following up on local versus external tensions as core to understanding success or failure in disaster response efforts. In Alaska the researchers found mixed opinions about civil defense, particularly federal civil defense, but also firm belief among local people that they could derive the risk and disaster protections they needed, and that they would get by in the face of disasters using the tools and the people they had.

In 1968 DRC researchers returned to the topic. They found that typical offices were small but had jurisdiction over large areas, crossing city and county boundaries. Directors spent a great deal of time on public relations work, running training sessions, showing films, and encouraging nuclear preparedness. Anderson and Dynes's research did little to support the claim that civil defenders were making themselves useful in both nuclear attack and other types of disasters:

> Our general thesis is that civil defense offices tend to be hampered by undue uncertainty with regard to many of their important organizational dimensions such as their authority relations, task domains, internal structures, and public support. And we will suggest that these sources of uncertainty generate operational difficulties for civil defense offices during disasters.[51]

In discussing organizational legitimacy specifically, a key concern for civil defenders vying for authority against other disaster experts, Dynes expressed the key problem for civil defenders. While the role of civil defense as a wartime organization was legitimate, Dynes found that "its involvement and operation during a natural disaster is generally not anticipated." Civil defense was systematically cut out of local planning, except as a "source of materials." Even here civil defenders found themselves at odds with their communities, as when it became known that in some cases civil defense offices had refused to allow their equipment—radios, for example —to be used for response activities in non-nuclear disasters. Civil defense generally "tends to be ignored in disasters because its operation is not seen as legitimate," Dynes concluded. Dynes raised a nettlesome additional point, as to "whether its attempted functioning in wartime situations would not also be hampered by the lack of community legitimacy." Because civil defense officials were not always community leaders they were often marginalized, and delay caused by this marginalization could lead to a need for emergent groups to perform relief functions.[52]

Anderson's further study of civil defense offices gives us a snapshot of the day-to-day work of these disaster experts. His research showed no significant changes since civil defense was created in 1950. "In the typical urban civil defense office," he observed, "the bulk of the membership is composed of volunteers and local officials who have been assigned roles to be activated in future civil defense situations in addition to their primary responsibilities in some other local government agency or department." Shelter management and radiological monitoring were two areas of expertise cultivated among civil defenders. Lists of volunteers often overlapped with fire and police auxiliaries. "However, most civil defense offices also keep lists of persons who are volunteers in name only since their involvement in civil defense programs is nominal or nonexistent. When asked about the size of their offices, civil defense officials tend to include such 'members' in their figure. Most of those included as 'volunteers' are not aware they are seen as a part of civil defense."[53]

While the absence of personnel might be troubling, one might assume that the problem could be remedied very rapidly if a nuclear showdown became a real concern. It was believed that the Cuban Missile Crisis effect might be part of civil defense, wherein citizen volunteers paid little attention to civil defense until U.S./Soviet relations became tense. Acknowledging this possibility, Anderson also found that "civil defense officials generally concede that their organizations lack many needed resources which require the expenditure of large sums of money. However, some offices are also without those resources—such as disaster plans—which do not require the direct outlay of large sums of money." Comprehensive, tested disaster plans "entail considerable time and effort and herein lies part of the explanation as to why they are seldom developed. The small civil defense staff often has little time to devote to disaster planning after the majority of a working day has been spent on other activities receiving higher priority such as stocking shelters and training volunteers in radiological monitoring."[54] Anderson advised that "to increase their chances for effective functioning during natural disasters, civil defense offices should ideally write plans specifically for this kind of disaster situation. However, in some instances, even nuclear disaster plans are not updated, and they would at least have some transfer value for natural disaster operations." If civil defense offices, in other words, were not prepared to respond to nuclear disasters, they were doubly unprepared for other types of disasters that cities faced. Dual use would spell dual failure.

Anderson's analysis noted that state level civil defense offices were in the same condition as city offices, and that overall the unstable budgets, reliance on volunteers, and lack of trust from the public and other disaster experts had rendered civil defense untrustworthy in disasters of more "common" occurrence. If civil defense could not respond to these disasters, Anderson concluded, it would not become magically capable and trusted in the event of a nuclear war.[55] Anderson's study—itself funded by federal civil defense officials—was one of many critiques that demonstrated a shift underway. The civil defenders were seeing their authority seriously questioned. By congressional and presidential action civil defenders could and would carry on, but their lack of resources and applicable local expertise was causing them to be shoved aside in favor of experts who could meaningfully prepare for and respond to disasters of all types.

DRC researchers found out that not just citizens, but also local civil defense experts and first responders were apathetic about preparations for nuclear war, because to them it was unthinkable, or they simply could not do anything about it—their interests were natural disasters. As time went on, the DRC found that the most successful interactions were with local responders who would use their reports as resources for shaping local disaster policies and response plans. Quarantelli, over a period of years and many trips to the Pentagon, came to believe that there were two types of officials among the federal civil defense elite: the hard-core "nuclear war types" and those who did not believe the propaganda. It was the latter group that kept the funding coming into the DRC. It was the former group that blocked DRC research from ever meaningfully shaping federal disaster policy in the 1960s. Eventually, it got to the point that Quarantelli and Dynes would simply cut and paste a boilerplate description of the "applicability" of their research findings for federal civil defense experts into their studies, while they went on and pursued the research questions and disaster situations they found most interesting.[56] Dynes traveled for years to the civil defense Staff College at Battle Creek, Michigan, to teach a "Disaster 101" course for civil defense personnel. To him it almost seemed like missionary work, and it was here that he concluded that the DRC's best chance of shaping the nation's *actual responses* to disasters was in helping educate local responders, the ones who were not fixated on nuclear war. The gulf between realistic preparedness and civil defense visions could sometimes prove humorous. As Dynes remembered:

> Many of them [local responders] . . . were getting tired of the sort of national security, you know the bomb . . . notion. In that same course, there was one guy in the country who was a Russian civil defense expert. He would come in and project what the Russians had. I think most of it was completely wrong, but anyway he was the only expert in the country, [and] they dragged [him] in.[57]

That a briefing from an expert on Soviet civil defense would prove useless to a sheriff or fire chief from small town America never seemed to have penetrated the federal civil defense mindset.

The other side of the research at the Disaster Research Center, particularly in the mid-1960s, involved Eugene Haas and laboratory research. The Behavioral Sciences Laboratory, as it was named, found its first student in Thomas Drabek, a sociology Ph.D. candidate from Colorado, who helped Haas outfit the facility with state-of-the-art behavioral observation tools, such as two-way mirrors, closed-circuit television, and audio recording technology. The goal was a difficult one, to get subjects in the lab to approximate a true organizational structure, then place them under stress and observe their responses.[58] Drabek undertook the most successful of these studies, a simulation of a plane crash in Columbus, Ohio, with different shifts of police dispatchers. The Columbus Police Department authorized the study, and told their dispatchers that some "new equipment" was being tested at Ohio State. Drabek and Haas put together a realistic call center in the laboratory and outfitted it with a full bank of telephones. DRC staff wrote and practiced hundreds of telephone call scripts, and called with "information" and requests for information about the crash from the unsuspecting dispatchers. The study was deemed a success, demonstrating that with increasing call frequency organizational stress also increased. To Quarantelli's fascination, though, the dispatchers remained mostly calm, and even used techniques to try to "catch" people they thought might be bogus callers, by asking for specific street locations and landmarks, for example. Despite this success, by the late 1960s the Air Force had lost interest in the lab studies, in part due to new applicability requirements for external research. Quarantelli and Dynes were not interested in pursuing this methodology, as they preferred fieldwork, and Haas left to go to the University of Colorado. The lab folded not long after, but while it lasted it marked the DRC as the only social science research center conducting both field and laboratory studies of human behavior under stress.

In 1970 Russell Dynes published *Organized Behavior in Disaster*, a monograph that summarized the methodological and theoretical achievements of disaster research to that point. Coming about ten years after Fritz's first assessment, it was a useful stopping point from which to review to what extent the paradigms of the field had been adequately proven. Popular conceptions of disasters' effects on individuals involved the sense that panic was common, rampant self-interest and aggression were common, and a "disaster syndrome" might occur where an individual would become childlike in his or her need for help. At the level of the community "the image of a 'social jungle' prevails. People, hysterical and helpless, gradually shed the veneer of civilization and exploit others. It is said that looting is common and that outside authority is perhaps necessary in order to inhibit these resurgent primitive urges. It is assumed that many will flee from the disaster area in mass panic, leaving the community stripped of its human and natural resources."[59]

The research findings were exactly the opposite of these suppositions:

After recognizing danger, the behavior of people is adaptive, aimed at protecting their families, others, and themselves. Panic is infrequent and does not occur on a mass scale. Disaster victims act positively, not irrationally or passively. Mutual help and self-help are frequent. Psychological disturbances do not render the impacted population helpless. Much of the initial rescue work is done by the victims themselves who do not wait to be told what to do. Contrary to the public image, movement toward the impact area is more significant than movement away. Those who converge on the impact area do present problems, but their actions are usually motivated by anxiety . . . by a desire to assist victims, and by a need to understand what happened, rather than by exploitation. Authenticated cases of looting are very rare. While disasters create personal and community problems, they do not result in chaos.[60]

Dynes noted the possibility that disasters could be both disruptive and integrative, depending on one's focus. They should be seen, he argued, as "dual aspects of the process of adaptation a community experiences when coping with disaster."[61] In other words, disasters reflected the broader social contexts in which they took place, and depending on what moment in time you looked at them, you could see a community coming apart and shortly thereafter a community coming together. The major findings of the disaster researchers Dynes spelled out should be seen as diametrically opposed to the core concepts held by civil defenders, especially their view that communities need strong outside leadership and defense against panic and chaos in the wake of a disaster. Working in the shadows of the larger civil defense effort, the disaster researchers had formed their own conceptually rigorous area of expertise. Their studies were often structured to render disaster knowledge that would be applicable under conditions of nuclear attack, and as with Anderson and Dynes, the work sometimes directly studied the civil defense organizations themselves under stress. The question remained, if the civil defenders were not going to apply the knowledge of human behavior under stress generated by disaster researchers, who would?

Discovering Vulnerability

A wave of civil unrest and violence unlike anything seen in the American city since the Civil War broke out in the 1960s. Pitched battles between rioters and police, and often the National Guard as well, broke out in African American neighborhoods of Philadelphia in 1964, Watts (Los Angeles) in 1965, Newark (New Jersey) in 1967, Detroit in 1967, and Washington, D.C., in 1968. Protests over desegregation, forced busing, urban renewal, housing policy, police brutality, nuclear war, and the war in Vietnam marked the 1960s as a decade when Americans took their grievances to the streets. The poor, racially segregated neighborhoods of the postwar American city harbored grievances that could explode into view with a suddenness and force just as damaging as any natural or technological disaster. In one sense these episodes seemed even less predictable than natural disasters—at least experts knew where the San Andreas Fault was, and that hurricane season came in late summer.

Taken from a different perspective, though, if one knew what he or she was looking at, civil disturbances were also quite predictable. Application of the research methodologies developed by social science disaster researchers seemed to offer a means to understand why some communities erupted into violence and others did not. Conversely, it was possible to apply disaster research methods toward understanding why communities might be differentially affected by the same disaster, why a hurricane might flood out one neighborhood and not another, or why poor and minority neighborhoods seemed time and again to suffer disproportionately the roughest effects of disasters. Through the late 1960s into the 1990s disaster researchers would shift their focus toward cataloguing and understanding the underlying structural risks inherent in certain communities, the dynamics of why and where vulnerabilities emerge, and the ways such vulnerabilities shape disaster impacts. Whereas the first wave of disaster research imagined disasters as external agents that provoked behavioral response and social change in a community, a new wave emerging in the 1960s–1990s theorized disasters as moments in time that revealed the preexisting strength or weakness in a community's social fabric.

In their 1968 article, "What Looting in Civil Disturbances Really Means," Dynes and Quarantelli noted that in more than 40 DRC field studies of disasters up to the mid-1960s, both in the United States and abroad, very few cases of looting had ever been verified. Several factors accounted for people mistaking normal behavior in disaster situations for looting, and they tended to fall into four general categories: "misinterpretations of observed behavior; misunderstandings over property ownership; inflated reports of looting; and sensational coverage of disaster situations by the news media."[62] With the mass outbreak of urban riots in the 1960s disaster researchers sought to reiterate that looting after natural disasters was almost nonexistent, and to also explore the underlying social causes of the real looting occurring in cities across the nation. In neither instance did human behavior reflect the propensity to wantonly take or destroy in the midst of social disruption, but arriving at this conclusion required distinguishing between disasters and civil disturbances, and understanding the underlying vulnerabilities in the communities where civil disturbances where taking place.

Disaster researchers beginning in the late 1960s turned attention to outbreaks of civil unrest and disturbance—they studied campus protests and urban riots and wrote provocatively on the topic of looting. It was an area where nuanced understandings of community and organizational behavior under stress could yield fresh and important (and controversial) insights, and where disaster research could use tools of social analysis to actively shape a debate over the causes and potential solutions to the urban crisis. In 1968 Dynes and Quarantelli published "Looting in Civil Disorders: An Index of Social Change." In the study they noted that looting was a very common fascination for journalists in press accounts of civil unrest, and that sensational accounts were, in fact, backed up by recent high numbers of looting incidents. For example, 600 stores were reportedly looted in the Watts riots, and in Newark 2,700 stores were attacked. They saw in the widespread public attention paid to looting the expression of a common and fearful worldview in which just below the surface "anti-social behavior" was always ready to emerge. "Such views," they argued "tended to reinforce calls for action which are repressive in nature."[63] Aggressive policing, for example, or urban renewal projects that concentrated and segregated urban poverty were two examples of "repressive" measures found commonly in American cities of the 1960s.

Dynes and Quarantelli rejected this sweeping notion of human nature, and instead sought to contextualize riot looting as a characteristic of an emerging reality in American urban race relations. In this new reality, "the spiraling outbreaks of looting are . . . indicative of the end of a particular era of accommodation between American Negroes and whites. In effect, the plundering and looting increasingly signal the end of a period of time when existing 'rights' in a community will be automatically accepted by a significant proportion of Negroes therein as being given."[64] Useful sociological evidence was to be found in the practice of looting if it was studied within the larger context of a riot. Here, the disaster research method was at work. Looking at riots via the phases of a disaster promised an analytical detachment to the process that militated against more simpleminded, reactionary, and racist interpretations. In this case the phases might include the conditions of inequality preceding the riot, followed by the social unrest and violence playing out over hours or even days on the streets (itself usefully divided into phases), and the recovery phase after the riot that might produce new chances for dialogue and community repair, or might lead the community deeper into a spiral of uncertainty and despair. The analysis proved enlightening. Looting incidents showed two main features of interest to Dynes and Quarantelli. First, only certain types of stores were looted. Grocery stores were most frequently targeted, as were furniture, apparel, and liquor stores, while banks, factories, schools, and homes were left alone. In other words, looting was not indiscriminate or chaotic, but reflected economic needs thrown into dramatic relief. Second, looting was usually done by people from within the community, not outsiders, and by different segments of society, not just the poor and unemployed. In other words looting seemed to reflect disquiet within a community that betrayed not just economic deprivation, but also more broadly shared frustration with the existing social and economic order.[65]

Though careful not to overlook the obvious criminality of looting, Dynes and Quarantelli pushed forward an analysis that went beyond the uninteresting "looting is criminal behavior" conclusion. In the looting of the 1960s it was in their view possible to witness the arrival of "a time of social change, particularly with regard to the distribution of valued resources in communities . . . The old accommodative order defining certain limits to property rights of American Negroes is being directly challenged to the point of collapse."[66] Looting provided only a "temporary" reordering of property rights, where looters seized the opportunity of a fracturing in the social order to change at least momentarily their material condition, but it could be seen as a harbinger of a more serious and sustained era of violence, a mode of dissent on the order of revolution, making it hard to bring the participants back into institutionalized democratic practice. Were middle-class and elite Americans, white Americans, listening? They were, in fact, or at least enough of them were to spur a federal response.

In the midst of the 1967 Detroit riots President Johnson created the National Advisory Commission on Civil Disorders, known as the Kerner Commission, to study the problem of urban rioting and racial violence, and give policymakers some insights into why it was happening and what could be done. In its very widely read and discussed 1968 report, the Kerner Commission (composed of many social scientists from different disciplines) came to the same conclusion as the disaster researchers—systematic economic disenfranchisement was the cause of the rioting and looting, not some simple breakdown of law and order or the expression of a genetic predisposition among the poor, or among African Americans to rebel against societal norms.[67] In a startling conclusion coming only three years after passage of the Civil Rights Act, the Kerner Commission report found that "our nation is moving toward two societies, one black, one white— separate and unequal."[68] It was, quite simply, a matter of economic inequality and racial segregation. The Kerner Commission called for redistributive policies along the lines of providing fair housing, jobs, and educational opportunities for America's poorest urban communities.

The political future of such recommendations would have fared better had the Kerner Commission made its report in 1964 instead of 1968. By the late 1960s the Great Society programs of the Johnson administration were being disassembled, with not even the president himself able to fight for them in the face of mounting costs from the war in Vietnam. Martin Luther King had been assassinated, and suburbanization and white flight from American cities continued at an accelerated clip. The entrenched poverty, racial segregation, and lack of economic mobility in the American inner city was reflected in the social practice of looting, and these conditions would get worse throughout the 1970s and 1980s before getting better (in some, not all cities, not all neighborhoods) in the 1990s.

Dynes and Quarantelli closed their looting study with a prescient warning:

a failure to see looting in current disorders as something more than "meaningless" or "criminal" behavior may eventually fragment the social consensus far more than it has been up to the present. This perspective upon looting as an index of social change may suggest alternative ways of dealing with property rights. In fact, if nonviolent ways are to be found, there may be no choice on how to think about the current disturbances sweeping American cities.[69]

The Disaster Research Center did not back away from this area of work, but explored the topic from, as might be expected, many different organizational and community-based perspectives.

DRC experience with following disaster trends over long periods and in different locations informed the methods used to expand the research mission into civil disturbances. In 1970, the year of the Kent State shootings, Dynes and Quarantelli did a major study of campus unrest in Ohio. Dynes and William Anderson published "Civil Disturbances and Social Change: A Comparative Analysis" in 1973, a study comparing riots and their outcomes in the United States and Curacao; the research took place between 1968 and 1972 and involved "semi-structured interviews with members of black groups and organizations." In 1974 a DRC research team including Quarantelli published "Police Department Perceptions of the Occurrences of Civil Disturbances." Many more similar studies followed, and additionally, many of the disaster studies of this time, even those not focused on social unrest per se, were centered on cities, providing for collection of data that might later reveal the underlying vulnerabilities in urban communities and how those vulnerabilities played out in disaster scenarios.[70] Disaster researchers were by the end of the 1960s making their way into areas of research that moved them into debates over some of the nation's most pressing social conflicts. Studies of organizational and community stress related to poverty, anti-war campus violence, and racism were moving the disaster experts a long way from checking up on civil defense officials in lonely Alaskan outposts. A new way of addressing the foundational question —"what is a disaster?"—was beginning to take shape.

Disaster researcher Claude Gilbert argues that the first generation of disaster research was performed in a "war paradigm." This paradigm took shape not only due to the heat of the Cold War environment at the time of the first critical work, but also because of the sources of disaster research funding. Civil defense funders played a significant role in the direction of studies done by Fritz and his colleagues in the Disaster Research Group, as well as the early work of the Disaster Research Center. "Disasters were viewed as situations likely to elicit the reactions of human beings and to allow an adequate test of them. The scientific approach to disaster," Gilbert continues, "is therefore a reflection of the nature of the market in which disaster research became an institutional demand." The "war paradigm" explained the ways the first social science disaster researchers conceptualized collective behavior under stress, how they answered the question "what is a disaster?" In this paradigm bombs "fitted easily with the notion of an external agent, while people harmed by floods, hurricanes, or earthquakes bore an extraordinary resemblance to victims of air raids."[71]

The DRC riot and campus unrest studies of the late 1960s and 1970s pointed the way to an emerging alternative to the "war paradigm," focused in the first place on understanding the underlying stresses within a given community. Rather than thinking only about an abstract set of human behavioral tendencies (like spontaneous mutual aid, or the problem of convergence behaviors) that showed up under stress across different geographies, researchers could also begin to assess the structural stresses within a community before disaster strikes. Such field work inventoried the stresses and strains of life in struggling American communities, it could be collected qualitatively or quantitatively, and it was pursued by researchers in fields across the social sciences from anthropology to social work. Within disaster research specifically, Gilbert sees with this shift of emphasis the eventual emergence by the 1980s of a coherent "vulnerability paradigm," an approach that "provides the basis for moving from disaster as an effect to disaster as a result of the underlying logic of the community."[72] One key strength of the new paradigm was the value it placed on social context. To assess social vulnerabilities researchers paid attention not only to the variable material conditions of community members, but also to their ideas of themselves and their neighborhoods, their memories and unique perspectives, that taken as a whole constructed both individual and aggregate views on a community's strengths, weaknesses, and shared values. A multiplicity of views could be collected, reflecting a diversity of vulnerabilities, and suggesting that disasters would visit variable effects across a region, a city, even within a given neighborhood.

Furthermore, vulnerability can emerge, rather than being a fixed and permanent feature of a community. Where a community might at one time do well in the face of disaster it might not in another. To take the example of urban riots again, the civil rights movements of the 1960s, the half-hearted economic policies of Johnson's "War on Poverty," misguided and backfiring urban renewal efforts, the stagnating urban economies of industrial cities in the northeast and Midwest—all were forces compressing a complex stratigraphy of tension underlying disadvantaged neighborhoods, and/or among disadvantaged groups in those neighborhoods. The context of their vulnerability was historically contingent; it evolved through public policy choices, the successes and failures of social movements, and economic cycles.

In the vulnerability model one sees disaster more as a moment when the curtains of daily life are pulled back to reveal the social dysfunction hidden just out of plain sight all along. The vulnerability concept is especially applicable to explaining why some urban settings give rise to riots, and others do not. Just being in a city, living in a high population density area or amid concentrated technological risks, is not sufficient to cause a riot. But in some parts of the city, a relatively small event like a routine traffic stop could escalate very rapidly into a full-blown riot that destroys large sections of the neighborhood—as happened in North Philadelphia in the summer of 1964, or Los Angeles in 1992. One has to know the details, the demographics, the economics, the history of arguments between the community and government authorities to know the real vulnerabilities of these communities. These were the conclusions of the Kerner Report, inso-far as they did not recommend more policing as the solution to urban riots, but urged policies that would reduce the inherent vulnerabilities of poor, largely minority communities.

Clearly the vulnerability paradigm and its answer to the question of "what is a disaster?" is not in full agreement with the Charles Fritz disaster definition, in which a community "undergoes severe danger and incurs such losses . . . that the social structure is disrupted." In vulnerable commu-nities the social structure is disrupted to begin with, and the researcher's job is to ascertain how, and why, and how this "preexisting condition" will affect a community's abilities in disaster response and recovery. Examining and describing vulnerability is an area of research where social scientists find themselves working against the most commonly understood causalities applied to disasters; as Claude Gilbert points out, it often seems counterin-tuitive to speak in terms of vulnerability. It "is simpler to say that a ship-wreck was caused by a storm, than to explain that the risks of a ship and its crew were revealed during a storm."[73] Critics of the concept cite the looseness of the terminology, with geographer Susan Cutter finding some 20 different permutations of "vulnerability" in use.[74] Other scholars, such as historian Greg Bankoff, worry that vulnerability reintroduces a centuries-old division of the globe into modern, "safe" zones and developing "unsafe" zones. Considering that the overwhelming number of lives and material losses from disasters occur in non-western countries, the applica-tion of vulnerability theory to this fact may have the tendency to impute a permanent victimhood in developing countries, and enable a "moral obli-gation on behalf of Western nations to employ their good offices to 'save' these vulnerable populations from themselves" through "the transfer and application of Western expertise."[75] In some vulnerability-inspired policy and technology interventions Bankoff sees the potential for a sort of disaster colonialism, an invitation for intrusion into countries where western con-ceptions of risk and standards of safety may not be economically feasible, or culturally desirable.

By the 1980s the second generation of disaster researchers would—without throwing away the powerful findings of the first generation "war paradigm" research—embrace vulnerability as a powerful new theoretical tool. Vulnerability was a means with which to understand risks and the reasons why some communities functioned very well, and others very poorly when disasters "from outside" struck—and why others seemed to bring disasters upon themselves in the form of riots and looting that destroyed what limited material wealth remained. Analyses of race, class, ethnicity, gender, mental health, and age identities began to appear in the disaster research literature at that time, and continue today. In sum, to explain a disaster in this paradigm, one does not ask: what was the disaster and how did it induce stress? Instead, one asks, why might this person or this community be vulnerable, and how will a stress event bring this vulnerability forward? One could go farther and also assess the localized hazards in the air, land, and built environment to craft an even more complete picture of a community's vulnerability to disaster. Vulnerability research today stretches well beyond the boundaries of one discipline or even one major field of inquiry. The interdisciplinary nature of risks and disasters enables variants of vulnerability research to take on different aspects of the broader problem of reducing negative impacts. Some vulnerability researchers focus more on the political and economic vulnerabilities of a community, some on the demographics and social structures that shape a community's resiliency. Others—particularly in the field of hazards research (discussed in Chapter 6) look more to the human-induced technological or underlying environmental vulnerabilities of a place, the dams or hazardous waste dumps next door, or the fault lines underneath communities that predisposed them toward disaster.

Even the most casual observer who watched five minutes of television coverage from New Orleans after Hurricane Katrina intuitively understands the vulnerability paradigm and the need for (among many other things) a more reliable connection between knowledge and power when it comes to controlling disasters in American cities. Some people got out (those who had the means), too many stayed put (mostly those who could not afford to leave for economic or health reasons), and the areas hit hardest were those with traditionally high exposures to flooding, such as the Lower Ninth Ward. Hurricane Katrina exposed vulnerabilities rooted in the region's deep historical traditions of racial segregation, economic disadvantage, and environmental risk built into the land in the form of an inadequate levee system. Political leadership at all levels was ineffective, and the rest of the nation watched stunned at how efficiently one monster storm could mete out destruction to the places and people who could bear it the least. The vulnerabilities were so obvious *after* the floodwaters started rising in socioeconomically disadvantaged and environmentally hazardous communities along the Gulf Coast and in New Orleans; why hadn't disaster experts and policymakers done something about those vulnerabilities ahead of time? It was not for lack of knowledge about American disasters that New Orleans drowned in August 2005.[76]

The social science disaster research tradition grew up in a Cold War context, in which civil defense experts wanted to know how citizens would react to nuclear attack. With little direct information to work from they set researchers to work studying proxy disasters to model human behavior under stress. The disaster researchers very rapidly came to a set of critical insights on the topic, insights that quite frequently undermined civil defense command and control fantasies of "panic-stricken" civilians and the crucial need for calm, technocratic experts to come in and save them and their cities from anarchy.

By the end of the twentieth century the field had grown well beyond its "war paradigm" foundation, and had expanded the purview of social science disaster research to include social vulnerability, opening the way for collaboration with researchers and practitioners well outside the social sciences —in hazards research areas like ecology, engineering, geophysical sciences, public and mental health, communications, and the expanding profession of emergency management. Whereas the civil defenders had significant authority to guide public disaster policy in the Cold War, the disaster researchers were steady advisors whose advice was often cast aside; of course, their field outlived the Cold War, and their methods found new applications. With the costs and human impacts of global disasters rising toward the end of the twentieth and into the twenty first centuries, the way is open for disaster researchers to explore new avenues through which to convert their expert disaster knowledge into best practices of emergency management and innovative policies of disaster mitigation and response. Many disaster researchers today hold out hope not only that the core knowledge at the foundation of their interdisciplinary field can lead to deeper insights into modern American disasters, but that the additional reach of the vulnerability paradigm, if employed effectively, might bring the results of disaster research into a broader sphere of policy relevance, quite beyond the civil defense boundaries of the field's founding era. September 11 and Hurricane Katrina have punctuated this need.

Writing in 1999, DRC-trained sociologist and Natural Hazards Center (University of Colorado) director Kathleen Tierney set forward the prospective research agenda for the next generation of disaster researchers. Thinking of the work ahead, Tierney cited a need for "a critical perspective on risk that focuses on the ways in which risk and power are related. Such an approach would recognize that political and economic power determine the ability to impose risks on others, shape public discourse about risks, sponsor and conduct research that presents risks in particular ways, and lobby for particular positions on the acceptability of risk."[77] Clearly this formulation of the potential societal value of disaster research is pretty far from civil defense headquarters. "This approach," Tierney concludes, "would build upon recent work that sees vulnerability to both natural and technological disasters as rooted in the operation of the political economy and in social inequality." Tierney's challenge to researchers to analyze the ways risks are allocated and the larger forces in society that shape and enforce those allocations—those "acceptable levels" of risk and disaster loss—moves disaster research squarely into politically volatile national debates over the proper balance between risk-making and profit-taking in modern America.

6

A Nation of Hazards

"That's quite an arm band you've got there. What does SIMUVAC mean?

"Short for simulated evacuation. A new state program they're still battling over funds for."

"But this evacuation isn't simulated. It's real."

"We know that but we thought we could use it as a model."

"A form of practice? Are you saying you saw a chance to use the real event in order to rehearse the simulation?

"We took it right into the streets."

"How's it going?" I said.

"The insertion curve isn't as smooth as we would like . . . we don't have our victims laid out where we'd want them if this was an actual simulation. In other words we're forced to take our victims as we find them."

—Don DeLillo, *White Noise*

What is it like always to live right on the edge of disaster? This is the question raised by Don DeLillo's 1984 National Book Award-winning novel *White Noise*. In *White Noise* the disaster is a "toxic airborne event," a billowing cloud of "Nyodene D" released in a rail accident exposing the protagonist, a college professor (of Hitler Studies) named Jack Gladney, and his family, as they attempt to evacuate. At the disaster relief center the SIMUVAC civil defense expert is on the scene, annoyed a bit that the reality of the disaster deviated from his computer prediction models, but able to engage Jack in friendly banter about his prospects for survival. Punching away at his computer (but still with the time-honored civil defense arm band) the expert gives Jack the news. He can't say for certain if Jack will die from the chemical exposure, but he will know more in fifteen years, the halfway point through the life span of Nyodene D in the human body. Perplexed by the uncertainty, Jack presses the expert for more information. "If I were a rat I wouldn't want to be anywhere within a two hundred mile radius of the airborne event," the expert tells him. Jack counters: "What if you were a human?"

It was a dark joke, and one Americans were certainly in on by the 1980s, just a few years after the Three Mile Island nuclear accident, the Love Canal evacuation, and in the midst of a Reagan-Era reheating of the Cold War. Metropolitan regions menaced by natural disasters, one slip-up away from a chemical spill or a nuclear accident, an "Evil Empire" with more thermo-nuclear weapons than ever before aimed at every conceivable target across the land—the hazards of modern American life could drive a person to question the difference between simulation and reality, between disaster and normalcy. Maybe uncertainty in the face of disaster was the best Americans could hope for after all.

By the end of the twentieth century American disaster experts knew more than ever before about the risks and disasters of modern urban indus-trial life. They could explain the behavior of fires and floods, predict the human impacts of disasters in different types of communities, and trouble-shoot problems in government disaster planning. And yet the pace of disas-ters remained brisk, and the toll in dollars and lives remained gruesome. The central conflict under examination in this book remained obvious and troubling with every passing hurricane season along the Gulf and east coasts, every fire season in the west, every time a factory exploded or a train car full of chemicals derailed or a tall building came under terrorist attack. The disaster experts were busy trying to stay one step ahead of the Ameri-can risk-taking that kept them in business. Seemingly unlimited in their research creativity, the limits to applying their knowledge often remained very real, following well-known patterns: professional turf battles, intergov-ernmental squabbling, laissez faire attitudes toward land development, and a penchant for technological risk-taking that brought the nation taller buildings, thriving metropolitan regions, and endlessly complex new set-tings for disasters.

A wave of new thinking about risks and disasters emerged in the 1960s, shifting the focus away from the nuclear threat and toward a deeper understanding of the underlying "hazards" of the American metropolitan landscape. In hazards research, disasters emerge as one part of a total ecology, a system of natural and human interactions made more and more dangerous with every subdivision creeping out into the flood plain, and every highway slicing a path across a fault line. Drawing its strength from methods in geography and the physical sciences, hazards research found willing advocates in citizens and policy-makers, who by the 1970s were less and less worried about the nuclear attack that never came and more and more startled by the costs of natural and technological disasters that arrived regularly.

By the end of the Cold War, social science disaster research and hazards research had been creatively melded into an interdisciplinary knowledge area that seemed to offer the possibility of holistic disaster mitigation (lessening impacts) and effective disaster response. Here was hard-won knowledge in ways to protect both people and structures from floods, earthquakes, fire, and other natural and technological disasters, fused with the social science disaster research that worked to understand human behavior under the stress of disasters. In this chapter I refer to each research area by its particular name—social science "disaster research" and geographical/technical "hazards research"—with the awareness that in very many cases the two were merging into one larger interdisciplinary research area that researchers more causally referred to as "disaster" or "hazards" research interchangeably. In the "All-Hazards Era," disaster experts combining knowledge in these areas moved toward a knowledge synthesis in which land, buildings, individuals, and even whole communities could be made more resistant to the effects of disasters.

The shift from the Civil Defense Era to the All-Hazards Era took place through a series of interconnected historical processes. First, interdisciplinary social science research conducted to model from real disasters the effects of nuclear attack had built over two decades toward mature understandings of individual, community, and organizational behavior under stress. The disaster researchers had been joined by hazards researchers studying technological and environmental risks, and an overall consensus had developed around the idea that disasters are not autonomous and unknowable but reflect the social and environmental conditions and vulnerabilities present when and where they occur or are created. The concept of the "natural" (separate from human action) disaster or the unavoidable industrial accident gave way in these years toward a more historically nuanced and holistic model of disasters as built-in features—"hazards"—of social and physical landscapes, not limited to single moments of destruction.

Second, the Cold War-centric federal bureaucratic structure of disaster preparedness and response was challenged directly in the wake of a wave of increasingly costly disasters—from earthquakes to urban riots—by municipal and state governments and Congress. The challenge culminated in the Carter administration's reorganization of federal disaster preparedness and response into one agency: the Federal Emergency Management Agency (FEMA). Third, a new interdisciplinary profession emerged—emergency management—guided by a legacy in civil defense but aspiring toward integration of mitigation, preparedness, response, and recovery as linked elements in a comprehensive approach toward protecting life and property from disasters. New degree programs in emergency management combined with research funding from the National Science Foundation and the National Academies helped expand the knowledge base at the center of the emerging all-hazards paradigm.

Last, it is critical to keep in mind the fundamental shifts in postwar American urbanism that created new hazards, and sometimes exposed old and perhaps forgotten ones. Postwar suburbanization led to a pattern of brisk metropolitan growth, with much of the new development in regions with significant inherent hazards like Southern California and the Gulf Coast. In 1950 only California and the industrial states of the Northeast and upper Midwest had metropolitan populations exceeding 50 percent of the overall state population; by 2000 this list included 37 states, with disaster-prone states like Texas, Louisiana, Florida, and Washington state among those having grown to a 75 percent metropolitan composition.[1] Whereas city governments before World War II were left to deal with such risks, often working hand in hand with fire experts, the risks of postwar suburbanization and metropolitan growth were left to thousands of suburban municipalities and unincorporated county governments to address. These were, to be sure, still urban problems, created from the transformation of land into real estate and high-density settlement. But the disaster experts were now facing urban problems at a metropolitan scale, compounding their longstanding knowledge creation challenges with enhanced problems of intergovernmental cooperation across urban/suburban boundaries.

Though much disaster research in the 1960s was carried out under the aegis of nuclear preparedness, in sociology, fire protection engineering, and geography in particular, the all-hazards mindset found nourishment through study after study showing the command and control precepts of the nuclear era to be outmoded at best, absolutely counter to reality at worst. Moreover, a new synthesis of sociological and geographical methods was seen, exemplified by the founding of the Natural Natural Hazards Center at the University of Colorado and its sustained funding by the National Science Foundation. This revolution in disaster knowledge might not have moved policy much, had it not found some allies in government questioning the strategy of Mutually Assured Destruction, and others decrying the ineffectiveness of federal civil defense as a comprehensive disaster relief approach in the 1970s, particularly the National Governors Association. Civil defense and the tangle of federal agencies that had competing oversight over its provision seemed more and more disconnected from the realities states and cities faced in coordinating disaster response and disaster mitigation efforts.

Nuclear attack preparedness aside, Americans were faced with the realities of the many natural and technological disasters that struck in the 1960s and 1970s. This was an era when—much like the first years of the twentieth century—a wave of disasters focused public attention, and brought forward difficult questions about the utility of nuclear civil defense as an appropriate means of response.[2] Hurricanes Betsy (1965), Camille (1969), and Agnes (1972) rank among the costliest hurricanes in American history. Devastating earthquakes hit Alaska (1964) and the San Fernando Valley (1971). Mt. St. Helens erupted in 1980. A "super outbreak" of tornadoes took place in 1974. Urban riots in Philadelphia (1964), Los Angeles (1965), Detroit and Newark (1967), and other cities, toxic waste in Love Canal, New York (1978), and the Three Mile Island nuclear accident (1979) all demonstrated that natural disasters were not the only type Americans needed to fear. These realities of postwar America—from suburban sprawl into low-lying areas and along fault lines to accelerating technological risks to urban decay and racial conflict—added up to a new era of wide-ranging disasters, none of which involved an exchange of missiles with the Soviets. With the signing of the Partial Test Ban Treaty (1963) and the Nuclear Non-Proliferation Treaty (1968) it was also more and more clear that U.S. defense policy was focused on reducing nuclear tensions with the Soviets, not stoking it, as had been the case early in the Cold War. These factors considered together show us why civil defenders and their consensus over the primary risk to the nation—nuclear attack—would be forced to share authority with a new wave of disaster experts in the 1970s.

Moving the all-hazards approach into the policy realm was a goal of many state and municipal officials, but in the federal structure the civil defense mindset was entrenched, and was in fact resurgent at FEMA in the Reagan years. To build their authority in the 1980s–1990s, emergency managers required more research, platforms to demonstrate their expertise, ways of replicating it through education, and policy avenues. The first degree-granting emergency management program was founded in 1983, and the emergency management profession began to grow rapidly in the 1990s, with its main claim to expertise being the ability to combine specialized knowledge of disaster causes and impacts with the ability to mobilize this knowledge on the scene as a first responder. This chapter follows the elevation of James Lee Witt to FEMA administrator, the subsequent move of FEMA to a cabinet level agency, and the rising profile of emergency management in the 1990s. With its success, emergency management at the turn of the twenty-first century nevertheless displayed a division at its heart between those who would focus on mitigating disasters in the first place and those who would emphasize disaster response functions. Squabbles with critics of the civil defense mindset and the ever-present difficulties presented in disasters by federalism remained in place—artifacts of the Civil Defense Era—impossible for emergency managers to completely cast aside.

September 11, 2001, and the year that followed the events of that day threw into plain view the competition that persisted, even with the Cold War over, between disaster experts focusing on all-hazards approaches and mitigation versus those wanting to revive the command and control mindset of the Civil Defense Era. In the post-September 11 United States, and particularly since Hurricane Katrina, a new uncertainty defines the always tenuous relationship between disaster experts and policy makers. In the midst of this uncertainty, a new era of "hazards realists" are working to get past the stale arguments over what "should have never been built," or "why people don't protect themselves against disaster." These disaster experts— drawing (as is familiar) from many disciplines and acting at different levels of government, and outside of government, are facing the nation's hazards with innovative solutions that might redefine the American disaster landscape for the twenty-first century.

Discovering Hazards

Hurricane Betsy crossed just south of the top of Florida into the Gulf of Mexico and hit the southeast coast of Louisiana on September 9, 1965, as a Category 4 storm. Storm surge swept up into Lake Pontchartrain and levees failed, causing extensive flooding of New Orleans, especially in its Lower Ninth Ward. Losses from Betsy totaled over a billion dollars. In the aftermath the issue of insurance arose—with Louisiana Representative Hale Boggs among others lamenting the fact that homeowners could not acquire adequate (or any) private market flood insurance on their standard home policies. President Johnson convened a task force that in 1966 called for legislation providing for a federally subsidized flood insurance program. Finding it "uneconomic for the private insurance industry alone to make flood insurance available," Congress passed the National Flood Insurance Act in 1968, creating the National Flood Insurance Program (NFIP).[3]

A significant feature of NFIP was that it mandated development of a flood plain management strategy to "encourage State and local governments to make appropriate land use adjustments to constrict the development of land which is exposed to flood damage."[4] Communities participating in the voluntary NFIP program were required to pass land use codes that would restrict development in flood plains, with the federal government aiding in the process of mapping and designating the flood plain boundaries. Under these terms, few communities participated. Category 5 Hurricane Camille destroyed the coastal communities of Mississippi in August 1969, killing 259 people and costing over a billion dollars.[5] As the second major storm in just a few years, Camille pushed NFIP more directly into the political and public consciousness. Under Richard Nixon, the program was made mandatory for all federally guaranteed mortgages under the Flood Insurance Act of 1972. NFIP was (and is) controversial, especially as it placed the federal government in a position to strongly influence land use policies at the local level. If citizens could be kept from settling in flood plains, then deaths and losses from floods would inevitably decline. Making such an approach politically viable over the long term meant making sure it was rooted in good knowledge about flood plain hazards.

The prerogatives of property owners have so frequently clashed with the advice of disaster experts that we might almost call this a naturally adversarial relationship. Fire experts had worked to use their risk knowledge in shaping development patterns and building methods before World War II, but with little help from government (there was no federal fire insurance program) they ultimately created private institutions that influenced the built environment through consensus codes, safety standards, and the suasion of insurance premium costs. However, NFIP demonstrated the emergence and policy implications of new thinking about how to deal with American disasters, an approach where property owners and builders were offered risk knowledge from the government (usually at no or little cost) to help them make decisions about where to buy, build, and live.

The emphasis on flood plain management exemplified by the NFIP was built on forty-plus years of natural hazards research, and no single researcher is more associated with the field than Gilbert White. White received a Ph.D. in geography with a focus on "Human Adjustment to Floods" from the University of Chicago in the early 1930s and went to work in the New Deal era Mississippi Valley Committee. His work in these years fit in with the "conservation" field, an interdisciplinary approach to land management pioneered in the late nineteenth century and first given power by the Theodore Roosevelt administration. The U.S. Forest Service under the leadership of Gifford Pinchot (1905–1910) demonstrated a science-based approach to adjudicating arguments over the most efficient ways to use federal lands. By placing emphasis on making inventories and maps of the ecosystems on federal lands, the Forest Service and agencies that followed it, such as the Bureau of Land Management (founded 1946), placed creation of geographical knowledge at the core of their claims to authority. Therefore, the government began supporting research, often through state universities, in geology, geography, hydrology, forest biology, meteorology, and other scientific fields that could help bureaucrats make decisions about how to manage federal lands. In this context White excelled as a young geographer, interested in the relationships between floodplains and settlement patterns, particularly in the West.

After World War II, White became the youngest-ever president of Haverford College, where he remained until 1955, at which time he returned to the University of Chicago to chair the geography department. At Chicago, White pursued his research interests vigorously in the areas of flood and water resource management. His research reflected a growing interest among geographers in thinking about natural processes as closely integrated with human choices about land use. White's work in these years

Figure 12. Major disasters of the All-Hazards Era. These disasters helped build the sense of urgency toward a reevaluation of civil defense as the predominant model of disaster preparedness in the United States, and paved the way toward the "all-hazards" model and the founding of FEMA. Top left: damage caused by the Alaska Earthquake, 1964. Bottom left: flooded New Orleans after Hurricane Betsy, seen from Air Force One on President Lyndon B. Johnson's visit to the disaster area, September 10, 1965, photo by Yoichi Okamoto, courtesy of LBJ Library. Top right: damage from Hurricane Camille in Biloxi, Mississippi, 1969, courtesy of National Oceanic and Atmospheric Administration. Bottom right: collapsed highway overpass at Interstates 5 and 14, San Fernando, California, Earthquake, 1971, courtesy of United States Geological Survey.

demonstrated a profound and influential insight into the dialectic between land development and risk, a clear-eyed realization that "vulnerability to the risk of a destructive storm . . . [is] the corollary of seeking beneficial use of land resources. Increased hazard accompanies increased material wealth." He was one of the co-authors of the 1966 task force report that created NFIP.

In 1969 White left Chicago for the University of Colorado and struck up a research partnership with Disaster Research Center cofounder Eugene Haas, who by that time had also joined the Colorado faculty. Their collaboration signals a key moment in understanding the trajectory of disaster research that would follow—in the Haas/White connection there was a coming together of the sociological, community-focused theoretical approach with a geography-centered approach to understanding disasters. Haas and his colleagues at Ohio State had spent years studying the relationship between community and organizations and their responses to disasters. White was interested in the hazards that lay inherent in specific geographies and the results that occurred when such hazardous geographies became settled and urbanized. These two methods, when synthesized, allowed researchers at last to think about hazards and disasters systematically, drawing together all the elements defining a given ecology: the land itself, development and construction, governance, and society.

From here hazards research became a very exciting area for scholars looking to develop interdisciplinary approaches, and to take their research in one or another special area—emergent social norms in disaster or hurricane storm surge effects, for example—and plug them into a larger theoretical framework. This hazards framework was and is based on two key planks. First, disasters are co-creations of human and natural systems in contact. Second, settlement and work in almost any geography entail risk of disaster, and research illuminates the likely frequency and magnitude of disasters by accounting for settlement patterns, density of settlement, and the characteristics of settlement. In terms of drawing policy-makers' attention, the timing for the hazards researchers could not have been better. The great wave of disasters was still underway—with the San Fernando Earthquake (1971) taking 65 lives and costing half a billion dollars and Hurricane Agnes (1972) killing 129 and causing $1.7 billion in damage. A looming question began to trouble disaster experts and average citizens alike: was the nation enduring a particularly bad run of luck with disasters, or were the disasters themselves becoming more dangerous as a result of suburbanization and the growth of metropolitan regions prone to hurricanes, floods, and earthquakes?

White and Haas proposed to conduct an assessment of natural hazards research in order to close the gap between the growing body of hazards knowledge and the necessity of using this knowledge productively. The new National Science Foundation Research Applied to National Needs (RANN) program funded the assessment. In 1975 White and Haas published *Assessment of Research on Natural Hazards.*[6] This landmark study was the first complete survey over the field of hazards research within the United States and internationally, reviewing hundreds of research works and concluding that additional research could and should be applied toward policymaking that would prevent or at least inform development in hazard-prone areas. Especially compelling were the three disaster scenarios sketched in the book: a hurricane in Miami, a flood in Boulder, and an earthquake in San Francisco. The scenarios draw stylistically from the civil defense "hypothetical attacks" of the 1950s and the Disaster Research Center's post-disaster studies of the 1960s, outlining the physical, social, and political impacts of each. In Miami, a Betsy-like storm causes severe evacuation problems and the loss of life is high. In Boulder, a flash flood takes 50 lives and leaves $38 million in damages. In San Francisco, an earthquake similar to the 1906 quake injures 22,000 people and causes $10 billion in damage. In each case, the authors created scenarios based on historical patterns of geographical vulnerability, cases where cities had gone right on building and rebuilding in harm's way. The difference was that by 1975 the losses would be several orders of magnitude greater than ever before, with the postwar processes of metropolitan growth happening without significant changes in land use restrictions or risk-aware construction controls.

White and Haas observed that hazards research at the time was "spotty, largely uncoordinated, and concentrated in physical and technological fields." They pointed out that while the discrete hazards from hurricane and tornado detection to forest fire control and hazard-resistant building design had all experienced strong research output, "relatively little is done in relation to the economic, social and political aspects of adjustment to natural hazards."[7] The National Academy of Sciences Disaster Research Committee, Institute for Defense Analyses, and Disaster Research Center had "only occasionally" seen "results in application of findings by public and voluntary agencies involved in disaster prevention or recovery." This social science work had been "sporadic and limited to an investigator's interest in local problems and narrow theory. No broad body of knowledge has been created, nor have earlier research findings been updated in terms of underlying social and economic changes in the United States."

The *Assessment* pointed out that "much time and effort properly goes into studying the physical mechanisms and properties of a hurricane, tornado, landslide or earthquake," but "relatively little goes into studying the human aspects of such geophysical phenomena." Most government agencies —like the U.S. Geological Survey, for example—that funded hazards research used it themselves, and the funds were often inadequate to produce much of lasting value. Most agencies could not support any research of this kind, a fact "especially true of state and local agencies and voluntary agencies. At present, no agency provides basic funding or coordination for natural hazards research." The *Assessment*'s case for the value of research relied on a few seemingly uncontrollable facets of postwar American life, most important, "shifts in population from country and city to suburban and exurban locations. More and more people live in unprotected flood plains, seismic risk areas and exposed coastal locations." The American suburban exodus had found "more people living in unfamiliar environments where they are totally unaware of potential risks."[8] In this, hazards researchers could make an even stronger case for their interventions. Americans were taking risks in unfamiliar terrains, the limited protections of local knowledge and disaster memory were nonexistent in the sparkling new neighborhoods of the American suburban frontier.

The *Assessment* was a call to action: take heed of the hazards in the land, the hazards under your cities, or face destruction on a scale reminiscent of the worst Cold War nightmares and the conflagrations of the 1900s. All-hazards research would emphasize studies of disaster relief and rehabilitation, disaster insurance, warning systems, technological aids like dams, and land use management. How such knowledge would be used, of course, was anyone's guess in 1975. With its emphasis on uniting social science disaster research with geography, engineering, and physical science hazards studies in hydrology, seismology, and meteorology, the *Assessment* signaled a new synthesis among disaster experts. White's work had already caught the eye of government officials in states like Louisiana, California, Florida, and Colorado—states with higher than average exposure to hazards. The *Assessment of Research on Natural Hazards* clarified priorities and a plan for action in research that would be directly applicable to public policy needs.[9]

The National Science Foundation responded to White and Haas's call for funding to create a clearing house for disaster research. The Natural Hazards Center at the University of Colorado was the result—the first center designed to incorporate the disciplines involved in all-hazards research in one location, and to foster studies that would investigate the "life-cycle" of disasters: mitigation, preparedness, response, and recovery. At its yearly workshops the Natural Hazards Center would become one of (if not the only) venue where civil defenders and first responders would interact with disaster and hazards researchers through formal exchanges of research and notes from the field, and also informally, forming relationships that would lead to collaboration on government panels. At the Natural Hazards Center there was hope that interdisciplinarity and intergovernmental collaboration would militate against hardened professional, disciplinary, and jurisdictional mindsets that had stood in the way of reducing the impact of disasters. William A. Anderson—a sociology Ph.D. graduate of Ohio State and a leading disaster researcher in the Disaster Research Center mode—went on to a high-profile career at the National Science Foundation, overseeing hazards research funding. In Anderson, Gilbert White, Russell Dynes, and many other researchers from this era we find disaster experts coming from the "disasters" and "hazards" research traditions working hard to break down the disciplinary boundaries. As always, though, the prerogatives of research funders strongly shaped the goals and applications of the research.

The NSF support for the Natural Hazards Center demonstrated a willingness to partner with researchers who could show real results in mitigation against natural disasters. The first major self-sustaining research centers growing out of the NSF interest were focused on earthquake research, with the National Earthquake Hazards Reduction Program (NEHRP), established by Congress in 1977, the most critical. This program spawned research sites at universities in New York, Illinois, and California, and in California particularly began to produce research that fed directly into land use and building laws on earthquake loss reduction. This was also among the first major federal expenditures on hazards research that was not focused on nuclear preparedness. The day of the civil defender had passed. Hazards researchers in geophysical sciences like seismology and soils science, as well as structural, environmental, civil, and earthquake engineers saw huge boosts in research funding, and accordingly their output in these years grew dramatically. The social science disaster researchers saw fewer gains through NSF funding at this time; their focus on disasters defined as "events" was still perhaps out of step with more the more "tangible" hazards concept of disasters, with its emphasis on mitigation politics that translated into built infrastructural protections like earthquake-resistant buildings or reengineered levee systems. The all-hazards disaster experts had managed to create interdisciplinary settings where new, systematic knowledge about hazards could be created. With willing government officials particularly alert to the political costs of inattention, they saw for the first time meaningful action in the area of disaster mitigation. Policy activity making use of this research was most brisk in the states that had the most to lose from "big ticket" disasters like earthquakes; California, for example, moved in these years toward rapid adoption of new standards for earthquake hazard mitigation in buildings.[10]

In addition to the hazards research funded by NSF, federal funding around this time became more available for fire research. In 1968, with passage of the Fire Research and Safety Act, set against the backdrop of Great Society era concern over consumer protection and the rapid expansion of suburban construction, the federal government allocated funds to solve what was termed the "national fire problem." The National Bureau of Standards was designated the center of federal research, with initiatives for fires in buildings, flammable fabrics, and fire technology. Fire research at NBS had been ongoing throughout the Cold War, but the majority of the work was on the nuclear attack "mass fire" problem. The major federal fire service report *America Burning*, released in 1973 in the midst of the emerging all-hazards consensus, demonstrated in great detail the ways fire had once again become a grave national threat to property and to lives.[11] Though the Conflagration Era had seen the end of city-leveling fires, the built-in fire risks of the American city (particularly in poorer neighborhoods) and the America home were showing fire to be a persistent threat. From dilapidated urban buildings to sprawling suburbs, children's sleepwear to furniture upholstery, postwar America was rapidly losing the gains it had made against fire risk before World War II, according to the report. Nuclear weapons were not discussed. Here we see a critical shift—similar to what was starting to surface in municipal and state governments—in which Civil Defense was losing its position as the dominant disaster paradigm. At this moment much of the research that had been done in the name of civil defense began to be revisited and reinvented with an eye toward its applicability to the other risks of urban life.

The 1974 Federal Fire Prevention and Control Act created the Center for Fire Research, with a state of the art fire research laboratory at the NBS campus in Gaithersburg, Maryland.[12] With the University of Maryland fire protection program close by in College Park, a symbiotic fire protection research and education complex emerged. Much as Armour Institute students had done research at Underwriters Labs in Chicago, Maryland students would conduct fire experiments at NBS. As John L. Bryan, longtime director of the Maryland program, explains, NBS training and opportunities for jobs at NBS were critical to the development of the program. Bryan remembers the excitement of the early days of the collaboration when he would drive students over to the NBS fire lab—it was necessary to go at night, because if the researchers set fires during the day, local residents would call the fire department thinking the building was on fire.[13] However, more was happening than just setting fires. While fire research had long been focused on developing standards and codes for buildings, it would come to encompass fundamental research on the chemistry of fires, novel fire suppression technologies, and digital fire modeling and computer simulation. Such interdisciplinary approaches would come to form a core body of expertise necessary for the next era of disaster experts, the emergency managers.

Founding FEMA

From the end of the Cuban Missile Crisis until the founding of FEMA, civil defense in the United States was hard pressed to make the case for its continued existence. With public fear of nuclear war neither increasing nor decreasing according to anything the civil defenders could control, the rationale for civil defense waxed and waned according to international conditions. A logical response to this uncertain hold on relevance was for civil defense officials to promote their work as applicable to natural disasters. This "dual use" strategy was at the center of arguments and research on civil defense in this era. Making the case in 1972 for a revision of the 1950 Civil Defense Act to include natural disasters, deputy director for civil defense Georgiana Sheldon (the highest-ranking woman in the Defense Department) renewed a well-worn argument.[14] Sheldon declared that the civil defense "nuclear-oriented program also enhances local capability for dealing with natural and other peacetime disasters, an amendment of civil defense legislation is needed only to make this aspect of the program 'legitimate.'" In a rather stunning reminder that civil defense experts were not reading the disaster research they had funded since the early 1950s, Sheldon pointed out that civil defense plans are needed as much "to stave off panic" in many types of disasters as they were in nuclear defense scenarios.[15]

In 1972 federal civil defense officials mounted a remarkable survey, taking stock of who they were, especially who composed the civil defense leadership outside Washington, D.C. Of 4,200 civil defense directors across the country polled, 2,442 responded. The numbers paint a very interesting picture. The oldest civil defense director was 86, the youngest 20, and a whopping 68 percent were 75 or older, with 17 percent under 40. The median age was 50. Two-thirds of directors had military experience, 12 percent had college degrees.[16] Demographics established, the survey continued to probe what the directors themselves thought, and what their constituencies thought, of civil defense. The civil defense mission, in short, had failed, with 79 percent of directors observing that by 1972 the public saw preparedness for natural disasters as "the primary local civil Defense mission; and "only 15 per cent felt the public rated nuclear preparedness first." Among the directors themselves by this time 65 percent were focused on natural disasters, with only 29 percent emphasizing nuclear attack as their priority.

With Congress raising the issue in the 1972 appropriations process and the House Armed Services Committee, civil defense director John E. Davis noted "Congress is trying to decide if Civil Defense needs more direct Federal support for its peacetime role in order to enhance its value as a strategic element of national defense." In that sense, Davis was bullish on the survey's findings, pointing out that his civil defenders had made the transition from nuclear to dual use thinking, and that "broad public and official support . . . for a stronger Civil Defense role in peacetime disaster could weigh heavily in any such congressional decision."[17] Before long Davis himself had adopted the language of the hazards researchers, referring to the direction he wanted to take civil defense as a "whole hazard" approach.[18]

Civil defense was formally assigned a dual role by defense secretary Melvin Laird in 1972, changing the name to the Defense Civil Preparedness Agency, and restructuring the agency to answer directly to Laird for both attack and natural disaster preparedness. The goal was to provide "total disaster preparedness . . . in keeping with President Richard Nixon's policy of making Federal government more responsive to the needs of both state and local governments." Civil defense would now teach the "'whole hazard' approach to local government," with the "federal government . . . helping the local government to make the best use of what it has to cope with in all types of disasters." The mission had changed, but the command and control mentality remained the same, and the founding of DCPA now posed a very real problem for civil defense—could they really do disaster preparedness? Actually making a difference in disaster mitigation and preparedness was something very different from preparation for nuclear attack, where plan after plan (after plan) took up shelf space but was never put to the test. Civil defense effectiveness would now actually be measured on a regular, though unpredictable, schedule from disaster to disaster.

In March 1972 a test for DCPA arrived in the form of a barge accident on the Ohio River near Louisville, Kentucky. Several barges broke loose, and one carrying 640 tons of liquid chlorine in four cylinders came to rest against a dam. Over the following month federal civil defense officials along with representatives of the U.S. Army Corps of Engineers, Environmental Protection Agency, and Atomic Energy Commission converged on Louisville to provide coordination and oversight of the operation to salvage the barge and remove the chlorine. On April 1 the mayor of Louisville ordered a mandatory evacuation of approximately 4,000 residents who lived closest to the chlorine barge while it was undergoing removal. The mayor took action in primary consultation with his local civil defense team and the police department.

The evacuation proceeded smoothly, but in the analysis after the fact two different versions of the disaster response came to light. Civil defense director Davis argued that the federal Office of Emergency Preparedness had acted as the coordinator and handled everything beautifully, and that the Louisville case was a perfect example of civil defense dual use preparedness in action. Davis especially noted that federal civil defense involvement had kept a generalized panic from setting in as the tense situation unfolded. Local officials and a Disaster Research Center (DRC) team came to a different conclusion. The researchers noted that local civil defense (CD) had been very well organized in the face of the disaster. They found that:

> far before the chlorine barge situation developed, the local CD office had conducted monthly meetings of approximately 20 emergency relevant organizations. This was part of the normal everyday

activities of the community. Officials from each of the participating organizations got to know officials from other organizations on a personal level. Lines of communication became regularized; role relationships were formalized. CD emerged as the coordinating agency and leader of the local groups. Where the normal activities were replaced by one of emergency and crisis, the formal and informal relationships that had been developed over time, were carried over into the new situation.[19]

This was from the perspective of disaster researchers an almost optimal case of community level preparedness, and the success of the evacuation emphasized the point. The role of the "outside" civil defense experts was less successful in their view.

When the federal agencies and civil defense officials arrived on the scene they had established their own emergency operations center, a rival to the local center at Louisville city hall. These officials were strangers to the community, converging from Washington, Atlanta, St. Louis, and other cities. "These federal people posed a threat to the local organizations. 'Problems of misunderstanding' as one local official called it, arose. 'It was the federal versus the local level' another local official commented.' "[20] The researchers found yet another example in the Louisville case where "in normal, everyday times federal and local community disaster organizations are not integrated into a functional working relationship. When a crisis occurs, these two levels are forced together and gaps show up, most notable at the level interface, the federal . . . and the local CD. Conflicts and misunderstandings ensue and the total crisis-containment effort suffers."[21]

The picture really could not have been any more clear—20 years of research on technological risks, and human and organizational reaction to disasters predicted exactly what the researchers witnessed. Locals were resourceful, they did not wait for outside help to begin addressing a disaster situation, their local organization could be creative and confident, and the convergence of outsiders, even outsiders with significant knowledge and resources, had hampered the response effort. The researchers wrote their report, federal civil defense officials wrote theirs, and they all went on with their lives. However, by this time city and state officials were becoming less and less likely to let such a situation slip away without noting the dysfunctional nature of the federal-local disaster expert relationship.

From the very beginning, Cold War civil defense faced real challenges in establishing legitimacy in municipal settings. A central question arose over expenditures—why should cities spend money needed for other priorities on civil defense readiness? As a political issue, civil defense readiness clearly played a more critical role at the federal than at the state or especially the municipal level. Winning the Cold War was not something any mayor was going to do, no matter how prepared his city was. Therefore, a critique began to build, bolstered by civil defense's own self-conscious desire to provide dual use preparations. If civil defense could be shown to be useful in peacetime, its legitimacy would be strengthened. Doing so would require adding new skills and administering a public relations campaign. Ultimately, though, governors and mayors rejected these efforts, and lobbied the executive branch for federal support in non-nuclear areas of disaster preparedness and response. In the shift toward all-hazards research and policy we also see the emergence of a new group of disaster experts at work in government settings—the emergency managers.

All-hazards research provided new ways of comprehending best practices in mitigation and recovery from disasters, and applying this knowledge was generally the work of policymakers who would pass restrictive land use laws and building codes to prevent or guide settlement and construction in hazardous geographies. Preparedness and response to disasters, though, even though all-hazards experts studied these areas, would still need to be carried out by responders on the ground. The civil defenders based their claims to authority on their special skills in understanding the nature of nuclear attack and their expertise in skills like shelter management and radiological monitoring. As we have seen, these skills were in light demand by the 1970s—states and municipalities were looking for new disaster experts, practitioners who understood and could apply best practices in all-hazards preparedness and response. What these skills would look like and how the practitioners would gain authority constitutes the history of the field of emergency management.

In the 1970s there was considerable unrest at state and municipal levels over American disaster policy. In 1977 this "concern prompted the National Governors' Association to form a Subcommittee on Disaster Assistance in 1977 to urge the president to establish a new Federal Emergency Management Agency and to undertake a comprehensive one-year project to analyze and make recommendations about the states' problems in managing all types of emergencies."[22] Disaster knowledge at the time was funneled through any number of congressional committees, as well as the Defense Civil Preparedness Agency. The governors wanted to streamline the process of obtaining relief for their states when disaster struck, and they wanted research that could help them direct disaster mitigation on the ground.

According to the National Governor's Association (NGA), the problem of disaster control at the state and local levels had a long history:

> The Council of State Governments recommended model state civil defense legislation in 1958. Most states have adopted it either wholly or in part. On the basis of this legislation, local and state governments implemented emergency programs for both attack and natural disaster preparedness. A serious conflict emerged, however, between the different orientations of the model state legislation on the one hand and restrictive civil defense attack preparedness and funding provisions on the other.
>
> States, which must deal with all kinds of emergencies with limited personnel, have found it very difficult to handle disasters effectively when they have to coordinate with multiple federal agencies, each with its own mandate and restrictions. Governors, therefore, have become increasingly concerned about the lack of a comprehensive national policy and organization for all types of emergencies. They began to voice their concern through NGA in 1977.[23]

In 1977 the NGA established a Subcommittee on Disaster Assistance. Nevada governor Mike O'Callaghan supervised the work. O'Callaghan, who had served as a regional director of the Office of Emergency Planning under Lyndon Johnson, brought to the work civil defense experience and a state-level point of view.

Over a year of research, hearings, and committee meetings NGA members discussed what they saw as the impediments and concerns. George Jones, Coordinator of the Virginia Office of Emergency Services pointed out that in natural disasters, nuclear war preparedness, peacetime nuclear technology, and earthquakes "each is going its own way with no coordination."[24] Greg Schneiders from the White House pointed to the possibilities he saw in adopting the "all risk" or "all hazard analysis." The task of making sense of the federal structure of disaster planning and response was not an easy one for the

NGA. An internal study revealed a staggering amount of agencies performing different, but sometimes overlapping, functions. In disaster planning, for example, federal agencies involved included the Federal Disaster Assistance Administration, Defense Civil Preparedness Agency (DCPA), Housing and Urban Development (HUD), Department of Energy (DOE), Department of Justice (DOJ), and the National Research Council. In disaster response, the collection included HUD, DCPA, the Small Business Administration, the Coast Guard, and Department of Transportation among many others.[25]

In the midst of the discussions Governor Milton Shapp of Pennsylvania proposed a "National Disaster Insurance Plan." Though this idea was rejected, its surfacing amidst the conversations about institutionalizing disaster mitigation reflected fresh thinking on the ways that the insurance industry and government might collaborate. A leading researcher in the topic was Professor Howard Kunreuther, an expert in insurance, risk analysis, and decision sciences at the Wharton School of the University of Pennsylvania, the same school that had early in the century fostered research on ways to effectively regulate the fire insurance industry in the Conflagration Era. Kunreuther had been researching the possibilities for federal involvement in hazards insurance since around the time of the first hazards *Assessment*. In a key 1974 article, Kunreuther compared 4 different options for adequately insuring the nation against hazards, these included: total federal responsibility, self-insurance by the homeowner, governmentally mandated insurance protection, and land use restrictions and building codes. Kunreuther cited the National Flood Insurance Program as a useful model, with its "dual system of premiums: federally-subsidized rates for present occupants of high flood-risk areas and actuarially sound rates for persons who propose to build new homes in these locations after the areas have been identified as subject to special flood risks." After analyzing the options Kunreuther concluded that "insurance supplemented by land-use restrictions and building codes appears to be an appropriate policy for shifting the cost burdens of disasters from the general taxpayer to individuals living in hazard- prone areas." Of course enforcing such a mitigation strategy would require a research effort to determine metrics for defining exactly what qualities made a region "hazard-prone." Here, Kunreuther cited the need for continued work through a "program of research supported by the National Science Foundation . . . currently underway to develop a data base for determining whether disaster insurance coverage should be voluntary or required."[26]

Ideas swirling around like total government insurance or federally-mandated coverage never moved very far in the NGA's deliberations, though they were provocative, and they did show another area of fusion in the creation of disaster expertise, bringing together social science-based economic analysis with natural hazards work. And, here was an echo of the Conflagration Era, in which the grave threats of business failure had prompted insurance companies to innovative research and policy-advocacy measures, culminating in the consensus code system and the founding of safety testing bodies like Underwriters Laboratories. Was such a consensus-based system possible in hazards mitigation, and if so, what new agencies or research centers could emerge as effective "honest brokers" of risk information, standards-creation, and policy advice? The NSF-sponsored research centers and programs and the Natural Hazards Center provided two possibilities, and perhaps the federal government itself could institutionalize these functions in a major agency—FEMA's proponents held out this hope.

In February of 1978 the NGA called for the creation of a new agency, a federal-level disaster management agency. There was concern about the lingering power of civil defense and the unwillingness of the Department of Defense to give it up. Committee members were concerned about inter-departmental obstacles, there was a concern among some, for example, "that if the Civil Defenders got organized they would make an incredible run on the federal budget. Will they have their way in continuing fragmentation?" These concerns aside, the NGA reached consensus. The NGA Emergency Preparedness Project took a year to prepare and stands out as a critical turning point in thinking about both key trends this book has studied: the development of disaster knowledge and the process of disaster standards and policymaking. The Preparedness Project called for a comprehensive national disaster policy that would direct federal aid for "nuclear, natural, and man-made disaster preparedness," consolidate federal programs related to disaster response into one agency, and appoint a director who could coordinate across agencies and levels of government while maintaining close direct ties to the president.[27] The creation of FEMA was now on the table.

In June 1978 President Carter—a former governor himself—submitted his Reorganization Plan #3 to Congress. Bureaucratically it proposed a feat of heavy lifting and demonstrated the degree to which civil defense had burrowed into agencies across government. By statute the Federal Insurance Administration would be moved from the Department of Housing and Urban Development; the National Fire Prevention and Control Administration from the Department of Commerce; and the Federal Emergency Broadcast System oversight from the Office of the President. By executive order DCPA would move from the Defense Department, the Federal Disaster Assistance Administration from HUD, the Federal Preparedness Agency from the General Services Administration, the National Weather Service Community Preparedness Program from Commerce, the Earthquake Hazard Reduction Office and Dam Safety Coordination Office from the Office of the President. Two new functions were also created by executive order: Coordination of Emergency Warning and Federal Response to Consequences of Terroristic Incidents.[28]

The strategies included dual use principles to be applied so that nuclear preparedness shared resources with all other types of preparedness, executive responsibility, state and local role emphasis, use of in-place federal resources, and mitigation.[29] Dual use had never worked in the past, but it was revived here and given another chance. The NGA also stressed the importance of coordinated mitigation efforts to go along with response and recovery efforts, concluding "the establishment of FEMA can provide an important foundation for a comprehensive national emergency management system wherein federal, state, and local emergency management organizations become equal partners."[30] With this in mind the NGA study focused on the comprehensive emergency management capabilities of states, commonwealths, and territories, emphasizing the needs for good disaster research and best practices at all levels of government, and FEMA acting as a clearinghouse for this information, as well as serving as a one-stop shop for relief services and funding.[31]

President Carter was careful not to send the message that he was loosening his resolve against the Soviet nuclear threat, but it was clear that FEMA's multiple missions would dilute the focus on Cold War disaster concerns. The *New York Times* reported it as a "shift in strategic policy": civil defense was taken away from the Defense Department and placed in the new agency. But civil defense was not shelved, over the objection of Carter's disarmament adviser Paul Warnke. Carter stated to the press that he was a believer in civil defense—an outmoded concept by 1979 when everyone from Robert S. McNamara to his own defense secretary Harold Brown thought civil defense gave the impression that a nuclear war could be survived, and even "won." A 1978 study had concluded that in a nuclear war 140 million Americans would die, leaving 80 million survivors. The *Times* article did not pay much attention to the more critical point that the creation of FEMA was a streamlining move to place authority over disaster mitigation and response in one agency, answering directly to the president—and that it could use its emergency management mandate to address all disasters. Such a move made sense to the former governor, knowing as he did the realities of dealing with disasters at the executive level, and accepting as he did that disaster preparedness could include more than just nuclear preparedness given the maturity of American disaster research. Additionally, presidential disaster declarations, a power granted the president in the 1974 Federal Disaster Relief Act, would ensure direct local involvement of the president after disasters, and certainly that could not be bad politics.[32]

In the midst of this restructuring effort, in March 1979, the Three Mile Island partial nuclear meltdown demonstrated—among other horrifying things—that disaster responders at the state and local level were simply overmatched by the risks and hazards in their communities, and that federal civil defense was too outmoded and diffuse to deal effectively with the nation's real hazards. The horrible serendipity of disaster pushed the creation of FEMA past any fears and obstacles, and President Carter signed the Executive Order creating FEMA on April 1, 1979.

When FEMA was created, the Civil Defense Staff College was moved from Battle Creek, Michigan, to Emmitsburg, Maryland, and renamed the Emergency Management Institute (EMI), "to reflect its new and significantly broader mission to train and educate the nation's emergency management community."[33] EMI established itself quickly as a clearinghouse for all-hazards research and best practices in preparedness and response. Conducting training for first responders on-site and publishing model syllabi and courses for teaching emergency management techniques, EMI provided a central hub for thinking about the translation of all-hazards research into emergency management practice. Under the direction of disaster research polymath Wayne Blanchard the higher education focus of EMI served as a crucial resource in helping to establish a core of knowledge and best practices in curricula and program development for emergency management educators.

In the period 1983–1998 two undergraduate programs in emergency management were created. The first, founded at the University of North

Texas (at that time North Texas State University) in 1983, began by offering continuing education credits, with classes taught by FEMA Region VI employees in the Dallas-Ft. Worth Metroplex. Citing the lack of college training among emergency managers and the generational reality that many of them were nearing retirement age, the university moved to establish the Emergency Administration and Planning Program (EADP). The Texas College Coordinating Board approved the new program, and in 1984 it began offering a bachelor of science degree in emergency management. The program was initially located in the Center for Public Service in the School for Community Service. Faculty included James Boswell from the Institute of Applied Sciences and Tom Fairchild from the Center for Aging. William A. Luker, dean of the School of Community Service, met with and was promised $100,000 in funds by FEMA administrator Louis Giuffrida. Though this money never materialized, lobbying the state worked out better and a $100,000 annual appropriation was passed.[34]

The early years of EADP were heavily influenced by Reagan era FEMA retrenchment into civil defense, but also reflected an emphasis on public administration, including courses in "American and Local Government, Public Administration, Public Management, Financial Aspects of Government, Accounting Principles, Principles of Management, and Personnel Management."[35] The goal was to train a new generation of emergency management practitioners, and classes were taught by instructors with military or civilian emergency management experience. All-hazards research was largely missing from the early curriculum. The first students stumbled on the program—they usually were nontraditional students with full-time jobs, and many were "older, white males seeking a career change from the military."[36]

The EADP program ran up against a difficulty at UNT when it became evident that faculty were not producing research. A sociologist—David Neal, a DRC graduate—was brought in as a joint appointment between the sociology department and EADP.[37] A great number of degreed emergency managers by the end of the twentieth century were graduates of the UNT EADP program. In the late 1990s George Washington University offered a graduate degree in emergency management. Oklahoma State University created a master's degree in fire and emergency management. Arkansas Tech, University of Akron, and Jacksonville State University followed suit.[38] The profession grew as states and localities began in the 1980s and 1990s to close their civil defense offices or reallocate personnel into all-hazards preparedness and response. The transition was complete by the late 1990s, when FEMA was elevated to cabinet level status, and hundreds of emergency management programs had opened or were in planning stages across the country, at the undergraduate and in some instances even graduate level.

In the 1980s, despite the surge of interest in hazards mitigation that buoyed the NGA process creating FEMA, the Reagan administration deemphasized mitigation at FEMA, and revived the Cold War civil defense mindset. Proponents of dispersal and shelter resurfaced—some like physicist Edward Teller had never gone away, but had been ignored with the national turn away from nuclear preparedness and toward hazards preparedness in the 1970s. Disaster and hazards research carried on in the various centers across the nation, but little was done at the federal level to bring the research into the core of emergency management policy formation.

The disaster experts—researchers and emergency managers alike—had an ally and fellow believer in all-hazards risk and disaster management in president Bill Clinton's FEMA director, former Arkansas state emergency management director James Lee Witt. Witt transformed the agency in the 1990s with an all-hazards approach into a successful risk and disaster mitigation and response institution; it was not an easy decade to do so, with Hurricane Andrew (1992), the Midwest Floods (1993), the World Trade Center Bombing (1993), the Northridge Earthquake (1994), and the Oklahoma City Bombing (1995) to contend with, the costliest natural disasters in American history to that point, and the most chilling harbingers of post-Cold War terrorism concerns yet seen.

Witt's steering of a federal agency that had become a sort of joke in Washington, D.C., mired in corruption scandals and trapped in Cold War amber, put on display Witt's firm grounding in all-hazards thinking, but also his "bureaucratic entrepreneurship," as noted by disaster policy expert Patrick Roberts. Under Witt, FEMA shelved most of the Cold War fantasy books and turned squarely to the project of bringing best practices in emergency management in line with the by then substantial findings of disaster and hazards research. Even in 1993, with the Cold War a memory, about 38 percent of FEMA's staff and 27 percent of its budget were focused on "national security emergencies," the most important being "all out nuclear war." As policy scholar Richard Sylves notes, the majority of that work was classified, and of the 3,000 full time employees of FEMA, a remarkable 1,900 had security clearances. Witt eliminated the National

Defense Directorate in FEMA, and set about reintegrating the split personality of the agency, a holdover from the longstanding Cold War dual use mission of the agency.[39] FEMA's newfound resourcefulness in the late 1990s was symbolized by elevation of the agency to cabinet level status, and programmatically in Project Impact, a local level mitigation program where cities designed their own mitigation plans and worked on them with seed money directly from FEMA.

With his background in the construction industry, as a local judge, and as emergency management director in Arkansas, Witt had arrived in Washington with an understanding of the various stakeholders that must be engaged to draft disaster mitigation policies that would not be hijacked by state governments and would also be credible in the eyes of local businesses and property owners. Whereas disaster relief funds and response planning efforts were relatively uncontroversial, mitigation—requiring as it did eminent domain takings, land use restrictions, and expensive, time-consuming planning efforts—was a much harder sell outside Washington.[40] Politicians were slow to warm to mitigation, with its slow and methodical assessments of hazards, research into local demographics and community contexts, and construction (or lack of construction) along lines prescribed by experts. Planning for disaster ahead of time, perhaps avoiding a disaster altogether through mitigation planning, is often not as politically electrifying as the prospect of a government official handing out relief checks or commiserating with disaster victims. Selling mitigation took personality, knowledge, and political skill.

In 1995 Witt pulled together representatives of local government, the private sector, including the insurance industry, and other stakeholders for a series of roundtables on disaster mitigation. Out of these conversations Witt pushed forward FEMA's "Disaster Resistant Communities" program, also known as Project Impact. Project Impact had four goals: (1) build community partnerships; (2) identify hazards and community vulnerability; (3) prioritize and complete risk reduction measures; and (4) develop communication strategies to make the case for disaster loss reduction.[41] Starting with seven pilot communities, Project Impact had increased to over 250 cities by 2000. DRC researcher Tricia Wachtendorf describes the "bottom up" disaster planning approach of Project Impact:

> citizens and organizations from all segments of the city, county, or
> region [work] to meet each of Project Impact's four objectives. . . .

Figure 13. The disaster experts. Top left: Russell R. Dynes and Henry Quarantelli, co-directors of the Disaster Research Center at Ohio State University (now at the University of Delaware), discussing looting in civil disasters, 1968, courtesy of Disaster Research Center, University of Delaware. Bottom left: FEMA director James Lee Witt and President Bill Clinton discuss Project Impact, Washington, D.C., February 26, 1998, FEMA News Photo, courtesy of FEMA. Right: Gilbert White, founding director of the National Hazards Center, University of Colorado, courtesy of the University of Colorado.

And, although FEMA provides seed money—the amount varies from between one hundred thousand dollars to as much as one million dollars—and other resources to designated communities, local participants must meet leveraging guidelines that are outlined by the federal agency; that is, communities must match the funds and resources provided by FEMA with alternative sources of funding.[42]

In Project Impact we see two trends coming together. First, spreading the all-hazards gospel of mitigation had been taken up by the highest disaster official in the United States. In the language of Project Impact's goals we can read the influence of disaster researchers, experts who had been describing "hazards in the land" and "vulnerability" of communities as powerful methods for reformulating disaster policy since the 1960s. Second, in its implementation, Project Impact reflects the 1990s rhetorical (and sometimes real) turn against "big government" solutions to vexing problems. By enabling municipal governments to apply directly for seed funding and encouraging public/private partnerships, James Lee Witt's FEMA was struggling to promote disaster policy that would have significant buy-in among the local stakeholders who were always at the front lines of disasters. In doing so, Witt also argued that the politically acceptable thing was also the right thing to do in this case. Though hard numbers on the efficacy of mitigation were not available, both Witt and his chief of staff Jane Bullock have recalled that they cited "reports" to any official who asked that mitigation saved four dollars for every dollar spent.[43]

The first major test of Project Impact came on February 28, 2001, when the 6.8 magnitude Nisqually Earthquake hit Seattle. Out of office by this time, Witt recalls watching mayor Paul Schell on CNN, responding to a question about why the city had seen such light damage from such a big quake. Seattle had in fact been among the seven pilot communities for Project Impact, and Schell cited the program as one of the reasons for the city's resiliency. On that very same day the Bush administration unceremoniously canceled Project Impact.[44]

Project Impact's overwhelming popularity pointed toward the possibility of mitigation and all-hazards emergency management as consensus methods of disaster control.[45] It even signaled that perhaps federally organized disaster preparedness and response might develop a place for itself as a publicly valued government function. The successful nationally coordinated preparations for the feared Y2K computer meltdown demonstrated that all-hazards thinking might meaningfully include technological and broader economic risks. Mitigation and the all-hazards paradigm, though they had worked their way from disaster and hazards research into federal policy, were not immune to political reality. The new facts of Bush era disaster policy were signaled by the suspension of Project Impact and the budget slashing of mitigation programs that would follow. September 11 and the months that followed witnessed a complete rethinking of American disaster policy, a renewal of Cold War fascinations with command and control, secrecy, and the imagination of disaster as an "enemy." The civil defenders were back.

September 11 and the Lessons in the Rubble

September 11 immediately changed the national conversation about disasters—and terrorism was now the primary fascination. There is no greater evidence for the important role of disaster experts in the modern United States than the outpouring of investigations and research publications following September 11. Witnessed by millions, the event was also studied by thousands. Military action was underway before any of the major September 11 studies were completed, but that did not dampen the zeal of disaster experts as they worked to understand the event and to use the lessons in the rubble to substantiate their paradigms of preparedness, or to promote new paradigms. Though almost all the experts would agree that terrorism should be reconsidered as a major risk to the nation, the agreement ended there. The main arguments swirled around the central concerns of disaster experts going back to the nineteenth century: framing a dominant risk, organizing and creating new knowledge to understand the risk, crafting new practices and policies to meet the risk, and defining clear roles for public and private actors at the local, state, and federal levels. In the case of September 11 the debate came ultimately down to how one answered the following question: was it primarily to be understood as a fire disaster or a terrorist attack?

The idea that investigation was a responsibility to the dead was heard everywhere. The *New York Times* editorialized that an internal review of fire department procedures was a good move: the department needed to "modernize its leadership structure and its tragically inadequate communication system." Lack of coordination between fire and police had led to police getting evacuation commands, but not firemen.[46] Writing in the *New York Times* on the one year anniversary of the collapse of the Twin Towers, Jim Dwyer pointed out that a year after September 11, "the public knows less about the circumstances of 2,081 deaths at the foot of Manhattan in broad daylight than people knew in 1912 knew within weeks about the Titanic, which sank in the middle of an ocean in the dead of night." Dwyer's critique foreshadowed the *9/11 Commission Report*—pointing out that intelligence failures needed study, but so did the city's building codes. He cited former World Trade Center director Alan Reiss as saying that because of building industry resistance almost no building code changes in New York or nationally were made after the 1993 bombing. "At least 1,100 people survived the initial impacts from the planes, but were trapped. How many might have been saved if the buildings had stood longer? The city has not explored that question." Mayor Michael Bloomberg was not focused on a disaster investigation. "Every single major event is different from all the others. . . . The training of how you would respond to the last incident is not really important," according to Bloomberg.[47] It was a cringeworthy statement considering the half-century of knowledge and practice created around mitigation of and response to urban risks and disasters ready and waiting to be consulted in the aftermath of September 11.

A major bipartisan panel—the National Commission on Terrorist Attacks upon the United States (the "9/11 Commission")—was convened by Congress in late 2002, conducted multiple hearings and interviews, and made an exhaustive report in 2004. The most thorough government study of a disaster in modern American history unfolded over those two years. The great majority of the Commission's work was focused on understanding the rise in organizational capabilities of the Al Qaeda network and the manifold ways the U.S. surveillance and counterterrorism community failed to recognize and prepare for the threat. Of the 13 chapters in the *9/11 Commission Report*, 12 are focused on these topics, with recommendations on reformation of CIA and FBI capabilities around meeting the terrorist threat worldwide—an awakening from a Cold War slumber and return to constant defense readiness.[48] Most critically, the *Report* advised that redundant and disorganized security functions be folded together into one mega-agency, the Department of Homeland Security, tasked with coordination across all levels of government and federal agencies to provide a comprehensive effort to thwart a future September 11 from taking place. It was a stunningly swift return to a civil defense model—with much of the planned research and lines of authority drawn from secret deliberations among defense experts in the offices of the Department of Homeland Security (including as it did the CIA and FBI), and the Pentagon.

One key chapter of the *9/11 Commission Report*—and the one of greatest interest to the emergency management community—traced the narrative of the attack on the Twin Towers and the attempts to save the people inside them. Problems in preparedness among fire and police responders and the city's emergency management system were cited. More troubling were the failings of the Towers themselves, a staggering list of technical defects ranging from the narrowness of escape stairwells to a lack of knowledge as to whether fireproofing of steel columns had ever been completed. Members of the fire protection, engineering, emergency management, and disaster research communities spoke out about the fact that knowledge had been available on how to make the Towers better, safer buildings; but best practices had not been followed in the construction and protection of the buildings or the regimes of preparedness necessary to respond to such a disaster. Herein lay the critical choice ahead for policymakers. Is money best spent mitigating all types of disasters, like preparing high rises for fires at upper floors? Or is it more effective to erase the risk at its origin, which was rapidly translating into the Bush administration's plans for a "War on Terror." A third option was also available: to revive the Cold War "dual use" strategy of civil defense, and fight the threat of terrorism while also trying to mitigate other risks facing the nation at the same time. It might be said that the American disaster clock had just been turned back to 1950.

The *9/11 Commission Report* was a best seller, and though much of it focused on terrorism, its broader take-aways for disaster experts generally could be stated simply in two points. First, the disaster might not have been avoidable, but it could have been much less horrific had existing disaster knowledge been applied. Second, the confusing array of government agencies—at all levels of the federal structure—presented an image of confusion, not confidence, in the nation's ability to protect itself from disasters through public action. That expert knowledge existed and was not used, that it was not embraced at the core of risk control and disaster policy, seemed to fly in the face of some of Americans' central assumptions about their strengths in the modern era. Risk knowledge was not flowing through expert channels into the halls of power, and the future of American disaster policy was in doubt.

Sociologist and director of the Natural Hazards Center Kathleen Tierney offered a scathing critique of the *9/11 Commission Report*. Tierney noted the 9/11 Commission's emphasis on the need for the "Incident Command System" to be fully adopted in emergency management practice. The need for better communications technology in disaster response emerged as another "useful" thing the Commission learned from the disaster response challenges that first responders and emergency managers faced at the World Trade Center. However, Tierney found the Commission paying almost no attention to the efforts needed to "engage the public in preparedness and response efforts," a glaring omission considering the key roles played by the building's occupants themselves in the midst of disaster. With firemen unable to reach the higher floors, many evacuees of the World Trade Center quite literally saved themselves and their colleagues. "On the contrary, the

Commission report is consistent with current trends that frame disaster management as a problem best addressed by people in uniform—law enforcement and the military," Tierney observed. Most important, Tierney spotted in the document a trend that hearkens back to the Cold War. "The increasing tendency to conflate disaster response and warfighting is among the most marked and alarming legacies of September 11," she argued. As evidence of the new reality in the brave, new post-September 11 world of emergency management, Tierney recalls that disaster researchers had recently received invitations to a conference "on needs associated with managing the 'domestic battlespace'—the place formerly known as our communities and homes—during terrorist attacks and disasters."[49]

In addition to the *9/11 Commission Report*, major studies were also conducted at the National Institute of Standards and Technology (formerly known as the National Bureau of Standards), growing out of the work of the Building Performance Assessment Team (BPAT) of 2002. Critics of the BPAT called for a thorough review of the entire fire safety network, the very system detailed in the first half of this book, which had been carried forward with few substantive changes since the 1930s, aside from the consumer protection and wildfire concerns that had arisen in the 1960s and been addressed in *America Burning*. Three major areas had proven particularly nerve-wracking to the fire experts: land development in the wildland-urban interface, high rise construction, and development of synthetic materials at such a rapid pace they could not be adequately tested. Added to this was a relatively new concept—performance-based standards—that had become more commonly adopted in local and state building codes. Performance-based standards are ad hoc standards created for specific structures or sets of components. On the plus side this strategy allows architects and engineers much greater latitude in design. On the negative side, the standards are unique and rely on very close scrutiny to determine safety. It is fair to say that the Twin Towers of the World Trade Center were "performance-based" in their design, a fact that showed the danger in the method.

Victims' families made common cause with critics within the fire safety network, and through the Skyscraper Safety Campaign they very insistently demanded greater scrutiny of Underwriters Laboratories, the National Fire Protection Association, and NIST. A story in the *New York Times* demonstrated that the NFPA "Life Safety Code" and some of the tests used for structural members of the World Trade Center dated to the early twentieth century and did not take into account the use of synthetic finishes and materials in office furnishings, for example. From this point of view it was time to consider wholesale building code revision for fire safety. As we know from the first half of the book, the building and fire safety consensus code system has a long and well-established history among experts in American disaster, so such a revision would challenge decades of expert tradition.

Glenn Corbett, a fire service veteran, former emergency manager, and fire science professor at John Jay College of Criminal Justice in New York City, testified that the NIST investigation had "fallen short." "Instead of passing a blazing torch of detailed recommendations," Corbett argued, "this lengthy marathon race has resulted in NIST giving our model code-writing groups a handful of flickering embers that although generally good in principle are entirely too vague. The model code-writing groups now have to wait even longer while NIST hires an outside organization to prepare a set of recommendations that can actually be assimilated into our construction codes."[50] Recognizing the longstanding power of the code councils in shaping American construction risks, Corbett focused his critique on the necessity of empowering them to do what they did best—collecting and integrating multidisciplinary risk information, and writing voluntary standards that could and would influence the next skyscrapers that might rise on the so-called "Ground Zero" site in Manhattan and elsewhere across the nation. NIST was in the way of this process, as Corbett, and many other fire experts believed.

The House Science Committee held a hearing in 2005, following up on its two provocative 2002 hearings to review NIST's World Trade Center collapse research efforts and findings. Sally Regenhard, representing victims' families through her Skyscraper Safety Campaign, now herself appeared before the Science Committee, where her tenacity was lauded by Chairman Sherwood Boehlert. Advocating for further research, building and safety code revisions, and accountability for the collapse of the Twin Towers, Regenhard had in the ensuing years devoted full time to putting the goals of skyscraper safety in front of the media, government officials, and disaster experts. She delivered her dim opinion of the investigation's outcome. "The recommendations, I feel, are very general and lack specifics. I feel that the vagueness of the language was influenced by a need for political correctness and a general reluctance or an inability to investigate, use subpoena power, lay blame, or even point out the deadly mistakes of 9/11 in the World Trade Center."[51]

Figure 14. Sally Regenhard and other families and friends of the World Trade Center dead at House of Representatives Science Committee Hearings, March 6, 2002. *New York Times*, March 7, 2002, B7. Courtesy of the *New York Times*.

The NIST investigations were innovative labor-intensive efforts that consumed a major share of institutional attention from 2002 to 2005. The final reports were extraordinarily detailed, pushing computer fire modeling to the absolute limits of its capabilities. Nevertheless, there was nothing the fire experts could do to bring back Christian Regenhard. The unwillingness to "lay blame," as Sally Regenhard argued, demonstrated what are perhaps irreconcilable differences between disaster experts, who often work at the patient pace of scientific consensus or government planning, and the citizens who demand more information, more accountability, and more guarantees that lessons from disasters like the World Trade Center collapse will be used to avoid such disasters from ever happening again.

Major public health concerns emerged after September 11, concerns that disaster experts rapidly developed into areas for interdisciplinary research and policy advocacy. Robyn Gershon at the Mailman School of Public Health at Columbia University set to work in trying to understand the myriad factors affecting people's abilities to escape the Twin Towers before the collapse. Though 87 percent of the people in the buildings got out, social and physical factors as well as designed-in elements of the buildings themselves shaped and in many ways impeded faster evacuation.[52] Gershon's work informed debate and reform on the requirements for high-rise building evacuation preparedness in New York City. Another area of research focused more on the rescue workers and communities that breathed the toxic dust from the collapsed buildings. The reporting of Juan González in the *New York Daily News* detailed the problems facing communities as they tried repeatedly to get information about whether their homes were safe. The EPA was accused of setting arbitrary standards, which González reported—and under extraordinary pressure his stories were buried deeper and deeper in the paper. González's resulting book, *Fallout*, shows the indecision and lack of knowledge at EPA as the situation played out.[53] Taking a somewhat longer view, public health experts Gerald Markowitz and David Rosner undertook a set of studies for the Milbank Foundation, concluding that city, state, and federal officials had not been prepared to assess the hazards in the air and water, and had not given adequate information or equipment to protect rescuers.[54] Based on these studies and other evidence of inappropriate health protections for first responders and workers at the site, a federal judge in 2006 awarded a rescue worker a judgment for health claims, tying those claims to the collapse—the first time this had been done.[55] This precedent was remarkable, as it opened the possibility that deaths and injuries as a result of lung disease related to the toxic Twin Towers dust might result in payouts to thousands of people. If this occurs, September 11 may someday be redefined as the most dangerous and expensive industrial accident in American history.

Terrorism Versus All-Hazards

Though the Bush administration was initially skeptical, by late 2002 it was clear that a new federal structure was going to be created, gathering up agencies that were in one way or another connected to counterterrorism. The result was the Department of Homeland Security, the largest federal agency of the postwar period—and FEMA was moved under the DHS umbrella. In line with the recommendations of the *9/11 Commission Report*, the entire federal risk and disaster structure was being refocused on terrorism.

This refocusing was first and most importantly seen in the patterns of federal funding for disaster mitigation. Grants now had be related in one way or another to the terrorist threat. This led to some creative grant-writing, and a trip back in time to the 1960s, as states and municipalities worked to receive federal funds for the multiple risks that faced them. The public became aware of the bizarre nature of this exercise as the media started reporting on the grant requests filed by small midwestern cities for chemical terrorism labs and similar questionably necessary augmentations to their disaster capabilities. Just as had been the case in the civil defense era, grants were for equipment, rarely for personnel or training. So even when funds were legitimately going for counterterrorism, cities and states often could not use the funds for to meet the needs they determined most pressing for their own communities.

The shift to a "terrorism paradigm," or rather the return to Cold War-style civil defense thinking, led to serious debates on the floor of Congress, as senators and representatives from urban centers complained about a federal funding scheme that allocated funds according to a federal "equal-ity" system for every state, rather than according to a "risk-based" system that might prioritize risks and vulnerabilities. Senator Hillary Clinton of New York was particularly forceful on this issue, but to no avail for over two years, as states like Wyoming found their per capita counterterrorism dollars coming in at seven or eight dollars per person, while New York and California found theirs at pennies per person. Within FEMA, leadership from the Clinton years had been completely replaced by non-expert politi-cal appointees like Joe Allbaugh and Michael Brown. Career FEMA employ-ees started to retire in large numbers, Project Impact was gone, and mitigation of natural hazards was demoted as a secondary concern.

Though the Cold War itself persisted into the 1960s, the central claims by civil defenders about the primacy of nuclear preparedness and the sur-vivability of a nuclear war were discredited in the eyes of citizens, local and state government officials, and disaster researchers. The creation of an all-hazards approach did not initiate a march toward ultimate safety from disaster—as evidenced by the quickening pace of costly and deadly earth-quakes, hurricanes, and wildfires in the 1990s as well as the attacks and building collapses of September 11, 2001—but rather reflected an emergent consensus among policymakers that nuclear attack should not be the domi-nant scenario shaping government disaster policy. The creation of the Fed-eral Emergency Management Agency in 1979 and the associated rise of the emergency management profession demonstrated a revision in goals and knowledge claims forming the nexus among research, practice, and policies in the face of disaster not seen since the early Cold War.

The immediate effect of September 11 seemed to indicate that a re-tooled Cold War civil defense approach to disasters was emerging. The new emphases of the federal disaster experts were centered around "fighting" external threats to communities, command and control, secrecy, federal supremacy over state and municipal prerogatives, and priority of effective military-style counterterrorism preparedness and rapid response over haz-ards mitigation. On September 10, 2001, it seemed clear to disaster experts that the long term shift in national priorities, priorities driving disaster research and disaster policy away from civil defense and to all-hazards was complete. But could a fifty-year historical evolution turn around in a single day? Was terrorism going to be the new nuclear threat, with all-hazards preparedness demoted to lesser concern while the civil defense establish-ment set about protecting American cities from attack? This, in many ways, remains an open question.

Not one single profession, branch or level of government, or academic discipline has managed to assert control over disaster knowledge, or disas-ter policy in modern United States history. In recent decades this has been made even more impossible by globalization and the increasing scale of risks in metropolitan regions. Risks, as we have seen, are products of devel-opment and historical contingency, not autonomous—disasters never arrive unannounced. Standards of safety reflect negotiations between the disaster experts, private development interests, policymakers, and citizens. Disaster experts have been most effective when they work in interdisciplin-ary settings, when they have strong advocacy tools at hand for policy influ-ence, or when they have intermediaries like insurance companies or grant agencies to translate their works into policy. Disaster knowledge like all expert knowledge may be wrapped in objectivity, but it is inherently applied in market and political settings. Risk taking in the United States often seems disturbingly amnesic—risks and disasters have, to some people, been worth forgetting if memory stood in the way of political or development agendas. Those who are not willing to forget, even the experts, have not always been successful in showcasing their knowledge and/or making their political case in a sustained way.

In August and September 2005, the Department of Homeland Security got its first major test of how it could react to "ordinary" disasters with the

new terrorism paradigm (or old civil defense paradigm) defining its structure. That it failed the test is an understatement. In the midst of the unfolding disaster of Hurricane Katrina, a Coast Guard general was interviewed
and pointed out that a hurricane is "a very active enemy." So, the goal was
"defeating" a hurricane and flood? Here was Cold War thinking dredged
up for the twenty-first century.

Hazards Realism in the Post-Katrina Era

It's the "weather of catastrophe," Joan Didion wrote in 1965 of the Santa
Ana winds that sweep down the California canyons every autumn—the
weather of firestorms that "shows us how close to the edge we are." Didion's "edge" sliced a line between sanity and madness, but it also marked
the borderline between the city and the wilderness. Out past the lights of
the metropolis, connected by a narrow two-lane highway, there was a land
before the cul-de-sac, before Wal-Mart and suburban creep. In those days
it was still possible to think of the city and its undeveloped hinterlands as
separate. But it's not 1965 anymore, and well beyond Didion's edge today
sits Rancho Santa Fe.[56]

In October 2007, when the Santa Ana winds returned to Southern California as they do every autumn, they caused 18 devastating wildfires to
rage through the region. The largest of these—the "Witch Fire"—charred
200,000 acres, consumed 1,125 homes, injured 40 firefighters, and killed
two people. And at the center sat Rancho Santa Fe. With a median home
price of more than $2 million, this unincorporated bedroom community—
described by a local real estate broker as "the new pleasure ground of America's landed gentry"—ranks among the most affluent in the United States.
Its 2,400 homes on the frontier of San Diego County are situated on two-
acre-plus lots where sidewalks and streetlights are banned. But Rancho
Santa Fe, despite its proximity to the fires, did not burn down. In fact, only
one house in the community was lost. The explanation is simple: a strict
set of land use and construction codes called "shelter-in-place."

Shelter-in-place is straightforward. First, accept that wildfire will be part
of your new home's ecosystem. Then, deprive it of fuel: avoid flammable
landscaping and construct a house that's as fire-retardant as possible. But
how do you get developers, construction companies, insurers, and homeowners to bear the costs of this new construction regimen? "It's real simple," says Rancho Santa Fe fire marshal and 37-year California fire service

veteran Cliff Hunter. "Don't approve the plans. If you don't approve the plans, they don't get a house."⁵⁷

Just like that, Hunter is helping to rewrite the drama that has long played out in communities from San Diego County to the Gulf Coast and the multitudes of other regions across America where disaster and construction are co-stars. This drama stars the "greedy developer" and the "sentimental environmentalist." Should we build or shouldn't we build? It's the land use equivalent of a Shakespearean dilemma, and just like Shakespeare's plays, it may seem real but it's ultimately fiction. Even with Hurricane Andrew and Hurricane Katrina firmly lodged in our collective memory, development in hazardous regions continues. Even if construction were to stop entirely in these regions, we would still have generations' worth of property and citizens to protect from a changing-risk environment that now includes the effects of climate change and aging infrastructure. Restriction by government has historically proved difficult to legislate and even harder to enforce. The question remains today, can best practices in mitigation show a more risk-sustainable way forward?

Disaster experts like Cliff Hunter are looking at the hazards in front of them, laying aside the "all things terrorism" mantra of DHS, and getting to work. Hunter's shelter-in-place gospel is only one of many possible solutions in the ongoing move among disaster experts toward mitigation and a sort of "hazards realism" that seeks to get beyond the age of "should we build or shouldn't we?" Many of these ideas have been around for a while, including shelter-in-place and the half-century of disaster research that it and other mitigation strategies build on, but they are only now being applied as the stakes of failure grow higher and higher. Others are less well known, intermingling sustainability theory and sophisticated new mapping and modeling technologies to profile hazards and predict their effects with greater accuracy. The trend cuts across the disciplines of planning, architecture, and ecology; it includes first responders and disaster experts. And, if successful, the hazard realists will more and more be shaping national trends of development in America's most hazardous regions.

Max Moritz sees a philosophical puzzle in the way Californians think about hazards. "We fight fires—it's very military—but we don't fight earthquakes," he says. "We avoid them or we engineer against them."⁵⁸ Moritz co-directs the Center for Fire Research and Outreach at the University of California, Berkeley. He wants to correct this inconsistency. Not fighting earthquakes, Moritz argues, has led to strong building codes and reasonable expectations of the built environment in earthquake-prone cities. It coincides with a century-old history—a post-1906 quake reckoning of the costs involved in rebuilding San Francisco or Los Angeles every generation. "We don't co-exist with fire and we need to," Moritz explains. "That's a fundamental difference."

Between 2000 and 2006, the United States witnessed five new records for acreage burned in wildfires, according to statistics collected since 1960 by the National Interagency Fire Center. The U.S. Fire Service reports that losses from "Outdoor and Other Fires" averaged $260 million per year over the past decade. The National Fire Protection Association estimates that in 2005 there were 800,000 fires in this category, resulting in 50 civilian fire deaths and 950 injuries.

Moritz has an explanation. "Part of this has got to be, while we are learning more, we are seeing the results of climate change, the accumulation of fuel and an expansion of the WUI." WUI is fire-ecology-speak for the "Wildland Urban Interface"—the region of development where the suburb meanders into undeveloped space. As people move out into the WUI they start doing what you would expect—they put out fires that threaten their homes. Fire season after fire season, this leads to the fight, with Herculean efforts by thousands of firefighters called out to save the day. Such efforts, even when successful, are costly.

To Moritz, who looks at the problem with a scientific eye, the real trick is not in denying development in the WUI outright, but in understanding when, where, and with what frequency wildfires strike. With this knowledge, a set of rational land use policies and building codes can be developed—policies that don't necessarily say no to developers but do entail accountability when developers and homeowners insist on taking risks with the full knowledge of what they are doing.

Moritz has spent much of his career studying the interactions among the large-scale forces that cause wildfires, the elements that make up a "fire regime"—like vegetation, geography, and weather patterns. While the fire regime changes over time, it can be mapped. And mapping means that decisions about fire-resistant building codes, for example, can be based on hard data. "The last real solid work on [fire weather patterns] was done in the '60s for civil defense reasons," Moritz notes. The federal government was worried about nuclear war-induced firestorms, so a set of fire maps was

developed. In the 1980s and again in the 1990s, California's Department of
Forestry and Fire Protection (CAL FIRE) commissioned Fire Hazard Severity Zone (FHSZ) maps after especially bad fire seasons, to assess risk in
wildland areas controlled by the state and to show areas where local residents are responsible for fire protection. But the pace of construction in
the WUI has been brisk since then, leaving these maps outdated.

In response to the accelerating threat of wildfires in recent years, the
California Building Standards Commission initiated a revised mapping
effort in 2007, intended to guide the next generation of development in the
WUI. A major break with past efforts is now possible thanks to computer-
based Geographic Information System (GIS) tools. Applying GIS to fire
hazards in California (think Google Maps for disasters) enables experts to
create maps that integrate potential fire locations with locations of buildings and the past fire history of a given area. The new FHSZ maps are
designed to give realistic probabilities for fire behavior in areas rated
according to "moderate," "high," and "very high" levels of risk. These areas
show up on a map in yellow, orange, and red bands that reflect not only
the history but also the possible future of the WUI.

Drafts of the FHSZ maps were discussed in localities across the state
for months, and they went into effect on January 1, 2008. The result that
Max Moritz and many in the fire expert community are betting on is a
science-based system of understanding risk and allocating responsibility
in a rational way across the state's WUI. This would echo the history of
fire protection in American cities during the era of industrialization and
conflagrations. Moritz's lab and CAL FIRE even co-host a website where
people can input a physical address and see where their property sits in
relation to fire hazard. If it is one of the highest risk zones, enhanced
building codes kick into effect. The state estimates the cost per home to
meet the new codes in the highest risk zones will run about $1,800. Enforc-
ing codes, of course, is another matter—but it will be more and more difficult to keep on building in the same old ways in the WUI. So, where will
development go from here?

From the individual structure up to neighborhood design, Moritz says,
"we can use what we know about fire in educating urban planners."
Moritz's lab holds workshops to demonstrate these new tools and has local
fire agencies and planners engage in cooperatively crafting the new building
codes. Better understanding of fire could also point the way to innovations
in architecture and construction. We can soon expect to see technological

revisions of household sprinkler systems, attic vent covers, and fireproof roof materials to protect against flying embers. We can also expect the prohibition of traditional favorites like cedar shake roofs, which tend to burst into flame at the slightest provocation.

Moritz's lab is also charged with providing information and outreach to homeowners—in a sense, the final frontier of fire hazard mitigation—and he has developed what he calls a Fire Information Engine Toolkit. The toolkit offers a web-based diagnostic allowing a homeowner to find out whether his or her home might be susceptible to fire and includes a fire mitigation guide with advice on fire protection for everything from decks to landscaping plants. Moritz expects that homeowners might be encouraged to use the toolkit by lowered insurance rates. Or by simple common sense, perhaps. Either way, Moritz's fire research lab is trying to accomplish something rather radical these days—making the products of macrolevel hazards research available at the micro level of the homeowner.

In 1993, the Mississippi River flooded for several months, from Minnesota to the Gulf of Mexico. It was a "500-year event" in the lingo of flood experts, costing $15 billion before all was said and done. In historical memory only the Great 1927 Flood matches it. As the waters receded, landscape architect and professor Anuradha Mathur and her husband, architect Dilip da Cunha, started getting interested in what they saw as a very narrow, very shortsighted, post-flood conversation about what to do next with the river. In the introduction to their 2001 book, *Mississippi Floods: Designing a Shifting Landscape*, they recall:

> From one side we heard calls for more control of the river; from the other, for the withdrawal of settlement from the floodplains; even as the Mississippi was erasing property lines and dissolving boundaries of all kinds, it was not shaking the distinctions by which this landscape has been looked upon and inhabited for the past three centuries: River and settlement, nature and culture, water and land.[59]

Shaking these distinctions would come to define Mathur and da Cunha's research method. They traveled up and down the river, conducting interviews, digging up old maps, and eventually riding along on one of the massive Mississippi barges for a week. They channeled Mark Twain, in whose *Life on the Mississippi* they found a respect for the water—as both resource and muse. That made more sense to them than the dry calculations of the Army Corps of Engineers. They met old blues musicians, studied the racial history of the land alongside the water, and at last came to a rather startling conclusion: the Mississippi River is not separate from the land through which it courses.

To say that land and water are part of one ecosystem with permeable boundaries is a rather difficult proposition in a country founded on the sanctity, and fixity, of property rights, and yet this simple idea undergirds all-hazards research and modern disaster mitigation strategies. Liberated from this "fixed river" concept, one immediately sees the road, or the stream, not taken. And, in fact, if one searches out the history of the river, the "fixed river" appears as an apparition. Rising water was a seasonal guest. Travel from New Orleans up the river to the sugar cane country and see the eighteenth-century Creole mansions. They were built to flood, with permeable basements and front doors that opened right to the river. Think about the land before industrial oil and gas production cut up the wetlands and real estate developers built houses in the lowlands. It's like the Nile in Egypt: flooding brings life, replenishes the land, gives rise to culture—a culture that values cycles and feels a deep shudder of memory and respect when the waters rise.

Moments of profound disruption in the American system don't come along often, but surely Katrina was one. In such a moment new ideas are often aired; and so, after Katrina, Mathur and da Cunha set about again to tear down the psychological boundaries between land and water along the Mississippi. The result was "New Orleans: Inhabiting a Fluid Terrain," a 2006 design project that developed into an exhibition. Mathur took her students from the University of Pennsylvania down to the Gulf, where they studied the geography and met the people and imagined the possibilities of the space for themselves. They developed plans that conjured up the city of New Orleans as a submersible space for living. The "Roof/Ramp" by Huiqing Kuang was one concept. It's an enormous multilevel ramp with housing, retail, and public space inside the structure, and on the roof is a garden. Day by day, it is a place to live, work, and play. But when the waters rise, as they invariably will again, the ramp becomes a lifeline to safety. And when the waters are high, the ramp could even be used as a temporary city, a place to locate housing for evacuees, keeping them rooted to the city where they live rather than dispersing them to the four corners of the nation as refugees.

High-density housing along the natural levees formed by the riverbank was another idea that grew from the process. Again emphasizing traditional use of land in New Orleans before the current levee system existed, the designers made use of a common sense proposition: build on the high ground and restrain development in the lowlands. Another proposal called for creation of new canals in the city that would simultaneously channel water to Lake Pontchartrain and discharge rainwater into the natural "bowl" that is New Orleans. Such a plan would "allow once more the Mississippi Water to flow through the city." This may seem counterproductive, except that the new canals will allow for more construction on high ground and the canal banks, and also return sediment to the city's naturally swampy areas, lifting the overall elevation.

At their core, the visionary designs of Mathur, da Cunha, and their students seek to remind us of two key lessons for life along the Mississippi. First, the city and the water are not separate. Second, separating them insults history, and, if the past is ignored, eventually you find yourself marooned on a rooftop in a sea of survivors who can't connect. Such lessons perfectly echo the thinking of Ivor van Heerden. "Be very careful of expanding the footprint of your city into wetlands, they are wet for a reason," he warns.[60] Like Mathur and da Cunha, van Heerden and his research team at LSU started with the history of the river and the history of its big floods to understand the bad planning that led to Katrina's devastation.

Sediment is a big player in van Heerden's analysis. Rather than turning the river into a canal, a process begun after the 1927 flood and renewed after Hurricane Betsy in 1965, van Heerden believes we need to allow periodic flooding of the Mississippi's surrounding lands. The flooding provides the sediment that builds land and nourishes the wetland ecology, land and plants that counteract subsidence and erosion that serve as powerful buffers against hurricane-induced storm surges. "We've lost over a million acres of protective apron," says van Heerden. "The river is in straitjackets, and it pours into 400 feet of water out in the Gulf. But, we could siphon the water and sediment out and into the wetlands, we can use diversions, we could even allow the river to take a different course."

Like Mathur and da Cunha, van Heerden laments the fact that the Army Corps of Engineers seems to be drawing just the opposite conclusion. It's "a mad rush to get a plan and start working, [with] very little thought to effectiveness. They've dusted off old Corps plans and put them in a shopping bag." Echoing Mathur and da Cunha, van Heerden believes that a fundamental philosophical shift—let the land and the water coexist—must come first. He argues, "Our river levees cause or exacerbate the flooding, because we don't look at it as a system, we have to start taking the European systems approach."

The European system to which van Heerden looks for guidance evolved from the greatest modern flood disaster to hit the Netherlands. In the winter of 1953, an enormous flood engulfed the country's vast lowlands, killing more than 1,800 people, destroying 4,000 homes, and causing evacuation of 100,000 people. Just as with Hurricane Katrina a half-century later, this was a disaster caused by a failed levee system, a disaster predicted and still sadly endured. The Dutch mitigation strategy was a highly technological one, involving construction of massive surge barriers at the meeting of land and sea. Rather than barring the two from meeting, however, the barriers have gates that can be raised and lowered, allowing saltwater estuaries and tidal zones to continue to exist. The gates are only closed when the seas are high and flooding is imminent. The Dutch looked at the hazards they faced after 1953 and calculated that they wanted to reduce the risk of serious flooding in their cities to an extraordinary ratio of 1:10,000. Within four years, the protective barriers were complete, and they continue to build and monitor them as the environment changes. Van Heerden laughs when he remembers showing pictures of the piecemeal Mississippi levee system to Dutch scientists. "Compared to the Dutch, ours are little sand castles," he says. The emphasis here is less on copying the Dutch exactly than on adopting the seriousness with which they approached the issue, and making a long-term societal commitment to protecting our cities. By cutting siphons through the current levee system, building serious levees where they are needed, and restoring the wetlands, van Heerden sees a way to coexist with the mighty Mississippi. He also cites the need to mimic the Dutch process of opening the levee design process to competition. The Corps of Engineers can build, in van Heerden's estimation, but visionary designs are quite another matter.[61]

As with Max Moritz's work in California, there is new promise in using computer modeling and GIS technology to project the implications of certain remedial actions or of taking no action at all. The Dutch, according to van Heerden, are once again showing the way forward, with sophisticated computer models allowing researchers to play out any number of scenarios and rediscoveries along the waterway. If van Heerden can get his models done in time, he might just be able to win over the politicians, engineers, and developers who are right now building the next generation of flood controls along the Mississippi.

Back in Rancho Santa Fe after the 2007 fire, fire marshal Cliff Hunter's gamble paid off. The local and even national press were jamming his phone line, wanting to know what the success of shelter-in-place meant for the rest of the country. Hunter is optimistic, but also realistic. "I don't recommend that people stay in their homes during a fire," he says.[62] Shelter-in-place is in fact a second line of defense, intended to protect people who can't escape because of age or illness. Still, he is obviously pleased when he explains he knows some people who stayed behind during the Witch Fire, despite the robocall warnings to evacuate. And they were fine, he says. The strict requirements of keeping a vegetation-free perimeter around the home, blocking attic vents from flying embers, and liberal use of fire-resistant building materials in addition to wider than usual escape roadways add up to a winning strategy for coexisting with fire, in Hunter's view.

The downside, of course, is the increased cost of construction and upkeep, and the risk that people will try this on their own but forget that shelter-in-place design must be maintained and monitored all the time. At Rancho Sante Fe, this is accomplished by inspectors who come around every fire season to catalogue code abuses, and through private restriction rather than public law. Recently, one woman put 22 forbidden cypress trees around her home and was flagged for a code violation. "Why did you do it?" Hunter wanted to know. "I never thought you would inspect," the woman replied. This attitude troubles Hunter, and especially agitates those who are concerned that shelter-in-place is unsustainable without costly and constant oversight.

Hunter sees another big problem: it's too expensive to retrofit all the homes in California's WUI that don't already make use of shelter-in-place. Such requirements, despite the new code structure and Max Moritz's fire maps, would take political courage that is currently untested but historically weak. This is the same sort of problem that faces the Gulf Coast. Those levees along the Mississippi? Not coming down any time soon. This means more living on borrowed time as the water and the land remain temporarily separated.

The modern urban history of the United States is in some sense a history of risk taking and unsustainable development. Every disaster necessitated more government oversight, more firemen and rapid reconstruction to demonstrate that the "fight" with nature was being won. Disasters also catalyzed eras of knowledge creation focused on understanding, mitigation, and responding to disasters. Connecting the research to policies of development and enforcement of those policies has been a constant challenge of modern American urban life. Now, as we settle into the twenty-first century, disaster experts are working hard to redefine how best to live with hazards. They know people want to live in disaster-prone areas, for cultural and economic reasons that are in many cases out of the control of any governing entity.

However, with new construction methods and more rational building codes facilitated by accurate map-making and computer models, it is unlikely that residents of the WUI will remain heedless. A fundamental realignment of construction with ecological reality—rather than feebly trying to push the ecology away from the construction site—will present new design options and ecological philosophies to be discussed in classrooms, town halls, laboratories, and firehouses. And as the discussion continues, hazards realists will make their case: You can live where you want to, but have a good, long look at a map first.

The All-Hazards Era is marked by the continued national apathy toward civil defense and the rising concern over technological and natural disasters, culminating in a deepening of knowledge about "hazards," and new policies directed at disaster mitigation and disaster response. FEMA and the profession of emergency management are the two outstanding artifacts of this era. It is the era we find ourselves in today as we mark the hundredth anniversaries of the Triangle Shirtwaist Fire and the Merritt Committee, and the fiftieth anniversary of the "hypothetical" nuclear destruction of Philadelphia. It is an era with more knowledge than ever before about risks and disasters, though hampered by difficulties in turning this knowledge into policy. In the aftermath of September 11 the rapid shelving of mitigation and reorientation of all-hazards thinking to place terrorism above all other concerns hearkens back to the early Cold War Civil Defense Era. It is perhaps too soon to know whether the trends toward a true All-Hazards approach to disasters can withstand the vicissitudes of national concern over "external" threats.

CONCLUSION

Even when they approach us silently, clad in numbers and
formulas, risks remain fundamentally localized, mathematical
condensations of wounded images of a life worth living. . . . sooner
or later the question of acceptance arises and with it anew the old
question: *how do we wish to live?* . . . Risk determinations . . . can
no longer be isolated from one another through specialization,
and developed and set down according to their own standards of
rationality. They require a cooperation across the trenches of
disciplines, citizens' groups, factories, administration and
politics. . . . There is no expert on risk.

—Ulrich Beck, *Risk Society*

Sally Regenhard holding a photo of her son, a fireman killed on September
11 (see page 285). It is a moment of collective grief, one in which we ask
ourselves: how do we wish to live? Is unwanted death and destruction
always the trade-off for technological risk-taking and relentless American
modernization? And if it is, then shouldn't we as a free society discuss that
bargain more frequently and more passionately, shouldn't it be a more
central debate in a modern democratic state? Shouldn't we know more
about the people and the institutions that frame these trade-offs for us—the
disaster experts—who they are, what they know, how they obtain and use
their authority, and whether or not they are good at what they do?

Like so many of my fellow New Yorkers after September 11, I felt compelled to sift the news for every new detail and anecdote. I roamed the city
looking for the "instant memorials" painted on the sides of buildings,
flowers and candles left on curbsides, photos of missing loved ones taped
to telephone poles. Poring over the "Portraits of Grief" in the *New York
Times* became a daily ritual. One I remember clearly. Crossley Williams, Jr.,

had called his parents when the first plane hit the World Trade Center—he saw bodies falling from windows. His mother told him to get out of the building, and his father said, "You heard what your mother said. Call me when you get out." The short tribute ended with a simple line that hit hard, and captured everything important—"'He enjoyed our company and we did his,' his father said."[1]

As a historian of modern cities I was especially eager to understand the debates around the collapse of the Twin Towers, and before long I was thoroughly confused and pretty angry about what seemed (and still seem) to me public discussions that miss the point. The public square was alive with officials and professional talkers shrugging off the collapse in favor of seemingly more satisfying conversations about the coming Freedom Tower, or hyping the war(s) as somehow appropriate symbols of vengeance, or yelling and screaming only about terrorism, or even worse crafting paranoid delusions of conspiracy when the central facts were all in the open. The tallest buildings in New York City were hit by hijacked planes, the buildings burned out of control, and collapsed, killing too many, and apparently stunning the experts and officials whose job it was to protect the public's safety. But why—aside from the suddenness and the horror if it all—were the disaster experts, the developers, architects and engineers, the politicians all stunned? It was as if the World Trade Center bombing of 1993 had been erased from memory, as if major fires had not wreaked havoc in American cities before. Somehow it was forgotten in the intensity of the tragedy that the Twin Towers were thrilling but also experimental architectural and engineering achievements; it was as if everyone believed that "acceptable levels" of safety in engineering and design could somehow predict the future and guarantee against all contingencies. Historical understanding was in very short supply.

Sally Regenhard and Glenn Corbett, Representatives Sherwood Boehlert and Anthony Weiner, and a handful of others inside the fire protection community, in the victims' family groups, in public health, and in the media could be heard in the background, asking serious questions behind all of the shouting.[2] I was listening pretty closely to them in those days. They wanted, I wanted, to talk about the fires, and the trade-offs in our risk and disaster control systems that made a fire disaster of that magnitude possible. In the end the World Trade Center disaster was a fire disaster, a vertical conflagration touched off by terrorists but impossible without the underlying vulnerability, a product of a risk-taking and risk-control system in modern America that constantly works to balance risk with profit, performance with disaster. The balance usually seems just right, until it doesn't. September 11 was a wake up call—for the threat of terrorism to be sure, but also for a reexamination of the other risks designed into the way we live, risks that shape every feature of our high-technology lives. It was and remains an opportunity to interrogate our disaster experts and our political leaders. It was a chance once again for Americans to think seriously about how we understand risks, how we plan for disasters, and whether or not that knowledge and those plans reflect our values.

There are historically identifiable reasons that in an age where fireproof buildings are possible we watched New York City's two tallest buildings succumb to fire on September 11. It was not a natural, inevitable result of progress or simply the actions of fanatics. It was the result of risks that were known and sanctioned by government, tended to by the disaster experts, and tolerated by the American public. No one wanted the disaster, but the conditions that made it possible—invention and risk-taking placing profit over precaution—were in many ways desirable, and in every way the results of a consensus over acceptable risk and disaster preparedness stretching back into the nineteenth century.

Where is the logic in erecting an elaborate structure of consensus-based fire codes for buildings, then allowing structures like the Twin Towers to go up as design experiments, tall, impressive, and risky? What is the sense, for that matter, in encouraging private development in areas where we know floods will carry away the homes, then providing taxpayer-funded subsidies for both the inhabitants and the builders? Why build on fault lines or in wildfire corridors, or live close to dangerous industrial facilities? Why prepare for "terrorism" above all else when floods, fires, and earthquakes pose far more consistent and grave threats to American life and prosperity? These are not rational decisions in the strictest sense, and yet each is built upon foundations of expert knowledge, expert professional judgments, and expert-advised policymaking that at a deeper level reflect the American public's preference for risk-taking over caution, even at great and repeated expense. This book provides historical context with which to answer some of these questions, but at its core it grows from an attempt to understand who the experts are, how they became powerful, and why they are only slightly closer today than they were on September 12 to protecting the public from disasters.

Did the Twin Towers collapse because of terrorism or fire? Was Hurricane Katrina a weather event or a technology failure? Is a disaster "natural" or human made? Depending on how one approaches these questions you will either find yourself accepting the inevitability of risk-taking and opting for explanations of disasters that do not fundamentally challenge the processes that make them. Or you will find yourself examining those risk-taking processes, thinking twice about blaming American disasters always on "external" threats and Acts of God. Attempting to answer these questions reveals the difficulties involved with applying disaster knowledge to public policy and urban development. Knowledge about risks and disasters drawn from the social and physical sciences, engineering and urban planning, insurance and public administration, has grown remarkably through both private and public research funding since the late nineteenth century. Application of the research into law has been very spotty, shaped by the politics of land development at every level, and most recently by a renewal of a "civil defense mindset" in disaster preparedness, updated by the Department of Homeland Security and myriad other agencies in order to move terrorism to the top of the list as the preeminent urban risk. A century's worth of disaster expertise—and a century's worth of policy development—have been shaped by the intertwined processes of urbanization, knowledge creation, and policy formation to control disasters. The broad trends have been at times towards creative and uniquely American solutions that intertwine public and private action, demonstrated clearly in the case of fire protection. Other trends demonstrate the persistence of dysfunction (or intermittent functionality), like the long life of fictional civil defense planning in the face of urban realities, or the frustrating inability of disaster researchers to strongly influence the policy process around hazard mitigation and emergency management.

Since World War II the strong federal role has not led to reduced risks. In fact the case has been just the opposite—but this is not a reason to abandon national mitigation standards or best practices in safety codes or emergency management. A consensus goal that emerged by the 1990s was the establishment of robust all-hazards mitigation with guidance from the federal government, but with policies and citizen inputs that fit into local realities. The experts in disaster can, in this way, serve to strengthen communities, and democratic practice more broadly, while also doing what they are trained to do: save lives and livelihoods from fire, rising water, and collapsing buildings.

The Disaster Experts builds on a generation of exciting scholarship in urban studies, sociology, geography, anthropology, and risk studies. Researchers have been very busy over the last few decades working to expose and critically examine the risk-taking systems that shape modern capitalism, the modern state, and the built environment. The work of Ulrich Beck, for example, forces us to consider risk as a feature of global capitalist development, a postmodern risk condition where the processes of modernization manufacture risks and disasters as a necessary accompaniment to profits. Beck's further hypothesis predicts an age in which threats like global warming or the collapse of interconnected financial markets force us in the west out of our protective cocoons of state, social class, and race privilege. Whereas "poverty is hierarchic," Beck warns us, "smog is democratic."³ Sociologists like Charles Perrow have shown us how "high-risk" has now become a normalized part of our technological systems, we live with "normal accidents" and internalize risk into our daily lives, often uncritically. Disaster and hazards researchers, working within the vulnerability paradigm, have been filling in the lines sketched out by Beck, arguing that in fact place and identity do still matter, and risks are unequally distributed across the democratic landscape, following the contours of traditional American divisions of poverty and segregation. Environmental risk hits the poor the hardest, and vulnerable populations always suffer more in disasters. Poverty is, to be sure, the longest disaster in American history.

Masters of synthesis like Carl Smith in his *Urban Disorder and the Shape of Belief*, Ted Steinberg in *Acts of God*, and Mike Davis in *Ecology of Fear* have presented us with coherent visions of a nation historically defined by risk-taking, Americans alternating between blissful ignorance and sputtering rage over the disasters that menace and destroy us again, and again, and again. In the most subtly powerful book yet on American risk and disaster—*The Control of Nature*—John McPhee interviews a long-time Louisiana hydrologic engineer, and in Raphael Kazmann's voice we hear the "numbers and formulas" of risk transformed into common sense fear over what's been created in the name of progress on the Mississippi River. "This is an extremely complicated river system altered by works of man," explains Katzmann. "A fifty-year prediction is not reliable. . . . Floods across the century are getting higher, low stages lower. The Corps of Engineers—they're scared as hell. This is planned chaos. The more planning they do, the more chaotic it is. Nobody knows exactly where it's going to end." McPhee lets the experts speak for themselves, and what they say rings true: we have to keep building, and we don't know where it will end. Or we do know, but we would rather not dwell on it.[4]

Much of the historical literature on American risk and disasters is wonderfully descriptive—a rich catalogue of studies including worker's safety and rights, auto safety, air quality, the consumer movement, environmental justice, and hundreds of specific disaster case studies. There is a danger here, though, of reading the analyses of specific disasters or public safety movements as singular, detached episodes, with "lessons learned" that don't significantly broaden or deepen our understanding of the broader historical processes at work in risk production, disaster, and recovery. We should take care not simply to adopt the idea of America as a risky place, as if that is some sort of genetic characteristic, rather than reflecting on the choices made in land use patterns, economic and political development, and broader spatial patterns of industrialization and urbanization.

In this book I was looking to develop a more synthetic treatment of the role disasters have played in American urban development, but more broadly in American political and economic development. Managing risk and disaster emerged as a signal feature of capitalism and democracy in the nineteenth century. It is useful also to trace the causes and impacts of risk and disasters across historical periods long enough to see that they are causal (and reactive) in and of themselves, and not just epiphenomena of urbanization or industrialization, or the rise of the modern state. With this in mind there were several possibilities for structuring the research. An obvious approach was to look at one type of risk, fire for example, and trace it over a long period. I started in this way, but found that what I initially expected to find—a story where knowledge creation led to professionalization and policy impact—was not the case at all. There were moments when the fire experts aligned what they knew with the power to do something about it, but there were also long periods, with horrific disasters throughout, when their knowledge and their authority were badly out of balance. This led me to the eventual conclusion that the long-term historical process of developing American disaster expertise has been shaped strongly by challenges to private commercial interests, and sometimes by public oversight, but never with great success by one profession. The expert has generally been a figure caught in between, working to add to his or her knowledge and authority without any guarantee of success over the long run in eradicating disasters. With this in mind I concluded that comparing three different broad types of experts—

fire experts, civil defenders, and disaster researchers—would reveal the fact that even in different historical contexts, American traditions of land use, local control, and risk-taking have strongly militated against a single profession or a single type of governmental actor seizing ultimate authority in risk and disaster control.

Additionally, while dividing pre- and postwar periods makes sense in terms of the major new threats of nuclear war and natural disasters at the regional level, there are two chronologies unfolding in modern American risk and disaster history, and I wanted to trace both. The first is a set of linked timelines that are always reactive to the major existential threats of a city. Among the many to choose before World War II, I chose fire, the risk with the most impact on both policy and the built environment. For the first twenty years or so of the Cold War the dominant threat was nuclear destruction. For the period following, nuclear threat jostled back and forth with natural disasters as threats of greatest concern, until the nuclear threat receded with the end of the Cold War and unrestrained postwar suburban and metropolitan development combined with natural and technological events to bring more and more people and property into harm's way. So, one set of timelines—roughly the chronological and sectional structure of the book—follows these three eras, the Conflagration Era, the Civil Defense Era, and the All-Hazards Era.

The second timeline of the book charts the broader development of cities, technological change, suburbanization, and regional growth all connected through continuous efforts to spot, learn about, and control risks and disasters—again to make such changes both economically and politically stable. When they are unstable we have seen experts arise, and when the concerns diminish the experts have either turned their attentions elsewhere, or held their ground as permanent stewards of their risk area. Combining these two overlapping chronologies (one divided into disaster eras, the other stretching over the modern era in total) was my analytical goal— not to arrive to the end of some long and inevitable historical process, but to understand why today we have simultaneously in our risk and disaster system consensus codes, private-sector development advocates, urban planners, military-influenced experts in command and control settings, and social and physical science researchers all staking significant claims to being the most critical "disaster expert." In truth, the experts of longest standing have been ones who could expand their professional boundaries through inter- and multidisciplinary work, and have expanded their reach through leveraging the built-in conflicts of federalism, where local knowledge retains power in America over some things, and federal power over others.

There is no singular "risk expert," as Ulrich Beck says, and that might be surprising to people in a nation where disciplinary expertise—think physician, lawyer, electrical engineer, investment banker—have staked strong claims toward controlling knowledge production and implementation. This book is in this sense, therefore, a continuation of work on the boundary disputes of disciplines and the futility of looking to professions as fixed markers of modernity.

The history of disaster experts takes us beyond that, though, into a nation in which risks and disasters, and the experts that study and tend them, are not easily lumped into categories of public or private, scientific or applied. The history leaves us in a place just like where Representative Weiner was in the 2002 World Trade Center hearings. He looked at the experts sitting at the witness table before him, thought about the collapse and the dead whose families were assembled in the chamber, and just wanted to know: where does the buck stop? To be fair to the experts, Weiner's question is not an easy one for them to answer. This book shows three cases where the question was answerable in broad terms, but even in disaster consensus eras, disputes over authority and responsibility are constant features of expert interaction. And the experts are not somehow autonomous actors—a major goal of the book has been to demonstrate that risk and disaster authority requires the constant creation of new knowledge, and strategizing on how to keep up with the forces of construction. The disaster experts are in microcosm fighting a battle that reflects a broader theme of modern American life: we want to take technological risks, profit by them, build inspiring modern environments, and stay safe from harm all at the same time. In their successes the disaster experts enable the faith that this is all possible and sustainable, in their failures they are called to answer for our disappointment.

Research into disasters matters, it has real human and economic repercussions, and when the research is productive but cannot influence disaster policy, cannot help shape the risks, then we have failed to live up to our obligations as social scientists, as technical experts, as those privileged enough to understand what's at stake. Sociologists and geographers have been self-critical in thinking about their roles as disaster experts, as have civil defense experts—particularly when they lament the inconsistency of their policy achievements. Historians have only begun the synthetic work that's possible to help us clearly see how risk-taking and the development of expertise to manage it compose a critical process in the modern United States. In its way this book hopes to build towards such an examination. Ultimately this book raises a couple of key questions of a more applied nature, questions whose answers will define the American vulnerability to disasters in the twenty first century, and may be useful in guiding policy debates and direct research funding decisions towards more democratic and productive outcomes.

First, should there be one profession to handle all disasters? Are webs of expertise sewn together with policy filaments possible, rather than one meta-level all-hazards profession? History shows that when disasters have been substantially reduced it has come as a result of disciplinary creativity and a tight fit between the experts and methods of policy creation. Where the policy process was closed off to disaster experts—often due to municipal deficiencies in legal authority or corrupt governance—novel third sector institutions like NFPA and UL have evolved to serve as connectors between risk knowledge and disaster control remedies.

A second question: will Americans embrace mitigation or continue to react, repeating well-worn patterns, to the same disasters? The second half of the book is focused on the history of mitigation—starting with Cold War civil defenders and ending with the hazards realists who have taken up this work more recently. Insurance companies may again show the way forward, as they begin to deny coverage in wildfire- and hurricane-prone areas. States and municipalities have started to fill this void, too, especially as the post-September 11 actions of the Department of Homeland Security leave many wondering if the federal government can effectively administer a sustainable, long-term national mitigation strategy. This is a big "if," considering that the "War on Terror" is still underway and counterterrorism still leads in federal grant-giving for disaster research, even after Hurricane Katrina. The future of mitigation, in short, remains uncertain. The civil defenders dreamed big, but failed in their mitigation strategies. If FEMA or state level disaster agencies can push mitigation, and the all hazards approach—even if it takes a voluntary form like the fire safety code councils—we may see a much more disaster-free century than the last one.

Thinking ahead, with the roots of our present condition firmly set in history, several lessons may be learned from the history of disaster experts that could and should have real implications for priority-setting in future research and for policy. These are areas where disaster experts and policy-makers could come together; and where historians would do well to play a role in providing detailed background and synthesis. First, let local knowledge win. When mitigation is working, when a municipality or state is connecting research to policy effectively, it should be unburdened with outside meddling, either by private developers working state government to shape local conditions, or by a federal bureaucracy that pushes one-size-fits-all solutions. This is not a call for some sort of "Disaster 10th Amendment," for just as with the history of American race relations or environmentalism, it is most certainly the case that some cities and some states will work hard for all the people, and others will not. A uniform national program of disaster control, though, is less manageable and less likely to succeed than linked local networks of mitigation and preparedness. Philadelphia should never have been expected to spend money on civil defense preparations that made more sense to experts in Washington than down at the local firehouse. Government and/or nongovernmental organizations could work to create and maintain reliable forums for public/private and citizen/ expert interaction at the local and state level. Such forums do have a history in the United States—but generally only in the form of expert panels and commissions assembled in the aftermath of a major disaster, like the Kerner Commission or the 9/11 Commission. Disaster mitigation and preparedness forums could facilitate the application of valuable risk knowledge into policies for protection at the local level.

A second recommendation: states and communities should invest in information technology first, ahead of massive infrastructural change, instead of waiting for restrictive land use policies to keep people from living in harm's way. Mass media, digital media and the internet, wiki culture, and GIS all make it increasingly possible that creative, local mitigation techniques may be made available in a way that avoids the disaster experts altogether, or at least speeds the process of knowledge creation. Disaster response itself is potentially much more nuanced now, more immediate— think of firefighters using hand-held GIS devices to follow the direction and speed of wildfires. Tools of information gathering, retrieval, and dispersal evolve rapidly, but that is no reason not to adopt them just as rapidly into emergency management practice. In many cases it may be that making maps available digitally, and training citizens and first responders to use the technology will be far more useful in saving lives and property than expensive investments like new dams and levees, water-delivery systems for fire protection out in the chaparral country, or other politically popular big-ticket items.

This leads to a third point. Make demographic and hazards information more readily available to the public and to emergency managers and first responders—make it downloadable into the hand-held devices firefighters will carry. Tell the histories of the people and the land in the context of disaster preparedness. This is hazards realism, and it must be addressed right now, and from here forward. The fact is that disaster mitigation requires poverty reduction, education, and land use restriction. Emergency managers all along, but certainly since Hurricane Katrina, have been reluctant to call these by name, recently promoting "homeland security" while in reality preparing for the hazards they must actually face, like the difficulties of evacuating people who lack transportation options from a flood, or getting medicine to the elderly in the midst of a snowstorm. Preparedness without attention to the known realities of the people and the land is sham preparedness, much like civil defense was throughout its history. There is a real opportunity post-Katrina to have a national conversation about the real threat of poverty, that in a disaster situation the weakest among us will drown. Though it may be politically risky to talk about poverty in the context of disaster protection, this conversation actually has a long history in American life, and since neither poverty nor disasters have been eradicated, there's no use avoiding the conversation now.

Fourth, the federal government, through coordination of risk and disaster research in national labs, in the university-based research system, through grants to nonprofit and nongovernmental entities, and through stimulation of private research, should be supporting hazards and disaster research more actively. Presently there is no centralized, well-funded center where risk and disaster knowledge across all hazards can be created side by side with public policy. Yes, mitigation should be privileged at the local level, but knowledge creation in the abstract must also be fostered to stay even close in to meeting new risks with technological and policy innovations. The emergence of Underwriters Laboratories and NFPA, in their way, demonstrate the effectiveness of centralizing a certain type of risk research. Had civil defense not been done under such a tremendous cloak of secrecy, the findings of disaster researchers as well would have been extremely useful to localities as they planned for real disasters like fires and floods. The hazards and disaster research centers, like those at the University of Colorado and the University of Delaware, are efforts that could be usefully scaled up to the federal level, perhaps in the creation of a new national lab. Presently the Department of Homeland Security "Centers of Excellence" are geographically dispersed, a good start, with local emphases; a national "risk" lab would commit resources in a serious way to interdisciplinary hazards and disaster research, alongside a policy and public administration division for intergovernmental policy formation and implementation research. The continued development and success of the interdisciplinary profession of emergency management hinges on fostering familiarity with hazards and disaster research among practitioners at all levels.[5] This will be done in university and college settings, and a national "risk lab" could also take this up as one of its key goals, building on the work already begun very effectively at FEMA's Emergency Management Institute.

Also, the development and applicability of consensus codes needs to be further explored. The consensus code system offers a uniquely American solution to problems that combine the need for authority and new knowledge in environments where government control and outright private control are impossible. In the case of fire protection, local control was disastrous because of laissez-faire attitudes to fire risk among municipal officials. In this instance the insurance industry worked to shape the built and policy environment, succeeding in both instances, but not without the creation of intermediary groups to develop new codes and standards. Today, just as then, technological change happens faster than precautionary research and policy formation—and an expansion of the consensus code process might assist in slowing the introduction of new technologies or land use prerogatives before they have been vetted by communities of experts representing different stakeholders. It will be necessary for government to provide incentives for the private sector to be involved in safety standard-setting and consensus code formation, especially in the construction and insurance industries. Such an approach may be usefully imported into community land use planning, emergency management, and mitigation efforts. The durable legal status of nonprofit consensus code groups presents a way forward when government regulation is untenable or the public voice is in opposition to commercial interests. The consensus code system is one where, also, the average citizen might meaningfully participate in risk and disaster conversations among experts.

Finally, we should not think wistfully back to the Cold War, a supposedly "simpler" time as many have suggested since September 11 and

Hurricane Katrina. Though cultural critics have presented that era as the punch line to a joke about how silly people were to hide under desks, we ourselves need to think about how we will look to observers fifty years from now with our "go bags" and duct tape, our body scans for toddlers at airports and our color-coded threat charts. Countenancing lies about preparedness because they make us feel safe is a weak response to government when it is at its worst, preying on our fears; and much worse, it makes it possible for policy makers to pursue actions that citizens may not approve or even be aware of, or if they are aware, may not fully understand due to "wartime" security measures. In the Cold War, civil defense was a rhetorical cover, a "band-aid for a holocaust" as one historian has called it, allowing the development of more and more offensive nuclear capabilities in the name of national security. If we build more bombs we will win, that "logic" went, and just in case this makes the public squeamish, we have our bomb shelters and evacuation plans to let us sleep at night. This dynamic is worth watching very closely, and people should not be afraid to speak out when they see it. Preparing our nation for terrorism above all other hazards is sensible only if we pretend the Cold War—and Hurricane Katrina—never happened.

In the end the disaster experts work in a nation grown powerful through taking risks. Theirs is the realm of safety, shaped by history—in them we place a trust that we may be only half-aware is ours to bestow.

NOTES

Introduction

1. *Portraits: 9/11/01: The Collected "Portraits of Grief" from the New York Times* (New York: Times Books, 2002), 413; Lisa Miller, "War over Ground Zero: A Proposed Mosque Tests the Limits of American Tolerance," *Newsweek*, August 8, 2010, http://www.newsweek.com/2010/08/08/war-over-ground-zero.html, accessed December 3; Eric Lipton, "Ground Zero: Building Standards; Mismanagement Muddled Collapse Inquiry, House Panel Says," *New York Times*, March 7, 2002, B7; Office of Chief Medical Examiner, City of New York, "World Trade Center Operational Statistics," January 30, 2009. See also Scott Gabriel Knowles, "Lessons in the Rubble: The World Trade Center and the History of Disaster Investigations in the United States," *History and Technology* 19, 1 (March 2003): 9–28.

2. "Learning from 9/11—Understanding the Collapse of the World Trade Center," Hearing Before House Committee on Science, 107th Cong., March 6, 2002, Serial No. 107–46, vols. 1–2, 98–100.

3. Ibid., 54.

4. Ibid., 24.

5. Ibid., 127.

6. Ibid., 131–33.

7. Therese McAllister, ed., *World Trade Center Building Performance Study: Data Collection, Preliminary Observations and Recommendations* (Washington, D.C.: FEMA, 2002), 3–4.

8. The New York City Fire Department had warned the Port Authority of the existence of a large diesel fuel tank in the building before September 11, 2001. The tank was ultimately blamed for the intensity of the fire and the collapse of Building 7. James Glanz and Eric Lipton, "A Nation Challenged: The Trade Center; City Had Been Warned of Fuel Tank at 7 World Trade Center," *New York Times*, December 20, 2001, B7.

9. McAllister, *Performance Study*, 5–6.

10. Author interview with Sally Regenhard, December 8, 2010.

11. "The Investigation of the World Trade Center Collapse: Findings, Recommendations, and Next Steps," Hearing Before House Committee on Science, 107th Cong., 2nd sess., May 1, 2002, Serial No. 107–61, 153.

12. House Committee on Science, Floor Statement on H.R. 4687, Congressman Sherwood Boehlert, July 12, 2002.

13. "Listening to the City," 2002. I attended this event, open to the public, and recall participating as more than 5,000 people in the Jacob Javits center "voted" for the designs they liked—none were liked. http://www.listeningtothecity.org

14. Josh Barbanel, "Explosion at the Twin Towers: Fire Safety; Tougher Code May Not Have Helped," *New York Times*, February 27, 1993, Late Edition, 1, 24.

15. Jim Dwyer, "Threats and Responses: Looking Back, Looking Forward, *New York Times*, September 11, 2002, A19; James Glanz and Eric Lipton, *City in the Sky: The Rise and Fall of the World Trade Center* (New York: Times Books, 2003), 132–33, 325–26.

16. There are some notable exceptions, works that have strongly influenced my methodological approach. Please see Conclusion for more discussion on literature and methods.

17. The argument that scientific research creates knowledge and knowledge applied brings solutions to societal problems is as old as the Enlightenment. It was explicated commonly in the twentieth-century United States, perhaps most influentially in Vannevar Bush, *Science: The Endless Frontier* (Washington, D.C.: Government Printing Office, 1945). Critique of the concept is rich and varied across the disciplines. I have found useful Max Horkheimer and Theodore W. Adorno, *Dialectic of Enlightenment* (1947; reprint, New York: Continuum, 1969); Philip Kitcher, "Public Knowledge and the Difficulties of Democracy," *Social Research* 73, 4 (Winter 2006): 1205–24; Kitcher, *Science, Truth, and Democracy* (Oxford: Oxford University Press, 2001); and Theodore M. Porter, "Speaking Precision to Power: The Modern Political Role of Social Science," *Social Research* 73, 4 (Winter 2006): 1273–94.

18. "Learning from 9/11," 180.

19. Thomas P. Hughes, *American Genesis: A Century of Innovation and Technological Enthusiasm* (New York: Viking, 1989); Olivier Zunz, *Why the American Century?* (Chicago: University of Chicago Press, 2000).

20. Russell R. Dynes, *Organized Behavior in Disaster* (Lexington, Mass.: D.C. Heath, 1970), 4.

21. E. L. Quarantelli, ed., *What Is a Disaster? Perspectives on the Question* (London: Routledge, 1998); E. L. Quarantelli and Ronald W. Perry, eds., *What Is a Disaster? New Answers to Old Questions* (Philadelphia: Xlibris, 2005); Ronald W. Perry, "What Is a Disaster?" in *Handbook of Disaster Research*, ed. Havidan Rodriguez, Enrico L. Quarantelli, and Russell R. Dynes (New York: Springer, 2006), 1–15.

Chapter 1. The Devil's Privilege

Epigraph: Lewis Mumford, *The City in History* (1961; reprint San Diego: Harvest Books, 1989), 447, 449.

1. Adjusted for inflation between 1880 and 1920, this difference reflects roughly a doubling in real dollar losses between the two benchmark years; the 1920 figure would

be $3.5 billion adjusted for 2009 values. Losses in the 1904 Baltimore conflagration year were $250 million ($5.8 billion in 2009); those for the 1906 San Francisco earthquake and fire year were $359 million ($8.85 billion in 2009). Statistics drawn from U.S. Consumer Price Index and calculated at *Consumer Price Index, Historical Statistics of the United States* (Washington, D.C.: Government Printing Office, 2008), http://www.measuringworth.com, 2011.http://oregonstate.edu/cla/polisci/download-conversion-factors, accessed January 14.

2. National Fire Protection Association, "Deadliest/Large-Loss Fires," 2010, http://www.nfpa.org.

3. For histories of fire protection technologies, fire insurance, and the fire service in the nineteenth century, see Amy S. Greenberg, *Cause for Alarm: The Volunteer Fire Department in the Nineteenth-Century American City* (Princeton, N.J.: Princeton University Press, 1998); Margaret Hindle Hazen and Robert M. Hazen, *Keepers of the Flame: Fire in American Culture, 1775–1925* (Princeton, N.J.: Princeton University Press, 1992); Christine Meisner Rosen, *The Limits of Power: Great Fires and the Process of City Growth in America* (New York: Cambridge University Press, 1986). See also Stephen J. Pyne, *Fire in America: A Cultural History of Wildland and Rural Fire* (Princeton, N.J.: Princeton University Press, 1982); Mark Tebeau, *Eating Smoke: Fire in Urban America, 1800–1950* (Baltimore: Johns Hopkins University Press, 2003).

4. Ulrich Beck, *Risk Society: Towards a New Modernity* (London: Sage, 1992), 17–50; for elaboration and expansion of the "risk society" critique, see Ulrich Beck, Anthony Giddens, and Scott Lash, *Reflexive Modernization: Politics, Tradition, and Aesthetics in the Modern Social Order* (Cambridge: Polity Press, 1994); and Ulrich Beck, *World Risk Society* (Cambridge: Polity Press, 1999). David Harvey has advanced a related critique in his work on the relationships between the development of industrial capitalism and urbanization. See especially David Harvey, *The Urban Experience* (Baltimore: Johns Hopkins University Press, 1989). Mike Davis has demonstrated in historical case studies the ways risk is unevenly allocated across the urban landscape in industrial society. See Mike Davis, *City of Quartz: Excavating the Future in Los Angeles* (New York: Vintage Books, 1990); and Mike Davis, *Ecology of Fear: Los Angeles and the Imagination of Disaster* (New York: Metropolitan Books, 1998). On the development of an elite culture of technocratic control in American cities, see Thomas Parke Hughes, *Networks of Power: Electrification in Western Society, 1880–1930* (Baltimore: Johns Hopkins University Press, 1993); and Miriam Levin, Sophie Forgan, Martina Hessler, Robert H. Kargon, and Morris Low, *Urban Modernity: Cultural Innovation in the Second Industrial Revolution* (Cambridge, Mass.: MIT Press, 2010).

5. Dalit Baranoff, "Shaped by Risk: The American Fire Insurance Industry, 1790–1920," Ph.D. dissertation, Johns Hopkins University, 2004; Dalit Baranoff, "A Policy of Cooperation: The Cartelization of American Fire Insurance, 1873–1906," *Financial History Review* 10, 2 (October 2003): 119–30; Howard Kunreuther, "Insurability Conditions and the Supply of Coverage," in *Paying the Price: The Status and Role of Insurance Against Natural Disasters in the United States*, ed. Howard Kunreuther and Richard J. Roth, Sr. (Washington, D.C.: Joseph Henry Press, 1998), 17–50.

6. Hazen and Hazen, 132.

7. Harry Chase Brearley, *Fifty Years of a Civilizing Force: An Historical and a Critical Study of the Works of the National Board of Fire Underwriters* (New York: Frederick Stokes, 1916), 8. See also National Board of Fire Underwriters (hereafter NBFU), *Pioneers of Progress: National Board of Fire Underwriters, 1866–1941* (New York: NBFU, 1941); and A. L. Todd, *A Spark Lighted in Portland: The Record of the National Board of Fire Underwriters* (New York: McGraw-Hill, 1966).

8. NBFU, *Proceedings of the National Board of Fire Underwriters, 1866* (New York: Styles and Cash, 1866), 1–8.

9. Ibid.

10. For a discussion of the ways nineteenth-century firms organized and analyzed information, see Alfred D. Chandler, *Strategy and Structure: Chapters in the History of the Industrial Enterprise* (Cambridge, Mass.: MIT Press, 1962); Naomi Lamoreaux and Daniel M. G. Raff, eds., *Coordination and Information: Historical Perspectives on the Organization of Information* (Chicago: University of Chicago Press, 1995); and JoAnne Yates, *Control Through Communication: The Rise of System in American Management* (Baltimore: Johns Hopkins University Press, 1989). For the rise of statistics in the service of transforming uncertainties into calculable risks, see Theodore M. Porter, *Trust in Numbers: The Pursuit of Objectivity in Science and Public Life* (Princeton, N.J.: Princeton University Press, 1995); and Arwen Mohun, "On the Frontier of *The Empire of Chance*: Statistics, Accidents, and Risk in Industrializing America," *Science in Context* 18, 3 (2005): 337–57.

11. H. Roger Grant, *Insurance Reform: Consumer Action in the Progressive Era* (Ames: Iowa State University Press, 1979), 74.

12. Carl S. Smith, *Urban Disorder and the Shape of Belief: The Great Chicago Fire, the Haymarket Bomb, and the Model Town of Pullman* (Chicago: University of Chicago Press, 1995), 19–22; see also Karen Sawislak, *Smoldering City: Chicagoans and the Great Fire, 1871–1874* (Chicago: University of Chicago Press, 1995); and Peter Charles Hoffer, *Seven Fires: The Urban Infernos That Reshaped America* (New York: Public Affairs, 2006), 106–52.

13. Eran Ben-Joseph, *The Code of the City: Standards and the Hidden Language of Place Making* (Cambridge, Mass., MIT Press, 2005), 47–57.

14. Rosen, 95–109.

15. Brearley, *Fifty Years*, 40–44.

16. NBFU, *Proceedings of the National Board of Fire Underwriters, 1875* (New York: Styles and Cash, 1875), 17–20; Brearley, *Fifty Years*, 45.

17. NBFU, *Proceedings, 1875.*

18. Ibid., 26.

19. Ibid., 27.

20. Ibid.

21. Ibid., 96–102.

22. Grant, 75.

23. Tebeau, 111–12.

24. NBFU, *Proceedings of the National Board of Fire Underwriters, 1889* (New York: Styles and Cash, 1889), 42.

25. The history of electrification is a broad and well-researched topic. See Hughes, *Networks of Power*; Forrest McDonald, *Insull* (Chicago: University of Chicago Press, 1962); David E. Nye, *Electrifying America: Social Meanings of a New Technology, 1880–1940* (Cambridge, Mass.: MIT Press, 1990); and Harold L. Platt, *The Electric City: Energy and the Growth of the Chicago Area, 1880–1930* (Chicago: University of Chicago Press, 1991).

26. NBFU, *Proceedings of the National Board of Fire Underwriters, 1892* (New York: Styles and Cash, 1893), 8. In the same speech Affeld called for a law to "prevent the city from being disfigured with unsightly and disproportioned 'skyscrapers,' which offend the eye and endanger the health of a city." This sentiment, outdated even in 1892, reflected the growing anxiety among underwriters of the day at the constantly changing infrastructure in the cities.

27. NBFU, *Proceedings of the Twenty-Sixth Annual Meeting of the National Board of Fire Underwriters, 1893* (New York: James Kempster, 1894), 98.

28. Edward Atkinson, "Speech to International Association of Fire Engineers," *Fire and Water Engineering* (June 24, 1903): 31. For a complete discussion of the history of the Associated Factory Mutuals, see Sara E. Wermiel, *The Fireproof Building: Technology and Public Safety in the Nineteenth-Century American City* (Baltimore: Johns Hopkins University Press, 2000), 104–37; Baranoff, "Shaped by Risk"; and J. Finley Lee, "The Competitive Role of the Associated Factory Mutuals," *Journal of Risk and Insurance* 36, 4 (September 1969): 401–18.

29. Marc Schneiberg, "Organizational Heterogeneity and the Production of New Forms," in *Social Structure and Organizations Revisited*, ed. Michael Lounsbury and Marc J. Ventresca (Oxford: Elsevier Science, 2002), 39–90.

30. Wermiel, 109–10.

31. Schneiberg, 43.

32. Ibid.

33. Harold Francis Williamson, *Edward Atkinson: The Biography of an American Liberal, 1827–1905* (Boston: Old Corner Book Store, 1934), 1–7.

34. Wermiel, 110.

35. Williamson, 106; John Ripley Freeman, "Autobiography of John Ripley Freeman," manuscript, John Ripley Freeman Papers, MIT Institute Archives and Special Collections (hereafter Freeman Papers), 141–47; Edward Atkinson, "The Factory Mutual System of Fire Insurance in Its Relation to Fire Resistant Buildings, Sometimes Called Fire Proof," *Insurance Monitor* (January 1903): 32–34.

36. Williamson, 104.

37. Atkinson, "Speech," 31.

38. Dane Yorke, *Able Men of Boston* (Boston: Boston Manufacturers Mutual Fire Insurance Company, 1950), 163.

39. Marshall B. Dalton, *Edward Atkinson (1827–1905): Patron of Engineering Science and Benefactor of Industry* (New York: Newcomen Society, 1950), 21. John Ripley Freeman, Woodbury's colleague at the Mutuals, remembered that he was technically trained, but had not finished his degree from MIT. Though Freeman saw him as "better at publicity and making business contacts than as a thoroughly scientific investigator . . . he [Woodbury] had performed more useful scientific research in the fire prevention field than any one else up to his time." Freeman, 142.

40. Yorke, 161–62.

41. C. J. H. Woodbury, *The Fire Protection of Mills and Construction of Mill-Floors* (New York: J. Wiley & Sons, 1882).

42. Insurance Engineering Experiment Station, *Report No. V: Slow-Burning or Mill Construction* (Boston: Manufacturers Mutual Fire Insurance Company, 1902), 3–7; Wermiel, 112–13.

43. Freeman, 142, 146.

44. Williamson, 109–10.

45. Andrew Abbott, *The System of Professions: An Essay on the Division of Expert Labor* (Chicago: University of Chicago Press, 1988), 112. See also, Andrew Abbott, *Time Matters: On Theory and Method* (Chicago: University of Chicago Press, 2001), 261–79.

46. Robert V. Bruce, *Bell: Alexander Graham Bell and the Conquest of Solitude* (Boston: Little, Brown, 1973), 92.

47. Freeman, 144.

48. Atkinson, "Speech."

49. Freeman, 147.

50. Ibid., 148–149.

51. Box 29, Freeman Papers.

52. Freeman, 148–49.

53. Ibid., 150.

54. Ibid., 152.

55. Ibid., 166.

56. Ibid, 152.

57. Ibid., 154–57; Wermiel, 129–30.

58. Atkinson, "Speech," 31.

59. Freeman, 157–58.

60. Ibid., 153.

61. C. J. H. Woodbury, "Conflagrations in Cities," delivered before the Franklin Institute, Philadelphia, January 23, 1891, 1–6.

62. Woodbury, *Fire Protection*, 7.

63. Ibid., 10.

64. Ibid., 11.

65. Ibid., 13.

66. Ibid., 26.

67. Ibid., 122.

68. Ibid., 122–23.

69. Wermiel, 127.

70. Edward Atkinson, "The Prevention of Loss by Fire and the System of Factory Mutual Insurance, Address by Edward Atkinson, Minneapolis, Minnesota," September 17, 1885.

71. Williamson, 125.

72. "In a Frame of Light," *Chicago Daily Tribune*, May 9, 1893, 1.

73. Daniel H. Burnham, *Final Official Report of the Director of Works of the World's Columbian Exposition* (1894; New York: Garland, 1989). On the context of Chicago's nineteenth-century growth, see William Cronon, *Nature's Metropolis: Chicago and the Great West* (New York: Norton, 1991); Donald L. Miller, *City of the Century: The Epic of Chicago and the Making of America* (New York: Touchstone, 1997). On the World's Columbian Exposition, see Henry Adams, *The Education of Henry Adams* (Boston: Houghton Mifflin, 1918), chap. 12; Dennis B. Downey, *A Season of Renewal: The Columbian Exposition and Victorian America* (Westport, Conn.: Praeger, 2002); Neil Harris, *Building Lives: Constructing Rites and Passages* (New Haven, Conn.: Yale University Press, 1999); and Neil Harris, Wim de Wit, James Gilbert, and Robert W. Rydell, *Grand Illusions: Chicago's World's Fair of 1893* (Chicago: Chicago Historical Society, 1993). The most complete histories of the nineteenth-and twentieth-century fairs remain Robert W. Rydell, *All the World's a Fair: Visions of Empire at American International Expositions, 1876–1916* (Chicago: University of Chicago Press, 1984); and Robert W. Rydell, *World of Fairs: The Century of Progress Expositions* (Chicago: University of Chicago Press, 1993). For the Columbian Exposition in the larger context of urban history see Timothy J. Gilfoyle, "White Cities, Linguistic Turns, and Disneylands: The New Paradigms of Urban History," *Reviews in American History* 26 (1998): 175–204.

74. Harry Chase Brearley, *A Symbol of Safety: An Interpretive Study of a Notable Institution Organized for Service—Not Profit* (Garden City, N.Y.: Doubleday, Page, 1923), 17.

75. William Henry Merrill, "The Story of Underwriters' Laboratories, Inc.," May 1, 1913, Underwriters Laboratories Archives (hereafter ULA); Casey Cavanaugh Grant, "The Birth of NFPA," unpublished paper, September 17, 1996, NFPA, 4, available in modified form in *NFPA Journal* (1996); http://www.nfpa.org/itemDetail.asp?category ID = 500&itemID = 18020&URL = About%20NFPA/Overview/History.

76. Brearley, *Symbol of Safety*, 17–18.

77. Ibid., 18.

78. W. H. Merrill, "Bill Rob," *Laboratories' Data* 2 (August 1921): 118, 120–21. Writing in memoriam after Robinson's death in 1921, Merrill gave him the ultimate compliment from a fire safety expert: "he has passed the test; he is approved."

79. Brearley, *Symbol of Safety*, 19.

80. Rachel Maines, *Asbestos and Fire: Technological Tradeoffs and the Body at Risk* (New Brunswick, N.J.: Rutgers University Press, 2005).

81. Brearley, *Symbol of Safety*, 18–19.

82. Norm Bezane, *This Inventive Century: The Incredible Journey of Underwriters Laboratories, 1894–1994* (Northbrook, Ill.: Underwriters Laboratories, 1994), 6–9.

83. William S. Boyd, "Early Days at Underwriters' Laboratories," *Laboratories' Data* 10 (November 1929): 256–57.

84. Ibid.

85. Merrill, "Bill Rob," 119.

86. Boyd, 255.

87. C. R. Alling, "Why Is Underwriters' Laboratories?" *Laboratories' Data* 3 (July 1922): 147.

88. A. R. Small, "Underwriters' Laboratories on the Pacific Coast," *Laboratories' Data* 4 (March 1923): 54.

89. For the history of engineering professionalization and education, see John K. Brown, Gary Lee Downey, and Maria Paula Diogo, "Engineering Education and the History of Technology," *Technology and Culture* 50 (October 2009): 737–52; Daniel C. Calhoun, *The American Civil Engineer: Origins and Conflict* (Cambridge, Mass., Harvard University Press and MIT Press, 1960); Monte A. Calvert, *The Mechanical Engineer in America, 1830–1910: Professional Cultures in Conflict* (Baltimore: Johns Hopkins University Press, 1967); Gary Lee Downey, "Low Cost, Mass Use: American Engineers and the Metrics of Progress," *History and Technology* 23, 3 (September 2007): 289–308; Thomas P. Hughes, *American Genesis: A Century of Invention and Technological Enthusiasm, 1870–1970* (New York: Viking Penguin, 1989); Robert H. Kargon, *Science in Victorian Manchester: Enterprise and Expertise* (Baltimore: Johns Hopkins University Press, 1977); Edwin T. Layton, *The Revolt of the Engineers: Social Responsibility and the American Engineering Profession* (Baltimore: Johns Hopkins University Press, 1971); A. Michal McMahon, *The Making of a Profession: A Century of Electrical Engineering in America* (New York: IEEE Press, 1984); David F. Noble, *America by Design: Science, Technology, and the Rise of Corporate Capitalism* (New York: Knopf, 1977); Terry S. Reynolds, ed., *The Engineer in America* (Chicago: University of Chicago Press, 1991); Bruce E. Seely "Research, Engineering, and Science in American Engineering Colleges: 1900–1960," *Technology and Culture* 34 (April 1993): 344–86; and Bruce Seely, "The Other Re-Engineering of Engineering Education, 1900–1965," *Journal of Engineering Education* (July 1999): 285–94; Amy E. Slaton, *Race, Rigor, and Selectivity in U.S. Engineering: The History of an Occupational Color Line* (Cambridge, Mass.: Harvard University Press, 2010). For current trends in scholarship on engineering education see *Engineering Studies*, particularly the theme issue "Locating Engineers: Education, Knowledge, Desire," ed. Gary Downey and Juan Lucena, 1, 2 (2009).

90. Victor C. Alderson, "The Progress and Influence of Technical Education," *Proceedings of the Thirteenth Annual Meeting of the Society for the Promotion of Engineering Education* (New York: Engineering News Publications, 1906), 132–38, 133.

91. Armour Institute of Technology, *Armour Bulletin* (Chicago: Armour Institute of Technology, 1894–1895): 19–22.

92. *Armour Bulletin* (1903).

93. Ibid.

94. *The Integral* (Chicago: Armour Institute of Technology, 1906).

95. *Armour Bulletin* (1932): 172.

96. Victor C. Alderson, "The Economic Needs of Technical Education," *Journal of the Western Society of Engineers* 7, 3 (June 1902): 307–18.

97. Robert H. Kargon and Scott G. Knowles, "Knowledge for Use: Science, Higher Learning, and America's New Industrial Heartland, 1880–1915," *Annals of Science* 59 (2002): 1–20.

Chapter 2. Reforming Fire

Epigraph: John Ripley Freeman, "On the Safeguarding of Life in Theaters: Being a Study from the Viewpoint of an Engineer" (New York, 1906), reprinted from *Transactions of the American Society of Mechanical Engineers* 27 (1906): 73, 74.

1. The historiography of the American Progressive Era is vast. I have found most useful Robert M. Crunden, *Ministers of Reform: The Progressives' Achievement in American Civilization, 1889–1920* (New York: Basic Books, 1982); and Maureen A. Flanagan, *America Reformed: Progressives and Progressivisms, 1890s-1920s* (Oxford: Oxford University Press, 2006). For the intertwined relationships among city, industry, immigration, and American reform, particularly via the disciplines of the social sciences, see Crunden, chaps. 2–3; Dorothy Ross, *The Origins of American Social Science* (Cambridge: Cambridge University Press, 1991), 143–71; and Louis Menand, *The Metaphysical Club: A Story of Ideas in America* (New York: Farrar, Straus and Giroux, 2001), 285–333.

2. Brian Balogh, *A Government Out of Sight: The Mystery of National Authority in Nineteenth-Century America* (Cambridge: Cambridge University Press, 2009).

3. "Eddie Foy Tells of Iroquois Theater Fire," *Laboratories' Data* 8 (March 1927): 74–77; Andrew M. Hayes, "The Iroquois Theatre Fire: Chicago's Other Great Fire," Ph.D. dissertation, University of Nebraska, 1999, 64–68.

4. "Tells of Horrors of Iroquois Fire," *Boston Herald*, January 11, 1904, 1.

5. "Burial for Dead Next Sad Duty," *Chicago Daily Tribune*, January 1, 1904, 1–8.

6. "Iroquois Theatre Souvenir Programme, Dedicatory Performance, 23 November 1903" (Chicago: Rand, McNally, 1903), 16, Collection of the Chicago Historical Society.

7. Henry Neil, *Lest We Forget: Chicago's Awful Theater Horror by the Survivors and Rescuers* (Chicago: McCurdy, 1904), ix–xii.

8. Edward R. Kantowicz, "Carter H. Harrison II: The Politics of Balance," in *The Mayors: The Chicago Political Tradition*, ed. Paul M. Green and Melvin G. Holli (Carbondale: Southern Illinois University Press, 1995), 16–32.

9. Nat Brandt, *Chicago Death Trap: The Iroquois Theatre Fire of 1903* (Carbondale: Southern Illinois University Press, 2003), 110–13.

10. "Many Theaters Violating Law Shut by Mayor," *Chicago Daily Tribune*, January 2, 1904, 1.

11. "Find Much for Censure: Aldermen Scathing in Their Criticism of Theater," *Chicago Daily Tribune*, January 2, 1904, 2.

12. "Laws Violated at the Iroquois," *Chicago Daily Tribune*, January 2, 1904, 4.

13. "Best House Ever Built: Building Commissioner Tells of the Iroquois," *Chicago Daily Tribune*, January 2, 1904, 2.

14. "Curtain Caught Because Cheap," *Chicago Daily Tribune*, January 2, 1904, 2.

15. "Every Theater in the City Shut by Mayor's Order," *Chicago Daily Tribune*, January 3, 1904, 1–2.

16. Ibid.

17. "Curtain Held by Board," *Chicago Daily Tribune*, January 3, 1904, 2.

18. Chicago City Council Building Committee, *Iroquois Theater Fire Investigation Testimony Report* (January 8, 1904).

19. Ibid., "Summary."

20. Hayes, 104–5.

21. "Firetrap and Cheaply Built," *Chicago Daily Tribune*, January 2, 1904, 2.

22. "The Truth About the Iroquois Theater," *Fireproof* 4 (February 1904): 6–8.

23. John Ripley Freeman to Jno. B. Schoeffel, February 5, 1904, Freeman Papers; David Hapgood, *Charles R. Crane: The Man Who Bet on People* (Philadelphia: Xlibris, 2000), 9–11, 25–26.

24. *Chicago Record-Herald*, January 8, 1904, 1.

25. Freeman, "Autobiography," 297.

26. E. V. French, "Memorandum on Reports, Feb. 22, 1904," Freeman Papers.

27. E. V. French, "Theater Inspection, Illinois Theater, Jan. 18 & 19 & Feb. 8, 1904," Freeman Papers.

28. E. V. French, "Theater Inspection, Academy of Music, Jan. 21 & 30, 1904," Freeman Papers.

29. E. V. French, "Memorandum for Mr. J. R. Freeman: Theater Reports, February 24, 1904," Freeman Papers.

30. E. V. French, "Theater Inspection, Bijou, Jan. 21 & 30," Freeman Papers.

31. G. F. Shaffer to John Ripley Freeman, 11 March 1904, Freeman Papers.

32. E. V. French, "Chicago Opera House, Jan. 28" and "McVicker's Theater, January 20," Freeman Papers.

33. G. F. Shaffer to John Ripley Freeman, March 8, 1904, Box 32: Chicago Theater Fire Study, Correspondence and Report, January–February 1904, Freeman Papers..

34. Chicago Theater Fire Correspondence, January–February 1904, sprinkler surveys.

35. John Ripley Freeman to E. A. Fisher, January 29, 1904, Freeman Papers.

36. "Tests Mean Much," newspaper clipping, January 19, 1904, 1, Freeman Papers.

37. *Chicago Chronicle*, January 10, 1904, 1.

38. Henry Evans to John Ripley Freeman, February 5, 1904, Freeman Papers.

39. Brandt, 124–34.

40. Ibid., 134.

41. Edgar Lee Masters, *Levy Mayer and the New Industrial Era: A Biography* (New Haven, Conn.: Rachel Mayer, 1927), 69–90.

42. Freeman, "Autobiography" 298.

43. Freeman, *Safeguarding*, 73–74.

44. For the business history context of the Progressive Era, see Alfred D. Chandler, *Strategy and Structure: Chapters in the History of the Industrial Enterprise* (Cambridge, Mass.: MIT Press, 1962); and Naomi Lamoreaux, *The Great Merger Movement in American Business, 1895–1904* (Cambridge: Cambridge University Press, 1985).

45. Louis Filler, *The Muckrakers* (1976; Stanford, Calif.: Stanford University Press, 1993), 190–202. The most artistic representation of the "mixed feelings" of the Progressives toward the technological and scientific achievements of big firms is found in the writings of Upton Sinclair. In *The Jungle* Sinclair describes immigrants in Chicago watching the automation of hog butchering in a meat packing factory: "It was all so very businesslike that one watched it fascinated. It was porkmaking by machinery, porkmaking by applied mathematics." Upton Sinclair, *The Jungle* (New York: Doubleday, 1906), chap. 3.

46. See Mark Aldrich, *Safety First: Technology, Labor, and Business in the Building of American Worker Safety, 1870–1939* (Baltimore: Johns Hopkins University Press, 1997).

47. See Harold Platt, *Shock Cities: The Environmental Transformation and Reform of Manchester and Chicago* (Chicago: University of Chicago Press, 2005); Martin V. Melosi, *The Sanitary City: Urban Infrastructure in America from Colonial Times to the Present* (Baltimore: Johns Hopkins University Press, 1999); and Joel A. Tarr, *The Search for the Ultimate Sink: Urban Pollution in Historical Perspective* (Akron, Ohio: University of Akron Press, 1996).

48. *Paul v. Virginia*, 75 U.S. 168 (1869).

49. Robert Riegel, "Rate-Making Organizations in Fire Insurance," *Annals of the American Academy of Political and Social Science*, (1917): 172–198.

50. Ibid., 183. In this climate we come to see why the Mutuals were so successful, focused as they were on very specific classes of risks and charging rates calibrated directly toward protecting property, not toward investment and return on investment.

51. Huebner, 5–6.

52. Ibid., 14–15.

53. Ibid.

54. *Report of the Joint Committee of the Senate and the Assembly of the State of New York, Appointed to Investigate Corrupt Practices in Connection with Legislation, and the Affairs of Insurance Companies, Other Than Those Doing Life Insurance Business*, vol. 1 (Albany, N.Y.: J.B. Lyon, 1911), 29.

55. Ibid., 1230.

56. Ibid., 1253.

57. H. Roger Grant, *Insurance Reform: Consumer Action in the Progressive Era* (Ames: Iowa State University Press, 1979), 124–28; Marc Schneiberg and Sarah A. Soule, "Institutionalization as a Contested, Multilevel Process: The Case of Rate Regulation in American Fire Insurance," in *Social Movements and Organizational Theory*, ed. Gerald F. Davis, Doug McAdam, W. Richard Scott, and Mayer N. Zald (New York: Cambridge University Press, 2005), 122–60.

58. Schneiberg and Soule.

59. Historian Mark Tebeau broke ground in his study of the relationship between the fire insurance industry and the fire service with his book *Eating Smoke*, in which he devotes some attention to NFPA as one of a fire prevention triumvirate including UL and the NBFU. Mark Tebeau, *Eating Smoke: Fire in Urban America, 1800–1950* (Baltimore: Johns Hopkins University Press, 2003).

60. Percy Bugbee, *Men Against Fire: The Story of the National Fire Protection Association, 1896–1971* (Boston: NFPA, 1971), 2

61. Ibid.

62. Ibid., 6.

63. Ibid., 8.

64. Ibid., 17.

65. Ibid., 18.

66. Ibid., 19.

67. Ibid., 20.

68. Ibid., 25.

69. *NFPA Quarterly* 16, 3 (1922).

70. Ibid., 227–29., Bugbee 39–40.

71. Ibid., 25.

72. *NFPA Quarterly* 25, 4 (1931): 344–45.

73. Ibid., 352–53.

74. See Charles Rosenberg, *The Cholera Years: The United States in 1832, 1849, and 1866* (Chicago: University of Chicago Press, 1962); James G. Burke, "Bursting Boilers and the Federal Power," *Technology and Culture* 7, 1 (Winter 1966): 1–23. On the dangers of nineteenth-century American industrialization, see also Aldrich, *Death Rode the Rails: American Railroad Accidents and Safety, 1828–1965* (Baltimore: Johns Hopkins University Press, 2006); Louis C. Hunter, *Steamboats on the Western Rivers: An Economic and Technological History* (1949; Mineola, N.Y.: Dover, 1993); Wolfgang Schivelbusch, *The Railway Journey: The Industrialization of Time and Space in the 19th Century* (1977; Berkeley: University of California Press, 1986); and Anthony F. C. Wallace, *St. Clair: A Nineteenth Century Coal Town's Experience with a Disaster-Prone Industry* (Ithaca, N.Y.: Cornell University Press, 1988).

75. Richardson Dilworth, ed., *The City in American Political Development* (New York: Routledge, 2009), 1–11. On trends in American political development scholarship more generally, see Karen Orren and Stephen Skowronek, *The Search for American Political Development* (Cambridge: Cambridge University Press, 2004).

76. William J. Novak, *The People's Welfare: Law and Regulation in Nineteenth-Century America* (Chapel Hill: University of North Carolina Press, 1996), 51–80, 62. Kevin P. Arlyck, "What *Commonwealth v. Alger* Cannot Tell Us About Regulatory Takings," *New York University Law Review* 82, 14 (November 2007): 1746–80; Daniel R. Ernst, "Law and American Political Development," *Reviews in American History* 26 (198): 205–19.

77. Christine Meisner Rosen, "Business, Democracy, and Progressive Reform in the Redevelopment of Baltimore After the Great Fire of 1904," *Business History Review* 63, 2 (Summer 1989): 283–328.

78. See Ben-Joseph, *The Code of the City.*

79. Arthur B. Jones, *The Salem Fire* (Boston: Gorham Press, 1914), 35.

80. "Salem's Awakening," *NFPA Quarterly*, 8, 1 (July 1914): 10–11. Franklin Wentworth had served on the Salem City Council and in 1910 had led an effort to get inflammable coverings for roofs passed. E. V. French, a key investigator of the Iroquois Theater Fire, took a train from Boston to take part in fighting the Salem conflagration, but was unsuccessful in saving a factory building owned by one of his Factory Mutuals clients.

81. Ibid., 134–36.

82. *American Political Science Review* 8, 4 (1914): 642–43.

83. *First Annual Report of the Fire Prevention Commissioner for the Metropolitan District, Massachusetts*, Public Document 107, August 1, 1914–August 1, 1915 (Boston: Wright and Potter, 1915), 35–43; Alice M. Holden, "Current Municipal Affairs," *American Political Science Review* 8, 4 (November 1914): 642–43.

84. Commonwealth of Massachusetts Supreme Judicial Court, *Ovide Boucher v. E.W. Longley et al.*, vol. 2, Part 2, July 8–December 30, 1916, 392–93.

85. *NFPA Quarterly* 20, 3 (1927): 211–12.

86. *NFPA Quarterly* 19, 1 (July 1925).

87. James Ford, "The Rebuilding of Cities After Disaster," *City Planning* (January 1927): 40.

88. *NFPA Quarterly* 26, 1 (1933): 325–29.

89. Ibid., 41–42.

Chapter 3. The Invisible Screen of Safety

Epigraph: Hubbard Hoover, "You Are Safer Than You Know," *Saturday Evening Post*, April 28, 1945.

1. W. H. Merrill, Jr., "Underwriters' Laboratories, Inc.," *Spectator* (May 1, 1913): 17–23.

2. Harry Chase Brearley, *A Symbol of Safety: An Interpretative Study of a Notable Institution Organized for Service—Not Profit* (Garden City, N.Y.: Doubleday, 1923), 29. Brearley was a very popular and prolific author in Progressive Era America, and his

works show an almost unbridled enthusiasm for the innovations of the insurance industry. He also wrote about New York harbor development and the history of time-keeping devices; see Harry Chase Brearley, *The Problem of Greater New York and Its Solution* (New York: Search Light Book Corporation, 1914).

3. Harry Chase Brearley and Daniel N. Handy, *Fifty Years of a Civilizing Force*.

4. Ibid., 190.

5. Ibid., 185.

6. Ibid., 188.

7. "Members of the N.F.P.A. Visit the Laboratories," *Laboratories' Data* 1 (May 1920): 76.

8. Brearley, *A Symbol of Safety*, 163–64.

9. Merrill to Shallcross, December 18, 1916, 3, Underwriters Laboratories Archives (hereafter ULA).

10. Merrill, "Underwriters' Laboratories, Inc.," 20.

11. *The Organization, Purpose and Methods of Underwriters' Laboratories* (Chicago: UL, 1916), 9.

12. Brearley, *Fifty Years*, 186.

13. Ibid., 189.

14. "On the Safe Side, Program One," Underwriters Laboratories, nd, 9.

15. "Underwriters' Laboratories, a Contribution by Stock Fire Insurance to a Public Cause, Fire Protection and Prevention," *Laboratories' Data* 3 (July 1922): 144.

16. Brearley, *A Symbol of Safety*, 39.

17. "Underwriters' Laboratories, a Contribution," 144.

18. *Manual of Instructions for Preparation of Reports Issued by Underwriters' Laboratories, Inc.* (Chicago: UL, June 1911), 1.

19. Ibid.

20. *Organization, Purpose and Methods*, 7.

21. "Visitors," *Laboratories' Data* 3 (January 1922): 31.

22. "Visitors," *Laboratories' Data* 6 (February 1925): 45.

23. "Players Watch Play of Automatic Sprinklers," *Laboratories' Data* 7 (February 1926): 47.

24. "Company Staff Members Inspect Laboratories," *Laboratories' Data* 10 (June 1929): 161.

25. Brearley, *Fifty Years*, 195.

26. Brearley, *A Symbol of Safety*, 32–33.

27. Joseph C. Forsyth, "Reinspection in New York City," *Laboratories' Data* 6 (July–August 1925): 143.

28. Ibid., 144.

29. Ibid., 143–44.

30. E. F. Reisenberger, "Qualifications and Duties of an Inspector," *Laboratories' Data* 3 (January 1922): 26.

31. Ibid., 27.

32. Chas. R. D'Olive, "Eliminating 'Unconscious Carelessness' in Inspections," *Laboratories' Data* 5 (February 1924): 48.

33. "Brief Review of Year 1916 at Underwriters' Laboratories," *Electrical Data* (February 1917): 11.

34. Brearley, *A Symbol of Safety*, 236.

35. Ibid., 31–32.

36. A. R. Small, "Service," *Laboratories' Data* 1 (May 1920): 65–68.

37. Brearley, *Fifty Years*, 193.

38. "Life and Fire Hazards of Electricity," *Electrical Data* 4 (July 1918): 21.

39. "Causes and Losses in Fires Due to Electricity," *Electrical Data* 2 (August 1916): 10–11.

40. "Fires and Accidents Reported Due to Electrical Causes," *Electrical Data* 1 (July 1915): 5–23.

41. "Fires and Accidents . . . ," *Electrical Data* 3 (July 1917): 16.

42. "Fires and Accidents . . ." (1915): 5.

43. "Fires and Accidents . . ." (1917): 16–19.

44. "Fires and Accidents . . ." (1915): 6–23.

45. "Fires and Accidents . . ." (1917): 16–19.

46. "Causes and Losses in Fires Due to Electricity," 10–11.

47. Brearley, *A Symbol of Safety*, 187.

48. G. T. Bunker, "Impressions," *Laboratories' Data* 1 (June 1920): 86.

49. "The Work of the National Board of Fire Underwriters," *Laboratories' Data* 9 (December 1928): 279–81.

50. "The New York Office," *Laboratories' Data* 3 (June 1922): 112.

51. "New York Testing Station," *Electrical Data* 1 (March 1916): 5.

52. "Tests on Material for New Fire Alarm Telegraph System of New York City," *Electrical Data* 3 (July 1918): 20.

53. C. J. Peacock, "Review of the Activities of a Service Engineer During the Year 1928," *Laboratories' Data* 10 (February 1929): 55.

54. "Meeting of Label Service Inspectors at Chicago Office, May 7, 1920," *Laboratories' Data* (May 1920): 62–63.

55. Gene Brockmier, "A History and Reminiscences of Underwriters Laboratories on the West Coast," manuscript, June 1993, 1–2, ULA.

56. Brearley, *A Symbol of Safety*, 18.

57. "UL letter," December 4–5, 1916, 2, ULA.

58. W. D. A. Peaslee, "Standardization Activities of Underwriters' Laboratories," *Annals of the American Academy of Political and Social Science* 137 (May, 1928): 60–61.

59. "Underwriters' Laboratories and Its Relations with the Acetylene Industry," *Laboratories' Data* 3 (November 1922): 215.

60. C. R. Alling, "Why Is Underwriters' Laboratories?" *Laboratories' Data* 3 (July 1922): 148.

61. Peaslee, 61.

62. Merrill, "Underwriters' Laboratories," 20.

63. Peaslee, 62.

64. David M. Hart, *Forged Consensus: Science, Technology, and Economic Policy in the United States, 1921–1953* (Princeton, N.J.: Princeton University Press, 1998), 18–20; see also Ellis W. Hawley, "Herbert Hoover, the Commerce Secretariat and the Vision of the Associative State," *Journal of American History* 61 (June 1974): 116–40.

65. Percy Bugbee, *Men Against Fire: The Story of the National Fire Protection Association, 1896–1971* (Boston: NFPA, 1971), 22–23.

66. Bugbee, 181–85, "NFPA Committee and Leadership Statistics". Major standards created by NFPA included Fire Sprinklers (first) 1896, Car Houses 1906, National Standard Hose Thread 1906, Skylights 1906, Municipal Fire Alarm Systems 1911, National Electrical Code 1911, Fire Drills 1912, Standpipes 1913, Automobile Fire Apparatus, 1914, Classification of Buildings According to Occupancy 1914, Construction of Private Residences 1915, Internal Combustion Engines 1915, Building Exits Code 1923, Fire Prevention Bureau Model Ordinance 1925. Laws and Ordinances passed included Electrical Current, Cleanliness of Streets, Motion Picture Machines, Garages, Heating Apparatus, Fireworks, Flues, Burning of Refuse, Explosives, Fire Limits, Fire Escapes, Flammable Liquids in 1913, City Planning and Zoning in 1933. Major Committees included: Automatic Sprinklers 1897, Building Construction 1901, Fire Records 1903, Municipal Fire Alarms Systems 1903, Theater Construction and Prevention 1904, Standard Hose Coupling Threads 1905, Common Causes of Fires 1910, Electrical 1911, Public Information 1913, Safety to Life 1913, Zoning 1926, Fire Protection Engineering Education 1939, High Value Districts 1916, Uses of Wood in Construction 1914

67. "W. H. Merrill in War Work," *Electrical Data* 4 (July 1918): 14.

68. Morton G. Lloyd, "The Bureau of Standards," *Laboratories' Data* 11 (May 1930): 163.

69. *Investigation of Cartridge-Inclosed Fuses*, Technologic Papers of the Bureau of Standards 74 (Washington, D.C.: Government Printing Office, 1916), 36–37.

70. Merwin Brandon, "Reminiscences of Underwriters' Laboratories, Inc.," unpublished book, April 1964, 43–44, ULA.

71. Amy E. Slaton, *Reinforced Concrete and the Modernization of American Building* (Baltimore: Johns Hopkins University Press, 2001), 67–71. On materials standardization and testing in the history of American technology, see Rachel Maines, *Asbestos and Fire); Jeffrey L. Meikle, American Plastic: A Cultural History* (New Brunswick, N.J.: Rutgers University Press, 1995); Thomas J. Misa, *American Steel: The Making of Modern America, 1865–1925* (Baltimore: Johns Hopkins University Press, 1995); Bruce Sinclair, "At the Turn of a Screw: William Sellers, the Franklin Institute, and a Standard American Thread," *Technology and Culture* 10, 1 (January 1969): 20–34. On "scientific management," see Frederick Winslow Taylor, *The Principles of Scientific Management* (1911; Mineola, N.Y.: Dover, 1998); Robert Kanigel, *The One*

Best Way: Frederick Winslow Taylor and the Enigma of Efficiency (New York: Penguin, 1997). The history of "accuracy" as a social construction is useful in the context of safety testing; see Donald MacKenzie, "Missile Accuracy: A Case Study in the Social Processes of Technological Change," in *The Social Construction of Technological Systems*, ed. Wiebe Bijker, Thomas Hughes, and Trevor Pinch (Cambridge, Mass.: MIT Press, 1987), 195–222; Donald A McKenzie, *Inventing Accuracy: A Historical Sociology of Nuclear Missile Guidance* (Cambridge, Mass.: MIT Press, 1990).

72. M. J. O'Brien, "History of Standard Time Temperature Curve," *Laboratories' Data* (November 1923).

73. R. E. Wilson, "Fire Resistance of Building Columns as Shown by Test," *Engineering News-Record* 87, 3 (July 21 1921): 106–10, 106.

74. "Fire Tests of Building Columns Issued," *Laboratories' Data* 2 (February 1921): 28.

75. *Fire Tests of Building Columns* (Chicago: UL, 1921).

76. Brearley, *A Symbol of Safety*, 28.

77. *Fire Tests of Building Columns*, 16.

78. Ibid., 17.

79. Ibid., 16.

80. *NFPA Quarterly* (1928); ASTM standard E119 was also created after these tests.

81. FEMA, *Promoting the Adoption and Enforcement of Seismic Building Codes: A Guidebook for State Earthquake and Mitigation Managers*, FEMA 313 (January 1998), Handout F; see also Ross E. Cheit, *Setting Safety Standards: Regulation in the Public and Private Sectors* (Berkeley: University of California Press, 1990); Harm Schepel, *The Constitution of Private Governance: Product Standards in the Regulation of Integrating Markets* (Oxford: Hart, 2005).

82. Colston E. Warne, *The Consumer Movement: Lectures*, ed. Richard L. D. Morse (Manhattan, Kan.: Family Economics Trust Press, 1993), 20–23; P. G. Agnew, "The Work of the American Standards Association," *Laboratories' Data* 11 (May, 1930): 168; Norman D. Katz, "Consumers Union: The Movement and the Magazine," Ph.D. dissertation, Rutgers University, 1977, 51–52.

83. Norman Isaac Silber, *Test and Protest: The Influence of Consumers Union* (New York: Holmes and Meier, 1983), 18.

84. F. J. Schlink to Landers, Frary and Clark, April 20, 1955, Box 881: 3, Consumers Research, Inc. (hereafter CRI) Collection, Rutgers Special Collections and University Archives.

85. A. B. Evans to Floyd-Wells Company, May 7, 1934, Box 1: 17, CRI Collection.

86. Letter to Mr. William D. Collins, May 29, 1934, Box 1: 17, CRI Collection.

87. Interview with Dewey Palmer, April 26, 1970, 6–8, Center for the Study of the Consumer Movement, Consumers Union, Mt. Vernon, N.Y.

88. Arthur Kallet and F. J. Schlink, *100,000,000 Guinea Pigs: Dangers in Everyday Foods, Drugs, and Cosmetics* (New York: Vanguard Press, 1933); Silber, 18–19.

89. Warne, *The Consumer Movement*, 76; Silber, 24–28; Katz, 105–11.

90. Alling, "Why Is Underwriters' Laboratories?" 147–48.

91. David A. Hounshell and John Kenly Smith, Jr., *Science and Corporate Strategy: DuPont R&D, 1902–1980* (Cambridge: Cambridge University Press, 1988), 37–44; Leonard S. Reich, *The Making of American Industrial Research: Science and Business at G.E. and Bell, 1876–1926* (London: Cambridge University Press, 1985).

92. "Underwriters' Laboratories, a Contribution," 145–46.

93. Ibid., 146.

94. Merrill to Shallcross, December 18, 1916, 3, ULA.

95. Ibid., 4.

96. "Underwriters' Laboratories and Its Relations with the Acetylene Industry," 216.

97. Ibid.

98. "Underwriters' Laboratories, a Contribution," 146.

99. Ibid., 144–45.

100. Alling, "Why Is Underwriters' Laboratories?" 149.

101. "Who Is at Fault?" *Laboratories' Data* 2 (December 1921): 206.

102. Ibid.

103. Ibid., 207.

104. C. J. Krieger, "Another Case of 'Get the Facts'," *Laboratories' Data* (April 1926): 75–76.

105. "Investigation of Cartridge-Inclosed Fuses," 37.

106. Ibid., 40–41.

107. Ibid., 42.

108. Ibid., 43–44.

109. Ibid., 44.

110. Ibid., 62.

111. Ibid., 66.

112. Ibid., 8–9.

113. Ibid., 16.

114. Ibid., 19–20.

115. Merrill to Shallcross, January 17, 1917, 3–4, ULA.

116. "Hose Monopoly Is Charged in Suit," *New York Times*, January 3, 1914; "Reports of Cases Decided in the Court of Appeals of the State of New York, V. 208 (Albany, N.Y.: J.B. Lyon, 1913), 583–84.

117. *Underwriters' Laboratories v. Commissioner*, 135 F.2d 371 (7th Cir.1943), 372–74.

118. Victor H. Kramer, "The Antitrust Division and the Supreme Court, 1890–1953," *Virginia Law Review* 40, 44 (May 1954): 444.

119. UL, "Fifty Years in the Service of Safety," 1944, 9.

120. Wendell Jamieson, "Incident On the 79th Floor Empire State Building Airplane Crash, 1945," *New York Daily News*, June 18, 1998, http://www.nydailynews.com/archives/news/1998/06/18/1998-06-18_incident_on_the_79th_floor_e.html.

Chapter 4. Ten to Twenty Million Killed, Tops

Earlier versions of parts of this chapter appeared in Scott Gabriel Knowles, "Defending Philadelphia: A Historical Case Study of Civil Defense in the Early Cold War," *Public Works Management and Policy* 11, 3 (January 2007): 1–16.

Epigraph: Stanley Kubrick, *Dr. Strangelove or: How I Learned to Stop Worrying and Love the Bomb*, 1964.

1. The historical literature on American civil defense has gone through two waves, one in the 1980s and one more recently, resulting in a shelf of very interesting and useful books. See Wayne B. Blanchard, "American Civil Defense 1945–1975: Evolution of Programs and Policies," Federal Emergency Management Agency, 1980, http://www.lrc.fema.gov/; Tracy C. Davis, *Stages of Emergency: Cold War Nuclear Defense* (Durham, N.C.: Duke University Press, 2007); Lynn Eden, *Whole World on Fire: Organizations, Knowledge, and Nuclear Weapons Devastation* (Ithaca, N.Y.: Cornell University Press, 2004); Dee Garrison, *Bracing for Armageddon: Why Civil Defense Never Worked* (Oxford: Oxford University Press, 2006); Andrew Grossman, *Neither Dead Nor Red: Civil Defense and American Political Development in the Early Cold War* (New York: Routledge, 2001); Thomas J. Kerr, *Civil Defense in the U.S.: Bandaid for a Holocaust?* (Boulder, Colo.: Westview Press, 1983); David Krugler, *This Is Only a Test: How Washington, D.C. Prepared for Nuclear War* (New York: Palgrave Macmillan, 2006); Langley Keyes and Jennifer Leaning, eds., *The Counterfeit Ark: Crisis Relocation for Nuclear War* (Cambridge, Mass.: Ballinger, 1984); Laura McEnaney, *Civil Defense Begins at Home: Militarization Meets Everyday Life in the Fifties* (Princeton, N.J.: Princeton University Press, 2000); and Kenneth D. Rose, *One Nation Underground: The Fallout Shelter in American Culture* (New York: New York University Press, 2001).

2. Federal Civil Defense Administration (hereafter FCDA), *An Hypothetical Narrative (February 13, 195_ attack) for the City of Philadelphia, PA*, 2, 1952, Box A-5311, Philadelphia City Archives (hereafter PCA). The City Archives hold substantial records of the Philadelphia County Civil Defense Council and civil defense records from the Mayor's Office from World War II to the 1960s. I have drawn heavily on these records, as they give valuable insights into the mindsets and actions of Philadelphia's public officials in the midst of the largest disaster preparedness moment in the city's history.

3. FCDA, 4; Philadelphia County Civil Defense Council, *Solution to Philadelphia Test Exercise*, March 12, 1951, 1, 6, Box A-5313, PCA.

4. Ibid., 10–13.

5. Krugler, 47.

6. United States Strategic Bombing Survey, *The Effects of Atomic Bombs on Hiroshima and Nagasaki* (Washington, D.C.: Government Printing Office, 1946).

7. OCDP, *Civil Defense for National Security* (Washington, D.C.: Government Printing Office, November 1948).

8. Kerr, 20–30.

9. "Federal Civil Defense Act," *Bulletin of the Atomic Scientists* 7, 2 (February 1951): 59–62.

10. "Civilian Defense Unit Opens Here," *Philadelphia Evening Bulletin*, April 13, 1950.

11. "Mayor's Message to Council on Civil Defense," August 10, 1950, Box A-5312, PCA.

12. J. M. McCullough, "Red Cross Picks 6 A-Bomb Relief Centers Here," *Evening Bulletin*, July 16, 1950.

13. J. M. McCullough, "Officer Pictures Phila. as Target for A-Bomb," *Philadelphia Inquirer*, June 13, 1950.

14. "Evacuee Areas Selected for A-Bomb Defense," *Philadelphia Inquirer*, May 14, 1950; F. Rosen, "Military Bases Also Alerted in Defense Move," *Philadelphia Inquirer*, August 20, 1950.

15. "Port on Alert for Sabotage," *Evening Bulletin*, July 28, 1950.

16. "City Defense to Screen Reds," *Evening Bulletin*, July 23, 1950.

17. "Here's What to Do if Atom Bomb Falls on Philadelphia," *Evening Bulletin*, August 13, 1950.

18. "Mayor's Message," 1950.

19. Russell R. Dynes, "Community Emergency Planning: False Assumptions and Inappropriate Analogies, *International Journal of Mass Emergencies and Disasters* 12, 2 (1994): 141–58.

20. R. A. Miller, *Division Commander: A Biography of Major General Norman D. Cota* (Spartanburg, S.C.: Reprint Co., 1989), 1–11.

21. Ibid., 93–94, 185–90.

22. City Council of Philadelphia, *Report of the Special Committee: To Investigate Civil Defense Program*, February 25, 1952, 6–7, PCA.

23. Ibid.

24. David A. Cavers, "Legal Planning Against the Risk of Atomic War," *Columbia Law Review* 55, 2 (February 1955): 127–57.

25. Ibid., 149.

26. Ibid., 146

27. Garrison, *Bracing for Armageddon*, 39–41.

28. City Council, *Report of the Special Committee*, 13.

29. J. C. Calpin, "Inside City Hall," *Evening Bulletin*, September 17, 1950.

30. City Council, *Report of the Special Committee*, 86–87; Philadelphia County Civil Defense Council, *Solution*, 4.

31. Philadelphia County Civil Defense Council, *Solution*.

32. Chicago Civil Defense Corps, *Chicago Alerts: A City Plans Its Civil Defense Against Atomic Attack* (Chicago: Chicago Civil Defense Corps, 1951), 2, PCA.

33. Tracy C. Davis, *Stages of Emergency*; Davis, a theater scholar, innovatively reads civil defense through the eyes of performance studies—pointing out the critical nature of "rehearsal" within the broader civil defense strategy of planning and public participation. As the weapons got more powerful it was harder to get people to stage evacuations—but "problem-solving conferences" persisted throughout the era, 66–67.

34. Chicago Civil Defense Corps, 1.

35. Ibid., 2.

36. Talia Whyte, "Irl D'Arcy Brent II, 90; Was CIA operative, Baird Executive," *Boston Globe*, December 15, 2010.

37. Chicago Civil Defense Corps, 20.

38. Ibid., 3.

39. Ibid., 20–21.

40. Ibid., 21.

41. Ibid., 6.

42. Ibid.

43. Ibid., 7.

44. Ibid., 2.

45. Anthony J. Mullaney, "German Fire Departments Under Air Attack," in National Fire Protection Association, *Fire and the Air War* (Boston: NFPA, 1946), 100, 110–11.

46. Ibid.

47. Eden, 1–11.

48. Arthur E. Cote, "History of Fire Protection Engineering," *Fire Protection Engineering* (online), http://www.fpemag.com/articles/article.asp?i = 375.

49. Norman D. Cota to Hon. Bernard Samuel, October 11, 1950, PCA.

50. City Council, *Special Committee*, 12, PCA.

51. "City and State Defense Heads Attend A-Bomb Exercise," *Evening Bulletin*, September 26, 1950.

52. Remarks of Mayor Bernard Samuel at Philadelphia Area Civil Defense Exercise Critique, Convention Hall, March 12, 1951, Box A-5311, folder "Test Exercise," PCA.

53. Agenda: Philadelphia Area Civil Defense Exercise, March 12–14, 1951, Box A-5311, folder "Test Exercise," PCA.

54. Philadelphia County Civil Defense Council, *Solution*, 5–7.

55. Ibid., 7.

56. "Officer Pictures Phila."

57. University of Michigan Survey Research Center, *Defense of Our Cities: A Study of Public Attitudes on Civil Defense* (Ann Arbor: the Center, 1951), 7–40, Collection of the National Emergency Training Center, Emmitsburg, Md.

58. Joseph S. Clark, Jr., and Dennis J. Clark, "Rally and Relapse, 1946–1968," in *Philadelphia: A 300-Year History*, ed. Russell F. Weigley (New York: Norton, 1982), 651–52.

59. Clark and Clark, 654–55.

60. City Council, *Special Committee*, 3–4.

61. Ibid., 15–16.

62. Ibid., 22.

63. Ibid., 110–11.

64. Ibid., 116.

65. Ibid., 177–79.

66. Ibid., 200.

67. Ibid., 58–59.

68. "Annual Report, 1943," Mayor's Office Files, Council of Defense, 60–101.1, PCA.

69. Ibid.

70. Remarks of Mayor Bernard Samuel, 1951, PCA.

71. "Civilian Defense Unit Opens Here," *Evening Bulletin*, April 13, 1950.

72. Frank P. Zeidler, "A Mayor Views Bomb Test," *Bulletin of the Atomic Scientists* 9, 4 (May 1953): 148.

73. Frank P. Zeidler, "A Mayor Looks at the Civil Defense Problem," *Bulletin of the Atomic Scientists* 6, 8–9 (August–September 1950): 250.

74. Joseph E. McLean, "Project East River—Survival in the Atomic Age," *Bulletin of the Atomic Scientists* 9, 7 (September 1953): 247.

75. Jennifer S. Light, *From Warfare to Welfare: Defense Intellectuals and Urban Problems in Cold War America* (Baltimore: Johns Hopkins University Press, 2003), 16–18.

76. Robert H. Kargon and Arthur P. Molella, *Invented Edens: Techno-Cities of the Twentieth Century* (Cambridge, Mass.: MIT Press, 2008), 88–89.

77. Donald Monson, "City Planning in Project East River," *Bulletin of the Atomic Scientists* 9, 7 (September 1953): 265–67.

78. Zeidler, "A Mayor Looks at the Civil Defense Problem," 249–50.

79. Michele Landis Dauber, "The Sympathetic State," *Law and History Review* 23, 2 (Summer 2005): 387–442.

80. Arthur S. Flemming, "The Impact of Disasters on Readiness for War," *Annals of the American Academy of Political and Social Science* 309 (Jan. 1957): 65; see also Carter L. Burgess, "The Armed Forces in Disaster Relief," *Annals of the American Academy of Political and Social Science* 309 (Jan. 1957).

81. Flemming, 69, 70.

82. "July 1, 1958: Office of Civil and Defense Mobilization (OCDM) Established," *History Commons* (online), http://www.historycommons.org/context.jsp?item = estabocdm#estabocdm.

83. Gary A. Kreps, "The Federal Emergency Management System in the United States: Past and Present," *International Journal of Mass Emergencies and Disasters* 8, 3 (November 1990): 275–300, 281.

84. Kreps, 284.

85. Garrison, *Bracing for Armageddon.*

86. Edward Teller with Allen Brown, *The Legacy of Hiroshima* (London: Macmillan, 1962), 243.

87. Ibid., 244.

88. Robert Jay Lifton, *Death in Life: Survivors of Hiroshima* (New York: Random House, 1968); see also Paul Boyer, "From Activism to Apathy: America and the Nuclear Issue, 1963–1980, *Bulletin of the Atomic Scientists* 40, 7 (August–September 1984): 14–23; Boyer, *By the Bomb's Early Light: American Thought and Culture at the Dawn of the Atomic Age* (Chapel Hill: University of North Carolina Press, 1994).

89. U.S. Civil Defense, "1966 Public Opinion Study," 18, National Emergency Training Center.

90. In fact public trust in government in postwar America reached its apex at roughly the time of the 1966 survey. See Pew Research Center for the People and the Press, "Public Trust in Government, 1958–2010" (online), http://people-press.org/trust/.

91. Lee Clarke, *Mission Improbable: Using Fantasy Documents to Tame Disaster* (Chicago: University of Chicago Press, 2001), 93.

Chapter 5. What Is a Disaster?

Epigraph: Charles E. Fritz, "Disaster," in *Contemporary Social Problems: An Introduction to the Sociology of Deviant Behavior and Social Disorganization*, ed. Robert K. Merton and Robert A. Nisbet (New York: Harcourt, Brace, 1961), 654.

1. FCDA, *Survival Under Atomic Attack*, film based on U.S. Department of the Army, *Survival Under Atomic Attack* (Washington, D.C.: Government Printing Office, 1951), http://www.archive.org/details/Survival1951.

2. Sociologist Thomas Drabek points out that these assumptions, questioned and downplayed at FEMA in the 1980s–1990s, are ascendant again since 9/11, under the terrorism planning agenda of the Department of Homeland Security. See Thomas Drabek, "Social Problems Perspectives, Disaster Research and Emergency Management: Intellectual Contexts, Theoretical Extensions, and Policy Implications," paper presented at American Sociological Association Annual Meeting, August 2007.

3. National Opinion Research Center, *Human Reactions in Disaster Situations: Report on Research Commissioned by Chemical Corps Medical Laboratories*, NORC Report 52 (Chicago: NORC, 1954), 7–8.

4. Ibid., 86.

5. See Carl Smith, *Urban Disorder and the Shape of Belief: The Great Chicago Fire, the Haymarket Bomb, and the Model Town of Pullman* (Chicago: University of Chicago Press, 1996).

6. Russell R. Dynes and E. L. Quarantelli, "The Place of the 1917 Explosion in Halifax Harbor in the History of Disaster Research: The Work of Samuel H. Prince,"

Preliminary Papers 182, 1992, Disaster Research Center, University of Delaware (hereafter DRC). The archives of the Disaster Research Center, formerly at Ohio State University, are an unmatched repository of published and unpublished reports and papers, as well as unpublished materials related to the hundreds of DRC research projects over the decades, and manuscript materials related to the 50-year history of social science disaster research in the United States. An enormous amount of these materials have been made accessible online; see http://www.udel.edu/DRC/ (particularly "Institutional Repository").

7. Lowell Juilliard Carr, "Disaster and the Sequence-Pattern Concept of Social Change," *American Journal of Sociology* 38, 2 (September 1932); E. L. Quarantelli, "Disaster Research: An Entry for an Encyclopedia," Preliminary Papers 167, 1991, DRC; David Neal, "Reconsidering the Phases of Disaster," *International Journal of Mass Emergencies and Disasters* 15, 2 (August 1997): 240–41.

8. Carr, 211–12.

9. Ibid., 212

10. Ibid., 215–16

11. Lynn Eden, *Whole World on Fire*; Gian P. Gentile, *How Effective Is Strategic Bombing? Lessons Learned from World War II to Kosovo* (New York: New York University Press, 2000), 16–18.

12. Gentile, 22, 24.

13. Ibid., 25–31.

14. Ibid., 34.

15. U.S. Strategic Bombing Survey (USSBS), *The Effects of Strategic Bombing on German Morale*, vol. 1 (Washington, D.C.: the Survey, 1947), 1.

16. USSBS, *The Effects of Strategic Bombing on Japanese Morale* (Washington, D.C.: the Survey, 1947), http://www.archive.org/details/effectsofstrateg00unit.

17. Charles Griffith, *The Quest: Haywood Hansell and American Strategic Bombing in World War II* (Maxwell Air Force Base, Ala.: Air University Press, 1999), 201–7.

18. Charles Fritz interview by Henry Quarantelli, May 19, 1993, DRC.

19. Ibid.

20. Gary Alan Fine, ed., *A Second Chicago School? The Development of a Postwar American Sociology* (Chicago: University of Chicago Press, 1995), 1–10.

21. David A. Snow and Philip W. Davis, "The Chicago Approach to Collective Behavior," in Fine, ed., 188–220, 192–93.

22. Jennifer Platt, "Research Methods and the Second Chicago School," in Fine, ed., 82–107, 102.

23. NORC, *America by Number* (Chicago: NORC, 1991), 1–3.

24. Ibid., 7.

25. E. L. Quarantelli, "The NORC Research on the Arkansas Tornado: A Fountainhead Study," *International Journal of Mass Emergencies and Disasters* 8, 3 (1998): 284.

26. Fritz interview.

27. Quarantelli, "NORC Research," 285.

28. Fritz interview; NORC, *America by Number*, 50–51.

29. Fritz interview.

30. NORC, *Conference on Field Studies of Reactions to Disasters* (Chicago: NORC, 1953), 14–16.

31. Ibid., 17.

32. Interview with E. L. Quarantelli, January 30, 1998, Tape 1, DRC.

33. Quarantelli, "NORC Research," 288–89.

34. Ibid., 304–6.

35. Anthony F. C. Wallace, *Human Behavior in Extreme Situations: A Study of the Literature and Suggestions for Further Research*, Disaster Study 1 (Washington, D.C.: National Academy of Sciences, 1956), http://www.archive.org/stream/humanbchaviorine00wallrich/humanbehaviorine00wallrich_djvu.txt.

36. Hersey's *Hiroshima*, first published in summer 1946 as a full issue of the *New Yorker*, was an overnight sensation, selling out at once. It was quickly brought out as an exceptionally popular book, and read aloud on ABC radio. From the perspective of disaster researchers the book was useful because it told the story of the Hiroshima attack entirely from the standpoint of the victims, and made use of first-person interviews collected on-site, close enough in time to the event to yield real clues into human behavior. In general Hersey found a strengthening of community, relative calmness and clarity of focus in the midst of the disaster as described by his interviewees, and prosocial, helping behaviors rather than panic and social chaos. See Michael J. Yavenditti, "John Hersey and the American Conscience: The Reception of 'Hiroshima'," *Pacific Historical Review*, 43, 1 (February 1974): 24–49.

37. John H. Powell, *Bring Out Your Dead: The Great Plague of Yellow Fever in Philadelphia in 1793* (Philadelphia: University of Pennsylvania Press, 1993).

38. Wallace, 7–12.

39. Knowles, "Defending Philadelphia," 13–14.

40. Fritz, "Disaster"; see also Charles E. Fritz and Harry B. Williams, "The Human Being in Disasters," *Annals of the American Academy of Political and Social Science* 309 (January 1957): 42–51.

41. Quarantelli Interview, Tape 4, DRC.

42. E. L. Quarantelli, "The Early History of the Disaster Research Center," n.d., 2, DRC; for DRC history see also E. L. Quarantelli, Russell R. Dynes, and Dennis E. Wenger, "The Disaster Research Center: Its History and Activities," Miscellaneous Report 35, 1986, DRC.

43. J. Eugene Haas, Russell R. Dynes, and E. L. Quarantelli, "Some Preliminary Observations on the Responses of Community Organizations Involved in the Emergency Period of the Alaskan Earthquake," Working Paper 2, 1964, 2, DRC.

44. Ibid., 4.

45. Ibid., 5.

46. Author interview with Russell R. Dynes, August 2007.

47. Ibid.

48. "Alaska Study," File 1532, 1965, 7–12, DRC.

49. "Alaska Study," File 2292, September 2, 1965, DRC.

50. "Alaska Study," File 1554, 1964, 4, DRC.

51. William A. Anderson, "Local Civil Defense in Natural Disaster: From Office to Organization," 1969, DRC.

52. Ibid., 202.

53. Ibid., 9.

54. Ibid.

55. Ibid., 55.

56. Author Interview with E. L. Quarantelli, August 2007. Quarantelli notes that some years later a graduate student noticed that DRC reports used boilerplate language in reference to civil defense applicability—it had apparently gone undetected or at least not remarked upon to that point.

57. Russell Dynes interview, 1997, Tape 2, DRC.

58. E. L. Quarantelli, "The Disaster Research Center Simulation Studies of Organizational Behavior Under Stress," Final Project Report 6, 1967, 1–14, DRC.

59. Russell Rowe Dynes, *Organized Behavior in Disaster* (Lexington, Mass.: Heath, 1970), 8.

60. Ibid.

61. Ibid., 204.

62. Russell R. Dynes and E.L. Quarantelli, "What Looting in Civil Disturbances Really Means," *Trans-Action* 5 (May 1968): 9–14, 10.

63. E. L. Quarantelli and Russell R. Dynes, "Looting in Civil Disorders: An Index of Social Change," *American Behavioral Scientist* 5 (March 1968): 132; see also Dynes and Quarantelli, "What Looting in Civil Disturbances Really Means."

64. Quarantelli and Dynes, "Looting."

65. Ibid., 134–35.

66. Ibid., 137.

67. The involvement of social scientists on the Kerner Commission study was necessary to establish the validity and stature of the study as social analysis, but the varying goals and methods of policy makers and social scientists forced restraints on researchers and tensions between the social scientists and staff directors charged with producing the final report. See Michael Lipsky, "Social Scientists and the Riot Commission," *Annals of the American Academy of Political and Social Science* 394 (March 1971): 72–83.

68. United States National Advisory Commission on Civil Disorders, *Report of the National Advisory Commission on Civil Disorders* (Washington, D.C.: Government Printing Office, 1968).

69. Quarantelli and Dynes, "Looting," 140.

70. See E. L. Quarantelli and Russell R. Dynes, "Disruption on the Campuses of Ohio Colleges and Universities," Spring 1970, 1981, DRC; Russell Dynes and William

Anderson, "Civil Disturbances and Social Change: A Comparative Analysis," 1973; E. L. Quarantelli, J. Rick Ponting, and John S. Fitzpatrick, "Police Department Perceptions of the Occurrences of Civil Disturbances," April 1974, DRC.

71. Claude Gilbert, "Studying Disaster: Changes in the Main Conceptual Tools," in *What Is a Disaster? Perspectives on the Question*, ed. E. L. Quarantelli (New York: Routledge, 1998), 4.

72. Ibid., 6.

73. Ibid., 7.

74. For discussion of Susan Cutter's discovery of the "twenty vulnerability definitions," and a more complete overview of vulnerability, see James M. Kendra, "Geography's Contributions to Understanding Hazards and Disasters," in *Disciplines, Disasters and Emergency Management: The Convergence and Divergence of Concepts, Issues, and Trends from the Research Literature*, ed. David A. McEntire (Springfield, Ill.: Charles C. Thomas, 2007), 20.

75. Gregory Bankoff, "Rendering the World Unsafe: 'Vulnerability' as Western Discourse," *Disasters* 25, 1 (2001): 27; see also Kenneth Hewitt, ed., *Interpretations of Calamity from the Viewpoint of Human Ecology* (Boston: Allen and Unwin, 1983).

76. For overviews of social science research into Hurricane Katrina, see "Understanding Katrina: Perspectives from the Social Sciences," Social Science Research Council (online), http://understandingkatrina.ssrc.org/; and Social Science Research Council Katrina Research Hub (online), http://katrinaresearchhub.ssrc.org/rdb/katrina-hub. See also Eugenie L. Birch and Susan M. Wachter, eds., *Rebuilding Urban Places After Disaster: Lessons from Hurricane Katrina* (Philadelphia: University of Pennsylvania Press, 2006), and Ronald J. Daniels, Donald F. Kettl, and Howard Kunreuther, eds., *On Risk and Disaster: Lessons from Hurricane Katrina* (Philadelphia: University of Pennsylvania Press, 2006).

77. Kathleen J. Tierney, "Toward a Critical Sociology of Risk," *Sociological Forum*, 14, 2 (June 1999): 236.

Chapter 6. A Nation of Hazards

Epigraph: Don DeLillo, *White Noise* (New York: Penguin, 1985), 139–41.

1. Frank Hobbs and Nicole Stoops, "Demographic Tends in the 20th Century," U.S. Census Bureau, November 2002, 43.

2. On "focusing events," see Thomas A. Birkland, "Natural Disasters as Focusing Events: Policy Communities and Political Response," *International Journal of Mass Emergencies and Disasters* 14, 2 (August 1996): 221–44; Birkland, *After Disaster: Agenda Setting, Public Policy, and Focusing Events* (Washington, D.C.: Georgetown University Press, 1997); and Claire B. Rubin & Associates, "Disaster Time Line: Major Focusing Events and U.S. Outcomes (1988–2008)," http://www.disaster-timeline.com/.

3. National Flood Insurance Act, 1968, 1.

4. Ibid., 2.

5. On Hurricane Camille, see Philip D. Hearn, *Hurricane Camille: Monster Storm of the Gulf Coast* (Jackson: University of Mississippi Press, 2004); and, Ernest Zebrowski and Judith A. Howard, *The Story of Camille: Lessons Unlearned from America's Most Violent Hurricane* (Ann Arbor: University of Michigan Press, 2005).

6. Gilbert F. White and J. Eugene Haas, *Assessment of Research on Natural Hazards* (Cambridge, Mass.: MIT Press, 1975).

7. Ibid., 5.

8. Ibid., 8.

9. Robert E. Hinshaw, *Living with Nature's Extremes: The Life of Gilbert Fowler White* (Boulder, Colo.: Johnson Books, 2006), 161–65.

10. On the development of disaster research into policy, see Louise K. Comfort, ed., *Managing Disaster: Strategies and Policy Perspectives* (Durham, N.C.: Duke University Press, 1988); Peter J. May and Walter Williams, *Disaster Policy Implementation: Managing Programs Under Shared Governance* (New York: Plenum 1986); and Robert K. Yin and Gwendolyn B. Moore, "Lessons on the Utilization of Research from Nine Case Experiences in the Natural Hazards Field," *Knowledge in Society: The International Journal of Knowledge Transfer* 1, 3 (Fall 1988): 25–44. On earthquakes and politics, see Carl-Henry Geschwind, *California Earthquakes: Science, Risk, and the Politics of Hazard Mitigation* (Baltimore: Johns Hopkins University Press, 2008).

11. National Commission on Fire Prevention and Control, *America Burning* (Washington, D.C.: Government Printing Office, 1973).

12. NIST, *Building and Fire Research at NBS/NIST, 1975–2000* (Washington, D.C.: Government Printing Office, 2003), 11–13.

13. Author interview with John L. Bryan, September 28, 2007.

14. "OCD Deputy Director Sees Federal CD Role in Peacetime Disasters," *U.S. Civil Defense Council Bulletin*, January 1972, 1.

15. Ibid., 8.

16. Ibid.

17. "The Director Speaks," *U.S. Civil Defense Council Bulletin*, January 1972, 3; "The Director Speaks," *U.S. Civil Defense Council Bulletin*, February 1972, 3.

18. "The Director Speaks," *U.S. Civil Defense Council Bulletin*, May 1972, 6.

19. Ibid., 3.; John S. Fitzpatrick and Jerry J. Waxman, "The March, 1972 Louisville, Kentucky Chlorine Leak Threat and Evacuation: Observations on Community Coordination," Working Paper 44, Disaster Research Center, Ohio State University, 1972.

20. Ibid.

21. Ibid., 12.

22. National Governor's Association, *Comprehensive Emergency Management: A Governor's Guide* (Washington, D.C.: National Governor's Association, 1979), 6.

23. Ibid.,10.

24. "Disaster Preparedness Subcommittee Meeting," December 19, 1977, 2, Mike O'Callaghan Papers, Nevada State Library.

25. Edmond F. Rovner, "Analysis of Federal Powers and Responsibilities in the Inter-Governmental Sphere of Emergency Planning and Response," February 1978, Table II, Mike O'Callaghan Papers, Nevada State Library.

26. Howard Kunreuther, "Disaster Insurance: A Tool for Hazard Mitigation," *The Journal of Risk and Insurance* 41, 2 (June 1974): 287–303; see also Kunreuther, "The Changing Societal Consequences of Risks from Natural Hazards," *Annals of the American Academy of Political and Social Science, Risks and Its Treatment: Changing Societal Consequences* 443 (May 1979): 104–16.

27. Nancy L. Ginn, *Energy Emergency Preparedness: An Overview of State Authority* (Washington, D.C.: National Governor's Association, 1978), ii–iii.

28. Ibid., iii–iv.

29. Ibid., iv–v.

30. Ibid., xii.

31. George D. Haddow and Jane A. Bullock, *Introduction to Emergency Management, Third Edition* (Burlington, Mass., Butterworth-Heinemann, 2008), 1–26.

32. Martin Tolchin, "Carter Seeks Civil Defense Plan in Reaction to Action by Soviet," *New York Times*, June 20, 1978, A1.

33. "A 58-Year Legacy of Training and Education in Emergency Management," xx, FEMA, Emergency Management Institute, www.training.fema.gov.

34. David Neal, "History of the Emergency Administration and Planning Program," report, University of North Texas, 2000, 3.

35. Ibid., 4.

36. Ibid., 5.

37. Ibid., 5–6.

38. Neal, 418.

39. Richard Sylves, "Review: Ferment at FEMA: Reforming Emergency Management," *Public Administration Review* 54, 3 (May–June 1994): 303–7.

40. Author interview with James Lee Witt, April 21, 2010; author interview with Jane Bullock, March 30, 2010. See also James Lee Witt and James Morgan, *Stronger in the Broken Places: Nine Lessons for Turning Crisis into Triumph* (New York: Times Books, 2002).

41. Tricia Wachtendorf, "Building Community Partnerships Toward a National Mitigation Effort: Inter-Organizational Collaboration in the Project Impact Initiative," University of Delaware, Disaster Research Center, Preliminary Paper 306, 2000, 1.

42. Ibid., 3.

43. Witt interview; Bullock interview.

44. Witt interview; see also Eric Holdeman, "Destroying FEMA," *Washington Post*, August 30, 2005.

45. Witt interview.

46. "Refighting the Fires of September 11," *New York Times*, July 12, 2002, A18.

47. Jim Dwyer, "Investigating 9/11: An Unimaginable Calamity, Still Largely Unexamined," *New York Times*, September 11, 2002, A19.

48. National Commission on Terrorist Attacks, *The 9/11 Commission Report: The Final Report of the National Commission on Terrorists upon the United States* (New York: Norton, 2004).

49. Kathleen Tierney, "The 9/11 Commission and Disaster Management: Little Depth, Less Context, Not Much Guidance," *Contemporary Sociology* 34, 2 (March 2005): 115–20. See also Claudia Dreifus, "A Conversation with: Kathleen Tierney: A Sociologist with an Advanced Degree in Calamity," *New York Times*, September 7, 2004.

50. "Statement of Glenn Corbett," House Science Committee, World Trade Center Hearings, 2005.

51. "Testimony of Sally Regenhard," House Science Committee, World Trade Center Hearings, 2005.

52. Robyn R. M. Gershon, Lori A. Magda, Halley E. M. Riley, and Martin F. Sherman, "The World Trade Center Evacuation Study: Factors Associated with Initiation and Length of Time for Evacuation," *Fire and Materials* (2011).

53. Juan González, *Fallout: The Environmental Consequences of the World Trade Center Collapse* (New York: New Press, 2002).

54. David Rosner and Gerald Markowitz, *Are We Ready: Public Health Since 9/11* (Berkeley: University of California Press, 2006); see also Irwin Redlener, *Americans at Risk: Why We Are Not Prepared for Megadisasters and What We Can Do Now* (New York: Knopf, 2006).

55. Anthony DePalma, "Many Ground Zero Workers Gain Chance at Lawsuits," *New York Times*, October 18, 2006.

56. Joan Didion, *Slouching Towards Bethlehem* (New York: Farrar, Straus and Giroux, 1990).

57. Author interview with Cliff Hunter, 2007.

58. Author interview with Max Moritz, 2007; see also Moritz Lab, University of California, Berkeley, http://nature.berkeley.edu/moritzlab/.

59. Anuradha Mathur and Dilip da Cunha, *Mississippi Floods: Designing a Shifting Landscape* (New Haven, Conn.: Yale University Press, 2001).

60. Author interview with Ivor van Heerden, 2007.

61. "Project New Orleans," University of Pennsylvania School of Design, 2006, http://www.project-neworleans.org/urbananalysis/betweenwaterandland1.html.

62. Hunter interview.

Conclusion: Experts in Disaster

Epigraph: Ulrich Beck, *Risk Society: Towards a New Modernity* (London: Sage, 1992), 28–29.

1. "A Nation Challenged: Portraits of Grief, Crossley Williams Jr.," *New York Times*, October 10, 2001.

2. There was a perhaps small but influential group of fire experts, academics, writers, and victims' family members after September 11 asking tough questions about

the safety of the buildings, and about the long-term health and psychological effects of the disaster on survivors, first responders, and the city as a whole. The *New York Times* was very active in reporting on the major questions and issues that led, ultimately, to the 2002 House Science Committee Hearings—issues like the premature recycling of the World Trade Center steel and the slowness and conflicts among federal agencies charged with the investigation. The *Times* also pursued the legal process required to open up the New York City Fire Department's 911 call records from September 11 to the public. Reporters Kenneth Chang, James Dwyer, Kevin Flynn, James Glanz, and Eric Lipton wrote detailed and critical articles that kept the safety question in front of the public. The *Times* covered the story of Abolhassan Astanch-Asl's attempts to investigate the World Trade Center steel, with the unforgettable description of the engineer looking outside his hotel window after just arriving in the city and spotting charred beams from the Twin Towers loaded on trucks parked in front of his hotel—he examined them on the spot. See Kenneth Chang, "Scarred Steel Holds Clues, and Remedies," *New York Times*, October 2, 2001; and Kenneth Chang, "Defending Skyscrapers Against Terror," *New York Times*, September 18, 2001. The *Times* also broke the story of Sally Regenhard and Glenn Corbett's first press conference, an event that also contributed to the call for a more complete investigation of the collapse. See James Glanz, "The Towers; Demand Rises For Widening Investigation Into Collapse," *New York Times*, December 15, 2001. For more on Regenhard's very influential victim's family organization, the Skyscraper Safety Campaign, see http://skyscrapersafety.org/. *New York Times* reporters also produced some of the best books about the World Trade Center, its construction, and its collapse. See Eric Lipton and James Glanz, *City in the Sky: The Rise and Fall of the World Trade Center* (New York: Times Books, 2003); and Jim Dwyer and Kevin Flynn, *102 Minutes: The Untold Story of the Fight to Survive Inside the Twin Towers* (New York: Times Books, 2004). In the first years after September 11 there were many other compelling articles, books, speeches, interviews, photographs, and websites covering the "dissenting" issues of safety, investigation, memory, and loss. See William Langewiesche, *American Ground: Unbuilding the World Trade Center* (New York: North Point Press, 2002); September 11 Digital Archive, http://911digitalarchive.org/; and "Mr. Beller's Neighborhood, 9/11 and Its Aftershocks," http://mrbellersneighborhood.com/tag/911-and-its-aftershocks." Charles Strozier has written provocatively about the survivor experience of September 11. I have been inspired by the compassion and creativity in his historical methodology, including his research into the "9/11 Survivor and Family Groups." Reporters, historians, and public health researchers worked to document and investigate the health effects of the Twin Towers' collapse, an interpretation of the disaster that was controversial at the time, and put pressure on government officials to address the working conditions at the recovery site, as well as the need for enhanced evacuation procedures in New York City high rise buildings. See Robyn R. M. Gershon1, Lori A. Magda, Halley E. M. Riley, and Martin F. Sherman, "The World Trade Center Evacuation Study"; Juan González, *Fallout; and Rosner and Markowitz, Are We Ready*.

3. Beck, 36. See also Charles Perrow, *Normal Accidents: Living with High-Risk Technologies* (New York: Basic Books, 1984).

4. John McPhee, *The Control of Nature* (New York: Farrar, Straus, and Giroux, 1990); Mike Davis, *Ecology of Fear: Los Angeles and the Imagination of Disaster* (New York: Vintage, 1999); Ted Steinberg, *Acts of God: The Unnatural History of Natural Disaster in America* (New York: Oxford University Press, 2000). Recent trends in disaster and hazards research are captured well in the books generated by the "Second Assessment of Natural Hazards"; see Raymond Burby, *Cooperating with Nature: Confronting Natural Hazards with Land-Use Planning for Sustainable Communities* (Washington, D.C.: Joseph Henry Press, 1998); Susan L. Cutter, *American Hazardscapes: The Regionalization of Hazards and Disasters* (Washington, D.C.: Joseph Henry Press, 2001); Howard Kunreuther and Richard J. Roth, Sr., *Paying the Price: The Status and Role of Insurance Against Natural Disasters in the United States* (Washington, D.C.: Joseph Henry Press, 1998); Dennis S. Mileti, *Disasters by Design: A Reassessment of Natural Hazards in the United States* (Washington, D.C.: Joseph Henry Press, 1999); and Kathleen J. Tierney, Michael K. Lindell and Ronald W. Perry, *Facing the Unexpected: Disaster Preparedness and Response in the United States* (Washington, D.C.: Joseph Henry Press, 2001). For recent overviews of "safety culture" and disaster research, see Susan Silbey, "Taming Prometheus: Talk About Safety and Culture," *Annual Review of Sociology* 35 (2009): 341–69; and Havidan Rodriguez, Enrico L. Quarantelli, and Russell R. Dynes, *Handbook of Disaster Research* (New York: Springer, 2007).

5. Emergency management educators have worked in recent years to bring the findings of disaster and hazards research into their curricula. In some programs the faculty are themselves disaster researchers. James Kendra, former director of the EADP program at the University of North Texas and now director of the Disaster Research Center at the University of Delaware, has discussed this challenge. See James M. Kendra, "So Are You Still Active in the Field, Or Do You Just Teach?" *Journal of Homeland Security and Emergency Management* 4, 3 (2007).

INDEX

ACKNOWLEDGMENTS

One name goes on the author line, but that is misleading. It is unthinkable that I would have finished this book without the consistent help and support of family, friends, and many close colleagues. I know many of them secretly wondered, when is he going to stop talking about John Ripley Freeman, or the "UL Falling Safe Test"? Ok, so, now we can move on to another topic—but the "Falling Safe Test," come on, you have to admit, that *is* pretty amazing.

It's an unbelievable bit of good luck to have a brilliant person in the office next door willing to read your work, and Amy Slaton is that person for me. She spent countless hours (days, months, years?) working through these chapters, offering insight, humor, and stern warnings to get the argument right up front and keep hammering away at it. She is a model scholar and much more, a treasured friend.

As an editor Bob Lockhart is one of the big league all-stars. When I convinced Bob that this project had promise the Phillies were an also-ran team. We worked together on the book (with several important strategy sessions at the ballpark) until they were the best team in baseball! We had better keep working together or who knows what might happen.

Friends and colleagues whose mentorship and big ideas over the years fostered the confidence and the subtle (best part of academia) competitive pressure to keep going are many. Eugenie Birch, Paul Bostick, Lee Clarke, Glenn Corbett, Russell Dynes, Bruce Hunt, Jim Kendra, Jeffrey Knowles, Jimmy McWilliams, and Chuck Strozier each read all or significant portions of the manuscript (sometimes more than once), and offered the "go ahead" and the "wait a minute" as needed. I learned a great deal from each of them, and did my best to incorporate their wise suggestions. My sincere thanks also go to: Lloyd Ackert, Rose Corrigan, Richard Dilworth, Greg Downey, Bob Kargon, Bill Leslie, Jerry Markowitz, David Munns, and Dick Rosen.

Drexel University has provided an exceptionally supportive (in resources and collegiality) environment, and I wish to thank specific administrators and staff who have encouraged me to do the research I needed to do, and helped me to stay on track. Special thanks to Mark Greenberg, Donna Murasko, Dave Jones, Don Stevens, Gina Waters, Sharon Grinnage, Ann Alexander, and Jen Britton.

In archives and libraries I found talented people who in many cases (in addition to being highly skilled) drove me to and from train stations, gave me books, fed me and told me about the histories of their organizations, dug up old, long-forgotten documents and images, and generally showed a sincere, and humbling interest in my project. In private archives and corporations thanks go to: Allen Haddox, American Insurance Association; staff of the Chicago History Museum; Janet Green, Factory Mutual; Colleen Petry-Johnson, International Code Council; Casey Grant and the staff of the Charles S. Morgan Library, National Fire Protection Association; and Kim Fuller, Witt Associates.

Underwriters Laboratories became a second home to me throughout this research—I returned several times, always uncovering more documents, and always meeting friendly people who know a great deal about and take pride in the history of their organization. Sincere thanks to James Beyreis, Mary Bolda, Sandra Collins, David Dini, John Drengenberg, Barbara Floyd, Tammi Gengenbacher, Don Mader, Pat Mamica, Traci Wellington, and the other staff members who assisted me with diligence. Gus Schaefer is UL's unofficial historian, carrying on a tradition established by the late Lee Dosedlo—it has been an honor to become friends with Gus.

At university archives and libraries I wish to thank: staff of the Drexel University Libraries; Lois Beattie, Nora Murphy and staff of the MIT Institute Archives; staff of the Temple University libraries; Wanda Headley and staff of the Natural Hazards Center of the University of Colorado; Pat Young and staff of the Disaster Research Center of the University of Delaware; Anne Turkos and staff of the Special Collections of the University of Maryland Libraries; staff of the University of Pennsylvania Libraries; Margaret Anderson and Rodney Obien, Worcester Polytechnic Institute University Archives and Special Collections.

At government archives thanks go to: Julie Beecken, Linda Krut, Edward Metz, and staff of the National Emergency Training Center (FEMA/U.S. Fire Administration) Learning Resource Center; Keith Martin, Terrie Wheeler and staff of NIST and the NIST Archives; staff of the Nevada

State Archives; David Baugh and the staff of the Philadelphia City Archives. Thanks also to Dr. Fahim H. Sadek of NIST for assistance in obtaining the book's cover image.

The precision and good nature of Alison Anderson and Julia Rose Roberts at the University of Pennsylvania Press are very much appreciated.

Thanks to Michelle Marchesano for timely and very helpful legal research.

Universities, professional conferences, journals and periodicals, and other venues opened their doors to me to present sections of the work in progress. My thanks for the valuable critiques provided by: the Barbara Bates Center for the Study of the History of Nursing; the Business History Conference; the Disaster Research Center; the Drexel University College of Arts and Sciences Dean's Seminar; the History of Science Society; the International Network of Engineering Studies, the Johns Hopkins University Department of the History of Science, Medicine, and Technology Colloquium; the John Jay College of Criminal Justice, City University of New York; the Natural Hazards Center Annual Workshop; the Social Science History Association; Society for the Social Studies of Science; the Society for the History of Technology; Underwriters Laboratories; *Annals of Science*; *History and Technology*; *Public Works Management and Policy*; and *Next American City*.

Many experts and colleagues gave very generously of their time and knowledge for interviews and discussions, these included: William Anderson, Wayne Blanchard, John L. Bryan, Jane Bullock, Dave Butler, Tom Castino, Glenn Corbett, Dilip da Cunha, Marino di Marzo, John Domzalski, Thomas Drabek, Russell Dynes, Charles Fisher, Robyn Gershon, David Hemenway, Cliff Hunter, Ana-Marie Jones, James Kendra, Howard Kunreuther, David Lucht, Anuradha Mathur, James Milke, David McEntire, James Milke, Max Moritz, John Radke, Pedro Ramos, Sally Regenhard, Antonio Ruiz, Harvey Rubin, Gavin Smith, Kathleen Tierney, MaryAnn Tierney, Henry Quartantelli, Susan Silbey, Carl Smith, Ivor van Heerden, and Earl Zuelke.

My family has been characteristically enthusiastic throughout this long process. Special thanks to my "coach," Jeff Knowles, and to the ultimate "Gram," Susan Meurling. To Gabriel, my little buddy, keep reading, and keeping telling jokes! And of course the wife, nothing is possible without the wife—all I can possibly think to say is "datchu," oh yeah, and watch out for the black ice!

DATE DUE

NOV 0 7 2013	

BRODART, CO.   Cat. No. 23-221